The Jews in Siedlce
1850–1945

JewishGen and the Yizkor-Books-in-Print Project

This book has been published by the **Yizkor-Books-in-Print Project**, as part of the **Yizkor Book Project of JewishGen, Inc.**

JewishGen, Inc. is a non-profit organization founded in 1987 as a resource for Jewish genealogy. Its website [www.jewishgen.org] serves as an international clearinghouse and resource center to assist individuals who are researching the history of their Jewish families and the places where they lived. JewishGen provides databases, facilitates discussion groups, and coordinates projects relating to Jewish genealogy and the history of the Jewish people. In 2003, JewishGen became an affiliate of the **Museum of Jewish Heritage - A Living Memorial to the Holocaust** in New York.

The **JewishGen Yizkor Book Project** was organized to make more widely known the existence of Yizkor (Memorial) Books written by survivors and former residents of various Jewish communities throughout the world. Later, volunteers connected to the different destroyed communities began cooperating to have these books translated from the original language—usually Hebrew or Yiddish—into English, thus enabling a wider audience to have access to the valuable information contained within them. As each chapter of these books was translated, it was posted on the JewishGen website and made available to the general public. In addition to Yizkor Books, this series includes memoirs and historical monographs. Some of these works were translated by professional translators.

The **Yizkor-Books-in-Print Project** began in 2011 as an initiative to print and publish Yizkor Books that had been fully translated, so that hard copies would be available for purchase by the descendants of these communities and also by scholars, universities, synagogues, libraries, and museums.

These Yizkor books have been produced almost entirely through the volunteer effort of researchers from around the world, assisted by donations from private individuals. The books are printed and sold at near cost, so as to make them as affordable as possible. Our goal is to make this important genre of Jewish literature and history available in English in book form, so that people can have the personal histories of their ancestral towns on their bookshelves for themselves and for their children and grandchildren.

A list of all published translated Yizkor Books can be found at:
http://www.jewishgen.org/Yizkor/ybip.html

Lance Ackerfeld, Yizkor Book Project Manager
Joel Alpert, Yizkor-Book-in-Print Project Coordinator

Edward Kopówka

The Jews in Siedlce
1850–1945

Translated from the Polish by Dobrochna Fire
Edited by Leonard Levin and Michael Halber

JewishGen, Inc.
An Affiliate of the Museum of Jewish Heritage
A Living Memorial to the Holocaust
New York

Supervisor
Prof. Zofia Chyra-Rolicz, D.Litt.

Reviewers
Prof. Regina Renz, D.Litt.
Prof. Piotr Matusak, D.Litt.

Published by **JewishGen, Inc.**
An Affiliate of the Museum of Jewish Heritage
A Living Memorial to the Holocaust
36 Battery Place, New York, NY 10280

Cover design and typesetting by **Monika Konopka**
Printed in the United States of America by **Lightning Source, Inc.**

Library of Congress Control Number 2014945512

ISBN 978-1-939561-23-7 (hard cover: 450 pages, alk. paper)

On the cover: Siedlce symbolic gravestone, part of the memorial monument in Treblinka,
designed by architect Adam Haupt, executed by sculptors Franciszek Duszeńko
and Franciszek Strynkiewicz, and unveiled in 1964. Photograph by Edward Kopówka.

To Izaak Halber, of blessed memory

CONTENTS

ON THE GENESIS AND TRANSLATION OF THIS BOOK
by Leonard Levin

This book had its origins in the 1980s when Edward Kopówka, a Christian Polish teacher, decided to study the history of the Jews of Siedlce while pursuing his master's degree. In investigating the subject, he developed a relationship with Izaak Halber, the last Jewish resident of Siedlce, who, after surviving the Holocaust, continued to live in Siedlce with his wife. As Kopówka progressed in his research, he consulted with Halber to learn more about the Jewish community of Siedlce from the Jewish point of view. After Izaak Halber died in 2000, Kopówka turned to Izaak's son, Michael Halber, who at that point was living in Canada and who assisted Kopówka in obtaining additional materials for his PhD research. The Polish version of the dissertation, Żydzi w Siedlcach 1850–1945, was published in Siedlce in 2009.

Isabel Cymerman can trace her ancestry in Siedlce to Rabbi Pinkas Zukierman (born in Siedlce, 1837) and to the Grynberg and Grynfarb families. The Grynfarbs were cap-makers as far back as the 1700s. Image 49 of the current book shows a cap-insignia of her grandfather's business. When Isabel learned of the publication of Kopówka's book, she approached JewishGen to inquire if the book could be translated into English. This initiative of hers was the first step in launching the translation project.

When Lance Ackerfeld, general coordinator of the translation projects of JewishGen, received Isabel's request, he turned to Dobrochna Fire, who had already served as Polish-language consultant and translator on a different project. Dosia tells of her motivation to engage in such work: "My parents endured World War II in Poland: my mother a righteous gentile; my father one of the Jews whom she helped to survive. This heritage of mine, which encompasses, as I see it, two parts of the Polish soul, the ethnically Polish and the ethnically Jewish, gives me a certain perspective on the events described in this book that I hope enable me to translate not only the words of the book but also its spirit." The narrative of the struggle for survival of the young Jews of Staszów, aided by the gentile Poles of Czajków, to which Dosia refers, is found in the Staszów Yizkor Book, translated by JewishGen.

Leonard Levin, a Judaics scholar who became the coordinator of this project, is married to Dosia's cousin Margareta Freeman, also descended of the Jews of Staszów. In the course of the translation phase of the project, Dosia and Lenny reached out to Michael Halber, who provided valuable assistance as historical and linguistic consultant. Thus all members of the team that put this work together can be said to have roots in pre-war Jewish Poland generally, and some more specifically in Siedlce itself.

Notes on the Translation
by Dobrochna Fire

A translator has the privilege of dwelling within the work that is being translated. In this case, I had the honor of being a resident of the Jewish community in Siedlce and of coming to know its people and its life. Although my father's family is from Staszów, not Siedlce, many names are the same, and much of the history is similar. I felt as though I were recreating my own family's past in making the lives of these people available to the English-speaking world.

Because there are so many variants in the spellings of Jewish names, I chose to leave the spellings of all the names of natives of Poland (as opposed to those of Russia or elsewhere) as they were in the original rather than to anglicize them. As for Jewish surnames, please refer to the translator's note to Appendix 3.

The reader might find an explanation of the naming of Polish streets helpful. Most streets in Poland are adjectives, thus describing "what kind of" street it is (*długa* [long], *targowa* [market], etc.). And since the word "street" in Polish is feminine (*ulica*), these street names more often than not end in the letter "-a." I have left the street names in this inflected feminine form. If a street is named after a person, that person's name is in the genitive case, thus meaning "someone's" street (named after the person). For these streets, I have used the nominative form of the name in English. Thus *ulica Piłsudskiego* in Polish would be Piłsudski Street; *ulica Orzeszkowej* would be Orzeszkowa Street; and so forth.

The Polish school system changed several times during the century examined in this book. In spite of these changes, the general structure remained the same: The most basic schooling was the primary school (*szkoła powszechna* or *szkoła podstawowa*), which lasted from 4 or 5 to 7 years. A child's education could then be followed, at various times during the past 150 years, by 7 years of what was either just secondary school (*gimnazjum*) or both secondary and preparatory school (*gimnazjum* followed by *liceum*), similar to middle and high school in the United States. My choice of translations for these levels of schooling will hopefully alleviate confusion.

ACKNOWLEDGEMENTS

The author was aided in the preparation of the Polish publication by Aneta Abramowicz, Łukasz Biedka, Witold Bobryk, Isabel Cymerman, Zofia Czapska, Andrzej Dąbrowski, Witold Duniłłowicz, Abraham Gome, Maria Halber, Michael Halber, Tadeusz Kaźmierak, Bogusław Mitura, Beate Stollberg (Trägerkreis Shoah-Gedenkstätten in Verbindung beim Kirchengreis Bielefeld), Helen Yomtov-Herman.

Additional help with the preparation of the English edition was received from Julian Dunwill, Maria Galas, Tali Geva, Al Stein, Amalia Strosberg.

The following contributed financially to underwriting the English translation: Isabel Cymerman, Margareta and Sarah Freeman, Lauren Lebowitz, Leonard Levin, Sara Mages, David A. Mink, Maurice Stein Potache, Ika Shneor, Rena Sonshine, Julia W. Tossell, Arleen Winkler, and Kol Zarember.

An additional contribution for the preparation of the printed edition was received from an anonymous donor.

INTRODUCTION

This work is the fruit of over a dozen years of research on the history of Jews in Siedlce. I decided to take on this subject because there has heretofore not been a systematic discussion of the history of the Jewish minority in Siedlce.[a] This issue was raised in contribution only by Paweł Śmieciuch[1] and Agata Dąbrowska.[2] My earlier publications merely indicated the state of my research and were in the nature of popularizations.[3] This study aims to fill in a gap in Polish research on the history of Siedlce. I limited my research temporally to the period from the second half of the nineteenth to the twentieth centuries since the majority of extant sources and publications relate to that period. The second reason for this choice was the rapid development of the city during this time and the influx of a large number of Jewish people. In this work I would like to answer the following question: How did Siedlce develop in the second half of the nineteenth century and in the twentieth century with this participation of this community as well as how it changed after 1942, when the Nazis murdered the Jews?

The words of Pope John Paul II on 10 June 1999 in Siedlce were a strong impetus to research on the history of the Jews: "In this martyrized Podlasie, I cannot fail to mention the martyrology of the Jewish nation, which inscribed its painful page during the Second World War."[4]

I made the years 1850–1945 the chronological bookends of my work. The year 1850 marked the opening of the Russian customs border to merchandise from the Polish Kingdom, which led to the rapid development of industry and trade. New conditions emerged for the economic development of the country and the enrichment of the population, of which the Jews were quick to take advantage, especially trade workers and merchants. Jews are a people who are very active, enterprising, and productive in the trades and small-scale production. Siedlce at that time became a city in which the Jewish population formed a high percentage and which teamed with a rich social, political, and cultural life. The end point was 1945. However, I mention the fate of Jews up to 2007, when the first organized group of young Israelis came to Siedlce looking for the roots of their ancestors. They toured the city, became acquainted with the history of local Jews, and paid homage to those murdered during the Holocaust.

This work is based primarily on Polish sources. These are materials that are held in the National Archive in Lublin (in the Provincial Offices unit in Lublin, Social-Political Department II), in the National Archive in Siedlce (in the County District unit in Siedlce and the County National Police Department unit in Siedlce, Collection of Posters from the Occupation of Siedlce County), as well as in other research institutes such as the Institute of National Remembrance in Warsaw, the Jewish Historical Institute in Warsaw, Yad Vashem in Jerusalem, and the Ghetto Fighters' House in kibbutz Lohamei Hagetaot in Israel. The Lublin archive houses materials created by the Siedlce district governor during the interwar period, which include, among others, semiannual and annual reports sent to the Lublin provincial governor. These documents also contain confidential information gathered by the local police. The Siedlce archive, on the other hand, contains the county administrator's monthly reports to the Lublin provincial governor. These acts contain very valuable information, thanks to which I was able to create tables representing monthly and yearly reports on the organizational activity of Siedlce Jews for the years 1934–1938.[5] During this period, Zionist parties and organizations dominated the life of the city. The activity of the Bund was also visible, along with the "Yiddishe Kunst" (Jewish Art), which was under its influence. Puzzling, however, are the infrequent initiatives of Agudah [Agudath Israel party—ed.], which had a large number of members and sympathizers in the city. Most likely the members of this party dealt with their political business during religious gathering and were for this reason not registered so frequently by the county administrator and the police. Of significant informative value are the acts of the County Headquarters of the National Police in Siedlce, but they also contain numerous inaccuracies and simplifications caused, I believe, by the inadequate knowledge of the affairs of the Jewish community by confidential informers. These acts often fail to distinguish among socialists from the Bund, socialists from the Zionist parties, socialist Jews active in the Polish Socialist Party, and independent activists with socialist leanings. They are all frequently given the same label of "Communists." To this are added the lists of actual Communists, and what results is a falsified political image of the city. Reading these acts, one gets the impression that socialism was equivalent to Soviet Communism for the policemen compiling these documents.

The Siedlce Archive also contains a rich collection of posters from the occupation. This is a very valuable resource for research relating to the period of the Second World War. The accounts and recollections found in the Institute of National Remembrance in Warsaw, the Jewish Historical Institute in Warsaw, Yad Vashem in Jerusalem, and Beit Lohamei Hagetaot also relate to this period.

I took three trips to Israel in pursuit of materials and a deepening of my knowledge of the subject. The first was in 1994. I met Siedlce natives Srul Lewin and Hercel

Kawe at that time, as well as the charismatic figure of Catholic priest Grzegorz Pawłowski.[6] In 1997 I took a study trip to Yad Vashem in Jerusalem. This course, designed for people working in museums of remembrance, was called "Judaism, the History and Culture of Polish Jews, the Holocaust." While completing the program of touring Israel, I happened upon Beit Lohamei Hagetaot, in which I discovered a very detailed map of the Siedlce ghetto. After computer editing, I am including it in this work. This is a new document in scholarly circulation. The earlier map of the ghetto that I had drawn on the basis of German materials, mostly posters from the occupation, was not exact. One might say that it was theoretical. In 2005, I took another, second level course in Yad Vashem in Jerusalem. At that time I had the opportunity to deepen my knowledge and to familiarize myself with the new, multimedia exhibit in Yad Vashem depicting the extermination of the Jews and the creation of the state of Israel. There is a 1939 photograph presented in this exhibit depicting the Siedlce synagogue in flames. This photograph was included to underscore the German extermination policy regarding the Jews at the very outset of the occupation.

Jewish sources were used in this work as supplementary material. It was primarily *The Book of Remembrance of the Siedlce Community* that supplied me with valuable information. Compiled in the late 1940s and early 1950s by Siedlce natives from various parts of the world, from Argentina, the United States, and Israel, it was published in 1956 in Buenos Aires in Yiddish and in a small number of fragments in Hebrew. The memoirs in Hebrew were written by Zionists. The editor-in-chief and the person who inspired this work's coming into being was Isaac Kaspi. In popularizing knowledge about the Jewish community in Siedlce, he played a role similar to that of Antoni Winter among Poles.[7] In fact, they corresponded, sharing information, yet each worked separately on the history of his own nation. *The Book of Remembrance of the Siedlce Community*, at my initiative and with financial aid from the Society of Supporters of Podlasie, was partially translated into Polish and is available in the National Archive in Siedlce. Adam Bielecki from the Jewish Historical Institute did the translation.

The majority of Jewish sources were destroyed during World War II. Copies of the *Shedletser Wochenblat* (The Siedlce Weekly), which were preserved in the Library of Hebrew University in Jerusalem, were an exception. Some issues of this periodical were sent to what was then Palestine. Michael Halber made an electronic copy of this journal and sent it to the Regional Reading Room of the Municipal Public Library in Siedlce.

The absence of sources makes it impossible to acquire additional information about the names of some of the people described in this book. Often only surnames appeared in documents. Some of them have variant spelling (Trzmielina/ Szmielina, Gudgelt/Gudgeld, Halbersztat/Halberszstadt, Jomtow/Jontow/Jom-Tow/ Jon-Tow). I standardized spellings when referring to one and the same person,

3

although I know there were instances of a variety of spellings of a surname within the same family. This also applies to the names Oszer/Uszer. I use the name Jakub or Jakób in this work in accordance with archival material.

Throughout this work, I consistently capitalize the word "Jew" [Żyd], out of respect, even though according to the rules of Polish orthography, "Żyd" is spelled with a capital letter when it refers to "member of a nation," whereas "żyd" is lower cased when it refers to "a follower of Judaism."[8] For the names of Jewish parties, associations, and so forth, I adhered to the spelling that was mostly in use in the interwar period. A change in the way many words deriving from Yiddish or Hebrew are spelled is currently observable in the Polish language.

This work is supplied with appendices. Included in them are sources that have not previously been utilized in Polish historiography (an interview with Hubert Pfoch and the account of Fritz Hoeft). The included literary works, particularly the stories of Bracha Kahan, depict characteristic Jewish types, their living conditions, and the atmosphere of old Siedlce. The work contains tables that portray the numbers of the city's Jewish residents during various time periods.

I would like to thank the late Izaak Halber, with whom I met many times and who was my source of plentiful information. After his death, I was helped by his wife, Maria Halber, who translated texts written in Yiddish. Their son, Michael Halber, provided me with guidance over several years and furnished me with much material, especially in English and Hebrew. I wish to give special thanks to Professor Zofia Chyra-Rolicz, who provided me with advice and assistance. An important source of inspiration and information were Jews who came from Siedlce but lived in various parts of the world; I corresponded with them both traditionally, that is, via the postal service, and with the aid of the Internet. These were Renia Pancerowa, Isabel Cymerman, Helen Herman, and Abraham Gome. Some of these people form a second and even a third generation connected by family tradition with Siedlce. These people sent me photographs and information, which I used in this work.

EDITOR'S NOTE, INTRODUCTION:

a. Although Jews were a minority (the second largest) in Poland as a whole, they formed a majority of the population of Siedlce for most of the period discussed in this book.

AUTHOR'S NOTES, INTRODUCTION:

1. P. Śmieciuch, "Społeczność żydowska w Siedlcach w latach 1919–1938 w świetle sprawozdań sytuacyjnych starosty Powiatu Siedleckiego (informacja o zespole)," in *Biuletyn Żydowskiego Instytutu Historycznego*, no. 1 (1992): 79–84.

2. A. Dąbrowska, "Przyczynek do dziejów Żydów w Siedlcach w latach okupacji hitlerowskiej. Nieznany pamiętnik z lat II wojny światowej," in *Szkice Podlaskie* 9 (2001): 228–244.

3. "Zostawiłem maskę przeciwgazową w Izraelu i przyjechałem do Siedlec—wywiad z Henrykiem Reise," in *Kurier Siedlecki*, no. 2 (14 March 1991); "Przełamać stereotypy," in *Kurier Siedlecki*, no. 14 (1991); "Trefne ryby," in *Kurier Siedlecki*, no. 18 (24 October 1991); "Bij Żyda—ratuj Rosję," in *Tygodnik Siedlecki*, no. 2 (1992); "Świątobliwy kaznodzieja," in *Tygodnik Siedlecki*, no. 20 (1992); "Getto w Siedlcach," in *Tygodnik Siedlecki*, no. 16 (1992); "Żydzi siedleccy—zapomniany świat," in *Gazeta Kulturalna*, no. 3 (1992); "Żydzi w Siedlcach do czasów I wojny światowej," in *Prace Archiwalno-Konserwatorskie na Terenie Województwa Siedleckiego* 9 (Siedlce 1995); "Żydowskie partie polityczne w Siedlcach w latach 1918–1939," in *Prace Archiwalno-Konserwatorskie na Terenie Województwa Siedleckiego* 10 (Siedlce 1997); "Polacy i Żydzi w Siedlcach podczas okupacji niemieckiej 1939–1944," in *Pamięć i Sprawiedliwość. Biuletyn Głównej Komisji Badania Zbrodni przeciwko Narodowi Polskiemu Instytutu Pamięci Narodowej* 40 (Warsaw 1997–1998); "Siedleckie kirkuty," in *Szkice Podlaskie* (Siedlce 1998); Żydzi siedleccy (Siedlce 2001); "Prasa żydowska w Siedlcach w okresie dwudziestolecia międzywojennego," in *Prasa podlaska w. XIX–XX szkice i materiały*, vol. 2 (Siedlce 2004).

4. Quotation remembered by the author. See also *I oto przybyłeś... Ojciec Święty Jan Paweł II w Siedlcach. Siedlce 10 czerwca 1999* (Siedlce 2000), p. 86.

5. See Tables 6–15.

6. Father Grzegorz Pawłowski (Jakub Hersz Griner) comes from an orthodox Jewish family. He hid as a child during the war by grazing cattle. After the war, he converted to Catholicism and later entered a seminary. In 1970 he left for Israel and there he preaches to Catholics from Poland and other countries of the former USSR. The Catholic church of the Spanish Franciscans in Jaffa has become a true support for Poles staying in Israel. In addition to hearing a weekly holy mass, workers staying in Israel utilized the Polish library here and obtained information about work opportunities or finding lodgings. In addition, Father Grzegorz offered missionary aid to the sick and needy. He arranged for access to medicine and in difficult instances served as a translator. For Polish laborers working illegally in Israel and not knowing Hebrew, this was an invaluable service. See *Sługa Mesjasza. Z ks. Grzegorzem Pawłowskim—Jakubem Herszem Grinerem rozmawia Lucyna Montusiewicz* (Lublin 2005).

7. Antoni Winter (1910–1988)—a long-time teacher in the Siedlce school district, social activist, and regionalist. He authored the historical monograph *Dzieje Siedlec 1448–1918* as well as numerous articles devoted to this city. During the German occupation, he was engaged in aid to the poor and to Children of the Zamość Region.

8. *Nowy słownik ortograficzny PWN*, ed. E. Polański (Warsaw 2000).

Chapter 1.

Siedlce and the Jews through the End of the Nineteenth Century

"A certain Jewish jokester, purporting to be well versed in the Hebrew language, figured out that Siedlce [...]—Shedlets [Hebrew שֶׁדְלֶץ—ed.] derives from two words: 'Shed' ('devil') and 'lets' ('jester'), together meaning an evil spirit, something that is the worst possible thing in the Jewish world."[1] This term served well-known Hebrew poet living in Israel Ilan Sheinfeld as the title of his fantasy legends called *Shedlets* (Siedlce). They are based on the experiences he encountered in his childhood listening to the tales of his mother and grandmother, who were from Siedlce.[2]

This joke notwithstanding, there are several versions of the source of the name of the city. "Siedlce" is the diminutive of the Old Polish noun *siodło* [saddle], which denotes a village, a settlement.[3] Koziorowski also derives the name "Siedlce" from the word *siodło*, indicating the analogous form in Old Czech.[4] Stanisław Wąsowski put forth a bold hypothesis. There are three villages close together in the vicinity of Checin: Siedlce, Sokołów, and Łukowa. It was this that justified the supposition that Siedlce, as well as the nearby cities of Łuków and Sokołów, were founded by colonists from those villages, who arrived here starting in the thirteenth century and settled on terrain that was at that time uninhabited.[5] Stanisław Litak derives the name "Siedlce" from the forest called Siedlisko, which surrounds nearby Pruszyn from the west and south.[6] There was also a legend in which Queen Bona, when traveling through these parts, marveled at the landscape and said that this would be a good place to found a settlement.

The first historical mention of Siedlce occurred in 1448. It is a power of attorney of the bishop of Kraków, Zbigniew Oleśnicki, given to the clergyman Mikołaj from the parish in Łuków, to which Siedlce belonged, for the purpose of collecting tithes from the village Siedlecz.[7] More information about Siedlce comes from the beginning of the sixteenth century, that is, the year 1503 and following. According to these records, the owner of Siedlce was Daniel Siedlecki, a member of the powerful Gniewosz family with the Rawicz coat of arms.[8] In 1532, thanks to the efforts of Stanisław Siedlecki, Siedlce became a parish. "The parish of Siedlce almost from the moment of its founding acquired many patrons and benefactors, among whom there were also Jews from Łuków who, wanting to secure peace for themselves,

7

offered a thousand Polish florens to the Siedlce church in 1675. Stanisław Siedlecki also saw to it that King Sigismund granted the rights of a city to Siedlce in 1547."[9]

The oldest signs of Jewish settlement in Siedlce come from the seventeenth century. This information in based on research performed in Jewish cemeteries by Maurycy Sztein in 1910. These cemeteries provided information about the earliest history of the Jewish community in Siedlce.

The oldest Jewish cemetery in Siedlce was located near the former horse market next to the city's synagogue. The date of its founding is not known. We do know, however, that up to the time of the Second World War, it contained a gravestone, a *matzevah*, from 1630. On 22 March 1798, Duchess Aleksandra Ogińska issued an order in which she confirmed the grant of land for the cemetery, making it development free. She brought about the closing off of the cemetery and ordered the community to put it in order by building a tall enclosure and planting linden trees.[10] In 1936, this cemetery was surrounded by a brick wall stretching along Żydowska Street (currently Berek Joselewicz[a] Street) from the synagogue building to Długa Street (currently Bishop I. Świrski Street) and then as far as Stary Rynek Street (this street no longer exists, as it is overlapped by an internal roadway among the buildings of the former Provincial Offices). The cemetery had an area of 2,412 square meters. Next to it was the synagogue.[11] The date of the building of the first wooden synagogue in unknown. What is known is that it burned down in 1851. A new, brick one was built on this same spot in 1856–1870. It was destroyed by the Germans in December 1939. The buildings of the BGŻ [Bank of the Food Industry] and the skyscraper of the former Provincial Offices are now located in this spot.

The next cemetery was located next to the Jewish hospital. It contained some gravestones from the years 1740–1822, but we know that people were buried there before 1740 as well. In 1926, this cemetery had an area of 4,780 square meters and was surrounded by a brick enclosure, stretching along Świętojańska and Sienkiewicz Streets.[12] It was completely destroyed during World War II. Only a fragment of the brick wall survived, against which the Nazis shot 10 Poles on 27 November 1943. Currently the wall contains a memorial tablet with the names of the murder victims and an appropriate bas-relief. After being recovered by the Jewish Religious Council in Warsaw, the hospital building was taken down and the land was sold. It is currently occupied by an apartment building. The destruction of the hospital by the legal owner was met with great surprise, and even with protests, by the residents of the city.[13]

The last cemetery, which exists to this day on Szkolna Street, was purchased by the Jewish community council, that is, the *kahal*, from the Christian Mateusz Skolimowski in 1826. The purchase was made on behalf of the Jewish community council by Josek Złotypierścień, Dawid Grynberg, and Mojżesz Nusbaum. In that year the cemetery was probably enlarged, because the archive of the Jewish community council contains documents confirming the functioning of this cemetery from 1807.[14] The oldest gravestone that was to be found there before World War II dates to 1827. Currently the oldest extant gravestone dates from 1855. Due to the expansion of the city in the vicinity of the cemetery, its closure was scheduled for 1 March 1867. The new one was to be created outside the city east of Stara Wieś. This intention was not, however, realized. On the contrary, in 1869 the cemetery was enlarged when a large area of land was purchased from the Mirkowski brothers. The next enlargement took place in 1910. In 1926, the Jewish community council bought two additional parcels of land connecting the cemetery with Cmentarna Street. Residents who owned property between these parcels protested, lodging a complaint with municipal and provincial authorities. In spite of this, burials took place on these two parcels at a distance of 30–80 meters from the cemetery proper.[15] The cemetery occupies an area of about 3,000 square meters.[16] It was desecrated on 22 March 1936. Headstones were painted over and pulled out of their footings. The perpetrators entered the cemetery after pulling several wooden slats out of the fence. This desecration took place during the period of emotional debates over the banning of ritual slaughter. The authorities linked the entire matter to these events. During the occupation, the Nazis committed mass executions of local Jews on the grounds of the cemetery. The shootings took place mostly against the cemetery wall. Additionally, bodies that were brought by truck were burned and buried there. It has not been determined where these transports came from. In 1942 the dead in a transport of Jews from Radom were buried here. As late as 1961, the Jewish Cemetery Inspection Commission counted as many as 18 mass graves, each of which was 5 and 10 meters long. About 3,000 murdered people are buried in them. These graves came into being after the majority of the signs of the criminal activities of the occupiers had been obliterated. In 1944 the Nazis exhumed the bodies of those they had murdered and burned them on pyres. The stench of burning bodies hung over the city for days. The older residents of Siedlce remember the event to this day.[17]

Materials that might more precisely document the history of the Jews in the beginning of their settlement in the city have not survived. Jews in Siedlce are first mentioned in a charter granted by Władysław IV on 8 December 1635. Thereafter they appear in all property inventories. Thus, in 1730 there were 39 Jewish families in the city, in 1755, 123 houses were recorded, of which 29 were Jewish. Siedlce was populated in 1765 by 631 Jews, and the function of rabbi was performed at that time by Meir, the author of a Talmudic commentary, "The Path of Meir." Subsequent years saw a drop in the Jewish population: 218 Jews resided in the city, along with Stara Wieś, in 1787, but in 1794 an increase occurred, with 375 people recorded.

A messianic movement arose in the seventeenth century among the Jewish population of the territory of eastern Poland. A universal expectation of the coming of the messiah spread among the Jews after the slaughter carried out by Chmielnicki's Kossacks. Such a movement developed in Podlasie as well. Its leader was Jehuda

He-Chasid. He was born about 1655, but it is not known with certainty whether it was in Siedlce. But he did live here a long time and surrounded himself with Jews from the city and its environs. Among his closest "brothers" were Gedalia from Siemiatycze and Abraham ben Gad Janower (Janowski). When Jehuda He-Chasid was 20, he left for Italy, where he studied the kabala in Verona for half a year.[18] After returning, he became a preacher in Szydłów by Grodno. Jehuda Chasid left Poland in 1699 along with 120 followers with the intention of heading for the Holy Land. On the way, on German territory, he was joined by other Jews, fascinated by his beautiful sermons. The number of his followers grew to 1,500 people. They called themselves the "Holy Society" (Chevra *Kadisha*). The foundation of his teaching was the announcement of pending salvation, which would befall only those Jews who did penance, were reborn morally, and turned to God anew. On regular days, they ate only bread and oil, only on Shabbat and holidays did they eat meat and other products deriving from living animals. They bathed daily in cold water and slept only on the ground, not in beds. The most zealous of them slept no more than two hours a day, spending the rest of the time on studying their writings. They were preparing for the arrival of the messiah by perfecting themselves morally and through frequent prayer, fasting, and penance (among others, by self-flagellation). Jehuda Chasid was an impassioned preacher with the ability to kindle a fire in the hearts of crowds of listeners and reach women as well with his messianic propaganda. There were instances when he would go into the part of the synagogue reserved for women and preach to them. He announced that the messiah would be revealed in 1706, but he never said who he would be, thanks to which he avoided the accusation of Sabbatianism.[19] In Nikolsburg in Moravia, the society divided into two groups. One, led by Chajim Malach and consisting of 150 people, took advantage of Samuel Oppenheim's offer and sailed down the Danube River to the Black Sea and from there to Jaffa. The other, larger group, under the leadership of Jehuda Chasid, went to Italy, from which it took ship in two groups to the Holy Land.[20]

It is interesting that the Chasidim were also joined by Christians who shared their messianic expectations. One of these was the mystic Hochmann von Hochenau. He believed that the Jewish road to salvation did not require that one change one's religion. The roads of Christians and Jews would converge when the messiah was revealed to one and the other. Hochenau agreed with the Chasidim that the messiah would appear in 1706 in Jerusalem, for they believed that no one would be saved outside Eretz Israel (Land of Israel).

Jehuda Chasid arrived in Jerusalem with his followers on 14 October 1700. There were only one thousand at that point, since 500 had died along the way. They settled by the old trading road in the ruins of cellars dating from the times of the Second Temple. They worked together to renovate the cellars, converting them into livable houses. The area occupied by the brothers was called the "Court of the Ashkenazim," that is, Eastern European Jews. Gedalia from Siemiatycze, the chronicler of the society, wrote down their first impressions: "The aforementioned Rabbi Jehuda Chasid set up a Midrash, a house of prayer, and constantly practiced in it both day and night with great penitential reverence, zealous prayers, sincere sorrow and tears. He also ordered that a spring or well be made, and every evening as well as every morning he would bathe in this spring or well and submerge himself three times, displaying great devotion in doing so. He did this for several days, and when, on the morning of the eleventh day, he submerged himself in this water, he fell ill and suddenly died."[21] The moment of death itself he presented in the following way: "Our teacher Rabbi Jehuda Chasid arrived in Jerusalem with his supporters on the day of the new moon in the month of Cheshvan 5461. [...] Most were ill from the great hardships of the voyage. The accommodations on the ship were very bad, and the space provided for all of us was much too tight. Our teacher went to the mikveh on the eve of Shabbat, and then he suddenly fell ill. He still said the evening prayer, but when he left the synagogue, he collapsed. Then he was delirious, repeating the morning prayer, constantly the same verses, without regaining consciousness. His brother-in-law, Rabbi Yeshayahu, finally said the Kiddush, and then a doctor was summoned. There was a wealthy Sephardic doctor in Jerusalem, equally versed in scholarship and in medicine, Reb Mordechai Molko. [...] When the aforementioned physician came, he said that he could do nothing now, that we would have to wait one day. On the morning of Shabbat, our teacher rose, washed, and said the morning prayer. Then he asked everyone's forgiveness for having disturbed their night's peace. He did not remember what had happened in the evening. He felt only that there was some sickness in him, but he felt almost recovered. Then he collapsed again. This time he was deprived of speech, he could not utter a word. He testament must lie somewhere under his writings; he often wrote on it. He was buried that very same day; many men and women of Jerusalem paid him their final respects. The Sephardic hazzan sang the Sephardic threnody, and all those who were gathered bitterly mourned the sudden death of our teacher and regretted that they were not worthy of seeing his saintly countenance. After every verse of the dirge, they beat their heads with their hands and called out: Woe! Woe! Even if someone had a heart of stone, he would have softened. Then the most distinguished Sephardim carried the litter to the cemetery on the Mount of Olives, and there he was buried, just as they do abroad, not in a tomb as was previously the custom here. His wife, the rabbanit, died a year later, and then his beloved little son. They moved on to eternity but left us in despair."[22]

Not all Chasidim, however, accepted the fact of Jehuda Chasid's death. As late as 1733, many of his followers in Poland, Germany, and Czechoslovakia sold their homesteads and set off for Jerusalem, believing that Jehuda was hiding in some cave and would be found. Some even believed him to be the messiah, who after his death would reveal his mission. The remaining brothers decided to build a synagogue in their neighborhood. They bought a large lot with this goal. One of the brothers described the situation at that time in the following way: "A huge amount of money was spent on the synagogue and its courtyard and many bribes were given to the Moslem rulers of Jerusalem before they let us build." The synagogue lasted a mere 18 years. Bitter religious tensions arose between the Sephardim, that is, the Mediterranean Jews, and the recently arrived Ashkenazim. The rulers of Jerusalem at the time supported the Sephardim, and in 1720 the Ashkenazim were driven out and the synagogue destroyed.

The site of the synagogue has a further history. In 1857, the building of a new shrine was begun. It was directed by Rabbi Mordechai Tsoref. The construction lasted seven years. More than half the cost was financed by a Jew from Bagdad, Joheskel Reuven. The rest was gathered from donations of the faithful. There was a saying that circulated among the donors: "Whoever buys one stone will see his life's ambitions fulfilled." This was an allusion to Rabbi Hanina ben Dosa, who carried stones during the construction because he did not have the money to make a donation. The erected synagogue had suggestions of medieval Ottoman architecture. A characteristic feature of the shrine was a cupola of large dimensions. The interior was ornamented with paintings containing motifs of the Shield of David, seven-armed candlesticks, as well as the tablets of law received on Mount Sinai. The synagogue was named Hurvat Rabbi Jehuda He-Chasid, from the surname of its original founder. Yet this structure also did not last. During the battles between the Jews and Arabs in 1948, the synagogue was destroyed, and the land was incorporated into Jordan. In 1967, after the six-day war, the Jews once again incorporated this part of the city into their country. They planned to rebuild the synagogue according to a new design. Yet none was accepted. A reconstruction according to the old design was also not undertaken. The place was simply reinforced, that is, the walls were torn down and one of the four arches holding up the cupola was reconstructed.[23]

The heyday of Siedlce did not come until the second half of the eighteenth century, during the time when Aleksandra Ogińska was the owner of the city. At her initiative, the stone palace was enlarged, the building of an arch of triumph was completed, a park was built, and many building were built that stand to this day. In order to gain funds for the renovation of city hall, Ogińska, on 1 April 1787, sold 28 stores that were in the ground-floor part of the building to the Jews in perpetuity. In 1783. King Stanisław August Poniatowski was visiting Siedlce. He was sumptuously greeted by Ogińska and two delegations: a Christian one, and a Jewish one. The Jewish delegation, in discussions with the king, touched on the matter of building a synagogue.

Jews were engaged primarily in trade and rental. We must assume that the Siedlce community council (kahal) existed in an organized form in the second half of the eighteenth century. In 1794, the community council started to construct its own building with an apartment for the rabbi and with a separate accommodation for a yeshiva (a higher Talmudic school for educating rabbis and teachers of religion).[24]

After the partitions of Poland, the city came under the rule of Austria. In 1804, Siedlce became an administrative city. Prince Adam Czartoryski turned Siedlce into the national property of the Austrian government. During the war of 1809, the city was incorporated into the Duchy of Warsaw and became a main city of the department, that is, the seat of local authorities. After the creation of the Kingdom of Poland in 1815, Siedlce became the capital city of Podlasie Province. When Podlasie Province was liquidated in 1845, [Siedlce] became a county seat of the Siedlce District of Lublin Province. From 1 January 1867 to 1912, Siedlce was the provincial seat of the newly created Siedlce Province.[25]

Not much is known about the Jews in Siedlce in the beginning of the nineteenth century. We know that three people had the exclusive right to sell kosher meat in 1812–1813: Abraham son of Dawid, Kalman son of Mosze, and Jakow son of Icchak.

In 1819–1823 the so-called Brześć Road was built. It led from Warsaw through Mińsk Mazowiecki, Siedlce, Międzyrzec, Biała Podlaska, and Terespol as far as Brześć and on to Russia. The city revived as a result of this road. A period of frequent contacts with Warsaw and Brześć as well as with other towns was initiated. Many people who traveled this route stopped in Siedlce. A brisk export of grain and other agricultural produce from the area ensued. This was noticed by Zofia Ścisłowska, who traveled this road and wrote down her observations in *Recollections from a Ride through the Country*: "Finally, Siedlce's being considered a small town can also be justified by the fact that all of trade remains in the hands of bearded speculators who, even after the city burned down in October 1854, work by baking commonplace bread, which was difficult to consume by residents accustomed to the famous Siedlce rolls that owed their existence to the cook of Her Excellency Ogińska, the Marshall's wife, once the heiress of this city, and that were at the time so famous that they were sent to Warsaw to the table of King Stanisław August. It is no small difficulty for the residents to become accustomed to Jewish bread and not so easy to forget about the rolls, which have passed into posterity! Yet on the other hand, one cannot deny the right that Siedlce has to being called a city, for it has a number of magnificent buildings. There is also a court of justice, before whose sentences many have bent their heads in humility. There is a credit society, a postal department, district authorities, and a treasury authority. There are schools with five grades, there is a girls' boarding school under the management of the respectable headmistress, Mistress Krzysztof. Siedlce also has a printing house and a bookstore, in which one can find a physic for boredom, if one suffers from that ailment. There are as many as two pharmacies, two confectionaries, two inns, one of which has the grand name of "Warsaw Hotel" and a cafeteria run by the firm of Mistress Najbelt, which has been well-known for a long time; this is a place for occasional evening rendezvous, the only social club for the residents. One can also find here several wine bars under the ownership of exiles, or rather, owners of the promised land: all this inclines one to call Siedlce a city, and henceforth we shall call it that."[26]

The German-language writer and astute observer of life Heinrich Heine also traveled along the Breść Road, describing his impressions in the book *About Poland*. Here is how he presented his observations: "I get shivers down my spine when I remember how I saw a Polish village inhabited primarily by Jews beyond Międzyrzecz for the first time. Even the *W— Weekly*, even if it were cooked to a pulp, would not be able to induce me to retch with such energy as the sight of these ragged, dirty individuals; nor would my ears be tormented to such a degree by the excruciating oration of a school kid enflamed by the love of physical education and fatherland as the Jewish jargon. Yet the disgust soon gave way to compassion when I looked more closely at the fate of these people and when I saw the pigsty-like burrows in which they live, jabber, pray, swindle, and—eke out an existence. Their language is Germanic, shot through with Hebrew, and cut to a Polish fashion. In olden times, due to religious persecutions, they migrated from Germany to Poland; for Poles were always distinguished by tolerance in similar cases. When some religious humbugs advised one of the Polish kings to force Polish Protestants to return to the fold of Catholicism, he replied, "*Sum rex populorum, sed non conscientiarum!*" [I am the king of people but not of their consciences!—author's note]. Jews were the first to bring trade and industry to Poland, for which Kazimierz the Great bestowed upon them extensive privileges. It seems they were much closer to the nobility than to the peasantry; for according to an old statute, a Jew gained nobility by converting to Christianity *eo ipso*. I do not know whether or why this statute was abolished and which of these two things lost their value. In those far-off times, Jews, both culturally and in education, certainly surpassed the nobleman, who pursued only the raw craft of war and did not yet have any French refinement. They, the Jews, on the other hand, at least were occupied with their Hebrew books in the fields of scholarship and religion, because of which they in fact had to leave their fatherland and a comfortable life. It seems, however, that the Jews did not keep pace with European culture, and their spiritual world became mired in unfortunate superstitions, which ingenious scholasticism forcibly squeezes into thousands of bizarre forms. And yet, in spite of the barbaric fur hat covering his head and in spite of the even more barbaric idea filling this head, I respect the Polish Jew immeasurably more than many a German Jew with a Bolivar on his head and Jean Paul in his head. The character of the Polish Jew, fated to complete isolation, became a compact whole; this Jew took on the stigmas of freedom. This man did not create within himself a quodlibetical mix of a variety of feelings and did not waste away, because he was not sentenced to choking in the tight walls of the Jewish streets of Frankfurt, in arch-intelligent urban regulations and merciful legal limitations. The Polish Jew, in his dirty gabardine, with his beard populated by vermin, with his garlic odor and gibberish, is dearer to me still than any number of Jewish potentates appearing in all their splendor of state debentures."[27]

Relations between the Jews and the Christian population varied. This is testified to by the fact that in 1816 a case of "ritual murder" took place in Siedlce.[28] The lack of understanding by the Christian population of Jewish religious practices was taken advantage of to spread anti-Semitism. It was in particular about the consumption by Jews of meat resulting from ritual slaughter. Jews consumed meat coming from animals and birds that the Bible calls clean and are popularly defined by the term "kosher" (in Hebrew *kasher*—"suitable"). The rules of slaughter had as their goal the elimination of blood, since its consumption was completely forbidden. The consumption of matzo, that is, unleavened bread, also became shrouded in legend. Jews consumed it during the holiday of Pesach, also called the Holiday of Unleavened Bread. It fell during the month of Nisan (March–April) and lasted 7–8 days. During this whole holiday, only unleavened bread, matzo, was to be consumed. Pesach was a spring holiday commemorating the exodus of the Israelites from Egyptian slavery. Religious Jews observe these rules in the present day, endowing them with great significance. Over the course of a number of centuries, libels were spread that Jews purportedly ritually murdered Christian children and added their blood to the matzo. Such libel often led to pogroms and lawsuits.[29]

It has been noted that an attempt was made in 1823 to create a zone for Jewish residents in Siedlce. A Podlasie Province commission worked out a special project as a result of which Jews were forbidden to live on the main streets, and the neighborhood in which they were to reside was demarcated as the western section of Piękna Street (currently Pułaski Street) and others, located in the southern or western parts of the city. The final deadline for relocation was set as the end of 1825 under threat of forcible removal of violators by the police as well as a financial penalty. No wooden, only brick, houses were allowed to be built in the Jewish neighborhood, and those according to approved designs. This project was never implemented.[30]

The November Uprising broke out on the evening of 29 November 1830.[b] The east-central location of Podlasie Province in the Kingdom of Poland made it an important area for operational reasons. In 1829, the territory of the province had a population of 362,331; of these, 37,939 residents, or 11 percent, were Jews, of which 80 percent lived in cities and 20 percent in rural areas. The percentage share of the Jewish population compared to the total population of Podlasie Province was 46 percent in cities and only 3 percent in rural areas. Most Jews were in Radzyń District, 31 percent, and in Siedlce District, 26 percent. In connection with the organization of new military formations by the insurgents, there was an increased need for footwear and sheepskin coats for the soldiers. As early as 19 December 1830, the Governmental War Commission called upon Piotr Strzyżewski, the deputy president of the Podlasie Province Commission, to take on the fulfillment of this responsibility with all due speed. In Siedlce, the requisite agreements were signed with Poles for the manufacture of footwear: ankle boots for the infantry and riding boots for the cavalry, but it was Jewish trade workers who took on their manufacture. The rallying point for the whole province was also set up in Siedlce. By 28 January, 527 pairs of ankle boots (57 from Siedlce, 120 from Międzyrzec, 164 froom Sokołów, 120 from Żelechów, and 65 from Biała) and 297 pairs of riding boots (125 from Siedlce, 123 from Żelechów, and 49 from Biała) had been manufactured and sent to the Military Station in Warsaw. The Supreme National Council imposed an obligation for Jews to supply 10 thousand sheepskin coats for the Polish army. The Jews of Podlasie Province were to supply 879. Their collection was carried out by Antoni Hincz, the mayor. By 2 February 1831, 673 sheepskin coats were taken in. The best at meeting their obligation were the Jews of Siedlce District, 100 percent, and Biała District, 83 percent, whereas the worst were those of the Łuków and Radzyń Districts, 62 percent.[31] It must be emphasized that to a large degree the speed of supplying the coats depended on the generosity and wealth of the Jews and to a lesser degree by the number of trade workers. Sandomierz Province, known for its slowness in supplying sheepskin coats, had the most furriers, and large numbers of sheep skins were tanned, according to data from 1827. So the Jews of Siedlce fulfilled their obligation superbly.

On 10 April 1831, a battle took place at Iganie with the goal of taking over Siedlce by the insurgents and crush the Russian units under General Grigory Rozen. The plan of attack was to hit the Russian units that were camped along the Brześć Road from two sides. General Ignacy Prądzyński attacked from the south, while the main attack was to come from the north under the command of General Jan Skrzynecki. Unfortunately, General Ignacy Prądzyński began the attack on his own, with only about seven thousand troops, intended for close combat, at his disposal. The Russians had a significant advantage; they threw 14–16 thousand soldiers onto the battlefield, among which were crack units of the so-called Lions of Varna. These were regiments of riflemen (thirteenth and fourteenth) that had won fame during the battles for Varna [in modern-day Bulgaria—trans.] during the Russo–Turkish War in 1829. They were decimated by the Polish artillery under the command of Major Józef Bem and the Polish infantry in a bayonet clash. In spite of serious losses (about five thousand men), the Russians retreated to Siedlce and prepared a defense. The Polish side sustained 400–500 deaths and many injuries. The Poles were in no condition to continue the attack on the city. General J. Skrzynecki arrived with his troops after the battle and the withdrawal of the Russians. Although it did not bring the intended military results, the victorious battle gained a permanent place in the history of the Polish and Jewish communities.

Between 1841 and 1843, a prison in the American style was built in the city with 117 cells. Its official opening was held 3 June 1844. The prison grounds contained a factory hall and the court building. The prison was modernized in 1882–1885 and

1891–1892. It contained two chapels: Eastern Orthodox and Catholic. Jewish prisoners held their devotions in the factory hall, and the Torah and necessary prayer accessories were kept in a special cell. During their holidays, Jewish prisoners were able to prepare their meals according to the dictates of their religion and their tradition. Many political prisoners served time in the prison. It exists and functions to this day.

Siedlce suffered an unsuccessful attempt at an uprising in 1846. The merchant Icchak Grinberg fought in the insurgent detachment commanded by Pantaleon Potocki.[32]

In 1851, the old, wooden synagogue burned down. The new, brick one was started in 1856, but in 1870 there was another fire, which destroyed the roof and the Aron Kodesh ([Holy Ark], the place where the Torah scrolls are kept). The work took several years and was completed in 1876. "The height of the synagogue was about four stories; two large windows in the shape of the tablets of the covenant, were placed on the eastern and on the western sides right under the roof. Beyond the entrance there was a large vestibule that led on the right to a small prayer house, known as the 'tailors' small prayer house,' and on the left was the women's gallery, which was part of the first floor on the northern and southern sides. The other part was located on the fourth floor of the synagogue. To the right and left of the vestibule, stairs led to the balcony, which was located on a level with the second floor. A large hall furnished with benches for 800 people stretched before a person entering the interior of the synagogue. Four or five steps led up to a podium (bima) in its center. The eastern wall around the Aron Kodesh was decorated with musical instruments of hammered copper. The Aron Kodesh was in the wall. In front of it gleamed two lions. Scenes from the Bible were painted around it."[33] The architect of the synagogue is not known; the Aron Kodesh was fashioned by J. Cwibak and his sons. Next to the synagogue was the city's Beit Hamidrash[34] as well as the home of the Chevra Mishnayot.[35] These buildings (or premises) were connected into one large structure. The synagogue was burned by the Germans on 25 December 1939. Next to the synagogue in Siedlce were numerous small prayer houses for trade workers, such as butchers (who engaged in ritual slaughter), cobblers, and so forth. The small prayer houses for trade workers were formed on the basis of occupational interests as a counterweight to Polish guilds.

Starting in 1820 and up to 1900, a very sharp dispute waged between the Chassidim (Chassid—"pious, God-fearing") and their opponents, called Mitnagdim (in Hebrew, Mitnaged—"opponent"). The opponents of the Chassidim came from Orthodox Jews who looked unfavorably upon any kind of religious novelty. The movement known as Chassidism, as has already been mentioned, arose in the first half of the eighteenth century in the eastern territories of the Polish Republic and very quickly found followers in Ukraine. In the years that followed, it spread in all directions, finding support everywhere. From the time Jews were slaughtered by

Chmielnicki's Cossacks, a mood of great uncertainty and grief reigned in Ukraine. It was halted by Israel ben Eliezer (c. 1700–1760), known as Baal Shem Tov, that is, a Man of Good Name. In its popular understanding, Baal Shem Tov signifies a man whom the people trust. In a religious sense, it is a man who communes with that which is godly, who lives with and for his neighbors. The master himself did not write down his teachings; they survive in fragments thanks to his students' notes.[36] "God, so the Baal Shem teaches, is in each thing as its primal essence. He can only be apprehended by the innermost strength of the soul. If this strength is liberated, then it is given to man at each place and at each time to receive the divine. Each action which is dedicated in itself, though it appear ever so lowly and meaningless to those who see it from the outside, is the way to the heart of the world. In all things, even in those that appear completely dead, there dwell sparks of life that fall into the soulds that are ready. What we call evil is no essence, but a lack. It is 'God's exile,' the lowest rung of the good […]."[37]

Chassidism was the common man's answer to formalized Judaism. Chassidic fellowships arose within official Jewish communities as groups whose aim was communal prayer. These fellowships were characterized by piety and joy of life, often exhibited through dance and song. Each fellowship was bound and distinguished by respect for righteous men, that is, *tzadikim*. The Chassidic fellowship did not constitute a community in the literal sense of this word but rather a gathering of the followers of one tzadik scattered in various places. The Chassidim regarded the tzadik as their greatest authority in religious and secular matters. A group resembling a court retinue gradually formed around the tzadik. The title of tzadik generally became hereditary, which contributed to the formation of various dynasties. A tzadik was supported by his followers, who visited him particularly during holidays. Sometimes this led to their living a very affluent life. But most tzadikim lived modestly and in poverty, gaining respect for themselves through knowledge and piety. There were many distortions in this movement, particularly in its later period. Rapturous love for the tzadik coexisted quite early on with crude adoration, treating the tzadik as a great miracle worker who "maintains an intimacy with heaven," can fix everything, and can secure a "comfortable" place in the other world. There was often hostility between the followers of different tzadikim. Frequently superstitions spread among the Chassidim. Currently, most Chassidim live in the United States and Israel.[38]

During 1823–1824, there were at least 30 Chassidim in a total Jewish population in Siedlce of 2,908 people living in 391 families. We find this out from an interrogation of Abraham Dawidowicz Kohen, in whose house local Chassidim gathered. He stated in the record of the interrogation that the Chassidim had been active "from Austrian times," which means from the years 1795–1804.[39]

The tzadik Symcha Bunim from Przysucha (?–1827) had a rather large number of supporters in Siedlce. The most influential of these was Zisie Siedlecer (of Siedlce).

Tzadik Bunin was a sensitive and intelligent man. He was connected with Jakub Icchak from Lublin, known as the Seer, and later with Yehuda–Jakub Icchak from Przysucha. After the death of Yehuda, a large number of the Przesucha Chassidim chose him as their rabbi.

Bunim was called the Knower of the Mystery. Throughout his entire life he strove for the renewal of Chassidism. His influential opponent in Siedlce was Meir Nisem (?–1810), the founder of the many branches of the Nusbaum family. A kind of trial arose over Bunim. It took place in Ostylec during the wedding of Opatów rabbi Abraham Yehoshua Heshel's grandson. This rabbi fulfilled the function of presiding judge of this court. Five students from Przysucha, chosen in secret balloting, went to Ostylec to defend Bunim. The delegation was chosen according to the following criteria: 1. wise man; 2. wise student; 3. pious Chassid; 4. wealthy man; 5. good speaker. Zisie Siedlecer was chosen as the wise man. Choosing him for such an important delegation testifies to the fact that he was known among the Chassidim, and the Siedlce followers of Bunim formed a considerable community. This was particularly true when Aleksander Zusja Kahan performed the function of rabbi in the 1820s. He was a close coworker of tzadik Symcha Bunim from Przysucha and known from the letter of protest he wrote in defense of the Chassidim to the representative of the Kingdom of Poland General Józef Zajączek asking him to rescind the decree delegalizing Chassidism.[40]

Yet it was the opponents of the Chassidim who led the Siedlce community in the nineteenth century. The opponents were the rabbis, the preachers, and the cantors. It was particularly the cantors who in Siedlce were the objects of quarrels and altercations between the discordant sides. Some believed that the cantor should be deeply religious and learned; other were prepared to disregard this under the condition that the cantor had a good mastery of the style of leading prayers and had a "sweet voice." Many Siedlce cantors were opponents of Chassidism. These included Szmuel Dawid Siemiatyczer, Ruwem Kantor, and Jakow Zelman Rubinsztajn. Rubinsztajn, who was feuding with the Chassidim, had to leave the city. Among the preachers who fought against the Chassidim were Monis and Izrael, called Izraelke the Preacher, who also left town in fear of attacks. During these years, the function of rabbi was performed until 1810 by Cwi Hersz Wajngarten and from 1853 to 1867 by Izrael Meisels. Israel Meisels was the son of Warsaw rabbi Duberisz Meisels. During his stay in Siedlce, he published the *Book of Commandments* by Rambam [Maimonides—ed.] with his father's commentaries. He died in 1876 in Kraków; these words were inscribed on his gravestone: " [...] He studied the Torah and the law of Israel day and night. As a judge, he judged Israel. He illuminated the sons of Israel with the light of his name [...]" One of the Beit Hamidrash in Kraków was named after him to honor his memory.

After Wajngarten and Meisels, the function of rabbi was performed by Baruch Lipszyc, the author of a religious book titled *Jakub's Covenant*.[41] They were all opponents of the Chassidim and held the highest offices in the community, thanks to which they were able to influence Jewish society. The battles between the Chassidim and their opponents not only brought much confusion but also contributed to the kindling of a religious life among Jews. The Siedlce opponent of the Chassidim Israel ben Jechiel Grinberg built a private Beit Hamidrash in 1878 because he did not want to pray in Chassidic houses of prayer. In 1903, Grinberg also built a religious Talmud-Torah school.

The battle between the Chassidim and their opponents ended when a new movement, Haskalah, or the Jewish Enlightenment, appeared among Jews. The supporters of the Haskalah were called Maskilim (the enlightened). Moses Mendelssohn (1729–1786) is considered to be the creator of the Haskalah. In the name of the implementation of assimilationist trends, he tried to prove the distinction between religious affiliation and a sense of national consciousness. The Maskilim had as their main goals the development of secular study, freeing Jews from the traditional attitude that is averse to any change, and gaining civil rights for Jews. The proponents of the enlightenment sent their children to Russian or Polish schools. This movement was elitist. All pious Jews fought against it vehemently.

In January 1863, there was an uprising on the territory of the Russian partition. Walenty Lewandowski along with a group of insurgents planned to attack the Russian garrison in Siedlce. However, the insurgents scattered before the attack took place.

The Jews, who had lived in the city for generations, had a positive attitude toward the uprising. They exhibited this support by cooperating with the representatives of the National Government. They sewed uniforms and sheepskin coats, they dealt in military equipment, and they transported mail. In the spring, on 26 March 1864, the tsarist authorities arrested the following Jews in Siedlce for sewing uniforms and coats for "the rebels": Sider Fagelman (a townsman from Sokołów, aged 60, father of four children), Jankiel Fridman (a townsman from Sokołów, age 40, father of three children), Simsza Futochman (a townsman from Sokołów, age 31, father of three children). Jankiel Snice (age 46, father of four children), however, a resident of the village of Trebień on the territory of Siedlce County, was arrested on 12 February 1864 for "making scythes in his home for the rebels." Altogether, 23 Jews in Siedlce County were arrested for aiding the insurgents.[42] The Siedlce Jew Michelson fought in an insurgent unit on the territory of Podlasie. Toward the end of the uprising, he was injured in battle and taken prisoner. In spite of being tortured, he did not betray his comrades in arms. He was hanged in Radzyń Podlaski on 18 August 1864.

Yet some Jews took an unfavorable view of the uprising movement. These were mostly arrivals from the depths of Russia, so-called Litwaks, who were imbued with Russian culture and language.

On 19 July 1851, the tsarist authorities issued a decree that bore the name

"Regulations concerning the use of clothing and specific characteristics of Jews and their women." The Siedlce chief of police at the time ordered that the decree be read three times in the city synagogue. It ordered the Jewish people to "resemble" Christians. Jewish men were to shave their sidelocks, beards, and hair; married women were to wear bonnets instead of wigs. Their attire was also to be more "European." Those who did not submit to the decree were fined. The authorities located the money from this source in a bank in Warsaw. In 1869, the sum collected amounted to 11,551 rubles. The Jewish community council, which was represented by Izrael Ber Liwerant, initiated efforts to have this money earmarked for the building of a Jewish hospital. The matter dragged on over twenty years. In 1880, a petition was sent to the tsarist authorities for the building of the hospital, signed by 233 Jews. The signees additionally committed themselves to paying 1,445 rubles annually for the benefit of the hospital. The hospital proposal was passed on to the minister of the interior in St. Petersburg. Only after four years, in 1884, was the proposal returned with the notation that technical flaws had been found in it and that the proposed sum of 1,445 rubles was insufficient for the maintenance of a hospital. Further efforts were made, which lasted another four years, that is, to 1888. The design was changed, the number of beds increased, and a commitment was made to cover all the hospital's expenses from their own donations. Abraham Kamiński, I.M. Lubelski, B. Kahan, as well as Rabbi Grohbard were engaged in conducting this case. The tsarist authorities continued trying to hamper matters, this time regarding the location of the hospital. Finally, approval was given for construction. In 1891 the hospital was ready. The following people were involved in this action: Juda Orzeł, Mordechaj Hajnsdorf, Tender Boksennbojm, Mosze Goldsztern, Nuta Zylberewajg, Note Rubinsztajn, Jakow Słuszny, Mosze Kelmenzon, Izrael Richter, Josef Zając, Gedalia Szapiro, Awigdor Solnicki, Beniamin Liwerant, Ch.D. Lichtenfacht, Meir Jona Rozencwajg, Jakow Grynszpan, Wolf Openhajm, Galman Kamienne, Kalman Wiśnia, and Kalman Jabłoń. Alter Słuszny was imposed as trustee, who managed the hospital and answered to the authorities. He did not have the support of the city authorities or the Jewish community council, which had wanted Doctor Rozental in this position. He was replaced after three years by Abraham Kamiński, who enjoyed the support of the community council. From 1902 to 1926, the position of trustee was held by Icchak Nachum Weintraub, a person who had great authority among local Jews. In order to assure income for the hospital, which was located by what was then the market square, fifteen stalls were set up. In 1892, a cholera epidemic broke out in Siedlce, and the hospital was converted to an infectious diseases hospital. The official opening of the hospital took place in 1893. In September 1906, during a military pogrom, the wounded and dead were brought to the hospital. During the shelling of the building by tsarist soldiers, the caretaker Jan Born, a Christian, and Judka Lipszyc, a patient, were killed, and paramedic Maria Łazarska was wounded. The hospital continued to function up to the World

War II. After the war, a children's hospital was located here for a time. Then for a number of years it served as a dental outpatient clinic.

In 1997, the process of restitution of real estate that had been the property of Jewish community councils began in Poland. The hospital building with the surrounding land was taken over by the Jewish Religious Council in Warsaw, which sold it in 2001 to the owner of a construction company and in the authenticated deed agreed to its demolition. The Union of Jews Originating from Siedlce in Israel and the city's public protested against such a decision. The protest against the demolition was signed by 246 people. The building was demolished in 2002 in spite of this, and apartment houses were built in its place.[43]

TRANSLATOR'S NOTES, CHAPTER 1

a. Berek Joselewicz—see chap. 5, n. 64.
b. November Uprising (1830–1831)—an armed uprising against Russia initiated by young officers at the military academy in Warsaw; supported by large segments of Polish society.

AUTHOR'S NOTES, CHAPTER 1

1. *Gazeta Podlaska*, no. 2 (1931): 7.
2. They were published in Tel Aviv in 1999 in Hebrew and contain 235 pages.
3. A. Brückner, *Słownik etymologiczny języka polskiego* (Warsaw, 1957), pp. 491–492.
4. S. Koziorowski, *Badania nazw topograficznych archidiecezji poznańskiej*, vol. 2 (Poznań, 1914), p. 185.
5. S. Wąsowski, "Koniec Podlasia," in *Gazeta Podlaska*, no. 2 (1932).
6. S. Litak, "Siedlce przed lokacją," in *Roczniki Humanistyczne*, vol. 11, book 2 (Towarzystwo Naukowe KUL: Lublin, 1962), p. 153.
7. A. Winter, *Dzieje Siedlec* (Warsaw, 1969), pp. 15–16.
8. Ibid., p. 16
9. Ibid., pp. 17–18.
10. Book of Remembrance of the Siedlce Community, ed. A.W. Jasny (Buenos Aires, 1956), pp. 14–15. [Published in Yiddish and Hebrew. The author used fragments translated from Yiddish into Polish by Adam Bielecki (see Introduction).—ed.]
11. Sąd Rejonowy w Siedlcach, Wydział Ksiąg Wieczystych (SR w S., WKW), księga hipoteczna no. 682.
12. SR w S., WKW, księga hipoteczna no. 697.
13. See Appendix 12.
14. M. Sztein, *O cmentarzyskach żydowskich w Siedlcach. Referat odczytany na posiedzeniu*

miesięcznym Siedleckiego Oddziału Towarzystwa Krajoznawczego dnia 14 czerwca 1910 r. (Siedlce, 1910–2008), p. 6.

15. Material in the author's possession.

16. SR w S., WKW, księga hipoteczna, no. 757.

17. W. Sobczyk, *Założenia projektowe na zagospodarowanie terenu cmentarza—pomnika męczeństwa Narodu Żydowskiego w Siedlcach przy ul. Szkolnej. Materiały historyczne i zdjęcia opracował Jontel Goldman*, typescript in the possession of the Nation Service for the Preservation of Landmarks in Siedlce; historical material and photographs compiled by Jontel Goldman.

18. Kabala—Hebrew *kabbalah*—"reception, acceptance, transmission, tradition." A mystical current of Judaism. The beginnings of the kabala should be sought in antiquity, among Jewish mystical groups occupied with questions of the beginning of the world and revelation. Its founding text is considered to be Sefer Yetsirah (Book of Creation—a treatise about the creation of the world). The greatest work of the kabala, Sefer ha-Zohar (Book of Radiance), was edited in the thirteenth century. It exists in many variations.

19. Sabbatianism—a messianic movement inaugurated in the middle of the seventeenth century by Shabetai Tsevi. It grew out of the kabalistic tradition. It preached that the Law of Moses and the institutions based on it were imposed on Israel by demonic forces and are contradictory to the tru e faith of the patriarchs. God's revelation is hidden in all religions that are based on the Bible and thus also in Islam and Christianity. Shabetai Tsevi converted to Islam in 1666, but he continued to preach his teachings clandestinely. [See Gershom Scholem, *Sabbatai Sevi: The Mystical Messiah, 1626–1676* (London: Routledge & Kegan Paul, 1973)—ed.].

20. J. Doktór, *Początki chasydyzmu polskiego* (Wrocław, 2004), p. 38.

21. Ibid., p. 38.

22. Ibid., pp. 38–39.

23. See photographs 17 and 18.

24. I. Kaspi, "History of the Jews in Siedlce," in *Book of Remembrance of the Siedlce Community*, pp. 20–21.

25. *Słownik geograficzny Królestwa Polskiego i innych krajów słowiańskich*, vol. 10 (Warsaw, 1889).

26. Z. Ścisłowska, *Wspomnienia z przejażdżki po kraju*, vol. 1 (Warsaw, 1857), pp. 86–87 (spelling consistent with original).

27. H. Heine, *O Polsce*, trans. Stanisław Rossowski (Lwów–Złoczów, n.d.), pp. 14–16 (spelling consistent with original).

28. I. Kaspi, "History of the Jews in Siedlce," p. 25.

29. The accusation of ritual murder in Siedlce appeared as early as the end of the eighteenth century. The design for a cemetery monument to the seven allegedly murdered people has survived. See *Katalog rysunków z Gabinetu Rycin Biblioteki Uniwersyteckiej w Warszawie* (Warsaw, 1969), vol. 2, item 796 (various localities; Siedlce, pp. 179–181).

30. A. Winter, "Siedlce jako ośrodek administracyjny w XIX w.," in *Szkice Podlaskie* (Siedlce, 1983), p. 12.

31. J. Warmiński, "Udział Żydów województwa podlaskiego w dostarczaniu obuwia i kożuchów dla wojska polskiego w czasie powstania listopadowwego 1830–1831 r.," in *Biuletyn Żydowskiego Instytutu Historycznego*, no. 2 (1975): 41–48.

32. I. Kaspi, "History of the Jews in Siedlce," p. 25.

33. Ibid., p. 30.

34. Beit Hamidrash—a house of study, a building containing its own library of religious works, designated for religious study, prayer, and discussion.

35. A building designated for the Brotherhood for the Study of the Mishnah.

36. M. Buber, *Opowieści chasydów* (Poznań, 1986). [Martin Buber, *Tales of the Hasidim* (New York: Schocken, 1947–48 / 1991).—ed.]

37. M. Buber, *Opowieści rabina Nachmana* (Paris, 1983), p. 17. [Translation used here is from Martin Buber, *The Tales of Rabbi Nachman* (New York: Horizon, 1956), pp. 12–13.—ed.]

38. W. Tyloch, *Judaizm* (Warsaw, 1987), pp. 244–252.

39. M. Wodziński, "Ilu było chasydów w Królestwie Polskim około 1830 roku?" in *Ortodoksja, emancypacja, asymilacja. Studia z dziejów ludności żydowskiej na ziemiach polskich w okresie rozbiorów*, no. 1 (2003): 39; Archiwum Główne Akt Dawnych w Warszawie, Centralne Władze Wyznaniowe (1871): 9–10, 42. Larger clusters of Chassidim, however, were found in neighboring cities, that is, 100 families in Sokołów, 60 in Żelechów, and 30 in Węgrów.

40. M. Wodziński, *Oświecenie żydowskie w Królestwie Polskim wobec chasysyzmu. Dzieje pewnej idei* (Warsaw, 2003), p. 111.

41. I. Kaspi, "History of the Jews in Siedlce," pp. 32–34.

42. T. Krawczak, "Nieznani powstańcy styczniowi na Podlasiu," in *Prace Archiwalno-Konserwatorskie na Terenie Województwa Siedleckiego*, issue 6, pp. 45–96.

43. This issue was discussed in the local and the Jewish presses; see *Głos Gminy Starozakonnych*, no. 1–2 (2003): 2–4.

CHAPTER 2.

THE SOCIAL AND POLITICAL LIFE
OF THE JEWS OF SIEDLCE
AT THE BEGINNING OF THE TWENTIETH CENTURY

After the fall of the January Uprising,[a] the Polish administration was abolished and was replaced by a new administrative division based on that in Russia. The country was divided into 10 provinces [gubernias]: Warsaw, Płock, Lublin, Łomża, Kalisz, Kielce, Piotrków, Radom, Siedlce, and Suwałki. Supreme authority was held by the Warsaw governor-general. He functioned as the commander of the Warsaw military district and stood at the head of the entire administration of the country. The Warsaw governor-general was the intermediary between the central authorities in St. Petersburg and the administrations subordinated to him on the territory of the Kingdom.[b]

Siedlce Province was founded on 1 January 1867 out of the northern part of the former Lublin Province and the small part of Stanisławów County that had been separated from Warsaw Province. In terms of area, Siedlce Province was the third largest in the Kingdom after Warsaw Province and Lublin Province. The province consisted of 12 cities, and Siedlce became the provincial capital. This event was followed by the city's development, which could be seen in the area of construction and the occupations connected with it: masonry, carpentry, woodwork, metalwork, and house painting. Arriving tsarist office workers needed housing of an appropriate standard. Houses were thus built for them or apartments rented. Housing rental became a good and regular source of income. A Municipal Credit Society was appointed, which issued construction loans. Between 1860 and 1890, construction work was mostly done by Jews. Only at the beginning of the twentieth century did Polish workers organize their own guild and successfully compete with Jewish trade workers, who were not successful in uniting and forming their own national guild. Shoemakers also enjoyed economic prosperity. They prepared whole transports of footwear, which was shipped into the depths of Russia. Master shoemakers were divided into two categories at that time. The first consisted of so-called authorized ones. These were trade workers who worked on their own and were distinguished by good, professional merchandise. The others were so-called outworkers [cottage workers]. These were shoemakers who worked for a larger middleman, who provided them with material and commissioned them to do the work. They

25

did their work in their homes, thus their name. Their sales were highest in the winter, when they sold inventory made during the summer. Shoemakers were well organized; there were about 150 "authorized shoemakers" and about 200 "out-workers," so at least 350 trade workers and their families in the city supported themselves through shoemaking. That was a considerable number in those days. If any one of them had financial troubles, he could get credit in cash or goods from such potentates as Orzeł or money changer S.B. Minel. Gaiter makers also experienced a period of prosperity. They were involved in the production of boot tops and gaiters. They were divided into two categories: authorized and trade. The "authorized" ones had the same status as authorized shoemakers. The "trade" ones, however, prepared merchandise for export. There were about 34 masters and about 100 workers among the gaiter makers. Unlike the shoemakers, the gaiter makers did not see a decrease in supply due to the outbreak of World War I because the military placed orders. Tailors formed another group of prosperous trade workers. There were about 35 master tailors in the city, and they were divided into five categories. The first were called "regimental" because they sewed for the needs of the army stationed in the city. Five masters and their helpers worked in this category. The second group contained twelve Jewish tailors and one Christian. They serviced the local Polish landowners and nobility as well as tsarist office workers. The third group comprised tailors for women, numbering five masters. The next group comprised nine so-called "cut-raters," who sewed using inferior materials and with less precision. The final group, comprising four masters, was specialized in servicing clients from the countryside and was thus called the "rural" group. About 100 people made a living at tailoring, including dressmakers and seamstresses.

Training someone for a trade took place in a practical way, when a boy was around 13 and his parents determined that their son has a "bad head for study." They then placed him in the care of a master, who was paid for four years. Such a youngster was called a "boy to be taught a trade." During this time he could learn very little, because he was more often used for housework than for the trade work itself. And so he would chop wood for fuel, carry water, buy produce for the master's wife, and even rock the cradle. After four years, he "got off training" and became a "yearly boy." He would get a small compensation once a year. After this he became a "time boy," that is, he would be paid for half a year after working through this time. Only after working through several half-years would he become a "weekly"—he would receive his pay after each week of work. The workday lasted from sunup to sundown during the summer and longer in winter. On Fridays before Shabbat, he worked shorter hours but without breakfast breaks. There were no vacations, and the master had complete power over the workers.

The post-uprising period in Podlasie was characterized by intensified Russification. Facts about the forcible conversion of the followers of the Uniate Church to Russian Orthodoxy are well known.[c] Jews were also subject to attempts at

Russification. A story circulated among the Jewish population of Siedlce, written down by Icchak Nachum Weintraub, about how the wife of a convert along with pious and less pious Jews sued her husband, Icchak Josel, who had converted to Russian Orthodoxy. He forcibly kidnapped and christened his younger son, who lived with his mother. The Jews, to whom the court did not return the child, kidnapped the boy from the home of the Russian to whom he had been entrusted and brought him up in the faith of his fathers so as to save him from Russification.[1]

The turn of the century found the Siedlce Jews in the situation that was described by Z. Zchuchit, correspondent for *Hamelitz* (The Advocate):

> Siedlce, one of the provincial seats in Poland, must be counted among the cities suffering such a bad fate. It is not often spoken of in the press, both to the good and to the ill, and it was for this reason that I decided to visit it and offer my impressions to public opinion. The number of Jews residing in Siedlce before the census was 18 thousand. Among them, thank God, are to be found both the wealthy and the very rich who could do much for the benefit of existing institutions and also to influence their brothers, impoverished both spiritually and materially. This is what the reader who is far from this city might think, but this is how the matter stands. Let us look just at the material condition of the population. The situation in commerce has worsened lately worldwide. Wages are low, especially since there is stagnation in trade and industry throughout Poland. Thus there is no industry or any branch of trade in a provincial seat such a Siedlce aside from booths and trade workers, whom we know from every small town and who earn their living through their hard work. Every resident of Siedlce who has any cash opens up a little booth, places his meager wares on the shelves, and sells it on credit. Understandably, he cannot get any earnings from this, but alas, what is he to do when there is no other way? This is why in Siedlce there are more booths than buyers and there is not a house in which one would not find a shop. The battle for existence is terrible. If someone crosses the street, he is set upon by hucksters who pull at him, each toward his own booth. The passer-by is stunned. People who have money in their pockets become moneylenders, and the helpless borrowers have no other way out and are forced to pay whatever interest is asked of them, and even interest for the interest. It is therefore no surprise that in a short time they become bankrupts and cannot make ends meet. [...] If they only understood they would start building factories, and thousands of Jews could find work there. Is in not laughable, that in a provincial seat such a Siedlce there is not a single factory? Every Jew likes to fake [imitate—author's note] another. If only one Jew would try to build a factory and be successful, many others would decide to compete with him. The proof is the stores that grow like

27

mushrooms after a rain. [...] The moral situation is no better than the material. Charitable organizations that could ameliorate the situation of the needy are completely nonexistent in the city. To the extent that there are societies called "Visiting the Sick" or "Medical Aid," they, too, are in a state of disorder. The directors do not issue reports, and no one requires them to be accountable. Does an institution such as a "Loan Fund," which is in such great need, even exist, especially now when the situation is so grave? Will anyone believe me when I say that even that institution is lacking? If someone becomes impoverished, then he should die of hunger. There is no prospect of a loan, except from those extortionists. To tell the truth, that are a few people here with good hearts who have willing hands for helping and improving the fallen and the impoverished, but one swallow does not make it spring... How distant are the rich Siedlce Jews from their brothers. The poverty of these people does not concern them in the least, about which we can be convinced by the following: In the published list of donors for the benefit of Bessarabian farmers who have suffered from the drought there is not one name from Siedlce! They did not offer even a kopeck. Why do the people of Siedlce distance and isolate themselves from the wider world and do not want to know what is happening under their noses?[2]

A [local branch of] the General Union of Jewish Workers in Russia and Poland—the Bund[d]—was founded in Siedlce in 1902. The Siedlce Socialist Committee stood at its head. It was created by Abraham Jabłoń, a woodworker, the grandson of the colonial merchant Chaim Szlomo Jabłoń, who was well known in the city at the time. The leading activists of the Committee were Eliasz Wicha, Zelman Jankiel Bursztyn, Tobiasz Kogan, Majer Liberand, Moszko Lias, Jankiel Ratyniewicz, Abram Lewin, Jakub Szczupak, Dawid Kunin, Etna Abramowicz, and Paja Leńska-Barszcz.[3] The Bund strove for a socialist revolution, as a result of which the proletariat was to take power. It also recognized the need for the dictatorship of the proletariat during the transitional phase. It fought against the emerging Zionist movement, whose aim was the formation of a Jewish state. The Bund saw the solution of the Jewish problem through the victory of socialism. Socialism was to bring the solution to their social and national problems to the Jews where they lived and where they would continue to live. This was to be achieved through the formation of national-cultural autonomy for them. It is for this reason that they voiced a need for the organizational autonomy of Jewish socialists. The Siedlce Bund at the beginning of 1906 was one of the more numerous organizations on the territory of the Kingdom after Warsaw, Łódź, and Białystok and counted about 200 members.[4] Bund combat troops for the province as a whole numbered about 80 people. These combat units were organized in Siedlce, Sokołów Podlaski, Węgrów, Parczew, Włodawa, and Biała Podlaska.

Just a year after its formation, the Bund was organizing a variety of efforts. During the night on 1 May 1903, Bund members distributed flyers calling for the celebration of Labor Day. Those who were in the Siedlce prison hung red flags from their windows, yelled out anti-tsarist slogans, and sang revolutionary songs during prison exercise sessions. Etna Abramowicz was the most active participant in these events.[5] What was happening in the Siedlce prison reached many people. It also reached Isaac Bashevis Singer, who wrote in *The Family Moskat*, "One of the men started to talk about the prison in Siedlce and the political prisoners confined there. They created their own self-rule. On 1 May, they dyed a piece of a white shirt with blood and made a flag out of it. There was a girl there, a consumptive, who was locked in a single cell. She poured kerosene on herself and set herself on fire."[6]

There was a poem, "In Battle," that was popular among Siedlce Bundists:

We are hated and expelled
We are persecuted and tormented
And all because we love
The people, poor and underfed.

They hang us and they shoot at us
They take our lives and our rights
Because we genuinely demand
Freedom for the hated peasants.[7]

In 1902, the Municipal Committee for Promoting Public Sobriety built a grand building that was popularly called the Public Teahouse. This was a cultural center for czarist functionaries and a place for propagating the Russian language and culture. One could there find all the most important newspapers appearing on the territory of the Russian Empire. It was important that one could get boiling water at no cost, and also tea and sugar at a small cost. This building, which exists to this day, became the meeting place for young socialists.[8] They would come here and over a cup of hot water or tea acquaint themselves with the official press, exchange conspiratorial writings, and discuss the revolution in a warm and esthetically pleasing environment. The tsarist gendarmes, however, discovered the true goal of these social get-togethers and put the building under surveillance. Several people were arrested, and some were searched. So the socialists went deeper underground. The head Bundist, Meir Wicha, rented an apartment in the attic on Przechodnia Street. The owner of the house was Mendel Liwerant. A signboard was hung on the front of the building announcing that this apartment housed a bookbinder's workshop. This was to justify the large number of people visiting this apartment, all the more so since Meir Wicha was a bookbinder by trade. Only initiated comrades, as the Bundists called themselves, met in this apartment, and a printing press was run with the use of a hectograph. Proclamations, flyers, and brochures were printed by

Zelman Bursztajn, Jakow Liwerant, and Ratyniewicz. When the socialist movement gained more and more followers, it was decided to form a so-called guild. At a designated time, especially on Saturdays after the midday meal, groups of conspirators would go out onto Warszawska Street (currently Piłsudski Street) and stroll between Szpitalna Street (currently Kochanowski Street) and Wojskowy Square (currently Pogoń Stadium). During these strolls, they would exchange papers and brochures. Agitators would try to talk young people into joining the party.

The intense agitation of the socialists soon led to the first strike. It was staged in the spring of 1902 among construction workers, especially carpenters. After agreements and secret balloting, it was decided that the following demands were to be presented to all the city's masters: 1. a twelve-hour workday; 2. a 90-minute break for the midday meal and a 30-minute break for breakfast; 3. work to take place during specific and constant hours; 4. masters should treat their workers better; 5. apprentices should be learning their trade and not be humiliated and exploited for household work.

Cards with the demands were stamped with a round stamp with the inscription "Org. Jewish Union of Russia, Lithuania, and Poland, Siedlce." In the middle of the stamp was a pair of clasped hands, a symbol of brotherhood. At first all the masters disregarded the demands. As soon as the season for construction work began, however, they acceded to the demands. The example of the construction workers influenced the house painters and the workers of the leather and tailoring industries. They all went on strike and won. After these successful strike actions, the tsarist police increased surveillance and in the spring of 1903 discovered the concealed apartment. Its owner, Meir Wicha, and Tojwele Kagan, an apprentice, were arrested. The police confiscated the hectograph, the party archive, and numerous brochures. During the investigation, Jankiel Ratyniewicz, Maks Szlomo Stołowy, Mosze Lias, and a person with the pseudonym "Long Kiwa" were detained. After spending a year in jail, Mosze Lias came home with advanced tuberculosis and soon died. His funeral turned into a demonstration. At the request of the family, the Bundists did not sing revolutionary songs or give speeches at the gravesite. When the funeral procession came to the "guild," that is, Szpitalna Street (currently Kochanowski Street), the Bundists unhitched the horse from the hearse and pulled it to the cemetery themselves. There they merely put down wreaths. The arrests did not stop the robust activity of the Bund. New activists appeared: Estera Mastbaum (the sister of Judl, "The Sloven"), Icie Stalow, Jehuda Liwerant, Herszel Liwerant, Jehoszua Szpigielman, and Izrael Chruściel. Their new leader was "Boris," sent from Warsaw. During the summer, larger party gatherings took place in the fields outside the city or in the orchard of the tailor Alter Bulc. In winter, they would meet in the apartments of party members; they also tried to organize meetings in houses of prayer,[9] but the religious congregants would chase them out or would continue their services during the meeting. Jostling and fighting would even break out. In connection with the many arrests that followed upon such energetic activity, a Committee for Aid to Political Prisoners was formed. Its main task was to collect funds to help the imprisoned. It was headed by a bookkeeper who worked in the S.B. Minz firm. He was helped, among others, by Jankiel Goldsztern "The Diplomat," Abraham Zygielwaks, Meir the son of Alter Słuszny, and Meir the son of Abram Słuszny.

In 1904, Siedlce had a population of about 24,000, of which 15,320 were Jews.[10] The cities of Siedlce Province, especially Terespol, Włodawa, Międzyrzec, and Sokołów Podlaski, were populated by Jews who had emigrated from Russia after the intense persecution that took place during 1870–1890.[11]

On the eve of 1 May 1904, the tsarist authorities, in an attempt to thwart the prepared demonstration, arrested PPS [Polish Socialist Party—trans. note] activist Romański along with his son and the apprentice Stępiński, as well as Bund activists "Georgii" and Pricel "The Squirt." The arrests did not frighten the socialist activists, however. Numerous groups with red ribbons appeared on the streets 1 May and forced the peddlers to close their stalls. In answer, mounted and foot military patrols appeared on the streets. A demonstration took place, which was described by a witness: "A multihued crowd of workers immediately appeared on Warszawska Street [currently Piłsudski Street—author's note]. Red flags flew. The street was flooded with slogans and workers' songs. In the front rank walked PPS members, workers, peasants, Jewish youths from Chassidic homes, and slaughterhouse workers. The parade walked down a few blocks. Siedlce was seeing such a unique sight for the first time. Mounted soldiers rode up and dispelled the demonstration with the hilts of their sabers. There were no casualties. It made a sensational impression on the city."[12] On 27 May 1904, the Bund organized a picnic in Ignanie Grove, where a battle had taken place on 10 April 1831 during the November Uprising in which the Poles were victorious. The location was not chosen randomly. By alluding to this historical battle, the socialists wanted to show that the Russian army could be defeated. About 200 people attended the rally. In his speech, Abraham Jabłoński presented the difficult position of workers and the needed solutions. After him, a "Litwak"[e] who had arrived for the occasion, discussed conditions in the Russo–Japanese War. The area on which the rally was taking place was suddenly surrounded by dragoons led by Kusakov, and the whole action was coordinated by chief of police Shedever. The members of the rally were surrounded by a double cordon. After they were all gathered in one place and tightly surrounded, the dragoons, with curses on their lips, rode into the crowd and hacked with their sabers, aiming for heads. The wounded and fleeing were stopped and arrested by the soldiers in the second cordon. About 50 people were wounded, among whom 11 severely. These were, among others, Grinka Isz, a student of the Public Secondary School [gimnazjum], who received a saber cut on the neck and was only just saved by Siedlce doctors; Golda Eta Simes, a young Bund activist, received head and chest wounds, as a result of which she ailed for several years and died; "Yellow Stelmach," a young man from Łuków, who received a saber cut on his hand; a young unknown woman, whose ear was cut off with a saber.

About 200 people were detained and taken to prison, where right past the gates they were brutally beaten. The prisoners were gathered in the yard, where the preliminary hearings were held. All the detainees maintained that this was not a political meeting but just a picnic. The judges, who sat behind a long, solid table, were Voikov, the deputy governor; Skariatin, the prosecutor; Shedever, the chief of police; V. Bilich, the captain of horse of the gendarmerie; Sawicki, a municipal doctor; Dawid Szwarc, a municipal paramedic; and Abraham Kamieński, a watchman of the Jewish community council.[13] The doctor and the paramedic directed the wounded to the prison hospital or the Jewish hospital, and watchman Kamieński confirmed or denied that someone was a member of the local community. The point was to catch and arrest "outsiders." The most severely wounded were taken to the Jewish hospital, which was manned by medical director Maurycy Sztein, his assistant and student Abramowski, paramedic Aharon Gran, and trustee Icchak Nachum Weintraub.[14] During the time the hearings were taking place, a crowd gathered in front of the prison, made up mostly of the family members of those who were arrested. The brutal action of the police and army caused greater sympathy to be felt by the residents of the city toward the Bund. The victims were given support in the form of monetary donations and food. The wounded placed in the Jewish hospital were ostentatiously visited and brought gifts and comfort. After these incidents, it was determined to expand the "self-defense," whose goal would be the prevention of future pacificatory actions of this kind as well as the implementation of retaliatory measures.

On 3 February 1905, the students of the Public Secondary School for Boys proclaimed a school strike. On the day before the strike, students of other nationalities were informed that the strike was of a national nature, which meant that participation in it was not compulsory for others, that is, Jews and Russians. The main demand was the Polonization of the school. In this situation the Jewish youth made an independent decision. At the end of February, 33 Jewish students of the upper classes stopped going to school and sent a letter by mail to the administration. They stated that they were joining the petition submitted by their Polish schoolmates. After this incident, Kazimierz Stein was made the Jewish delegate on the strike committee. The school was attended at that time by 314 children, including 53 Jews, of which 33 supported the strike, even though in the early period it was run by supporters of the National Democratic movement.[f] Twenty-three students were expelled for participation in the strike, while ten were able to present "important circumstances for [their] absence."[15]

An intensification of the revolutionary movement took place in 1905. During that year, under the influence of the Seventh Conference of the PPS, this party became more closely connected with the Bund. A joint action was the celebration of 1 May in the form of a general strike. The planned demonstration did not take place in Siedlce because a large number of Russian troops were stationed in the city. In the evening, however, a small demonstration took place spontaneously as well as a clash between the Jewish population and the military on Warszawska Street. These people hid from the street into the synagogue, where clashes also took place. Twenty-three people were wounded; forty members of the Bund and one member of the PPS were arrested. The demonstration was joined in a symbolic way by the political prisoners in the Siedlce prison. They hung red scarves and flags from the windows of their cells.[16]

For the terror of the tsarist authorities toward the revolutionaries, the PPS and the Bund issued several death sentences against the most zealous tsarist functionaries. The first organized terrorist act of the revolutionaries was the successful bomb attack against police chief Shedever on 22 May 1905. The attack was carried out by one of the "combat ten" of the PPS led by Tytus Bobrowski.[17] Within the framework of these acts, the Bund combat unit headed by Mendel Rychter was successful in assassinating Bartniczuk, a member of the Rural Guard. The Rural Guard fulfilled a role similar to the gendarmerie. On 21 and 28 June, the combat units assassinated the guard Muszyc and cavalry sergeant Michalewski.

On 28 June 1905, a sympathy strike took place in Siedlce connected with demonstrations by the Jewish population supporting the workers of Łódź. On 23–25 August, another strike took place that also encompassed the railroad station. The authorities took energetic action to combat it. Ten "agitators" were arrested, half of whom were Bund members and half were from the PPS. In retaliation, a squad of dragoons were fired upon that evening on Wojskowy Square (currently Pogoń Stadium on Piłsudski Street), and Grzegorz Kubik, a patrolling guard, was fired upon on Piękna Street (currently Pułaski Street). On 25 August on Wojskowy Square, Feliks Zaremba from the PPS carried out an armed assassination attempt on an officer of the dragoons, and the following evening the patrols on Długa Street (currently Bishop I. Świrski Street) and Ogrodowa Street (currently Sienkiewicz Street) were fired upon.

In addition to political battles, the Bund also fought against the "criminal underground." The Bundists performed their first action on 10 October 1905. This was the day for setting the cornerstone under the new Catholic church, which is currently a cathedral. The ceremony attracted a large number of the faithful. The Jewish thieves and burglars from Mińsk Mazowiecki decided to take advantage of this occasion. The Siedlce Bund members found out about this and scattered volunteers from the "self-defense" group throughout the gathered crowd. They noticed that a certain Josel (characteristically called "the Louse"), a pickpocket, was stealing from the assembled people. The attempt to apprehend him led to fierce fighting, as a result of which Josel was taken to the hospital. After this physical and moral victory, the Bundists decided to wage war against brothels and prostitutes. At that time the so-called Moscow Cottage was functioning legally in Siedlce. It was called that because its owner was a veteran of the tsarist army who "serviced" the officers and noncommissioned officers of the Siedlce garrison. A Bundist combat unit chased out the prostitutes and burned down the house. The workers also tried to convince the prostitutes to change their occupation. There were apparently positive cases where the ladies abandoned their occupation and developed relationships with their "benefactors."[18] In response to the attacks, the criminals made retaliatory attacks, but not in the city, where the Bund controlled everything. Those who were attacked were Siedlce trade workers and merchants in nearby towns such as Mordy, Łosice, or Sokołów Podlaski. The criminals were supported by the merchants from these towns, who pointed out the "outsiders." In response, the Bund combat units, especially on market days, would blockade the roads leading into Siedlce and turn back residents from the above-named towns who were coming to the provincial seat. In this way, they not only prevented them from engaging in trade but also from taking care of official business. The conflict ended with an agreement reached with the delegates from the particular towns and the leadership of the party. A fierce conflict occurred during the strike at the shoe factory belonging to the Seber brothers, Szmilke and Icie, called "Koszeces."[19] The factory was automated. Its owners were known for the brutal treatment of their several dozen workers: they would swear at them and even beat them. Knowing the brutality of the Seber brothers, the Bundists long delayed taking up action against them. However, their roughness toward their workers and the prestige of the party tipped the scales in favor of calling a strike. The Bund sent the Seber brothers demands whose goal was a bettering of the lot of the workers. The "Koszeces" reacted with derision and threats against the Bundists. So when one of the brothers, Szmilke, went to Warsaw, the Bund combat units there sentenced him and exacted "corporal punishment." After returning to Siedlce, the Seber brothers along with other "Koszeces" severely beat two Bundist activists: Chaim Goldberg "Bone" and Zalman Bursztajn "Priel," who sustained a head injury. Other Bund and Poalei Zion activists hid from them because they were in danger of a similar fate. Combat units made up of "Koszeces" workers dispersed the "guilds" on the streets with revolvers in their hands. The Bund decided to use force to deal with the Seber brothers and brought in members of combat units from Kałuszyn and Mińsk Mazowiecki. The fight against other merchants connected with the "Koszeces," namely, Wiktor Koszec, who was a monopolist in the fruit trade in the region, and Ibl Hol, dealing in fish. Ibl Hol was attacked, severely beaten, and robbed of his merchandise. This attack had broad repercussions because not enough fish was delivered to the city for Shabbat. The fruit stalls of selected merchants were demolished. Some serious incidents seemed inevitable. Seeing this, the "Koszeces" offered a proposition of coming to an understanding and easing the situation. The leadership of the Bund accepted such an outcome of the matter with pleasure. The prestige of the party grew substantially among the residents.

A heightening in a revolutionary mood took place before 1 May 1906. Red flags and banners appeared with the signs "Away with the Cossack Duma" and "Long live the revolution." The banners were "decorated" with mock-up bombs. The demonstration on the day of 1 May did not take place because the military and the police were placed on high alert.

As part of the Duma boycott on 2 May 1906, a Bund combat unit intended to launch an attack in Siedlce on the province-wide meeting that was called in connection with the opening of the Duma session. This meeting took place in the building of the Rural Credit Society. The action did not succeed. The bomb slipped from the hands of the assassin on the street and exploded. The tsarist police managed to arrest two assassins: Josek Międzyrzecki and Jankiel Rychter. During the arrest, an exchange of fire took place between the police and the cover group.[20]

In Siedlce there was also a Jewish Organization of the Polish Socialist Party [hereafter referred to by its Polish acronym: ŻO PPS—trans. note]. It was most influential among the gaiter makers. ŻO PPS had about 70 members and about 100 sympathizers. It was founded by Abraham Kadysz.[21] The most active members were Mosze Kalmanowicz (the son of the well-known Chassid, the follower of the tzadik from Kock), Isroel Cymerman, Michał Agresbaum, Mosze "the Chassid," Abraham Federman, Oszer Levite, Josel Sztos, and Chaim Serbaj. The regional leader was Mendel Radzyński.[22] The calling of a meeting for 22 December 1905 that was attended by about 3,000 people attests to its activity. At this meeting, a resolution was adopted postulating the convocation of a Constitutional Assembly in St. Petersburg and in Warsaw.[23] In April 1905, with the cooperation of Judl Mastbaum "the Sloven," the ŻO PPS organized a combat unit consisting of 15 combatants.[24] The ŻO PPS acted in the shadow of the Siedlce PPS and Bund. The socialist movement had significant support in Siedlce. Joel Mastbaum, Judl's brother, who along with his mother was the only one in the whole family who did not support the socialist movement, thus described his father's views in his characteristic memoirs titled *Red Years*: "My father was wont to lean his hands against the taproom bar and either himself tell or listen to heroic tales of Christians and Jews about the uprising against the Russians. He would listen to the peasants cursing the Russian tsar or would swear himself and tell the peasants that Jesus was only a man and the Jews that Moses the Law-Giver was a socialist."[25] In 1904, an attempt was made to establish a secret press for "Robotnik" [the Worker—trans.], the mouthpiece of the PPS. The press was to be housed in the apartment of Doctor Majerczak, a Polonized Jew and member of the PPS. A large house was even bought in the doctor's name that would be suitable for this purpose. A typesetter, Mojżesz Chirurg, even came to Siedlce to set it up properly. Unfortunately, as a result of the start of the Russo–Japanese War, Doctor Majerczak was mobilized into the tsarist army and left Siedlce.[26] This is how Józef Piłsudski recalled that time: "During the Japanese war, I happened upon Siedlce in my underground work. The address of a certain factory was recommended to me; it was actually a plain dye workshop, and the owner [Garbiec—author's note], a kind-hearted chubby man, was to receive me. [...] After a lengthy conversation, when I had already taken care of all my business, he felt some kind of exceptional sympathy toward me and turned to me before my departure: 'We cannot part like this. Allow me to share with you the greatest souvenir as a farewell gift.' And from behind the ceiling of his little factory he pulled out two small pieces of tissue wrapped in a multitude of small sheets of paper. One could see on them the stamp of the National Government. I asked where this came from. He told me the story: These tissues had survived the hell of Siberian penal servitude and then returned to Poland. A certain mayoral aide, a Jew, returned from penal servitude and could not find a place for himself in his new life, having left one shore and not arrived at the other. When he was dying in cramps and pain, he gave this sacred relic to the father of this trade worker. Now this heir to the tradition of Rawicz's work is sharing this holy relic with me as one would share a communion wafer; he kept one tissue and gave the other to me for my later life."[27]

The Siedlce ŻO PPS ceased to exist at the end of 1909. At that time the most vigorous Jewish activists were arrested: Michał Agresbaum, a Bundist and coworker of the ŻO PPS; Mendel Radzyński, the leader of the ŻO PPS; as well as Judel Mastbaum, Modest Zieliński, and Moszko Kalmanowicz.[28] The activity of the ŻO PPS died out after the arrest of these activists. Only the distribution of PPS declarations printed outside of Siedlce in Yiddish continued. Jankiel Langer and Jankiel Frejlich took care of this. Jankiel Langer was arrested in 1913.[29]

In 1903, a group of ten people, with Izrael Tabakman at their head, was removed from the Bund. In his memoirs, he justifies this action in the following way: "We were all politically educated on Bundist propaganda brochures, books that told us of the battle of the heroic Russian proletariat against the tsar, of the huge strikes of many thousands of workers against the capitalists, of the arrests, imprisonments, and executions. All of this had an effect on our moral sensibilities, and we were prepared for the battle against tsarism and the exploitation of workers. This was the battle we waged on the 'Jewish street' in Siedlce, a battle against a long workday, for better pay, and for better treatment of us. But as soon as we encountered our opponents on the 'Jewish street,' our 'pitiful' Siedlce capitalists, whose workshops were located between their beds, when during a strike we met the tears of the wives of the 'manufacturers,' who lamented, 'What do you want from us? Do the opposite, get my husband work; then at least I'll have something for Shabbat'—then we started to look at this reality with different eyes."[30] After another 20 people joined them, they created an organization called New Workers—Zionists. It was headed by Izrael Tabakman and Motl Korzenicki. Their goal was to create a Jewish state in Palestine with a socialist political system. For agitational purposes, they set up their guild on one of the streets of Siedlce. Then they became part of the Zionist organization that was operating in Siedlce, Ha-Tkhiya ("Rebirth"). Izrael Tabakman, Motl Korzenicki, and Abraham Zilbersztajn were coopted into the existing Ha-Techiya Committee, which was composed of Górewicz, the leader of the Siedlce Zionists and a teacher in the Hebrew school; Perec Komar, a shoemaker; Szlomo Weintraub, a secondary-school student; Mejer Rozenwaser, the son of a cigarette producer; Luba Ajzensztat, a secondary-school student; and Motl Berenbojm, a bookbinder.[31]

In 1905, the Siedlce Zionist community was enlivened by Alter Gotlib. The meeting place for various Zionist groups was the Beit Hamidrash at Icie Mały's on Piękna Street. There propaganda campaigns were led by local Zionists, such as Górewicz or the above-mentioned Gotlib, as well as by invited activists, among them Josef Szpryncak and Jakow Szajnberg, delegates to the Sixth Zionist Congress. A large group of Zionists with socialist views took part in these discussions. A result of these meetings was the emergence of the Poalei Zion party, which brought together dissatisfied members of Ha-Techiya. The dissatisfaction stemmed largely from the differences of opinion on the subject of the social program. The split was brought about by the group of activists who were under the influence of the articles of Dov Ber Borokhov printed in *Evreyskaya zhizn* [Jewish Life, Russian periodical—trans.].[32] This is how Izrael Tabakman recalled that day: "Róża Lerner, a member Ha-Techiya, made available to us premises in a new house that her father, Jakow Lerner, had built on Ogrodowa Street. There were no tenants there yet. A discussion took place in this house that lasted from Friday evening to Saturday night without interruption. All the Zionist groupings, including the Socialist Zionists, were present at this discussion. Speeches were made by Górewicz, the two delegates, and Alter Gotlip. The next day, at the last session, after a short report and a brief discussion, we decided to form the Poalei Zion party.[33] The Poalei Zion committee was made up of Izrael Tabakman, Mejer Rozenwaser, Gabiel Szlechter, Motl Tajblum, Motl Korzenicki, Luba Ajzensztat, and Motl Berenbojm.[34] In 1905, Poalei Zion supported the shoemakers' strikes and fought against the so-called Koszeces family. Dov Ber Borokhov was on the side of combining the socialist and Zionist ideologies. He considered the mass emigration of Jews and the creation by them of a Jewish state in Palestine to be an inevitable process, being an expression of the aspirations of the Jewish proletariat. He considered Jews living in diaspora (dispersion) to be a transitional and inappropriate situation. Regardless of the progress of emancipation, he was also an opponent of assimilation.

Between 1903 and 1905, [a branch of] the Zionist-Socialist party was created in Siedlce at whose head was Bojarski, a student of the Siedlce secondary school. Mosze Cukier, Abraham Giebel, and Zilkie Kawa were active members of this party.[35] The Zionists-Socialists supported the immediate need of creating a Jewish state with a socialist system. They did not specify the place where this state was to be formed. The Zionists-Socialists formed armed combat units, buying arms from the Ostrołęka Regiment that was stationed in Siedlce. Bojarski 's arrest and deportation to the place of his birth, that is, to the depths of Russia, slowed the developing activity of the Zionists-Socialists. They continued to be active but no longer found as many followers. In 1907, Apolinary Hartglas gave a speech to them. This is how he recalled those moments: "Shortly thereafter I received an invitation to a meeting of the local Zionist-Socialist Organization in Siedlce. I went there out of curiosity. The meeting at a secret location was quite large. There were quite a few workers, members of this organization, but present also were members of other organizations, particularly workers from the Jewish section of the PPS [Revolutionary—trans.] Fraction, and there were also Christian members of the PPS Fraction. I listened to papers and discussions. This was all rather paltry and on a low level: well-worn clichés and desperate efforts to pull in by the hair and tie together a worldwide socialist revolution and the realization of Zionism. The only thing I got out of this visit was to become acquainted with the representative of the PPS, who was present there, the sympathetic and handsome polytechnic student Girtler, a Pole and a Christian.[36]

EDITOR'S NOTES, CHAPTER 2

a. An uprising against the Russian Empire. It began on 22 January 1863 and lasted until the last insurgents were captured in 1865.

b. Kingdom of Poland (Congress Poland)—a part of Poland under Russian rule from 1815 to 1918.

c. Uniate Church—a branch of the Greek Orthodox Church in the Polish-Lithuanian Commonwealth that united with the Catholic Church in 1596.

d. A good resource for the Bund is Nora Levin's *While Messiah Tarried: Jewish Socialist Movements 1871–1917* (New York: Schocken, 1977).

e. "Litwak"—A Russian Jew, as opposed to a native Polish Jew. Litwaks arrived in two waves: in 1881–1882, as a result of repressions following the assassination of Tsar Alexander II; and in 1905–1907, in connection with the 1905 revolution in Russia. Litwaks were often looked upon with suspicion by the more orthodox Polish, "genuine" Jews.

f. The National Democratic party was always, from its founding in the late 19th century, a nationalistic organization, so anti-Semitism was inherent. It did not become militantly anti-Semitic, however, until the time of the Second Republic. Perhaps not ironically, its support for Zionism was based on its desire for all Polish Jews to emigrate.

AUTHOR'S NOTES, CHAPTER 2

1. I.N. Weintraub, "A Siedlce Story of Conversion," in *Book of Remembrance of the Siedlce Community*, pp. 604–605; see Appendix 18.
2. Z. Zchuchit, "Korespondencja z Siedlec," in *Hamelitz* (The Advocate), no. 149 (1900).
3. Archiwum Państwowe w Siedlcach (hereafter APS), Siedlecki Gubernialny Zarząd Żandarmerii (hereafter SGZŻ), sig. 192, pp. 5–6.
4. APS, SGZŻ, sig. 192, pp. 13, 24, 25.
5. U. Głowacka-Maksymiuk, *Gubernia siedlecka w latach rewolucji 1905–1907* (Warsaw, 1985), p. 64.
6. Isaac Bashevis Singer, *Rodzina Muszkatów*, vol. 2 (Warsaw, 1996), p. 12.
7. Its author is Edelsztats; translated from the Yiddish by Adam Bielecki.
8. This building still exists today. After the Russians withdrew from the city, it functioned as a Community Center. After World War II, it functioned as the cinema Podlasie, and currently it is in the possession of the Municipal Center of Culture.
9. That is, Beit Hamidrash—in Judaism, a house of prayer serves for the acquisition of knowledge and the study of the Bible; it does not have the sacral nature that Christianity does.
10. U. Głowacka-Maksymiuk, *Gubernia siedlecka w latach rewolucji 1905–1907*, pp. 22–23.
11. B. Wasiutyńska, *Ludność żydowska w Królestwie Polskim* (Warsaw, 1911), pp. 19–25.
12. I. Kaspi, "History of the Jews in Siedlce," p. 90.
13. A member of the prayer house watch, a self-government body of the Jewish community council, created by a tsarist decree. The Russian authorities wanted tighter control over Jewish community councils.
14. I. Kaspi, "History of the Jews in Siedlce," p. 92; Głowacka-Maksymiuk, *Gubernia siedlecka w latach rewolucji 1905–1907*, p. 92 (the author, however, gives the year as 1905).
15. S. Lewin, *Żydowska młodzież w strajku szkolnym 1905 r.* (Warsaw, 1996), pp. 79–80.
16. I. Kaspi, "History of the Jews in Siedlce," p. 93.
17. APS, SGZŻ, sig. 192, pp. 24, 40.
18. In 1905, the Bund led similar actions in Warsaw, Lublin, and Łódź. The problem of Jewish prostitutes at the turn of the nineteenth and twentieth centuries is addressed by Małgorzata Kozerowska and Joanna Podolska in the article "Piranie czekają na kadisz," in *Wysokie obcasy*, no. 3, issue 404 (20 January 2007): 10–17 (supplement to *Gazeta Wyborcza*).
19. The name "Koszeces" comes from the Polish *koszyk* or *kosz* [basket—trans.], usually made of wicker, from which goods were sold in the market.
20. It has not been explained why this assassination attempt was made by Jewish fighters. Their main demand during this period was the acquisition of broad cultural autonomy. They did not, however, fight against the opening of the Duma (parliament), which was done intensely by the PPS.
21. In later years, he left for the United States, and in 1947 he opened a Cultural Center

in Acre (Akko), Israel, which he called "Siedlce," to honor the destroyed Jewish life in this city in this way.

22. H. Piasecki, *Żydowska Organizacja PPS* (Wrocław, 1978), p. 214.

23. Ibid., p. 215,

24. Ibid., p. 216. The pseudonym "Sloven" stuck to him from his childhood, when as a young boy he stubbornly looked for a button he had lost in the city's gutter. He was 17 when he commenced his political activity.

25. I. Kaspi, "History of the Jews in Siedlce," p. 79.

26. M. Król, "Dr Wiktor Majerczak (1875–1919)," in *Kronika Ruchu Rewolucyjnego w Polsce*, vol. 3 (1937), no. 4 (12), pp. 167–169.

27. J. Piłsudski, *1863* (Warsaw, 1989), pp. 152–153.

28. P.L. Maksymiuk, *Konspiracja w Siedlcach w latach 1907–1914*, p. 58 (typescript of a master's thesis in the possession of the National Archive in Siedlce). Judel Mastbaum was exiled for life to a camp in Siberia and was not heard from again.

29. Ibid., p. 59.

30. I. Tabakman, "The Activity of Poalei Zion in Siedlce," in *Book of Remembrance of the Siedlce Community*, pp. 371–374.

31. Ibid., p. 375.

32. Dov Ber Borokhov lived from 1881 to 1917. He was an ideologue and leader of the Poalei Zion party. He came from a family of the intelligentsia, and he also received a traditional religious education. Independently he studied languages, philosophy, history, and the natural sciences. He did research on the subject of the Jewish labor movement and the Yiddish language. Among other things, he wrote *The Jewish Labor Movement in Numbers 1895–1904* and *The Economic Movement of the Jewish Nation*.

33. I. Tabakman, "The Activity of Poalei Zion in Siedlce," p. 377.

34. Ibid., p. 377.

35. Ibid., p. 376.

36. A. Hartglas, *Na pograniczu dwóch światów* (Warsaw, 1996), pp. 101–102; Jan Girtler (born 1879, date of death unknown) was a PPS activist starting in 1904. He came from Łuków. He studied at the Warsaw Polytechnic. He was arrested in 1905; after his release he headed the work of the PPS organization in Siedlce. He was arrested again in early 1906 and spent half a year in the Siedlce prison. From 1907, he was a lecturer of technical subjects at the University for Everyone [Uniwersytet dla Wszystkich—trans.]. He was evacuated to Russian in 1915. During that time he was active in Kiev in the Committee for Aid to Victims of War. In 1918 he returned to Poland and was employed as an office worker in Warsaw.

CHAPTER 3.

THE POGROM OF 1906

The successful assassination of chief of police Captain Aleks Goltsev took place on 21 August 1906.[1] The assassin, dressed as a Jew, was Józef Wasilewski, pseudonym "Sparrow," a member of the Combat Organization of the PPS; he ran away after completing the act. Goltsev, along with the sanitary commission, which included the Polish doctor Anastazy Sawicki and the Jewish paramedic Dawid Szwarc, were performing an inspection of the soda-water factory of Samuel Josef Goldsztern. It was located on Piękna Street (currently Pułaski Street), which was inhabited completely by Jewish residents. The first to exit the factory gate was Sawicki, who was approached by an unknown person and told, in Polish, to quickly walk away. When Goltsev appeared at the gate, the assassin threw a bomb in his direction. The chief of police died on the spot, and the badly wounded Szwarc, a few days later in the hospital. The guard Szulżyk was also wounded. The army stationed in the city was placed immediately on emergency combat alert. Patrols were sent to Piękna Street, and the tailor Ch.M. Frydman, who was the owner of an apartment located near the location of the assassination, was arrested. It was suspected that the assassin may have used these premises. That day the soldiers opened fire on groups of people who appeared on Piękna Street. In this way, six people were killed: Szlomo Zalman Goldsztern, Ita Miriam Macielińska, Icchak Milgram, Dawid Macieliński, Baruch Mordechaj Morgensztern, and Mrs. Sukniewicz; about 40 people were wounded. A few days later, in the afternoon, the army surrounded the "Jewish neighborhood," which was located between Piękna Street and Ogrodowa Street (currently Sienkiewicz Street), and a search was conducted looking for revolutionaries and socialists. Jakow Jabłoń, a Bund activist, was killed during this raid, and about 60 people were beaten and wounded. The soldiers had come across them in the local Beit Hamidrash at the evening prayer. They broke into the building and beat the men gathered there with the butts of their rifles. When they left, they shot out the windows of the building. After this incident, the entry door locks were reinforced and metal shutters were installed in the windows.

The assassination of Goltsev became the pretext for mounting a pogrom against the Jews of Siedlce. The raid that resulted in the deaths of several people and the

41

wounding of a dozen was only a portent of what was to take place. At the encouragement of the tsarist authorities, there was an attempt as early as June to stage a pogrom by instigating Christians. But things did not go as easily in Siedlce as they had in Białystok.[2] The Christian community of the city, both Catholic and Eastern Orthodox, did not succumb to the provocation of the tsarist authorities thanks to the decisive anti-pogrom stance of the PPS and the clergy.[3] The residents did not allow themselves to be dragged into the provocation that was attempted on 17 June; it was supported neither by the railroad workers nor by the soldiers. At that time one provocateur was killed, a policeman who was shooting at a soldier, as well as a gendarme who was agitating in favor of the pogrom. The soldiers of the Ostrołęka Regiment, which was at the time stationed in Siedlce, sent out heavy patrols onto the streets of the city to prevent any disturbances. Soldiers were particularly targeted for provocation because two years previously, on 6 November 1904, about 800 recruits had started robbing Jewish stores. Soldiers also became involved when the Jews organized a self-defense, having clubs and rocks at their disposal.[4]

Also refusing to be provoked were the young people of Siedlce, who remembered their Saturday battles with the "Jew kids" on the roads outside of town and on Wojskowy Square across from the prison, where they played stickball and where several dozen youths would gather on one or the other of the two sides. It is characteristic that the participants in these events were condemned for these battles by their older friends and parents.[5]

In September 1906, a state of emergency was declared in Siedlce. The Ostrołęka Regiment, which the tsarist authorities did not trust, was moved away and replace by the Libava Infantry Regiment, seasoned in pogroms and punitive expeditions in Livonia.[a] Foot and mounted patrols appeared on the streets. A police curfew was imposed, lasting from 8 P.M. to 6 A.M. Colonel Tikhonovsky took charge of the city, which was placed under the special protection of the *Okhrana* [Russian secret police force—trans.]. Proclamations, signed by the St. Nicholas Society for Reformed Order, were distributed among the military and civilian populations and contained the so-called Protocols of the Elders of Zion.[6] This proclamation contained the so-called speech of the head rabbi, which had the following content: "We have been fighting against the cross for the past nineteen centuries, and our nation is not giving up on this and is not kneeling. We are scattered in all parts of the world in order to conquer the whole world. Our power increases each day. The golden calf, which the priest Aaron created in the desert, is at our disposal, and this is the true God in our time. Only when we are the sole possessors of gold shall we seize power."[7]

On 7 September, the patrols were strengthened starting in the morning. The rumor was spread throughout the army that sixteen revolutionaries had arrived in Siedlce. In the evening, the army surrounded the entire city. It had earlier been divided into zones for which particular officers were responsible: Bolikhov,

Vesyolov, Aleksandrov, Musaratov, Bialer, von Kleist, and Sumarkov. Telegraphic communication was turned off, and no one was allowed to leave or enter the city. The signal for the start of the pogrom was the hanging of a flag from city hall. About 8:30 in the evening, several shots were fired in the center of the city, and these were followed by gunshots from the 39th Narew Dragoon Regiment and the Libava Infantry Regiment. Shots were heard in the city from 7 to 10 September (old calendar), that is, from Friday evening, the beginning of Shabbat, to Monday at 2 P.M. On the night of 7 September, soldiers set fire to houses, stores, and stalls using kerosene. The stores of Grinberg, Rosen, Solarz, Liwerant, and Stołowy, among others, were burned down. That night, the head of the Okhrana, Tikhonovsky, summoned Rabbi Szymon Dow Anolik;[8] two community council clerks, Nachum Weintraub and Mosze Temkin; as well as the secretary of the community council Czaczkes and demanded that they give up those who were shooting at the army. The rabbi responded that he knew nothing about this. Tikhonovsky then gave them two hours to provide an exact list of the addresses of the revolutionaries. The next day a delegation went to see the provisional governor-general Engelke with a demand to explain the situation that had arisen and to stop the murder and robbery. In response, Engelke arrested the delegates, accused them of espionage, and threatened to have them shot. He even allowed them to write farewell letters to their families and then handed them over to Tikhonovsky. Tikhonovsky placed them facing the wall of the police building and arranged soldiers with rifles ready to fire across from them. He did not, however, give the order to fire. After this "game," he let them go with a repeated demand to provide him with a list of the revolutionaries. The delegation once again stood against the wall; this time they were saved from certain death by the tsarist officer Stayanov, who arrived at the order of the Dubienecki Regiment commander in order to obtain information about events in the city.[9] The next day, that is, 8 September, gunfire lasted all day with small interruptions. Soldiers with officers at their head broke into apartments, robbed and murdered. On that day, Meir Wolf was killed, the father of six children. The soldiers killed him while he was praying with his children. Soldiers wounded Chana Liebhaber and Chaim Liberman for refusing to pay a ransom, and then they murdered them while taking them to the hospital. They did the same to Romanowicz, who sustained burns but saved himself from his burning house. The soldiers took him to the hospital and there finished him off with their rifle butts. In the courtyard of the Jewish hospital, the guard Jan Born, a Christian, was killed when he was admitting the wounded and the murdered. Inside the hospital, a shell wounded the paramedic Maria Łazarska and the patient Judka Lipszyc, who subsequently died of his wounds. Even a tsarist soldier, Abraham Rafał (age 22), who had come home on leave, was killed. He tried to defend his parents when the soldiers broke into their apartment. He was shot by rifle fire. Mendel Tajblum (age 34) had his eyes poked out before he was shot. The teacher Mordechaj Josef Miller (age 40) was murdered using bayonets and sabers. The youngest victim of the pogrom was three-year-old Jehoszua Rozen, whom the soldiers killed in the arms of his mother while taking her to the prison.[10] Not only was the Jewish hospital shelled but also the synagogue, the Catholic church, the Polish school building, and the building of the Rural Credit Society.[11] The soldiers used 30,000 rounds of ammunition during these incidents, according to "Petukhov's Report."[12] Jewish homes on Prospektowa Street, Sokołowska Street, and Jatkowa Street were burned down, altogether over a dozen buildings as well as ten stalls belonging to the hospital and located near the square. The stores of Szmul Solarz and Ball Rozen were also burned down.

Icons of Nicholas the Wonderworker and the Black Madonna of Częstochowa appeared in the windows of terrified Christians. Stolen items were traded next to the railroad station, where you could buy a pair of bloody earrings for next to nothing.

Drunken soldiers, who had been supplied with half a railroad car of pigs, held a free-for-all on Warszawska Street, where they murdered animals and people to the accompaniment of songs. Colonel Tikhonovsky, "in order to uplift the mood of the troops," ordered a choir to be assembled so as to spur on the battle. Among others, "God, Protect the Tsar" was sung.[13] Tikhonovsky was worried that he might be the victim of an assassination, so he ordered his subordinates to arrange a "real memorial and bathe in blood to their ears" in the event of his death.[14]

New divisions of the army were brought to Siedlce; the Vladimir Regiment, famed for its pogrom in Białystok, arrived, and on 8 September the 195th Infantry Regiment was summoned telegraphically from Dęblin as well as the 48th Artillery Regiment, which fired upon the houses on Piękna Street at 7 A.M. The result of the shelling was damage to the houses of Estera Rabinowicz, Rachela Groch, Brajna Czestodna, and Mosze Eliahu Solnica.

The bloody balance sheet of the pogrom may have been as many as 50 murdered, 100 wounded, and about 500 arrested.[15] Many families were left without a roof over their heads. About 40 stores and many apartments were robbed. The desire to rob by drunken soldiers was so great that, even a day after the pogrom, Wiktoria Radzikowska was shot sitting at the table in her own house on Stodolna Street.

In spite of searches conducted in almost all the houses in the city, the solders failed to find any evidence of the activity of revolutionaries. They found no weapons or any publications of illegal publishing houses. It was stated officially that the army and police sustained no losses. The records of the gendarmerie, however, show two wounded: one in the hand and one in the head.[16] As became evident subsequently, one of the soldiers was injured by his colleague while breaking into a store when the latter tried to pry open the door with the butt of his rifle. During this action, the rifle went off. The other wounded soldier was one who was struck with a sabre by an officer while the dragoons were demolishing the buffet in the Victoria Hotel. The drunken dragoon refused to listen to his officer's summons to desist from robbing because officers lived in the hotel and it was the property of a Christian.[17]

Right after the Siedlce pogrom, the governor-general, Evgeny Sykalov, issued a proclamation to the residents, ending with the words, "Residents and Citizens! I call upon you for mutual amicable work to calm our agitated lives. Let us heed the voice of truth and humanity residing in each soul, and let us direct our common efforts toward making our heretofore calm and hard-working Siedlce no longer resemble a prison watched over by the authorities."[18]

The public reacted to the pogrom by creating the Committee for Those Who Suffered during the Disorder in Siedlce. The authorities did not permit the use of the correct name, which was the Committee for Aid to the Victims of the Pogrom. The Committee comprised the most eminent representatives of the city, both Jews and Poles: Stanisław Sunderland (chair, an attorney by profession), Dawid Czaczkis (secretary of the Committee and secretary of the Jewish community council), B.D. Anolik (Anulik, rabbi), I.N. Weintraub, J. Scipio del Campo (a Catholic canon), M. Minc, A. Chrzanowski (an attorney), Korsak (mayor of the city), and N.D. Glizberg. The committee had two goals: first, aid to everyone who had suffered in any way during the pogrom; second, the preparation and publication of a memorandum to the government in St. Petersburg with a request to explain how the pogrom could have taken place, to punish the guilty, and to free those who had been arrested.

The memorandum to the government was prepared by three attorneys: Fiszbain, Luria, and Warszawski, signed by Aleks Chrzanowski, Dawid Czaczkis, and Stanisław Sunderland, and delivered through a delegation to Prime Minister Pyotr Stolypin. Here are some fragments: "Your Excellency. We are appealing to your Excellency in connection with the events that took place in Siedlce on 8–10 September 1906. We do not wish to present atrocities or give the names of people and complain about them. We wish only to establish facts that no one can deny and from which Your Excellency will draw the proper conclusions. [...] During the entire time that this military action was taking place, the city was cut off from the world. No one was allowed to enter Siedlce. Permanent residents, who had left the city for fear of misfortune and wished to return to Siedlce due to distress about the fate of their families, were forced to remain at the railroad station. The telegraph was closed to clients. [...] During the shooting, soldiers fell upon every Jewish apartment, and in every instance of a failure to open the door, they broke it down with the aid of huge firehouse crowbars. Immediately upon breaking into the apartment, the soldiers demanded that revolutionaries be handed over and took the opportunity to demand greater or lesser sums of money. Everyone who had the courage to resist was mercilessly beaten. During searches in houses, these poor wretches were also tortured. Of all the cruel acts of the soldiers, we wish to emphasize only one incident. A young Jew, the father of six children, Meir Wolf, was accosted in his apartment during prayers. Contrary to the officer's testimony, he was very cruelly tortured. He was thrown from wall to wall until his skull was crushed. It must be emphasized that no weapon was found on him or in his apartment. [...] Altogether, 59 stalls were robbed and 12 buildings went up in flames. An uncountable number of private apartments were robbed and destroyed."[19]

The response to the memorandum was the creation of a new commission, which arrived in Siedlce and took two weeks to familiarize itself with the matter. After the commission returned to St. Petersburg and its results were assimilated, another commission was immediately formed, which arrived in the city in December 1906. During its stay, those who had been arrested started to be released from prison. This was the only result of the activity of these two governmental commissions, and in a secret report it was ordered that soldiers be searched and all looted objects be seized. It was maintained that the pogrom was not a military action but only a reaction of soldiers who were hostile toward the revolutionary movement and especially Jews after the assassination of Captain Goltsev.[20] The investigation ended with a press announcement of Colonel Tikhonovsky's receiving thanks from the Warsaw governor-general. The Vilnius newspaper *Dos Yiddishe Volk* aptly summed this up at the end of 1906, writing, "The Siedlce slaughter ended as all slaughters of Jews do. Investigating commissions arrived, then a government declaration follows, in which everything is blamed on the revolutionaries, the perpetrators of the pogrom are promoted, and everything moves on."[21]

According to Committee data, 1,502 families suffered, amounting to 7,306 people. Material costs were assessed at 334,584 rubles.[22] In the published proclamation asking for aid, the members of the Committee appealed, "You who are human beings, you in whose hearts burns the sacred fire of love for your fellow man, a sense of justice and brotherhood, open your hearts to the Siedlce Fellowship, open your fraternal arms, and when you cannot return to them the price of blood, tears, and suffering, avert from them the torment of hunger and cold, poverty and sickness. But hurry! Hurry because right behind poverty walks the angel of death!"[23] The response was moral and material aid in the amount of 120,000 rubles. For a population of the region that was not too prosperous, this was a significant amount. These funds were earmarked for the repair of vandalized houses, the rebuilding of burned down stores, the purchase of stolen stock, and the purchase of ship tickets for immigrants departing for Denmark (mostly Copenhagen), America, or Palestine. One thousand rubles were appropriated from the collected funds and used to found a Savings and Loan Fund, which was later changed into a Joint-Stock Bank and prospered well among the largest cooperative banks in reborn Poland.

The tsarist authorities intended to court martial 150 people who were arrested earlier and were being held in the Siedlce prison. However, as a result of protests from national opinion and from abroad, they abandoned this intention, but the majority of the prisoners had to leave Siedlce and emigrate.

Right before the pogrom, the activists of the Jewish self-defense left the city, rightly suspecting that they would be the first to be sought. With a military operation of this scale, they would have had no chance to stage an opposition to the great strength of the shelling and could only serve as a pretext for even greater repressions.

The military pogrom in Siedlce made everyone aware that the authorities had decided to squelch the revolutionary movement with force. The fears that a similar pogrom, but with the benefit of greater experience, could take place in Warsaw were well founded. The Siedlce pogrom had far-reaching repercussions throughout the country and abroad. Maurycy Minkowski, a graduate of the Fine Arts Academy in Kraków, came to the city right after the pogrom in company with Noach Pryłucki. At the railroad station they saw hundreds of terrified Jews, sitting on their bundles and waiting for the train to flee the city. After this experience, the artist painted two moving paintings titled "Fugitives" and "After the Pogrom," which were displayed in many exhibits abroad.[b] The city was also visited by the writer Lejb Perec[c] and the poet Menachem Borejsza.[d] A folk song also arose that was sung in Yiddish and contained 12 to 14 verses. Only six of them were written down, and they have survived. I cite it here in a loose translation:

On Saturday during the day after dinner,
The Jews were rejoicing,
They had no idea
That a disastrous night awaited them.

We sat hidden in attics and basements,
Our hearts in our throats[24]
The pigs from Libava[25] were rampaging in the courtyards
Lurking in wait for our lives.

Icchak the butcher put up a strong resistance,
They smashed his head with their rifle butts,
And took all his goods.

Listen, you goy,
Don't think this is how it's going to be:
You killed small children,
Many will pay for the children's blood.

In your own city
Watch yourself carefully,
So that a bomb is not thrown at you.[26]

The day after the pogrom, Józef Bekker, at the time a journalist for the Warsaw

Dos Leben (Life), arrived in Siedlce. He described his observations in the paper and in a memoir, fragments of which were published. They have great value because Bekker talked to the witnesses of those events and wrote them down:

> The train stops. Everyone, even those who fear returning to the city, decide to leave the train. It is impossible not to enter the city. In all the doorways there are soldiers and gendarmes, who search everyone. I walk between two rows of soldiers. Fat hands groped me. One of the gendarmes left me alone, but another wanted to show his power as well so he also groped me. Finally, the search ended. But the soldiers are not letting anyone out—they are waiting for the train to leave. Time is dragging on remarkably slowly. Finally the train moved and left. The soldiers open the doors. We want to run, but then a shout is heard: Stop or I'll shoot! Stop at once! There is a new order: all the droshky drivers who had gathered by the railroad station were to leave. Let no one dare leave in a droshky. As soon as the droshky drivers left, the soldiers ordered us to line up in rows and start moving under the guard of the police. Everyone arriving in the city, regardless of sex or age, was taken to the police station. [...] Regardless of the fact that the authorities insist that everything is the fault of the revolutionaries, who instigated the pogrom, none of those present with whom I spoke blamed the Bund. Even the elderly were very well aware of the prevocational fictions of the authorities, who wanted to place the blame for what had taken place on the revolutionaries. Not a single person, not even those whom the pogrom left naked and barefoot, not one of them dared place the blame for the pogrom on the Bund or the Bundists. [...] One old Jew told me that he had tolerated all the beating that the soldiers inflicted on him in the house. On the street—it was an unbelievable miracle—no one touched him. After arriving at the police station, he hoped that here the end of his suffering would come and that here he was safe. There were many officers in the police station. Now they won't beat me, I thought, and I was sorely mistaken. Suddenly one of the officers shouted, Beat all the Jews! I immediately got such a blow to the head with a rifle butt that I fell to the ground. Some officer ran up and started to kick my head with his foot. I stood up and with all my might started to run, but along the entire length of the corridor I was bombarded with blows, and all of this took place right next to a large group of officers. A large group of people were gathered at the police station, another old man told me. The whole floor was covered in blood from sabre and rifle wounds. There was not a drop of water to wash the wounds. An officer came, who separated the men from the women. The young people were also separated. This last group was beaten with particular brutality and then led off to jail. Then an officer came out and in the name of Tikhanovich, the head of the

Okhrana, announced that if the revolutionaries are not surrendered immediately, then everyone at the police station would be killed. He repeated this
several times. Everyone started preparing for death. But when the indicated
time limit was reached, those at the police station were not killed but taken
to jail, where they stayed until Monday. During that entire time the prisoners were not fed. Bread had to be bought from the criminals. [...] Those
who remained in basements or attics were in an immeasurably most difficult situation. Several families hid in a certain basement. These were the
old and the young. They were there from Saturday evening until noon on
Monday without food or water. The children cried and asked for something
to drink, but the older people were afraid these cries might reach the ears
of the soldiers. In this horrible situation, the Jews were even prepared to
smother the crying children. Fortunately, it did not come to that. In some
basements, children were give urine to drink. It is not difficult to imagine
in what a horrible situation and under what conditions people found themselves if they were prepared to take such actions.

[...]One shopkeeper was approached by a certain colonel who needed
some cigarettes. He didn't pay for them. After not paying for them, he said
that the shopkeeper would soon receive his payment. The colonel barely
left when the shooting started. Soldiers broke into the store, wounding the
shopkeeper and looting everything. An officer came to another Jew and
asked for change for a ten-ruble note. When the shooting started, the shopkeeper wanted to flee, but the officer calmed him. But when the shopkeeper
opened his cash register to break the ten-ruble note, the officer grabbed all
the money in the drawer and yelled, "Here's for all your work, boys!"

The most horrible pillaging was on Saturday and Sunday. As soon as the
shooting started, the soldiers ran into one of the stores, looted everything,
and raped the girl who worked there. That same evening, soldiers herded
a whole family to the police station, a father, mother, and daughter. On the
street in front of the parents, the girl was raped and then shot. The parents
were wounded and led to the police station. Stores that were closed suffered even more brutal pillaging than those that were open. At the head of
the soldiers and firefighters walked the police, who pointed out the Jewish
stores. The firefighters broke down the doors and immediately started open
looting. They took everything down to the shoddiest trinket. Then they
doused the store with kerosene and set it aflame.

[...] In one house, all who were still alive hid in the back rooms of the
apartment, where bullets did not reach. The soldiers broke into the house,
and after taking everything of value that was there, they took the cooked
food from the cupboard and, spreading themselves out at the table, gobbled
up everything. Then they broke all the dishes and turned the room into

49

a toilet. [...] In front of officers, soldiers mercilessly beat children who fell on the street to avoid the bullets. The soldiers exhibited particular cruelty toward those unfortunate wounded who were lying helpless in the street.

A certain G. was wounded while he was being taken to the police station. He fell to the street. The soldiers wanted to determine for sure whether he was still alive. They shoved a lighted cigarette up his nose and forced his eyes open, but G. gave no sign of life. The soldiers threw him onto a wagon, drove him to the hospital, and again tried to find out if he was still alive. They finally decided he was dead and ran off. Even in the hospital, G. tried not to show any sign of life. They were about to send him to the morgue. Finally feeling that the soldiers were no longer there, G. started to show some signs of life. A few days later, when he was telling me about what he had experienced on the way to the hospital, G. was himself surprised that he had enough willpower to put up with all the adversities he had endured.

P. was not so lucky. The dragoons who were taking him to the hospital kicked him the whole way. They decided that P. had died, but when he made a noise, the dragoons threw him to the ground and finished him off.

An elderly man of 69 was searched, robbed, beaten, and then he and his wife where driven to the police station. On the street the old man sustained such a beating with a rifle butt that he fell. One of the soldiers hit him on the head with his *shashka* [Cossack saber—author's note], while the other fired. The bullet hit him in the face, and the old man stayed in the street. With great difficulty and agony the old man crawled to the gate of some house, where he was pulled inside. There they washed his wounds, helped him, and the unfortunate old man survived. The soldiers drove a pike [a kind of spear in the Russian cavalry—author's note] through another seventy-year-old man and took four rubles from him. Upon leaving the poor wretch, they threatened him that if he shot at soldiers again, they would finish him off!

[...] But there were those people in Siedlce who in those doleful days dared to show their humanity toward Jews. The saleswoman in a liquor store on Długa Street [currently Bishop I. Świrski Street—author's note] hid several Jewish families in her place. When the soldiers needed some vodka, she didn't open the store so as not to reveal the Jews but gave the vodka out the window, explaining that she's afraid a stray bullet might get into the shop. The wife of an officer in the Dubieński Regiment hid several Jewish families in her apartment. [...] The Jews who told me about this unusual humanism in Siedlce said with envy, "What lucky people; in a few moments they earned the right to life in paradise for themselves!" There were very few people in Siedlce who were so eager for a heavenly reward.[27]

After the pogrom, the activity of all Jewish parties ceased. For the most part, their activists emigrated. The Jews of Siedlce fell into an apathy that lasted over a dozen years. On the other hand, religious life blossomed. Rabbi Szymon Dow Anolik, Meir's son, started a reform of religious education. On the 9th day of the month of kislev in 1907,[28] he issued a proclamation in which he appealed:

> Many people have long since realized that it is essential to convene special committees in all cities for supervising *cheders* and for taking care of the concerns of teachers and their students. They should mainly give exams to students and assign them to the appropriate teacher. Parents should pay tuition to the committee, and the committee should pay the salaries of teachers. I found out the Rabbi Lajb Hunter, may he live, the son the head rabbi Reb Josef Zindl from Warsaw, may he live, has authority to act in this matter, which started in Warsaw a long time ago and has even achieved some success. He is doing the honorable thing for scholarship, and there is much benefit from this. I have long been acquainted with the respected the rabbi Reb Lajb, who does everything as the Torah commands. That is why it is important to aid him, to strengthen his hands in all his endeavors, and may education spread among the Jews. Parents and teachers will see the benefit that this matter brings in a very short time. Things will become brighter for Jews.[29]

A few weeks after issuing this proclamation, Rabbi Anolik died, and the text of the proclamation was treated as the testament of this venerable man.

In January 1911, Siedlce had a population of 31,153, of which 17,157 were Jews, 12,090 were Catholics, and 1,792 were Eastern Orthodox (this figure does not include soldiers stationed in barracks).[30] In 1911, 27 houses of prayer, among which 24 were private, functioned in addition to the synagogue.[31] During this period, an increase was noted in the number of Jewish students in all types of schools that existed in the city.

The general stagnation of the city intensified after 1912, when Siedlce Province was liquidated and Siedlce County was added to Lublin Province. During this time, there were seven hotels in Siedlce, five of which were run by Jews. These were the Litewski Hotel of Chaim Wyszkowicz, the Węgierski and Warszawski Hotels of Moszek Zubrowicz (all three on Piękna Street), the Europejski Hotel of Mendl Goldfarb (on Warszawska Street), and the Nadwiślański Hotel of Ester Szapiro (on Alejowa Street).[32]

TRANSLATOR'S AND EDITOR'S NOTES, CHAPTER 3

a. Livonia—currently Latvia. See also author's note 25 below.

b. For information about Minkowski's paintings, see http://www.yivoencyclopedia.org/

article.aspx/Painting_and_Sculpture; http://www.thejewishmuseum.org/home/content/exhibitions/special/emergence/emergence_zoom/emergenceL7.html; and http://www.flickr.com/photos/magnesmuseum/sets/72157629588665079.

b. Isaac Leib Peretz (1852–1915) was one of the "Big Three" of classic Yiddish literature, together with Mendele Mokher Seforim and Sholem Aleichem.

c. Menachem Goldberg-Borejsza (1888–1949)—poet and journalist, born in Brześć Litewski; moved to Warsaw in 1905 as a teacher of Hebrew; initially published under his birth name of Goldberg, later added his mother's maiden name, Borejsza; convinced by Peretz to write in Yiddish rather than Russian.

Author's Notes, Chapter 3

1. APS, SGZŻ, sig. 192, pp. 24, 40.
2. On 10 July 1905, the tsarist authorities in Białystok, with the participation of the Christian population, executed a pogrom, as the result of which 12 Jews died and about 100 were wounded. The pogrom in Białystok was repeated a month later, that is, 12 August; this time over a dozen people were killed and about 200 were wounded. The August pogrom used the police and military troops.
3. The PPS issued five proclamations in which it warned the Jewish residents about a pogrom: on 3 May 1905, in June 1905 (day unknown), on 10 November 1905, on 7 December 1905, and on 14 June 1906 (it condemned the pogrom in Białystok; see U. Głowacka-Maksymiuk, "Odezwy Siedleckiego Komitetu Robotniczego PPS z okresu rewolucji 1905–1907," in *Szkice Archiwalno-Konserwatorskie na Terenie Województwa Siedleckiego*, issue 3 (1982), pp. 123–136. Among the Catholic clergy, the most ardent anti-pogrom stance was taken by Canon Józef Scipio del Campo.
4. B. Mark, "Proletariat żydowski w okresie walk styczniowo-lutowych 1905," in *Biuletyn Żydowskiego Instytutu Historycznego*, no. 17–18 (1956): 11.
5. K. Dębiński, "Gimnazjum siedleckie w latach 1870–1877," in *Księga pamiątkowa Siedlczan* (Warsaw, 1927), pp. 119–120; F. Kuropatwiński, "Ze wspomnień młodości," in *Księga pamiątkowa Siedlczan*, pp. 140–239.
6. *The Protocols of the Elders of Zion* was published for the first time in the St. Petersburg periodical *Russkoe Znamya* in 1903. Two years later, they appeared in book form. This date coincides with the events of the 1905 Revolution. Everything points to the fact that the *Protocols* were drawn up on the initiative of the tsarist Okhrana, which wanted to use them to combat the revolutionary movement. For more on this subject, see Janusz Tazbir, *Protokoły mędrców Syjonu* (Warsaw, 1992).
7. I. Kaspi, "History of the Jews in Siedlce," p. 107.
8. Szymon Dow Anolik (Anulik), son of Meir—a righteous and learned rabbi. He was an opponent of the conservatives, but he was honored by them for his wisdom. Before he came to Siedlce, he was the rabbi in Szorki, Ostrów, and Tykocin. He published many of his sermons. He died in 1907. His book containing the basics of Hebrew grammar appeared in 1912.

9. I. Kaspi, "History of the Jews in Siedlce," p. 107.

10. Ibid., p. 111. It is noted in the police reports that Rozen died in the flames of his house on Warszawska Street (APS, SFZŻ, sig. 158, pp. 23-24, 26-30).

11. "Interpelacja posła do Dumy, znanego adwokata siedleckiego Stanisława Sunderlanda," in *Gazeta Podlaska*, no. 25/26 (1931).

12. The secret report of the captain of the Siedlce police Petukhov to the governor-general in Warsaw was stolen by a certain Bakaj. In Petukhov's report, he mentions that as early as 11 August, that is, a month before the pogrom, Tikhonovsky demanded a meeting during which the most appropriate way of accomplishing a mass search of houses was discussed. This meeting was attended, besides Petukhov and Tikhonovsky, by colonel of the gendarmerie Virgalich, captain of horse Potocki, the deputy Siedlce chief of police Protopopov, and Aleksandr Grigorov. Tikhonovsky was then supposed to have said, "We will respond to terror with even greater terror." Bakaj is a very unclear figure in the revolutionary movement. He worked for the Warsaw Okhrana, but at the same time he cooperated with the socialists, especially Burtsev. For more information about him, see Czesław Miłosz, *Człowiek wśród skorpionów. Studium o Stanisławie Brzozowskim* (Paris, 1962), p. 94; "Fragmenty Raportu Pietuchowa," in *Gazeta Podlaska*, no. 25/26 (1931).

13. S. Martynowski, *Pogrom w Siedlcach* (Łódź, 1936), p. 24.

14. I. Kaspi, "History of the Jews in Siedlce," p. 117.

15. S. Martynowski, *Pogrom w Siedlach*, pp. 21-22; in the records of the gendarmerie, APS, SAZŻ, sig. 158, pp. 23-24, 26-30; these numbers are reduced: 26 killed, 76 wounded, and the correct number of 500 arrested. Jewish sources, that is, Kaspi, "History of the Jews in Siedlce," pp. 112-119, give 31 killed and 600 arrested.

16. APS, SAZŻ, sig. 158, pp. 23-24, 26-30.

17. S. Martynowski, *Pogrom w Siedlach*, p. 26.

18. bid., p. 27.

19. I. Kaspi, "History of the Jews in Siedlce," pp. 124-125.

20. S. Martynowski, *Pogrom w Siedlach*, pp. 26-27; *Gazeta Podlaska*, no. 25/26 (1931).

21. I. Kaspi, "History of the Jews in Siedlce," p. 140.

22. Ibid., p. 121.

23. *Tygodnik Ilustrowany*, no. 38 (1906), p. 18.

24. Literally: We were holding our souls in our hands.

25. This is a reference to the Libava Regiment, whose soldiers distinguished themselves by their cruelty. [Libava, or Liepaja, a Baltic port city in the southwest of what is currently Latvia, previously known as Livonia.—trans]

26. I. Kaspi, "History of the Jews in Siedlce," p. 139. Translated into Polish by Adam Bielecki.

27. *Nazajutrz po pogromie*—a fragment of the memoire of Józef Bekker. Preparation for print and introduction by Dora Kaneleson. Translated and annotated by Krzysztof Gębura, in *Prace Archiwalno-Konserwatorskie*, issue 14 (2004), pp. 183-193.

28. Kislev—the ninth month of the Hebrew lunar calendar, counting from Passover, or the third after Rosh Hashanah (New Year)—begins at the end of November or

the beginning of December. The holiday of Hanukkah begins on the 25th day of this month.

29. I. Kaspi, "History of the Jews in Siedlce," p. 65.
30. S.D. Kaszyński and H.H. Tiliński, *Gorod Sedlec, istoriko-statistichesky ocherk* (Siedlce, 1912), p. 12.
31. Ibid., p. 42.
32. Ibid., p. 42.

CHAPTER 4.

THE REVIVAL OF JEWISH SOCIETY
DURING THE PERIOD 1915–1920

The political revival of Siedlce Jews occurred in 1915 after the Russian withdrawal. There was not much fighting over the city, yet during the brief battles one house was demolished and seven were damaged. Two farm building were also burned down and three were damaged.[1]

On 2 August 1915, the Civic Guard of the city of Siedlce was created; its goal was to maintain order and cleanliness. Among the 23 sergeants mentioned are the surnames Berg and Sonnschein (unfortunately, first names were not included on the list), and among the 79 militiamen there are two Międzyrzeckis, Mendel Drachły, Alberg, Bursztyn, Szeflan, Cukier, Merchenlein, Kramarz, Tuchmacher, Eszyk, Goldberg, Aldmann, and Rosenbaum. It is interesting that in the next listing in December 1918, after Poland had regained its independence, all 47 surnames are Polish sounding.[2]

On 27 January, a municipal "meat monopoly" was introduced, and only eight people were given permission to slaughter and bring live inventory into the city; among these eight were Moszko and Jankiel Jedwab, Icek Sarnowski, Berek Lubelski, and Moszek Włodawski.[3]

The new occupational forces permitted the activity, albeit controlled, of many Jewish organizations. Because of the large number of refugees in the city, a Jewish Soup Kitchen was set up. Its management consisted of N. Neugoliberg, trustee; J. Turyn, deputy trustee; J. Gutgeld, member; Lejzor Śliwka, member; P. Rubinstein, member; Kiwa Lewartowski, cashier; Sz. Suchatolski, secretary; U. Celnik, inspector; B. Rotenberg, agricultural division; J. Altszuler, agricultural division; and M.M. Landau, auditing committee; A. Kwiatek—auditing committee; and M. Rydel—auditing committee. In its report for the five-month period from 11 January to 19 June 1916, the Soup Kitchen reported that it had an income of 14,879 rubles, which was spent on meals in the following amounts: local residents were issued 50,054 meals without bread and 5,898 with bread; the homeless from Brześć were issued 11,156 meals without bread and 22,117 with bread; the homeless from Pińsk were issued 2,438 meals without bread and 8,526 meals with bread. Altogether, during the period of the report, 100,189 meals were prepared and issued to

1,054 people. Among individual donors, N. Weintraub, J. Rydel, and Dz. Steinitz distinguished themselves.[4]

The economic and sanitary conditions in the city were very difficult. Cases of typhus were noted in the spring of 1916. The "List of Beggars Detained Today on 16 I 1917," prepared by the Municipal Militia, testifies to the difficult material conditions of the residents. The list contains 35 names, of which 13 are of local Jews and 1 of a Jew from Warsaw.[5]

In 1916, Jewish Art enlivened its activity. The Germans, as the new occupational forces, were received sympathetically by the residents of the city. The society rented a large space at 66 Warszawska Street, where its premises became a real Jewish cultural center. The following divisions operated: literary, dramatic, and musical. Moreover, there was a library and a reading room. Jewish Art had 450 dues-paying members. The German authorities did not obstruct its activity in any way; on the contrary, it facilitated it. "A ticket to some event at Jewish Art was like a pass and allowed one to be out after the curfew."[6] The society also engaged in political activity. Its representatives, Josef Rozenzumen, Abraham Zigielkwas, Abraham Grinszpan, Szaul Zubrowic, Jehiel Jabłoń, and Mosze Mandelman, wearing blue and white armbands bearing a Star of David and the name "Jewish Art," took part in a patriotic demonstration on 3 May 1916.[a] The several-thousand strong parade headed by the most distinguished Siedlce activists walked through the city. It stopped in front of the premises of the society, where it sang the song "Boże, coś Polskę"[b] and a Hazomir march, "Sing, Sing." As Mandelman recalled, "And indeed, that day was filled with the spirit 'Let's love one another.' Jews and Poles felt united in brotherhood. The 'community of fates' that tied Jews and Poles together on the Polish Land over dozens of years was especially emphasized in speeches."[7]

A young participant of those events, Anna Kahan, noted in her *Diary*:

Wednesday, 3 May 1916.

We decorated the balcony over our store with red-white and blue-white flags in honor of the Polish holiday. We also hung up a blue and white Star of David. All the balconies and windows are decorated with banners and the Polish eagle in a wreath of flowers and leaves. On some balconies there are signs: "God save Poland!" and on others, "Awake!"[c]

No wonder the joy of the Polish people is great—they have waited 125 years for this holiday.[d] I wonder whether the Jewish people will ever celebrate their own national holiday.

The Rabbi and all Jewish institutions have been invited to take part in the celebration. There is a large sign over the synagogue on which the Star of David and the Polish eagle are painted below quotations from Jeremiah. It is surrounded by many small white and blue flags.

The streets are lined with people waiting for the parade. Services are held in all churches and synagogues. Itke and I are standing on Hospital [Szpitalna] Street.[8] The procession begins with the militia, carrying Polish banners. Then come priests in their vestments, carrying holy pictures and singing. A student's band marches, playing patriotic Polish songs. Delegations from Polish and Jewish organizations follow. The Jews wear white and blue arm-bands and badges in their lapels. Students, wearing tri-cornered caps[e] and multicolored ribbons streaming down their shoulders, pass. They are followed by children from all schools. Firemen are the last in the parade.

Now the civilians fall in behind the procession, a huge crowd marching in perfectorder.

As the procession approaches the Hazomir building,[9] a mandolin orchestra on one balcony, and a chorus on another, play and sing.[10]

Itke proposes we have a look at the arc of flowers and leaves erected on Stodolna Street. It is magnificent. A work of art. A sign above it reads: "For your freedom you shall act!" Close to the ark is a speakers' platform. All the buildings around are decorated with colored silks, flags and flowers.

Barg spotted us from his balcony across the street and he came down to take us up on his balcony where we can watch the rest of the parade. It's certainly something to see! Thousands of people, colorfully dressed, moving, playing, singing. A group of girls dressed in Cracowian costumes are especially attractive.

After the parade passes, we go down to march along with the crowd. I see Tovye running around, taking pictures with his camera. Many German officers are taking pictures, too, from balconies and rooftops.

The lawyer, Hartglas, speaks on a raised platform outside the big synagogue.[11] I can hardly hear what he says, I catch broken phrases. Then Rozenbaum takes me to a spot close to the speaker.

Mr. Hartglas greets the Polish people in the name of their Jewish neighbors. He elaborates on the significance of the 3rd of May for the Jewish people, giving all kinds of historical data. At the end, he expresses the hope and wish for a free and friendly life for both nations, living in harmony and peace.

There is applause.

It's hot. I'm tired and I go home. I'm glad I'm off today and will be able to attend school for the first time.

But my hope is shattered. As I stand barefoot, washing my hair, I receive a message that all stores are open and I must come to work.[12]

In the fall of 1916, elections to the City Council were held for the first time in Siedlce. A united Jewish electoral committee was formed, which chose as its headquarters the building of the society. Here is where the representatives of Zionists,

Bundists, Folkists, Orthodox Jews, and Chassidim gathered. The members of the society set out for the city and campaigned. They had one goal: to seat as many representatives of the Jewish community on the City Council as possible. They attained their goal: of 24 council members, 14 Jews were seated.

Jewish Art was experiencing a blossoming. Meetings at which papers were delivered were important events. These often led to heated discussions in which various political and philosophical concepts clashed. So, for example, Sz.I. Stupnicki was sojourning in Siedlce and delivered a series of papers about the Folkists. Mosze Mandelman remembered one of his presentations:

> I remember an interesting episode that is worth emphasizing: on Saturday evening, when Szulim Jankiel Stupnicki was speaking with youthful verve to a packed room in Jewish Art about the rights and aspirations on the "Jewish street," Leo Belmont, a well-known Polish writer, entered. He was in Siedlce at that time and was to speak about the Russian revolution that same evening. He noticed a poster on the street about Stupnicki's paper. Then he said to himself, let's hear how the Jews discuss such matters in Yiddish. For a long time he attentively listened to the paper and the discussants, among whom were Dawid Nojmark (Bund), Dawid Grinfarb (Poalei Zion), Mordechaj Jafe (Zionist), and Jakub Tenenbaum (no party affiliation). After the paper was delivered, Belmont went into the wings and introduced himself to Stupnicki. He warmly shook his hand and announced that he had understood everything and was delighted with the high level and insightful depiction of the problems. He would never have believed that among the common people one could debate socio-political issued in such a civilized fashion "in jargon."[13] He invited Stupnicki and several of our other members to his own paper titled "Tsarism and Revolution" (this was after the outbreak of the revolution in 1917). We accepted the invitation, but his paper did not excite us.[14]

Philosophical-religious issues were addressed in the papers of, among others, Hiles Cajtlin. Meetings and discussions were a good education for the Jewish activists of Siedlce. The society also expanded its concert activity. U. Kipnis and Z. Zelikfelt organized a series of concerts that included Jewish folk songs. During this period, when literature in Yiddish was just coming into being, this was a novelty. The years 1918–1920 saw the further development of Jewish Art, which took on the building and running of its own secular school. In his "Report on the Political and Social Situation" during this time, the Siedlce county administrator wrote, "The Jewish population, in regards to both its political as well as its social life, significantly surpasses the Polish population."[15]

The divisions of the Jewish Art Society expanded significantly. The literature division included Jakub Rodak, Dawid Nojmark, Jakow Fiszman, Jahiel Groman, and Mosze Mandelman. The music division also expanded, comprising a choir (numbering 50 people and the conductor Josef Zonszajn), a string orchestra, a brass band, and a mandolin orchestra—altogether about 120 people. In the summer, these orchestras gave concerts in the city park under the baton of Eliahu Szpilman, and after his death, A. Szpilfidel. The drama division, with Jakub Tenenbaum at its head, grew to 30 people.

November 1918 arrived. Apolinary Hartglas, who was in Siedlce at the time, recalled the end of the German occupation in the following manner:

> On 12 November small groups of legionnaires along with soldiers from General Sikorski's Polnische Wermacht[f] appeared on the streets of Siedlce, and sporadic exchanges of gunfire would take place between them and the German soldiers. In fact, the majority of German soldiers walked around the city unarmed and drunk, wore red ribbons, and cheered the legionnaires. On 13 November the panicked fleeing of the Germans commenced. I happened to witness a genre scene in front of City Hall. Two fat and huge field gendarmes rode up, armed from head to toe, on tall horses. Suddenly a small, maybe ten-year-old, boy ran out of the vestibule of City Hall, ran up to the horses, and ordered the gendarmes, in Polish, to dismount. The two began to laugh, and one of them jokingly threatened the boy with a pistol. The boy then pulled a revolver out of his pocket and aimed it at the gendarme. The gendarmes scratched their heads, dismounted, and handed their weapons and horses to the boy. The boy called over several urchins, no bigger than he, and together they took the weapons and horses to City Hall. A few hours later, I was in court, and suddenly we heard the rattle of wagons and cannons and the clomping of horses. We looked out the windows. It turned out that a large German division was entering the city: over a dozen cannons with an appropriate number of artillerymen and several dozen wagons with baggage and troops. All this was coming from the east... When they reached the courthouse, several city militiamen and a couple of boys hopped onto the first cannons and wagons and stopped the horses. The Germans jumped down to the ground and left peacefully, leaving the baggage and weapons in the hands of the militia. In the afternoon, a German soldier came to me and asked on behalf of the Kreischef that I come to him right away. As I approached County Hall, I encountered bank director Urbański and the president of the Agricultural Society, Godlewski, whom, as it turned out, the Kreischef had also sent soldiers to summon. [...] When we walked together into County Hall, we found him at the telephone surrounded by several senior county clerks. The Kreischef told us that he had been trying since morning to make telephone contact with Governor-General Beseler in order to receive instructions about what he should do, stay or

go, but he could not get a connection. Then when we found out that General von Beseler had fled to Germany the previous day, the Kreischef decided on his own responsibility to depart along with the clerks on the next train, but he did not want to leave everything unprotected, at God's mercy, so he sent for us and asked that we count and take over the cash box, documents, and inventory and give him a receipt. He also asked if we would, if we could, issue him a certificate stating that the population did not file any complaints against him during the time he held his office. Since that was indeed the case, we issued him the appropriate certificate and receipt, all of which the three of us signed, and we called in several militiamen and a sergeant to take charge of the property left behind. Next the Kreischef started to ask us if we would agree, the three of us, to escort him and the clerks to the train station for fear that a crowd might attack them on the way. We answered this request in the negative, assuring him that there was not the least fear, since the population had the best opinion of him and these several clerks. We said our goodbyes, and they left. After our departure, the militiamen on their own initiative took the Germans' sabers, and the Germans went to the train station. No one harassed them along the way or caused them any harm whatsoever.[16]

Further political, cultural, and social revival took place after 1918 and the strengthening by Poland of independence and democracy. A veritable flowering of civic initiatives took place. By 1919, five Jewish associations had already been registered officially in the city.

The Jewish Musical-Literary Society, with offices at 66 Warszawska Street, took on the objective of supporting music and literary activity. The management board consisted of chairman Abraham Zygielwaks and members Wulf Frydman, Chil Jabłoń, Jakub Tenenbaum, Izaak Alberg, Szyja Goldberg, Jakób Liwerant, Abram Grynszpan, and Ber Czarnobroda. The society had 400 members.

The Office for Aid to Jewish Workers, with offices at 22 Warszawska Street, offered assistance to Jewish workers who were laid off from work. Froim Celnik was the chairman of the management board, and its members were Wulf Fridman, Josek Wiśnia, Srul Tabakman, Pinku Langier, Moszko Altszuler, and Josek Lebensglik.

The Society of Jewish Workers, with offices at 27 Ogrodowa Street, was engaged in cultural and economic activity. Its chairman was Ela Celniker, with members Jankiel Zonszajn, Josef Zonszajn, Naftul Kozienicki, Icko Rosen, Jankiel Liwerant, Moszko Altszuler, and Moszko Grabie. There were 300 people in the society.

The Siedlce Jewish Savings and Loan Society, with offices at 20 Długa Street, engaged in economic activity consistent with its name. Kliman became its chairman, while Lejzor Śliwka, Mendel Liwerant, and Lejbko Szapiro became members. In addition, there was a council comprising chairman Gliksberg and members Tejwel

Grinszpan, Herc Halbersztadt, and Szmuel Cukier. The society brought together 3,000 people.

The Siedlce Commercial Society for Mutual Credit, with offices at 62 Warszawska Street, engaged in extending loans to its members for industrial-commercial goals. Its chairman was Nachum Weintraub, with members Moszko Landau, Dr. Maurycy Stein, and Mojżesz Wołonicki. The council comprised a chairman, who was Apolinary Hartglas, the deputy chairman, in the person of Stanisław Teigenbaum, and members Srul Gutgeld, Icko Rotgold, Mosze Abe Ajzensztadt, Wolf Barg, Kiwa Lewartowski, Munysz Sukiennik, and Abram Judel Rosen. The society had 328 members.[17]

In this year, as police records indicate, the **Union of Jewish Workers in the Trades**, led by Abram Figowy, was also active and had 250 members. The **Siedlce Merchants Club**, in turn, had about 200 members, headed by Samuel Cejtlinek. This club functioned as a social organization. The Zionist charitable organization, which was yet to be registered officially, was the **"Ezra"** (Aid, Support) **Auxiliary Union of Jewish Women**, which had 700 members and was headed by Tyla Głowiczower.[18] The **Zionist Committee**, under the aegis of Apolinary Hartglas, had slightly fewer members, at 600. There were also two organizations that brought together young people: **"Hashomer Hatzair" Youth Association**, which had 140 members under the direction of Berł Rejman, and the **"Tzeirei Mizrachi" Orthodox Youth Association** under the direction of Nachman Rubinstein.[19] There were also the **"Workers' Center" Jewish Association**, with 476 members headed by Jakób Groman, and the **Central Bureau of Labor Unions Affiliated with the "Workers' Center,"** with 500 members and Srul Tabakman as chairman.[20]

In 1919, two of the four printing houses in the city were Jewish: Wiktoria, at 31 Kiliński Street, whose owners were Haskiel and Gdala Goldberg; and Artystyczna, at 27 Kiliński Street, whose owner was Szyja Lichtenpacht. There were several dozen bakeries, most of which were Jewish. There were nine registered goldsmithing-jewelry stores, all of them Jewish. The city had nine bookstores, five of which were Jewish: Szyja Celnik's, Icek Gotfarb's, Mozes Miodownik's, and Abram Szeflan's [author lists only these four—trans.]. They were located either on Warszawska Street or on Kiliński Street.

The city was divided in 1919 into eight police districts.[21] There were seven gastronomic enterprises in the fourth district, two of which were Jewish: Liberman's restaurant on Floriańska Street, and Hersz Grynwald's restaurant on Kiliński Street. There were also seven gastronomic enterprises in the sixth district, and they were all Jewish. Jankiel Tomkin was the owner of a restaurant at 28 Warszawska Street; Mejer Frydman, a restaurant at 17 Długa Street; Pinkus Ajzensztejn, a beer house at 35 Długa Street; Matys Zylbersztejn, a tea house at 30 Długa Street; Hersz Sztejnberg, a restaurant at 34 Długa Street; Benjamin Naterman, a restaurant at 36 Długa Street; and Jankiel Goldsztejn, a tea house at 21 Prospektowa Street.

Of the six gastronomic enterprises, one belonged to Ida Rotfarb, a cafeteria at 13 Roskosz Street. Three of the seven enterprises in district three were Jewish: Leja Międzyrzecka ran a restaurant at 19 Piękna Street, Mendel Cukierman had a restaurant at 5 Piękna Street, and Szmul Wajsman had a beer house at 8 Floriańska Street. There were eleven enterprises in the first district, and they were all run by Jews.

Metal warehouses were run by Mejer Modnykamień at 8 Mała Street, Icko Duła at 35 Piękna Street, Icko Asman at 25 Piękna Street, Szaja Bomblat at 25 Warszawska Street, Jankiel Cukierman at 21 Warszawska Street, Mejer Nusym Frydman at 19 Warszawska Street, Icko Kulicki at 15 Warszawska Street, Lejb Szyfer at 11 Warszawska Street, Tobja Szyfer at 14 Piękna Street, Lejbko Asman at 8 Przyjazd Street, Jankiel Goldberg at 8 Przyjazd Street, and Dawid Kucharski at 11 Przyjazd Street.

The following Jewish mills were located on the territory of the city in 1919: Berek Jakubowicz's at 9 Brzeska Street, Moszek Feder's at 33 Floriańska Street, and Jankiel Uberman's at 69 Ogrodowa Street.

Mozes Szmidt and Szymon Goldberg were dentists of Jewish descent who practiced their profession during this time.

Bohdan Korzeniewski remembered the critical period of the founding of the Polish Republic in Siedlce.[g] He characterized it in the following way:

> Siedlce was a city with a population at that time of probably 40 thousand. It was completely lacking any industry and was surrounded by rich villages. The wealthy peasantry belonged to right-wing peasant unions, supporting Witos. This period, as I remember it today, was quite instructive. One could draw the conclusion that society develops best, most vigorously, when it is given complete freedom. The government, in the initial period of its existence, gave people the initiative, and they instantly organized themselves. I remember vividly the disarming of the Germans, which took place as if some secret order were at work. We don't know why the legionnaires who had been hiding up to that point and former soldiers from various armies, mostly the Russian, suddenly came out onto the street and in a moment appeared with weapons, carrying three, four rifles. They took them from the Germans calmly, with a smile. This took place without one shot being fired, without any defense. The German would hand over his rifle, shake hands, and ask where the train station was. The city was mostly National Democratic. There were many followers of this party, or of the right-wing branch of the peasant party. But there were also poorer, or more enlightened, peasants who joined left-wing peasant parties. Wici immediately started to develop very nicely.[h] They engaged in educational campaigns, and peasants went to school. Siedlce was the only educational

center in Podlasie, along with Biała Podlaska. It had at that time, starting immediately in 1918, two state secondary schools: the Hetman Żółkiewski Secondary School (mathematics and natural sciences) for boys, to which I was admitted; and another, the Prus Secondary School for the humanities. There was also a private secondary school run by a director whose name was Szwec (we called it the "Swedish" secondary school),[i] where Jacek Woszczerowicz's father, old Woszczerowicz,[j] taught Latin surrounded by grim respect. There were also two schools for girls, a public one and a private one, and also an agricultural vocational school. No industry, a little trade in the hands of Jews—and this was Siedlce. That is why all of life was concentrated around the school, which had excellent teachers. Today I wistfully recall the culture, tactfulness, and wisdom of these people. My principal was Mieczysław Asłanowicz, of Armenian descent. A natural scientist, he was a man of immeasurable kindness, wisdom, and determination at the same time. He was the one who reared us. The school was filled with peasant children: in my entering class of 40, only 5 or 6 were from the intelligentsia.

[…] It was probably the spring of 1918 that we returned to Siedlce. We found our wooden house (a kind of manor house) unchanged, as though we had just left on an outing. We returned to the same apartment, to the same furniture, but to completely changed circumstances. My father did not return to his job in the court but worked at first in the bank as a bank clerk, but very quickly he started to be a social activist. First, in 1920, he was elected mayor of Węgrów, where he stayed for a short time, during the Bolshevik invasion (that is where he rescued Jews from looters). After his return he was mayor of Siedlce for a while, briefly. I remember that a very elegant two-horse chaise would drive up to pick up my father. He soon had to resign, however, because he, like [Gabriel] Narutowicz, was elected by left-wing forces and national minorities.

Mostly it was Jews who voted for my father. He had many friends among them, and hence our affectionate memories are tied to this community. My father was invited to weddings, to almost all the Jewish ceremonies, and often he would take us with him. Siedlce was almost half Jewish; all commerce was in their hands. At the same time, these were Jews who were Polish patriots, tied to the ideals of the January Uprising, to such a degree that they Polonized their last names. Sometimes this led to some amusing things, such as a signboard would display the name Różany Kwiat [Rose Flower] instead of Rosenblum. Very few stores were Polish, but the coffee house was Polish. We went there every Sunday. My father drank coffee and bought us, I remember, two vanilla cupcakes each.[22]

The period of the city's dynamic growth ended with the arrival of the Bolsheviks. On 11 August 1920, the Red Army occupied Siedlce for a period of eight days. The detachments marching in via Brzeska Street were greeted enthusiastically by a group of Communists, among whom was a fairly large Jewish delegation. A welcome gateway was even set up. "Authority was handed to the people by Feliks Dzierżyński himself, who came to Siedlce on 14 August 1920. It was received by Stanisław Krasuski, a former employee of the Agricultural Syndicate and Municipal Council, who had re-emigrated from Russia. Józef Lewandowski, a worker and member of the PPS, was made military commissar, representing the interests of the Red Army. And a certain Alperowicz was made chairman of the Revolutionary Committee in Siedlce."[23] As we see, Feliks Dzierżyński, the creator of the Chrezvychaika—the Extraordinary Commission for Fighting Counterrevolution and Sabotage—felt a certain sentiment for the city in which he had spent almost two years: he spent time in the local prison from March 1900 to January 1902. The tsarist authorities determined at that time that he was dangerous for society. The Revolutionary Committee (Revkom) appointed by him contained 22 Communist activists. Some Jewish activists supported him, some from Poalei Zion stalled for time, while some decided to wait things out. These were positions that were characteristic for the whole Jewish population of occupied Poland. One of the activists of Poalei Zion described those days as follows: "Seeing that one used rolls of paper with numbers on them to pay, people slowly started to hide goods and more important items. Panic broke out in the city. The Polish militia, wanting to show how Communist it was, constantly caught Jews with hidden goods. The Revkom demanded workers, carpenters, locksmiths, and bakers, but these only hid and did not want to go to work."[24]

During the retreat of the Red Army, some of the Siedlce Communist activists evacuated with it. After Polish troops entered, provost courts dealt with the Revkom sympathizers and collaborators who had remained in the city. The French officer Charles de Gaulle was a witness to these events:

> We marched into Siedlce on the heels of the victors. The city was in turmoil. The Bolsheviks had set up a Soviet in it with the aid of local Jews (more than half the population in fact). Currently the citizens of Siedlce want the Jews who were on the side of the enemy to be punished; there are constant arrests accompanied by the howls of huge crowds. That morning, many Jews were executed by firing squad because here they do not delay in carrying out executions. Surrounding the wagon containing those sentenced to death, their family and friends walked at a certain distance, echoing their laments. Then the Jewish community took the bodies and, in conformity with Jewish tradition, quickly buried them. It is said that when a Jew dies his body must be placed in the earth before a church bell tolls. If this is not

done, an evil spirit will torture the unfortunate deceased and bring much woe to the bereaved.[25] Yet these poor fellows have enough troubles in their lives, ever filled with disquiet in fear of failures and with their passion for trade.[26]

The Mobile Court of the Command of the Warsaw General District, sitting during 23 and 27 August, condemned to death by firing squad ten former soldiers of Jewish descent and two civilians, Abraham Grynszpan and Nusek Piła, "for the crime of desertion and treason."[k] The sentence was carried out. The execution of Abraham Grynszpan—who had served as secretary of the Revkom for two days before he was dismissed because he was deemed to be a "bourgeois and Zionist"— had especial repercussions within the Jewish community. His father had hidden a wounded Polish officer in his apartment during the entire period of the Bolshevik occupation.[27]

The courts additionally sentenced ten people to from five to ten years of hard labor. There were also instances of lynching. In the Golice Woods, 20 massacred bodies of Jews were found. The reports of representatives Hartglas and Farbstein describe exactly what took place in the city.[28] Instances of beatings, looting, and rapes are cited.

The opinion that Jews supported only the Bolsheviks during the Polish–Bolshevik War predominated among some politicians of the interwar period. When Wincenty Witos came to Siedlce in August 1920 and saw Jews in the civic guard with white-and-red armbands, this immediately seemed both strange and suspicious:

> In Siedlce it struck me at the very outset as strange that the responsibilities of the civil guard were being carried out almost exclusively by Jews. They wore white-and-red armband and bowed low to everyone they met on the street. The city was rather a sorry sight. The streets were completely littered with trash, the houses were shabby, and stores were closed. Jews timidly looked out of their apartments, starting to gather in small groups. All the Jewish houses were heavily decorated with Polish flags. This did not prevent red Bolshevik banners from having waved on these very same houses but a few days ago. [...] The Polish military authorities, after entering the city, imprisoned a large number of Jews in Siedlce and had them indicted. Several sentences were passed and executed, but many Jews escaped justice because the courts, supposedly at the request of Mr. Piłsudski, conducted lengthy investigations, and an international commission arrived before these were concluded, leading to their discontinuation. And so the Jewish culprits went free. [...] Further on, around Przygoda [Suchożebry Township—author's note], we met a division of volunteers numbering about 150 people. They were all from Poznań. They remained under the command of

a former Prussian cavalry sergeant, who still spoke Polish poorly. [...] The soldiers were resting after a two-day forced march, having their fun with a Jew, supposedly a spy, whom they had met on the road. They were very surprised when I reprimanded them for this, recommending that they let the Jew go.[29]

The Jewish population in its majority behaved passively, taking a wait-and-see approach. Such an approach during times of historical turning points did not save the Jews; on the contrary, it often led to pogroms. They took place during the Polish–Ukrainian War, in Lwów, for example, where pogroms were carried out by both Poles and Ukrainians.

After the Polish–Bolshevik War, peace and order were maintained in the city, attempting to prevent disturbances and riots from taking place. Especially those planned "from the outside." A note from a police agent of 14 July 1921 to the commissioner of police testifies to this fact: "I am reporting that on the 13th of this month in the evening I was in the Summer Theater in the Park, where there were about 12 Upper Silesian insurgents with whom I struck up a conversation on the subject of the Kingdom of Poland; in the process I found out from them that on Saturday and Sunday there was to be a party in the Park for the benefit of the Upper Silesian insurgents, but they unanimously said that after the party in the Park they would have a party with the Jews, whom they must eradicate in Poland, just like they did the Krauts in Upper Silesia, even though there is only one battalion of them in Siedlce, but they must accomplish their task and once and for all take care of the Jews in Poland because there are too many of them here, and they firmly promised themselves to have a little uprising with the Jews in Siedlce on Saturday and Sunday."[30] In the light of extant sources, no anti-Semitic incidents took place on those days. However, in April 1922, there were incidents of cutting off the beards of Jews by conscripts from Poznań who were passing through the city.[31]

Translator's Notes, Chapter 4

a. 3 May—Patriotic celebration of the Constitution of 3 May, adopted by the Great Sejm of the Polish-Lithuanian Commonwealth on 3 May 1791; the document's adoption led to the second and third partitions of Poland among the neighboring absolute monarchies due to its very democratic (for the times) content; called the "first constitution of its type in Europe" by British historian Norman Davies, it is the world's second oldest codified national constitution after that of the United States (4 March 1789). This day acquired great significance during the 123 years of Poland's nonexistence as a state as a symbol of a high point in the country's political and national aspirations. Although its celebration was banned during the Communist period, it has retained its significance to this day.

b. "Boże, coś Polskę"—patriotic song in the form of a prayer, loosely translated as "God Save Poland." For a further explanation of the history and significance of this song, see http://www.usc.edu/dept/polish_music/repertoi/boze.html.

c. Czuwaj!—Polish scout greeting, meaning "On guard!" or "Be vigilant!" being a Polish adaptation of Baden-Powell's "Be prepared"; the Polish greeting harkens back to that used by medieval Polish knights and castle/city watchmen.

d. Waited for this day for 125 years—Strictly speaking, this should be 123 years, i.e., since the third partition in 1795 that deprived Poland of its statehood. The two previous partitions were in 1772 and 1793.

e. Tri-cornered caps—in Polish *rogatywka*, usually a four-cornered cap used in the Polish military in some form since the 14ᵗʰ century; also adopted as part of boys' school uniforms; considered by many even today to be a Polish national head covering.

f. *Polnische Wehrmacht*—also called *Polska Siła Zbrojna* [Polish Armed Forces], originally a World War I military formation created as part of the German Army. Poles became combatants in the armies of all three partitioning countries, although Russia withdrew before the end of the war. The group that was formed by Józef Piłsudski as part of the Austro-Hungarian army was called the Polish Legions (*Legiony Polskie*). General Władysław Sikorski (1881–1943) was one of the commanders of the Legions. Both the *Polnische Wehrmacht* and the Polish Legions formed the backbone of the Polish Army formed in 1918. Should not be confused with the World War II *Polnische Wehrmacht*, which was a unit of Polish volunteers formed in 1944 within the German army as an anti-Soviet espionage and guerrilla force.

g. Bohdan Korzeniewski (1905–1992)—Siedlce native; Polish director, theater historian and critic, translator from Russian and French, writer, and teacher.

h. Wici—Name of what would become the Union of Rural Youth [Związek Młodzierzy Wiejskiej, ZMW], which focused in this period on furthering the education of rural youth and on inculcating a spirit of social responsibility and patriotism in them.

i. A pun on the similarity in pronunciation between *szwedzki*, "Swedish," and *szwecki*, an adjective formed from the nonexistent noun "szwec." The correct Polish form for Szwec's, however, would be *Szweca* (possessive of the name/noun "Szwec"), not *szwecki*.

j. Marian Jacek Woszczerowicz—Siedlce native (1904–1970); famous theatre and film actor.

k. Mobile Court (*Sąd Lotny*)—a team of military judges that followed the front lines of the Polish Army in 1920 and punished Polish citizens for cooperation with the enemy, maily treason, desertion, and other offenses. Its goal was maintainance of discipline within the army and on the front lines.

AUTHOR'S NOTES, CHAPTER 4

1. APS, County National Police Department in Siedlce (KPPPS), sig. 105, "Wykaz nieruchomości miejskich m. Siedlce uszkodzonych lub zrujnowanych podczas działań wojennych w sierpniu 1915 r.," fol. 21.
2. APS, KPPPS 1915–1933, sig. 1.
3. APS, KPPPS 1915–1933, sig. 2, fol. 62, 149–150.
4. APS, KPPPS, "Sprawozdanie żydowskiej taniej kuchni z 5-miesięcznej działalności od 11 stycznia do 19 czerwca 1916 roku," sig. 105, fol. 2–5.
5. APS, KPPPS, sig. 2, fol. 136–137.
6. Mosze Mandelman, "The Library and the 'Jewish Art' Society," in *Book of Remembrance of the Siedlce Community*, p. 510.
7. Ibid., p. 510.
8. The parade route led from the new church (cathedral) on Długa Street (currently Bishop I. Świrski Street), then along Szpitalna Street (currently Kochanowski Steet), Warszawska Street (currently Piłsudski Street), and Świętojańska Street, up to Stodolna Street, which on that day was renamed 3 May Street.
9. Hazomir—the cultural center of the Jewish Art Society, whose offices were at that time at 66 Warszawska Street. [Hazomir (also Hazamir, from Heb. *zemer*, song)— a common name for Jewish choral societies, which of course were central to Jewish Arts centers.—ed.]
10. The choir sang "Boże coś Polskę" and the Hebrew hymn of Hazomir, "Zamru" (Sing).
11. Apolinary (Maksymilian) Hartglas (1883–1953)—a lawyer, Jewish politician, journalist, member of parliament (Sejm, 1919–1930) representing the Universal Zionist Party, close co-worker of Izaak Grünbaum. In Israel a high official in the Ministry of Internal Affairs. Born in Biała Podlaska, he practiced law in Siedlce between 1907 and 1919, taking an active part in the social life of the city. In his memoirs, *Na pograniczu dwóch światów* [On the border of two worlds] (Warsaw, 1996), Hartglas gives an account of this event and includes a brief summary of his speech (pp. 173–174).
12. Anna Kahan, *The Diary of Anne Kahan: Siedlce, Poland, 1914–1916* (New York: YIVO, 1983), pp. 141–371. The original was written in Yiddish and translated into English by the author and in that version published in the bulletin *YIVO Annual of Jewish Social Science*, vol. 18 (1983) [reprinted here—trans.]. The cited fragment was translated into Polish by Michael Halber.
13. That is, in Yiddish. [The Yiddish language had a low reputation ever since the time of the German-Jewish Enlightenment, when it was considered nothing more than a bastardized form of German. One of the main goals of the Yiddish literary revival from the 1860s onward was to dispel this negative prejudice.—ed.]
14. M. Mandelman, "The Library and the 'Jewish Art' Society," pp. 512–513.
15. APS, SPwS, sig. 2, p. 3.
16. A. Hartglas, *Na pograniczu dwóch światów* (Warsaw, 1996), pp. 179–180.
17. APS, KPPPS, "Spis stowarzyszeń działających w Siedlcach w 1919 r.," sig. 105, fol. 27.
18. The name of the union referred to the tradition connected with the return of the Jews

to their homeland. Ezra was the leader of the group of exiles that returned in 458 BCE from the Babylonian captivity.

19. Tzeirei—literally means "young people" [from Hebrew *tzeir* (young)—trans.].

20. APS, KPPPS, sig. 116.

21. Their exact division and borders are described in Grzegorz Welik, "Akta siedleckiej policji w AP Siedlce jako źródło do dziejów miasta," in *Prace Archiwalno-Konserwatorskie na Terenie Województwa Siedleckiego*, issue 10 (1997): 168–169.

22. B. Korzeniewski, "Było, minęło, nie wróci. Wspomnienie mówione," part 2, in *Znak*, no. 403 (1988): 38–39; no. 404 (1989): 59.

23. *Tygodnik Siedlecki*, no. 3 (1988), J. Garbaczawski's letter to the editor.

24. I. Tabakman, "The Activity of Poalei Zion in Siedlce," in *Book of Remembrance of the Siedlce Community*, p. 391.

25. A folk superstition having nothing to do with the religion of Moses, which requires that the deceased be buried as soon as possible, preferably on the same day.

26. Ch. De Gaulle, "Bitwa o Wisłę. Dziennik działań wojennych oficera francuskiego," in *Zeszyty Historyczne*, no. 9 (Paris, 1971), p. 15.

27. M. Dauksza, "Siedlczanie w obliczu bolszewickiej inwazji 1920 r.," in *Prace Archi-walno-Konserwatorskie na Terenie Województwa Siedleckiego*, issue 10 (1997): 103–134.

28. Centralne Archiwum Wojskowe w Warszawie (CAW), I 440, 12/6–7.

29. W. Witos, *Moje wspomnienia* (Warsaw, 1990), pt. 2, pp. 115–116.

30. APS, KPPPS, sig. 58, fol. 21.

31. APS, KPPPS, sig. 59, fol. 15.

CHAPTER 5.

POLITICAL ASPIRATIONS OF JEWS
DURING THE PERIOD 1918–1939

5.A. ZIONIST PARTIES

The political aspirations of Jews during this period in regard to their attitude toward the future and the issue of creating their own state were very diverse. I have divided them into two trends. The first represents the parties striving toward the resolution of the Jewish problem by creating an independent Jewish state. They were made up of the Zionist parties. The movement that was later called Zionism was founded by Theodor Herzl (1860-1904). He united some loose small groups that had previously been acting out of religious impulses and created a movement of a political nature. In his youth, Herzl was not occupied with Jewish problems. It was only under the influence of the Alfred Dreyfus affair, when an officer in the French army was falsely accused of treason, was convicted in 1894, and was rehabilitated in 1906, that he lost faith in European liberalism. After a personal observation of the development of events in France, he became convinced that assimilation did not protect against anti-Semitism and that the only resolution of the Jewish problem was the establishment of a state. He contained his musing on this subject in the book *A Jewish State* (Der Judenstaat), published in 1896. Herzl felt that the creation of a Jewish state would benefit not only Jews but the entire world. In fulfillment of his idea, he convened the I Zionist Congress in Basel in 1897. The political program of the new movement was formulated at this congress and took the position that Zionism strove toward the establishment of a publicly and lawfully guaranteed homeland for the Jewish nation in Palestine. At first the creation of such a state on the territory of Africa or South America was contemplated. However, under the influence of eastern European religious Zionists, they concentrated on Palestine as the land of their fathers.[1]

Zionism had adherents in Siedlce as early as the nineteenth century. At first they were gathered in the movement Lovers of Zion [Hovevei Zion—ed.]. At its first conference, which took place in Katowice in 1884, the delegates from Siedlce were Mosze Goldberg and Jehoszua Goldfarb. The city had a branch of the Society for the Support of Jewish Farmers and Artisans in Syria and Palestine, known as the

Odessa Committee. In reality, this was a branch of the Lovers of Zion, an organization that was officially banned in Russia and was backed in Siedlce by a rather numerous group of young Chassidim. Larger gatherings of members took place during engagements or weddings. This was a typical camouflage from the tsarist police. In later years, after heated polemics inside the Lovers of Zion, its offshoots appeared: Sons of Moses, Political Zionism, and Spiritual Center. Zionism underwent many transformations and internal divisions. Several parties emerged from it.

The following parties having this orientation functioned in Siedlce: the Zionist Organization in Poland, the Zionist Labor Party, Right Poalei Zion, Left Poalei Zion, and the Organization of Orthodox Zionists "Mizrachi." The Siedlce Zionists had a worthy pioneer in Abraham Abrahams. He was born in Siedlce in 1801. After coming of age, he took up ritual slaughter and became a butcher. At the age of 36 he left Siedlce for London. There he developed his skills connected with slaughter and wrote several theses dedicated to this subject. His best known book was titled *Abraham's Covenant.* This was a commentary on the *Shulkhan Arukh,* the traditional law connected with slaughter. Abrahams also published an autobiography titled *Memory for Abraham.* In 1878 he left for Jerusalem and built a house there. After a time, he donated it to the society Abode of Israel. Abraham Abrahams died in Jerusalem in 1880.

The next well-known Zionist activist that left for Palestine was Jehoszua Goldfarb. He was born in 1867 to a Zionist family; his father, Mosze, was an activist in the Lovers of Zion movement and owned an oil processing plant in Siedlce. As a young man, Jehoszua was also active in this organization and then in the organization Sons of Moses. He left Siedlce several times to visit Palestine as a tourist and then settled there permanently in 1909. Together with Zejwele Klusek from Warsaw, he founded the Carmel Society and initiated the founding of the settlement Rehovot (Streets), in which he lived for a certain time. Next he moved to Tel Aviv (Mound of Spring) and initiated the founding of the Kadmat Haaretz Association, whose goal was to purchase land around Tel Aviv. During World War I, he lost the money he had invested in Siedlce. But he did well in developing his financial interests in Palestine, helped organize the National Treasury in Tel Aviv, and set up an almond garden in Rehovot.

In the 1930s, a group of Zionist youths left for Palestine; among them was also the later leader of Left Poalei Zion in Siedlce, Josef Słuszny. Some of the new arrivals had to return to their native city. Some had health problems in tolerating the change in climate, while others returned for economic reasons because they could not find means for supporting themselves. Josef Słuszny also returned and became engaged in political activity.

The Polish government expressed its favorable position toward the idea of Zionism officially, among others, in a letter of Prime Minister A. Skrzyński of 31 March 1926, "To the President of the Zionist Executive Board, Nachum Sokołow."

The following words were used in it: "The government is following with interest the development of the efforts of Zionist organizations directed toward the rebirth of Jewish national and cultural individuality on the soil of Palestine..."[2]

The Zionist Organization in Poland—Histadrut Haziyonit be Polonia

It had about 600 members in Siedlce in 1922 and about 500 sympathizers. On 27 July 1922, it organized a rally at which Dr. Jehoszua Gotlib from Warsaw spoke.[3] About 2,000 people were present. Jehoszua Gotlib's lecture touched upon the matter of Palestine's mandate and the need for general agreement among all Jews for the building of a Jewish state. He said at that time, "Friends! We have finally lived to the happy moment when we are the citizens of our own country; the Palestinian Mandate has been confirmed. From this moment on, we shall be looked upon completely differently; they will have to treat us as they do every other nation. But we must put forth every effort to rebuild our own country as quickly as possible and start dwelling in it. Our wandering has now ended. We have to stop dividing ourselves into different parties, such as the Orthodox, the Poalei Zion, Tzeirei Zion, and others. We have to arrive at there being only one Jewish people and one Jewish front. Our Orthodox brothers desperately want everything to be set up religiously, in accordance with their program. Very well, I agree, that if our country, Palestine, is to be rebuilt by donning yarmulkes, I will gladly put one on myself. But in the meantime, nothing will come of this. We have to get on with the work of rebuilding."[4] The overall income from the rally, that is, 400,000 marks, was earmarked for the support of economic and cultural work in Palestine. That same day, in the evening, Wajman held a banquet in Dr. Gotlib's honor. One and a half million marks were brought in during the event, which were sent directly to Palestine. After the Palestinian Mandate was confirmed, the Secretariat of the Provisional Jewish National Council was convened, with offices at 24 Ogrodowa Street. Members of the council included Maksymilian Schleicher as chairman and Uszer Liwerand, Srul Cukier, and Nachum Weintraub. The secretariat conducted a very energetic campaign in favor of leaving for Palestine. In the period from 26 July to 26 August 1922 alone, it sent nine families there. Officially, the Siedlce branch came into being only in 1924 and had about 200 members. At its head were Uszer Orzeł, chairman (merchant); Maksymilian Schleicher, vice-chairman (doctor); and Lew Gutgeld.[5] The Zionist Organization had as its goal the direction of the efforts of all Jews "toward the rebuilding and development of Palestine as the public-legal guarantee of a Jewish homeland in national, cultural, and economic respects."[6] The main offices of this party was in Warsaw. "Its methods of action: propaganda in word, letter, and print."[7] With the goal of raising money for their activity, they organized concerts, dances, and courses in, among others, Hebrew, agriculture, trade, and tourism. A membership subscription, called a shekel in Hebrew, was 6 zlotys annually. The highest authority in the Zionist Organization was the Representative

Congress, then the Central Committee, and then the Auditing Committee. The Congress met once a year. One representative was selected during the General Assembly from every division of the party that had 200 members, and an additional representative was selected in divisions containing over 250 people. Every delegate had the right to one vote for a candidate to the governing body of the party as well as the right of a passive and active vote. The Central Committee consisted of 15–25 people elected by a majority of the votes of the delegates. The Central Committee took care of the totality of the party's activity and oversaw the correct development of the following departments:

1. The department of fundraising for the purchase of land for immigrants in Palestine, the so-called Keren Kayemeth LeIsrael.
2. The department of donations and contributions for the support of all economic and cultural work in Palestine.
3. The department for the support and recruitment of immigrants to Palestine, the so-called Palestinian Department.
4. The department for cooperation among landowners in Palestine, the so-called Hachsharat Hayishuv.
5. The department for the vocational and moral preparation of candidates for settlement in Palestine, the so-called Hechalutz Hamerkaz.
6. The department for the support of Hebrew culture.[8]

Before the Tenth Congress of the Zionist Organization, the Histadrut, in 1929, a division into three factions occurred within its ranks: Al Hamishmar, Et Livnot, and Revisionist Zionists.

Al Hamishmar (On Guard) paid a great deal of attention to the immediate activity in Poland, the goal of which was to prepare emigration recruits for the future Israel. The members of this faction demanded national autonomy through the creation of secular Jewish communities. They considered Hebrew to be their national language, although they allowed for the use of Yiddish. They cooperated with other national minorities in Poland with the aim of protecting common interests. This faction was similar to the Folkists. It placed great emphasis on diplomacy, although it demanded a rapid resolution of the Jewish question. Izaak Grünbaum stood at the head of this faction in Poland. The Siedlce Al Hamishmar had 50 members, headed by Lewi Gutgeld and Fiszel Popowski.[9]

Et Livnot (Time to Build) concentrated its activity on preparing skilled workers for Palestine, to which it organized immigration. It placed great emphasis on diplomacy, connecting their hopes for obtaining a state through this means. It treated Jews differently than other minorities in Poland. It was close to the Orthodox group and the Mizrachi. This faction was headed in Poland by Leon Reich and Abraham Ozajasz Thon. The Siedlce Et Livnot had 30 members, at the head of which were Makymilian Schleicher and Abram Szloma Englader.[10]

Revisionist Zionists believed that the Zionist movement should avoid becoming involved in Polish matters. In their view, the Polish authorities should be supported when they took a positive attitude to the concept of Zionism. The Revisionist Zionists had as their only goal the building of the Jewish state in Palestine within its historical borders and on religious principles. They saw the coming into being of their state in armed battle with the British, since they were the ones who held the mandate over Palestine and made the immigration of Jews to it difficult. They demanded the following: handing over gratis any uncultivated state land in Palestine to Jews, the conduct of agrarian reform, an appropriate customs policy, protectionism for Jewish industry, the creation of Jewish armed forces in Palestine, and the appropriate manning of national offices in Palestine by Jews. This faction was characterized by nationalism and militarism. Their leader was Vladimir Jabotinsky. In 1931 the Revisionist Zionists broke off from the Zionist Organization and created a separate Union of Zionists, and in 1935 they broke off from the Worldwide Zionist Organization and formed their own central one—the New Zionist Organization. The Revisionist Zionists, under the influence of increasing anti-Semitism, gained ever greater support among Jews, particularly in the 1930s. They treated anti-Semitism as a positive phenomenon for them because it contributed to the growth of the number of their followers. The Polish authorities supported the New Zionist Organization and aided Jewish armed organizations because they believed that emigration was advantageous for Poland in resolving the Jewish problem. On Polish territory, the Revisionist Zionists wanted to play the same role in Jewish society as Piłsudski's followers had in Polish society. Reemigrants, who had had to leave Palestine because of an unfavorable attitude toward them by the British authorizes, had a particularly radical attitude. They intended to return with rifles in hand. After Hitler came to power in Germany, Jabotinsky promoted the slogan "evacuation of Jews to Palestine," which would have encompasses 1.5 million Jews over the course of ten years, with half the emigrants coming from Poland. With this goal, as early as 1933 "nests" of Beitar—a youth organization of revisionists, among whom were members of the oldest groups—participated actively in Military Preparedness training. The exercises, under the direction of officers of the Polish Army, lasted for four weeks over two years. Upon completion, members of the MP underwent an intense course in one of the military camps. On the basis of an understanding between the leadership of the MP and the leadership of Beitar, members of this organization were allowed to participate in exercises in their uniforms and could march fully armed under the command of their commanding officers during ceremonies. From November 1937 to September 1939, the Poles provided arms and explosive materials to the National Military Organization (Irgun Zvai Leumi), which was transported illegally by sea to Palestine.[11]

The offices of the Revisionist Zionist in Siedlce were located at 11 Błonie Street. The executive board consisted of Jakub Obersztejn, Zelman Frejlich, and Srul Rozenberg. They had rather extensive support, particularly among the youth. On

25 August 1935, the Revisionists held elections to the First International Congress of the New Zionist Organization. Eight hundred seventy-two people participated in the election, which amounted to an attendance of 85 percent. The revisionists organized lectures, such as, Dawid Morgenstern from Siedlce and Dr. Szachtman from Paris presented a paper on 11 December 1935 in the presence of 220 people titled "What Caused the Revisionist Zionist to Leave the Old Zionist Organization." Because of their efforts to act conspiratorially, no broader information about them has survived.[12]

All the factions were united by a common goal—the building of Palestine. Every grouping, however, saw a different road leading to its realization. The faction Et Livnot, which affected Jewish society through the *Shedletser Wochenblat* (The Siedlce Weekly), had the greatest influence, with a circulation of 800. The Zionist Organization as a whole had influence in the City Council (in 1932, M. Schleicher and U. Orzeł were councilors on its behalf), the Home for Orphans and Seniors, the Society for Health Care, the Joint-Stock Bank, the "Tarbut" Society and School, the Alliance of Small Merchants, the Union of Workers in the Trades, the Committee for Aid to Jewish Students (so-called Auxilium Academicum Judaicum), the Jewish Scouting Organization (Hashomer Hatzair), the Jewish Athletics and Sports Union, and the Jewish Art Literary-Musical Society.[13] The Zionist Organization had a 3 percent share of influence in the society of Siedlce County (counting society as a whole). In terms of numbers, they were second only to the Orthodox Jews, who had a 6.5 percent share in the totality of the county population.[14] Yet it was active on a larger scale than the Orthodox Jews.

The Zionist Organization organized lectures on subjects of a national content and meetings with interesting activists. Rallies in which thousands of Jews participated were a very important manifestation of its activity. They were usually called as a reaction to events in Palestine, for example, during periods when the British authorities limited immigration by Jews or during anti-Jewish riot by Arabs.[15] Such rallies took place in Siedlce in May and August 1929. In August of that year, there was a funeral service in the synagogue for Jews who died in Palestine. About 2,000 people took part in it. After the service, the young people formed a procession that moved from the synagogue into the street. The police scattered the demonstrators. That same day, in the evening, a rally was held in a closed establishment. About 1,000 people took part in it. Speeches were delivered by, among others, Landau, Mordechaj Gotesdiner, Mozes Jon-Tow, Lejb (Lewi) Gutgeld, and Fiszel Popowski. After going out into the street, another attempt was made to hold a march. The police intervened this time as well and scattered the demonstrators. As an act of protest and solidarity with the Palestinian Jews, a strike lasting from half an hour to an hour was held that day in Jewish stores and companies.[16]

So-called Saturday cultural evenings gained popularity. On Saturdays, after the end of Shabbat, gatherings were organized dedicated to culture, the press, and music. Lejzorowicz gave a lecture titled "The Jewish-Polish Salon at the End of the Eighteenth Century in Germany" at the turn of January and February 1924. On 9 February that same year, Dr. Szyper gave a talk on "Jewish Culture," and 1 March Lejb (Lewi) Gutgeld read a paper, "The Jewish Press." On 13 April 1925, Dr. Szyper came to the city again, with Apolinary Hartglas, the parliament member well known here. Szyper gave a talk on the life and literary work of Perec, while Hartglas talked about the current political situation and reported on the work of the Sejm [parliament—trans.]. The next important meeting with Sejm member Apolinary Hartglas was organized on 17 October 1926. It took place in the hall of the Municipal Club with an audience of 100 people. Hartglas reported on the activity of the Jewish Circle of Sejm members and explained the causes of the unrest that arose after the confirmation by the Circle of the agreement reached with the government by Dr. Reich and Thon. He also explained the reasons why Dr. Reich had resigned from his post as chairman of the Jewish Circle. He presented the postulates put before the government and emphasized that "the Jewish nation places high hopes in Marshal Piłsudski and trusts that it will not be disappointed, in exchange for which the Jewish nation is prepared to support the current government." He described the course of the May events [reference to the so-called May Coup—trans.], expressing high regard for the troops of Marshal Piłsudski, from whom the Jewish population did not experience any unpleasantness, even though Jews were often wrongly accused in Warsaw of shooting at the marshal's troops. In connection with the fact that the former prime minister Bartel promised to meet the Jewish population's demands, "the Jews promise to give the present government their aid and cooperation in rebuilding the economy of the state."[17]

Apolinary Hartglas, as a Sejm member, became engaged in the matters of other minorities in his district. In 1919, the Polish authorities took over all the shrines and buildings belonging to the Eastern Orthodox Church. The Eastern Orthodox priest Jan Charłampowicz turned to Sejm member Apolinary Hartglas with a request to plead with the state authorities in Warsaw for the return of at least one of the shrines located in the city. Hartglas interceded in this matter several times in the Ministry of Religious Denominations and Public Education. Despite receiving a favorable response from the central authorities in Warsaw, the city authorities did not return a single building to the Eastern Orthodox population, which at that time numbered about 1,000.[18]

The Zionist Organization supported the Polish authorities, trying to help the state by, among other things, supporting the subscription of a national loan in 1933. In order for this action to have a social character, a General Jewish Committee was convened that issued a proclamation asking for support for the government. As we read in this proclamation, "We Jews, who suffer most during times of unrest, should respond most fervently and stand in the first ranks of the appeal of the Government, which always safeguards law and order in the country. [...] With this deed we should document our attachment to this country and prove that during any time of state necessity we will stand in the ranks of our own free will to demonstrate our help."[19] There was also no lack of Jews in strengthening the defense of the country.

On 26 February 1933, a convention of Podlasie Zionist Organization delegates was held. Six hundred delegates arrived at the hall of the Komet [Comet—trans.] Cinema in Siedlce. The proceedings were opened with the singing of the Polish anthem. The participants spoke in Polish, Yiddish, and Hebrew. When member of the Sejm Izaak Grünbaum[20] started to deliver his paper titled "The Current Situation of Zionists in Poland and Palestine," a group of Communists shouted, "Away with the fascist government, away with Grünbaum, the lackey of the fascist government!" Several chairs were thrown onto the stage. Lejb Gutgeld sustained a head wound. Order was restored by the arrival of the police. The organizers of the meeting did not, however, reveal to the police who was responsible for the incident. The outraged Grünbaum changed the subject of his paper. He spoke about the battle with communism from the national point of view of Jews. The next part of the convention took place in the Jewish Home for Orphans and Seniors. There, in a smaller gathering, papers were read by Master of Arts H. Polakiewicz, "The Activity of the Central Committee of the Zionist Organization in Poland"; Master of Arts Muszkatblit, "Cultural and Tarbut [see chapter 7—trans.] Activity"; Natan Asz, "Emigration to Palestine"; and Lejb Gutgeld, "Work on Rebuilding Palestine." Wizenfeld from Biała Podlaska, Dr. Menasze Zylberman from Łosice, Josek Frydlub from Sokołów Podklaski, and Dr. Hersz Goldfarb from Radzyń took part in the discussion that ensued after the papers were read.[21]

On 16 June 1934, the Zionist Organization organized a memorial service in Siedlce in honor of Chaim Nachman Bialik, who had died in Palestine.[22] Approximately 400 people attended. Siedlce residents Kiwa Goldfarb, Eugeniusz Brandt, an attorney, and Lewi Gutgeld spoke at this gathering. The speakers emphasized the achievements of the deceased for the Zionist movement and described his poetic and social activity.[23]

On 28 June 1935, the members of various Zionist groups, with the exception of the Revisionist Zionists, held an election for delegates to the Nineteenth Zionist Congress. Five lists were voted on; 1,184 voters participated in the elections, which was an 86 percent voter turnout.

On 18 May 1936, the Zionist Organization organized a memorial gathering to honor the memory of the deceased president of the Worldwide Zionist Organization, Nachum Sokołow. It was attended by 350 people. It was probably members of the Zionist Organization that in the beginning of October 1936 plastered the walls of the city with posters bearing the following content: "Jews! How many years have passed since we were forced to leave our Homeland. From that moment dates our national downfall. We wandered over countries and seas, we were oppressed and exploited, but our spirits did not fall. We defended ourselves bravely against the terror of foreign countries: against the Spanish Inquisition and against German persecution. We have long waited for the moment when our dreams of returning to Eretz would be fulfilled. And finally the day that is to be our liberation has finally arrived. We must use our joint forces to pave our way to our Homeland and fix the work that we put in place thousands of years ago. Jews! We call upon you with your obligation to work with clasped hands for the good of the Jewish Nation. Away with Arab terror! Let us bring help to our brothers in Eretz and in the whole world."[24]

In October 1938, the Zionist Organization, having 300 members, was headed by Nachum Weintraub, chairman; Dr. Henryk Bergman, vice-chairman; Moszko Judenglauben, treasurer; and Kiwa Goldfarb, secretary.

The World Zionist Labor Party—Mifleget Avodah Zionit Hitachdut

This party strove to create a future Jewish state that would be based on the idea of democratic socialism. It emerged in 1920 at the initiative of moderate socialists. It accepted the formation of the Polish Republic, although it did not concern itself much with Polish politics, placing its main emphasis on its activity in Palestine. It strove for the creation of solidarity within the Jewish community. It was anti-Marxist in its outlook.

The Zionist Labor Party, Hitachdut, started its activity in Siedlce in 1925. It had 25 members and about 30 sympathizers. The leadership of the party consisted of Icko Freilich, chairman, a member of the editorial staff of *Shedletser Wochenblat*; and Abram Altenberg, secretary, co-founder of the Jewish Bank in Siedlce. Members paid dues in the amount of 50 grosz [Polish currency; 1 grosz = 1/100 of a zloty—trans.] per month. Hitachdut cooperated with the Zionist Organization, particularly with the "Tarbut" Educational Society as well as within the framework of Keren Kayemeth LeIsrael (Land Purchases) and Keren Hayesod (Economic Work [Foundation Fund—trans.]). It had little influence in society and had a negative attitude toward the activity of Left Poalei Zion, Right Poalei Zion, and the Bund. Hitachdut functioned in the extra-party Zionist accord, League of Working Palestine.[25]

Jewish Social-Democratic Labor Party—Right Poalei Zion

The Jewish Social-Democratic Workers Party Poalei Zion (Workers of Zion) arose in the Russian partition during the 1905 Revolution. During the early 1920s, the Poalei Zion party split into a left wing and a right wing. Right Poalei Zion espoused the idea of Zionist democratic socialism and supported the Polish authorities, although it did not take part in Polish politics. Its main goal was the building of a Jewish Palestine. It was a member of the League of Working Palestine.

It was not officially registered in Siedlce. It functioned through the Labor Union of Unskilled Workers, which existed since 1918. This union had 20 members at the time; its executive board consisted of Mozes Grynfarb, chairman, and Chaim Dawid Kamienny, secretary. Union members paid dues in the amount of one zloty per month. The police estimated the influence of Poalei Zion (left and right combined) at about 300 members and an equal number of sympathizers.[26] In 1927, Right Poalei Zion, along with Zionist Socialists, took part in the election to the City Council, creating a Jewish Workers Election Committee "Poalei Zion." Its election platform emphasized the building of cheap housing, defense of renters' rights, the extension of the sewerage system and electrification of the city, regulation of emigration by facilitating departure and help for all those heading for Palestine, increasing productivity by subsidizing Hechalutz, and the right to use Yiddish in communal institutions. The party was opposed to capitalism, reactionary politics, anti-Semitism, and assimilation.[27] Right Poalei Zion influenced Hechalutz (Pioneer), Hashomer Hatzair (Scouts), and the "Freiheit" Cultural-Educational Society. This party cooperated with the Zionist Organization.[28]

Jewish Social-Democratic Labor Party—Left Poalei Zion

The revitalization of the leftist Zionist movement in Siedlce took place in 1916 when the German occupants permitted political and social activity. At that time the adherents of this movement created the Worker's Home, which was located on Ogrodowa Street (currently Sienkiewicz Street). Its executive board consisted of Mosze Międzyrzecki, Icie Altszuler, and Henech Zalcman. The Worker's Home was under the influence of Borochov Jugend—Borochov's Youths. This was a left-wing organization referring to the idea of Dov Ber Borokhov. Its goal was the preparation of future party members and settlers in the Palestinian state. The Worker's Home had a large and well-equip88]ped reading room. It ran a soup kitchen for the poor. Party and social activity was carried out even on holidays, which was a cause of friction with the "religious" members of the Jewish community and the rabbi. In its initial phase, the Worker's Home was supposed to function as a "nonparty club" and to serve all workers. A sharp dispute arose between the Bundists and the Zionists, however, as a result of which Bund followers were expelled. They therefore created their own home called the "Tsukunft" (The Future) Workers' Society, and then they gathered around the Jewish Art Society. During this time two independent committees arose spontaneously constituting Poalei Zion. They joined into one party and commenced intensified activity. Among its activists were Melech Heinzdorf, Zawl Górnicki, Awremele Zilbersztajn, Mejer Zalcman, Śliwka, and Rozenzumen.

During the interwar period, Left Poalei Zion voiced the need to stage a Marxist revolution, acknowledged international struggle, supported Soviet Russia, and strove toward the creation of a Communist Palestine. It did not belong to the Polish Communist Party since the Polish Communists did not acknowledge the idea of Zionism, which Left Poalei Zion espoused. Toward the end of the 1930s, this party

distanced itself from communism and moved closer to other socialist-Zionist parties, and in 1937 it entered the League of Working Palestine. In Poland, Left Poalei
Zion strove toward equality of rights of Jews and Poles in the sphere of access to
public offices, the judiciary, and education.

In 1922, Left Poalei Zion, together with the Bund, created a local Jewish Workers
Election Committee within the framework of preparations for the national election.
The committee consisted of Abram Kleinrerer, Josef Słuszny, Szlama Kamiński,
Szlama Hochberg, and Izrael Tabakman.[29]

In the beginning of the 1920s, the leading activist of this party was Zamwel
Rozenzumen. Left Poalei Zion manifested its presence in February 1926 during
the strike held by the Leather Industry Union. There were two separate unions in
Siedlce: the Polish and the Jewish. Both unions acted jointly making two demands:
higher wages, and payment for work in cash and not promissory notes. A large
number of workers agreed to take promissory notes for their work instead of
cash. Businessmen claimed that they could not pay in cash since cash was needed
to pay for goods that were indispensable for production. They started to pay for
work with promissory notes. Those who did not agree were not given any more
orders. So-called "percentagers" immediately appeared, usually from the families
of businessmen, who bought out the promissory notes at 80 percent of their value.
The strike lasted two long months. The businessmen tried to place orders on the
existing terms with workers in the trades living in the vicinity of the city, but the
determined stance of members of the PPS thwarted these intentions. The strike
ended in success.

This party was not officially registered in Siedlce. It functioned through the
Society of Evening Classes, which was registered from 1927 and was subordinate to
the central branch in Warsaw. It had 86 members. Its executive board consisted of
the chairman, Szlomo Kamieński, the owner of a box manufacturing company; the
secretary, Zamwel Rozenzumen, a collector for the Siedlce Healthcare Fund; and
members Chil Gutowski, a tailor, Chana Handlarz, and Dawid Orzech. Everyone
who belonged to the party paid dues in the amount of one zloty a month; aside
from this, resources for its activities were raised by organizing various events. Left
Poalei Zion ran the "Star" Sports Club, whose soccer team performed at a particularly high level. There was also a choir under the direction of Josef Zonszajn,
and a drama circle, whose director was Heinsdorf. Josef Słuszny, Hochberg, Izrael
Tabakman, Zamwel Rozenzumen, Froman, Awremełe Zilbersztajn, Melech Heinzdorf, Meier Zalcman, Dawid Orzech, Bronia Mozes, Dawid Grinfarb, Chana Handlarz, Śliwka, Szlomo Kamieński, and Abraham Josel Kornicki were energetic
activists.

In the 1927 elections to the City Council, Left Poalei Zion received 614 votes,
earning two seats won by Zamwel Rozenzumen and Abram Zylberberg. Their election platform supported transferring city taxes solely onto the wealthy, battling

against high prices, electrification of the poorest streets, building a water-supply system and a sewerage system, protecting renters from eviction, hiring both Jewish and non-Jewish workers in public-works projects, financing Jewish secular schools out of the city budget, and publication of all city announcements also in Yiddish.[30] In 1930, during elections to the Sejm and Senate, Left Poalei Zion submitted their list and won 952 votes in Siedlce and the county. I had influence in the Icchak Lejba Perec Jewish School and in the Garment Industry Workers Union, Textile Industry Workers Union, the Wood Industry Workers Union, and the Retail and Office Workers Union.

Left Poalei Zion affected Siedlce Jewish society by organizing lectures. Speakers were drawn mostly from Warsaw. One such meeting took place on 2 June 1933 in the hall of the cinema Lux and had an audience of 200. Comrade Zubrowel from Warsaw gave a talk titled "What Does Palestine Look Like in Reality?" In his presentation he attacked all the Jewish parties and claimed that only Left Poalei Zion with its workers could rebuild Palestine.[31]

Organization of Orthodox Zionists "Mizrachi"

The Mizrachi Party arose in 1902. *Mizrachi* in Hebrew means "eastern," that is, the direction a person faces during prayer. They believed in the principle "The country of Israel for the people of Israel in accord with the law of Israel." Its guiding slogan was "Religion, Study, Work." They strove toward the founding of a Jewish state in Palestine based on religious principles.[32]

The motivator of the movement of religious revival among Jewish youth in Siedlce was Szalom Jeleń, the son of Mosze Księgarz. In 1915, along with Aron Nelkienbojm, Lejb Rotwajn, and Pesach Rozen, he assembled religious youths. At first they gathered on the premises of the Mishna Brotherhood.[33] The brighter ones among them taught Bible study courses for religious workers in the Talmud-Torah school. The Agudah (Union of Israel), fearing for their influence in the school, intervened and caused the authorities to ban these meetings. The movement, however, found many new followers. The following activists joined them: Abraham Frydman, Jeszajahu Zelikowicz, and Jehanatan Ajbeszyc. They opened a House of Study in the apartment of B. Altenberg at 28 Kiliński Street. About 60 boys gathered there in order to acquaint themselves with and deepen their religious and literary knowledge. They did not limit themselves only to religious matters but were open to all kinds of literary trends. On this basis, the religious-cultural union called "Tvuna" (Wisdom) was created and was legalized in 1916. Its founders were F. Jeleń, Abraham Frydman, and Dawid Zusman. The goal of Tvuna was to deepen knowledge and piety. The union's offices were on Ogrodowa Street in the house of Mrs. Słuszna. Tvuna united about 200 members. It organized lectures, various kinds of courses, for example, Polish language and calculation, and ran a biweekly wall newspaper called *Our Little Cultural Corner*. Tvuna was a local idea; Siedlce housed its central offices, which maintained contact with 15 branches, including a branch in Warsaw.

In 1918, under the influence of pogroms in Ukraine, Jewish young people started wondering about the idea of a nation whose goal would be to create a state of Israel. After such discussions and a vote, Tvuna officially united with Mizrachi, which already existed in Siedlce but did not have much support.[34]

Mizrachi's significance rose after that. A new executive board was chosen that included Dawid Zusman, A. Frydman, Jehanatan Ajbeszyc, G.M. Karpin, Jeszajahu Zelikowicz, I. Folszpan, and I. Kamienica. In this new grouping, a recruitment campaign was started among young people. To this end, well-known speakers were brought in, proponents of the idea of the formation of Israel. Among those who spoke in Siedlce were Rabbi Awigdor Emiel from Grajew, who was later the chief rabbi in Tel Aviv; Rabbi Brot from Lipna; and Rabbi Nojfelt from Nowy Dwór. Mizrachi was in favor of the reform of Judaism, and with this goal organized religious meetings between young people and progressive, that is, German, rabbis, among them Kochem and Karlbach.

This party ran a soup kitchen for the poor, located in the house of Majzlisz at 22 Ogrodowa Street. Toward the end of 1919, with the help of Elimeleh Nojfelt, the son of the rabbi from Nowy Dwór, a committee called the Daughters of Mizrachi was organized. The Daughters of Mizrachi had 60 members, the most active of whom were Frajda Nusbojm, Aina Arżel, Sara Rodzińska, Sara Słowiatycka, and Małka Srebrnik.[35] In 1919, Mizrachi founded an orphanage for Jewish children with the name Home for Orphans on Ogrodowa Street (in what is currently the location of Podlaska Academy at 24 Sienkiewicz Street). About 40 children resided there. These orphans were taken care of by Fajga Lewartowska.[36] Mizrachi attempted to create Mizrachi Worker, an organization whose goal was to train skilled workers and send them to Palestine. They managed to train and send off a group of eight carpenters.[37] In 1920, at the initiative of Mizrachi, a cheder was founded, a religious school for 6- to 7-year-old children called Torah and Knowledge located on Ogrodowa Street. It was run by Efraim Celnik and Alter Ajzenberg. In ensuing years, Mizrachi was enlivened only during elections to the community council (kahal). In its later activity, it concentrated on running the Home for Orphans and the cheder.[38]

In the 1920s, the members of this party met rather frequently in the establishment at 24 Ogrodowa Street. Religious matters and the future Palestine were discussed. Active speakers were at that time Kamienica, Fela Berg, Abram Żyto from Łuków, J. Szylman, and Gotesdiner.[39] In the 1930s, Mendel Ajzenberg and Iser Rozenberg headed the party. They had three representatives in the Community Council Board: Szyja Beniamin Zelikowicz, Medel Ajzenberg, and Jankiel Mandelbaum.[40] The general meeting of this party that took place on 22 January 1933 in the restaurant at 8 Szpitalna Street brought together 37 people. A new executive board was elected: Mordko Czarny, chairman, a merchant by trade; Iser Rozenberg, secretary,

a merchant; Mendel Ajzenberg, a tailor; Szloma Pryzent, a tailor; Boruch Berko-
wicz, a cobbler; and Lejb Srebrnik, a merchant.[41] At the next meeting, 2 March
1935, in which 30 people participated, Rabbi Chaim Zysman from Knyszyn and
Dr. Szlema Szapiro from Warsaw debated the rebuilding of Palestine. In July 1935,
the Mizrachi group organized a talk titled "The Zionist Congress in Lucerne and
Religious Live in Palestine." The issue was presented jointly by Szyja Zelikowicz
from Siedlce and Zarach Warhaftyk from Warsaw in the presence of 250 people.
Among the activists of the party who survived the war thanks to having emigrated
to Palestine were, among others, the brothers Abraham, Menachem and Zachor
Frydman, Iser Rozenberg, Gotesdine, and Ridel.

The Pioneer Movement—Hechalutz

The Pioneer movement appeared in 1916. Its goal was to prepare pioneers who
would go to Palestine and work there. A kibbutz (commune) was created for the
needs of agriculture in the village Patrykozy, where young people learned the
hard work of a farm. In Siedlce at the home of the Wajman brothers, who lived
in the Rozkosz quarter, a worker commune was created, where trades were taught
that would be useful in Palestine. The Jews who live in Diaspora (dispersion) were
mostly workers in the trades and merchants, so they were not properly prepared
for the difficult living conditions in Palestine. The kibbutzim were to give them
a practical preparation for their new path in life and to toughen them physically
(hachshara).

The activists of Pioneer (Hechalutz) were Mosze Jon-Tow, the main founder of
Hechalutz in Siedlce; Dawid Ben Joself-Pasowski; Benjamin Czarny; and Dawid
Furajter.[42] Through the Podlasie Regional Committee, the Chalutz movement
assembled in Siedlce all the Zionist youth organizations: Hashomer Hatzair
(Scouts), Freiheit-Dror (Freedom), and Hechalutz Hatzair (Young Pioneer). Each
organization had its own separate premises and executive boards, and each engaged
in its separate activity; the goal of the Committee was mutual coordination. In
the years 1930–1933, the Committee was headed by Dawid Pasowski (he adopted
the surname Ben Josef after leaving for Palestine). The Committee managed the
Hechalutz funds, which were earmarked for financing emigrants heading for Palestine. A great deal of importance was given to developing brotherly ties among
the members of Hechalutz. Rallies were organized to this end that took place in
the village of Krynica, in the manor house of the owner of the estate, Cynamon. By
the light of a campfire, with linked hands to form a circle, they danced the hora,
sang Hebrew songs, and made friends. First loves would then blossom. In 1930
a regional assembly was held in Krynica in which local activists of the Chalutz
movement took part along with guests from Palestine. Hechalutz led the choir and
drama circle and organized lectures with the participation of the guests invited
from Palestine. The members of Hashomer Hatzair (Scouts) wore uniforms and

had merit badges and ranks, in a word, they adhered to the principles of scouting. In Siedlce, Hashomer Hatzair was organized by Herszel Słuszny, who directed it for many years. His assistants were Małka Lewin, Jehuda Liwerant, Dawid Jon-Tow, Bunin Czarnobroda, and Josef Kacpan. From 13 June 1936, the executive board consisted of Chaim Begagon, chairman; Ber Lederman, vice-chairman; Uszer Trzmielina, treasurer; and Chana Gropman, secretary. This organization brought together school children from various communities. They inculcated in their members the principles of mutual aid. Collections of money were organized for the purchase of books and school supplies for members from poor families. In July 1936, Hashomer Hatzair organized two street drives, from which the income was allocated for summer camps for children. The woods in the Rozkosz quarter provided a place for playing, holding meeting, and having parades. During vacation, camps were organized in surrounding villages.[43]

The Zionist Socialist Chalutz Youth Organization "Freiheit-Dror" ran the Hapoel (Worker) sports club; several of its members in the bicycling division took part in a trip to Palestine in 1932 and stayed there. This organization later united with Hechalutz Hatzair.

On 11–12 May 1935, Hechalutz organized a two-day gathering of its members in Siedlce County. There was a trip to the woods in Wólka Wołyńska on the first day, and sporting competitions were held on the second day. In August 1935, the organization was run by an executive committee that consisted of Maksymilian Witarysz, chairman; Berko Redenburg, first vice-chairman; Szmul Apelbaum, second vice-chairman; Dawid Frydman, treasurer; and Szmul Rak, secretary. Beniamin Czrny, Dawid Furjter, and Szymon Jabłoń were also activists and organizers. Hechalutz had 70 members. The general meeting of members that took place 10 January 1936 provided a new executive board consisting of Izaak Jabłkowicki, chairman; Benjamin Czarny, vice-chairman; Benjamin Szapiro, secretary; and Chaim Kisielewski, treatsurer.

The Siedlce Hechalutz cooperated closely with the pioneers in Łosice, Mordy, and Mokobody. Work was coordinated and instructions were given by Jechil Halpern from Warsaw.

5.B. Parties Rejecting Emigration as a Solution to the Jewish Question and Striving for Equal Rights within the Framework of the Second Republic

This trend was represented by the following parties: Union of Israel—Agudath Israel, the Jewish Folk Party, General Union of Jewish Workers in Poland—Bund, as well as an assimilationist movement. In this subchapter, the KPP [Communist

Party of Poland—trans.] is also discussed; its goal was to overthrow the political system of the Second Republic.

Union of Israel—Agudath Israel, known as Agudah

On Polish territory, the orthodox (i.e., right-believing adherent of Judaism) movement was organized in 1916 as the Orthodox Union. In 1918, it changed its name to Peace to Loyal Israelites, and in 1919 it adopted the permanent name Union of Israel. The goal of Agudah was the "resolution of all matters relevant to the general Jewish public in the spirit of faith and tradition."[44] This was the party's most important task.

Agudah was the largest party in Siedlce and had the greatest influence. It began its activity in 1918. In 1922 is had about 400 real members and about 200 sympathizers. The dynamic activists included Josek Czytelny, Motys Rubinsztajn, and Dawid Jabłoń. On 23 March 1922, they organized a meeting in the butchers' house of prayer on Jatkowa Street. It was attended by 2,500 people, including women. The speakers were Rabbi Zelig Morgenstern from Sokołów Podlaski and Jojna Naj from Łuków. In their talks, they opposed the Zionist idea of building a secularJewish state in Palestine. They also protested against the Zionists taking over all positions in the Jewish government in Palestine. They asked the faithful to resist Zionist agitation and to stand by people who observe religious precepts. On that same day and at almost the same hour, the Zionists arranged a lecture in the hall of the Lux Cinema titled "Orthodoxy and the Rebuilding of Palestine." About 200 people came. A. Zyte and J. Sylman spoke, arguing that the Orthodox were a "backward nation, whose goal is to set up a government in Palestine on the Biblical model, which they, as a faction of enlightened Jews, could not allow."[45] After the meeting, about a dozen "hot-blooded" Zionists went to the Orthodox house of prayer to break up their meeting. They did not achieve their goal because the Orthodox group was protected by the police. In turn, it was the Bundists who tried to disrupt the next gathering of the Orthodox group, which took place in the hall of the Lux Cinema on 23 July 1922, by starting fights and making noise. After they were removed from the hall, Mordko Zysman finished delivering his paper in peace. Mordko Zysman's next talk, titled "Palestine and Religion," which was organized on 29 July 1922, also did not take place peacefully. Zysman turned to the assembly with these words: "We Jews have to devote ourselves less to commerce and rather more to work in order to prepare ourselves for physical labor in Palestine. We in particular, the Orthodox, will show that we can work. We are not a party that has existed for a few years; we existed at the beginning and we will exist to the end. We knew and felt that the Jewish worker was not doing well, but we could not help him then for a variety of reasons. But the Most High did not forget about the Jews; the worker is doing well today, he is prospering, but surely in his own country, in Palestine, he will prosper even more."[46] About 800 people, who were gathered in the city synagogue, listened to his remarks, among them a sizable group of Bundists and Zionists. They were the ones who interrupted his lecture, yelling, "Away with him! We know how the Orthodox wanted to help the workers! We know you well!" After this incident, everyone started to leave the synagogue. Zysman completed the delivery of his lecture to only a small handful of his followers.[47]

On 1 February 1925, in the hall of the Lux Cinema, a gathering of the Orthodox took place at which Sejm deputy Rabbi Meir Szapiro spoke.[48] The meeting was presided over by the chairman of the executive board of the Siedlce Jewish Religious Council, Srul Gudgeld. Rabbi Szapiro and editor Frydman talked about the necessity of a religious upbringing among Jews "so as to protect in this way the young generation against the harmful influences of postwar corruption."[49] They were listened to by about 200 people.

The intensive development of Agudah started in 1925 when a youth division, Tzeirei Agudath Israel, and a workers' division, Poalei Agudath Israel (1926), were created. Altogether, Agudah had about 300 members. Its executive board consisted of Srul Gutgeld, chairman (merchant); Jakub Szczerański, vice-chairman (bank director); and Mozes Zakon, treasurer (merchant).

On 4 March 1934, Agudah organized a lecture in the building of the Home for Orphans titled "The Task of Orthodoxy in Relation to the Rebuilding of Palestine." The speakers at this meeting were Myszkowski, who lived in Krynki in Białystok County, Morgensztern from Sokołów Podlaski, and Całka from Mokobody. They had an audience of 150 people.

The Union of Israel had the following divisions:

1. **Beit Agudath Israel** (an organization for young women) had 30 members and about 150 sympathizers between the ages of 18 and 25. Its executive board consisted of Dwojra Perla Rubinowicz, chair; Brucha Lewin, vice-chair (teacher); Doba Kramarz, secretary; Estera Solnica, member; and Ryfka Gitla Goldfeder, member. The offices of the women's organization were at 24 Sienkiewicz Street.

2. **Tzeirei Agudath Israel** (an organization for young men) had 70 members and about 100 sympathizers between the ages of 18 and 26. Members of the executive board were Srul-Meir Kleinlerer, chair; Mojżesz Cukier, vice-chair (bookkeeper); Abram Lejbko Jeleń, secretary (editor of *Unser Weg*); Szmerl Nusbaum, member (merchant); Moszko-Leib Blumengranz, member (merchant); and Lejb-Srul Golszoch, member. The offices of the organization were located at 7 Szpitalna Street (currently Kochanowski Street).

3. **Poalei Agudath Israel** (Workers of the Union of Israel) was an organization that had 80 members and about 150 sympathizers between the ages of 18 and 30. The executive board consisted of Mojsze-Aron Nelkinbaum, chair; Juda-Lejb Iberman, vice-chair (office clerk); Szmul Rot, secretary (shipping clerk); Szyja Rybka, treasurer (watchmaker); Towia-Josef Jakubowicz, member (office clerk); Srul-Szloma Cukierman, member (shipping clerk), and Szymon Stok, member. The

organization's offices were located at 7 Szpitalna Street. It was officially registered from the beginning of 1935 and was incorporated.[50]

The Orthodox Jews believed that the foundation of the existence of Jews is religion and that the state in which they lived was merely a place to stay until they return to the Promised Land. They had significant influence among the religious population.[51] In Siedlce during the interwar period, rather large groups of Chassidim were active and were under the influence of tzadikim from Góra Kalwaria, Kock, Parczew, and Kozienice. The most numerous were the Chassidim who were followers of the tzadik from Góra Kalwaria; they had three prayer houses, on Piękna Street, Długa Street, and Szkolna Street.

The Orthodox Jews observed their religious precepts by being active in a variety of organizations. These included the following:

1. Central Association for the Care of Children and Orphans came into being in Siedlce in 1926. Alter Kamiński, Binem Rotenberg, Aron Jabłoń, Dawid Konopny, and Izrael Cukier formed the executive board.

2. "Shomrai Shabbos V'hados" Society, whose main goal was to observe the sanctity of the Sabbath (Shabbas) as well as the main precepts of Judaism. It came into being at the end of 1926, with an executive board consisting of Mordyks, rabbi; Sławatycki, rabbi; Srul Gutgeld, chairman of the Jewish community council; as well the more renowned Orthodox known for their piety: Elkenbaum, Spektor, Żelazny, and Ratyniewicz. In the 1930s, the association took up the battle against illegal ritual slaughter. At a meeting that took place on 26 October 1935 in the presence of 70 people, a resolution was adopted calling for a battle with this business. I. Zakon, J. Ekielbaum, and H. Borek spoke in this spirit.

3. Charitable Society for Aid to the Sick "Bikur Cholim." This society had a rich history. It is not clear exactly in what year it was formed. In 1843, its activity was reactivated and took on the name "New Society for Visiting the Sick." Its members were mostly tailors. The responsibility of each of them was doing good deeds by visiting the sick, which was "one of the largest columns holding up the world." Their task was also to lend money for treatment and also, in the event of the death of a member of the Society, to pray for him for 30 days in the evening and the morning and in the absence of children to say kaddish (prayer for the dead) for a period of one year. In the event, however, that one of the members of the Society is taken ill, the remaining members were to gather in the Beit Hamidrash and recite psalms for the Creator to grant the patient mercy and return him to health. They were also to collect dues for the activity of the Society. During the interwar period, the executive board consisted of Pinkus Bursztejn, Hersz Halbersztat, Icko Miodownik, Szyja Rozengarten, Mendel Mandelbaum, Berko Srebrnik, and Icko Rozengarten (all of them merchants). The term of honorary chairman lasted three years. He did not receive any remuneration for fulfilling this function, but he was obliged to fulfill all the obligations of the Society in an exemplary fashion, including the systematic payment of dues. The chairman was elected in the following manner. A meeting of all the members of the Society took place on the 18 of Adar.[52] An urn was produced into which slips of paper were thrown with the names of the members of the Society present at the meeting. Next, the so-called monthly chairman would pull six slips out of it. Those whom he drew were called "the trusted." They then selected the members of the executive board, including the chairman, the treasurer, the chronicler, and three accountants and three auditors. They had three days to fulfill this function; if after the passage of this time they had not fulfilled their obligation, the procedure was started from the beginning. The admission of new members took place with the support of the chairman and the rest of the members of the Society; the decision was made by democratic vote. In the event of the illness of a member of the executive board, all the other members of this board must gather at the Beit Hamidrash and pray for the recovery of the sick person. In its many years of activity, the Society was "renewed" several times and functioned until the extermination of the Jewish population in 1942.

4. **Society for Looking after the Sick "Linas Hatzedek."** The society implemented its goals by providing free medical care, constant care for the sick, and provision of medicine and spiritual comfort. The executive board in the 1920s consisted of M. Miodownik, H. Lewin, M. Grynfarb, L. Gutgeld, A. Libman, Sz. Fiszer, D. Nelkenbaum, A. Górnfinkiel, J. Jagodziński, Konopny, and others (they were all merchants or workers in the trades). In November 1935, a new executive board was elected: Józef Alberg, chairman; Symcha Sztajberg, vice-chairman; Mojżesz Eksztejn, secretary; Abram Rotfarb, treasurer; as well as Nuchim Lubliner, Berko Liwak, Józef Jagodziński, and Szmul Winer as members.

5. **Society for Aid to the Poor of Siedlce "Beit Lechem" (House of Bread).** The goal of the society was to provide aid to Jews who lived in poverty. The activity was carried out rather efficiently. The society ran a soup kitchen in which unemployed and impoverished Jews could eat. A meal consisted of soup, which was obtained free of charge or for a small contribution. The executive board during the 1920s consisted of Abram Milberg, Srul Rozenblum, Szmul Wakasztejn, and Szmul Rajsman. The auditing committee was composed of Berko Gorzałka and Szlomo Kiszenbaum (all those named were either merchants or workers in the trades).[53] In August 1935, a new executive board was elected at a meeting attended by 45 people: Benjamin Bomblat, chairman; Józef Konopny, vice-chairman; Wolf Milgram, treasurer; Józef Żelazny, secretary; Matys Nurman, member; Lejb Stański, member; and Szymon Kawa, member.[54] During the twenty-year interwar period, at the initiative of the society, the executive board of the Jewish community council in Siedlce determined that, with the aim of helping the poor during the holiday of Passover, bakers, salesclerks, and customers would donate to the society two matzos for each pud (16.38 kg) of flour.

6. SZAS Society (six books of the Mishnah). The society was engaged in studying the Mishnah. It came into being in Siedlce in 1838. Members had to study a page of the Gemara early in the morning at the Beit Hamidrash, because, as was written in the chronicle, "The Talmud is great and not comparable to anything." One of the commandments stated that a page of the Talmud should be studied only in a group, at one table placed to the east and the north of the Aron Kodesh (the place where the Torah was stored); one could not study it alone. Each member paid dues to the society noted down in detail in the statute, and penalties were even paid for missing a single day of studying the Mishnah. New members were admitted only after completing the study of all the books of the Mishnah, that is, every seven years, or during elections of new members to the executive board. The executive board could consist of three people who were unrelated to each other. A new member of the society paid in a so-called induction fee. After completing the study of one book of the Mishnah, a feast could be held only with the consent of a majority of members, but after completing the study of all the books, a feast should be held during which this moment was ceremoniously celebrated. From sources we know of a ceremony that took place on the twenty-second of the month of Adar in 1879. It opened with the singing of cantor Abraham Chaim Efron along with the choir and playing by the folk group of Lajbisz and his son Jancie. Thirty chapters of the Psalms were read. The ceremony lasted all night and had about 300 participants. Among those present were the governor and his whole retinue. The community council was at that time administered by Szymon Grinberg, Cwi Cebula, and Izrael Dow Liwerant, and the executive board of SZAS Society was composed of Fajwel Bojm, Cwi Josef Czarnobroda, and Dawid Szymon Kapłan.[55]

7. "Lodging House" Jewish Charity Society. This society engaged in activity consistent with its name and the goal contained in it. On 30 July 1936 it organized a public collection for the benefit of the society.

8. "Beit Ya'akov" (Jacob's House) School of Religious Courses. It was located in the premises at 38 Piękna Street. This was an evening school for girls in primary school.[a] Rabbi Chaim Jehuda Ginzberg felt that studying in such schools was harmful to girls and they should supplement their education with a traditional Jewish upbringing.

During the entire period of the functioning of these societies, chronicles were scrupulously kept. Unfortunately, they were all destroyed during World War II.

Agudah was engaged in running the religious Talmud-Torah school. It had great influence in the Jewish community, the Merchants Union, and the Union of Workers in the Trades. The Union of Israel fought against all other Jewish parties, especially the Zionists. However, toward the end of the 1930s, on a wave of intense anti-Semitism, it started to cooperate with others to make sure that the future Palestinian state has a religious character.

This is how Apolinary Hartglas characterized the chairman of this party:

"Among other Siedlce Jews, I can recall Srul Gutgeld. A rich merchant in a long coat, the leader of the local Agudah who spoke Polish, he would appear at my place once a year and place into my hands a rather large sum for Keren Hayesod and Keren Kayemeth, much larger than that given by the Zionists, who were no poorer than he, asking only that this remain a secret between us."[56]

The Jewish Folk Party in Poland—Yiddishe Folks Partei in Poylen, known as Folkists

This party arose in 1917. Its platform supported the permanent existence of Jews in a democratic Polish state, connecting it with the acquisition of national-cultural autonomy. The Folkists represented secular aspirations, limitation of the role of religion in life, and transformation of the religious community into a secular representation of Jews. They spoke mainly against the Orthodox, but they were equally against the Zionists and the socialists. They acknowledged Yiddish as the national language of Jews. During the twenty-year period, this language became a literary language thanks to the Folkists.

The party started its activity in Siedlce in 1918. It did not, however, have much of a following. The Folkists based themselves mostly on the intelligentsia. The party had its greatest support in nearby Międzyrzec. Altogether in Siedlce County it had from 50 to 300 members and about 200 sympathizers. This party was led by Menasze Czarnobroda, chairman (merchant); Hersz-Mendel Szapiro, vice-chairman; and Chaim Kawa. In addition to them, Icek Altszuler, Josek Jabłonka, Jakub Zając, and Abram Słuszny were vigorous activists. The Folkists concentrated mostly on running the Icchak Lejb Perec School and on the activity of the Jewish League of Popular Education cultural-educational society. They had certain influences in the Jewish Art Literary-Musical Society, a member of the board of which was their representative, Pejsach Kapcan, and in the Retail and Office Workers Union.[57]

On 26 August 1922, in the hall of the cinema Moderne, a paper was given by Dr. Cyper titled "Folkists and Democracy." About 100 people attended. Dr. Cyper from the outset spoke against the departure of Jews to Palestine. He supported this by saying the Jews in Poland had fought for it and spilled their blood enough, so now they had the right to live peacefully on its territory. All the more so since they had property here that they should not dispose of, and in Palestine they had nothing. Dr. Cyper also argued that among those leaving for Palestine were many Bundists, who during the battle for the "rudder of power" in that country will want to start a revolution, "and what it has brought about we can see in Russia." As Dr. Cyper argued, the Zionists are shortsighted, because they do not see the behavior of the Arabs. They will not allow a sizable influx of Jews into Palestine, and England will take a passive position, asserting that Arabs have long inhabited this land. The Orthodox, on the other hand, as he argued, imagine that with the aid of religion they will achieve everything in Palestine, but they do not want to go themselves. At the end of his exposition, Dr. Cyper stated that Jews should not be active in various parties but should form "one Jewish people that could demand rights for itself, and in these times Jews should stay where they are and not listen to those who talk about Palestine."[58] Dr. Cyper received rousing applause from the gathering for his conclusions.

On 16 February 1923, Szulim Jankiel Stupnicki from Warsaw gave a talk titled "Attack of the Sejm Jewish Circle on Yiddish Schools and the Yiddish Language." Present were about 50 Folkists, who were chaired by Mosze Mandelman. Szulim Stupnicki referred in his lecture to the initiative of Representative Noach Pryłucki, who made a motion in the Sejm of the Republic of Poland to institute schools in Poland with Yiddish as the teaching language. This motion was not supported in the Sejm by the Jewish Circle, which claimed that this is a "jargon," and the language of Jews is Hebrew. Szulim Stupnicki declared this position of the Circle to be a betrayal, and in the following part of his talk he demonstrated that Hebrew was a dead language and difficult to learn. Yiddish, on the other hand, was a language that was currently being used by Jews. His conclusions were supported by Moszko Mandelman and Menasze Czarnobroda. The meeting concluded with the signing of a protest resolution against the harmful activity of the Sejm Jewish Circle.[59] On 8–10 March 1924, the Folkists organized a "School Week" during which they collected funds for the school and school supplies for poor Jewish children. The authorities hindered this effort and stopped the fundraising on the pretext of "formalities." This did not discourage the Folkists, who organized a concert in the Municipal Club for this purpose. The Bund and Poalei Zion, as well as most of the labor unions, supported this effort, but the Zionist Organization did not, justifying their position with the fact that the Folkists did not include the study of Hebrew in their schools. The Zionists organized competing gatherings and parties during these days, during which they collected money for the Palestine Fund. It was undoubtedly this rivalry that brought about, on the initiative of the Folkists, a meeting in Siedlce in April 1924 between the Zionist representative Izaak Grünbaum and the Folkist representative Noach Pryłuski.[60] Grünbaum gave a lecture on "Socialism and Zionism" and Pryłucki on "What Is Jewish Culture." The meeting took place in a peaceful atmosphere.[61]

The Folkists continued to organize a series of talks. Thus, on 10 May 1924, Perec Markisz gave a lecture with the humorous title "Italy, Egypt to Palestine!" He argued that "there is poverty and hunger in Palestine, and Jews have no reason to go there."[62] He criticized the Zionists and claimed that departures for Palestine are a misfortune for Jews. Then on 15 April 1925, they organized a rally in the hall of the Municipal Club with the participation of the representative to the Polish Sejm Noach Pryłucki. He talked about the cultural-educational efforts that were being made in Jewish society and how they were opposed to the Zionists, "who earmark the funds they have collected not for Jewish schools but for various objectives in Palestine, where living conditions for Jewish émigrés could not be worse."[63] His remarks were listened to by about 100 people.

Most likely at the initiative of the Folkists, and with the support of the Bund and Poalei Zion, the City Council changed the name of Żydowska [Jewish—trans.] Street to Berek Joselewicz Street. This is one of the oldest streets in the city. It arose on the eastern frontage of Old Market Square, probably during a period of residential regulation. Next to it, on the plot that was called Old Market Square, was the synagogue. The name Żydowska Street appears as early as 1811 in what was called the survey registry of the city. The change in the name took place at the beginning of the 1920s. This is confirmed by the preserved registration books in which the first entries come from 1925.[64]

For a time in 1926, that is, during the time that elections to the City Council and the Township Council took place, the Folkists published a weekly, *Dos Vort* (The Word). Its editorial board consisted of Jakow Tenenbojm, Menasze Czarnobroda, and Mosze Mandelman, whom the authorities considered to be the chief organizer of this movement in Siedlce.[65]

During the 1930s, the activity of this party declined. The Jewish League of Popular Education was disbanded by the Polish authorities, and the Perec School failed due to a lack of financial means. The increase in anti-Semitic sentiments also did not offer prospects for the attainment of autonomy by Jews.

General union of Jewish workers in Poland—Algemener Yiddisher Arbeter Bund in Poylen, known as Bund

In 1897 the General Union of Jewish Workers in Russia and Poland—Bund was founded at the initiative of Jewish socialists in Vilnius, and in 1905 the Jewish Social-Democratic Party Bund was founded in Galicia. In 1916 the Bund on the territory of the former Russian partition detached itself from the all-Russian head office, and in 1920 in was joined by the Jewish Social-Democratic Party [ŻPSD—trans.]. The Bund rejected the vision of a mass emigration of Jews to Palestine. It was building socialism, which was to bring a solution of social and national problems through the creation of national-cultural autonomy. The Bundists acknowledged the need for an organizational separation from Jewish socialists, and so mostly Jewish assimilationists were active in the Polish Socialist Party. The Bund foresaw that the socialists would gain power with force, using battle formations in their campaign, basing themselves on workers, and attracting various others who were disillusioned with capitalism. The transition period after they gained power wound function under the dictatorship of the proletariat controlled by workers.

The Bund did not specify the form in which power would be exercised but rather limited itself to stating that the Soviet system was not universal. In the sphere of the economy, it anticipated the expropriation of big industry and trade, high finance, and owners of the means of communication, transferring them to the state, to local communes, or to cooperatives. Large agricultural property was to be partly parceled out to peasants and partly transferred over to cooperatives. The Bund assumed that the economy would be managed by authorities composed of representatives of the state, producers, and consumers. This was a search for a middle road between communism and parliamentary democracy.[66]

After Poland gained its independence in 1918, the Siedlce Bund began work to organize Jewish socialist institutions. The following were organized: labor unions, which until 1920 had their offices at 14 Warszawska Street; "Tsukunft" (The Future) Youth Organization, with offices at 20 Długa Street (currently Bishop I. Świrski Street); Home for Children; "Konsum" Consumer Cooperative; and a library, which functioned within the framework of the Jewish Art Society. Until 1920, the Bund's activity was vigorous. Its leaders at that time were Mosze Altszuler, Jakow Fiszman, Dawid Nojmark, Abraham (Abram) Słuszny, and Szulka Zubrowicz. Tsukunft, which had about 500 members and sympathizers, was especially active. At its head were Jeheskiel Lublinerman, Dawid Kuperant, Sane Waszelbojm, and Alter Nauczyciel.[67]

This expanding activity was interrupted by the Polish–Bolshevik War. In July 1920, the Polish authorities detained the following Siedlce Bund activists and placed them in an internment camp in Dębie near Kock: Abraham Słuszny, Froima Kuszer, Abram Jociuk, Abram Gerszt, Leni Aldfedor, Pinkus Longer, and Chaim Śliwka.[68]

Some of the Bund activists supported the Revolutionary Committee in August 1920, which came into being when the Red Army occupied Siedlce. After the Red Army withdrew, the majority of the activists who was becoming Communists left the city with it. The Polish authorities looked with suspicion upon this party for many years afterward. Those who had been interred were released in December 1920 after signing a "Declaration" that stated, "I hereby solemnly pledge not to participate actively or passively in any action directed against the Polish State."[69]

The support of the Bolsheviks by a part of Jewish society during the military actions of 1920 caused a divergence in the erstwhile cooperation of the two societies, the Polish and the Jewish. The Jews in Siedlce and its surroundings had taken a very active part both in the 1863 uprising and in the patriotic manifestations in 1916. The 1920 war was a mortal threat to the renascent Polish state. At such a historic moment, the support given to the Red Army by local revolutionary activists had a powerful impact on the whole of later Polish–Jewish relations.

After the Bolshevik war, there was an attempt to rebuild previous structures. "Konsum" Consumer Cooperative and the Leather Workers Union once again arose, and the library continued to function. New institutions were formed, such as the "Morgenstern" (Morning Star) Sports Club, "Tsukunft" Youth Organization, and SKIF (Socialist Children's Union).

SKIF was a branch of Tsukunft. Schoolchildren from the age of 12 belonged to it. In 1922, Jugendbund Tsukunft had about 100 members from the ages of 8 to 18. They were led by Alter Nauczyciel and Chaja Wolman. But the Bund was no longer very active. It was more active only during elections to the City Council, to which it added two representatives, Beniamin Kramarz and Rachela Berg. The Bund received 629 votes. At that time, an agreement was reached between the PPS, the Bund, and Poalei Zion, and what was called a socialist majority was formed. Thanks to this, Jewish schools, the Home for Children, and the Jewish poor received aid from municipal funds. During this same time, the Bund had representatives in the Healthcare Fund: Josef Rozenzumen and Jakow Icchak Lajbman.[70]

Before the Sejm elections in 1922, this party organized a rally for women in the cinema "Moderne." Five hundred ladies came to hear the lecture by Comrade Diena from Warsaw. Diena and her assistant Altszuler from Siedlce called upon the women to vote for ticket no. 4.[71]

The Bund carried on broad campaign activity through meetings and lectures. Thus on 8 December 1923 in the cinema "Lux," a lecture was organized titled "A Year of Work by the Jewish Circle in the Sejm." The lecturer was Szlema Zygelbaum, pseudonym "Artur," from Warsaw. He believed that the activity of the Jewish Circle in the Sejm was harmful to Jewish workers and "oppresses the proletariat as much as the defense [department] and the gendarmerie" and in conclusion called for "gathering under the banners of the Bund organization, which strives truly and sincerely to improve the existence of the working class."[72]

Toward the end of 1923, strikes of Jewish workers took place and were supported by the Bund. The gaiter workers went on strike from 4 to 7 December, demanding a 100 percent wage increase, and they got it. On 18 December, tailors went on strike, demanding a 125 percent increase. They got a 100 percent increase. The strikes took place peacefully, and only wage demands were made.

On 9 April 1925, in the hall of the cinema "Ognisko," Comrade Zybert from Warsaw gave a talk, "The Jewish Question in Poland." There were about 100 people present, and the income received was earmarked for the Sanatorium for the Children of Workers in Otwock.

The Bund tried to affect the community council (kahal). They boycotted the first elections to the Jewish community council in 1926 because it had denied voting rights to nonreligious Jews.

In the 1920s, the Bund was active mostly in trade unions. Under its influence were the Garment Industry Workers Union, Retail and Office Workers Union, Leather Industry Workers Union, and Primary School Teachers Union. At that time, Szmul Szymański (director of the Worker's Cooperative), Mose Grynberg (gaiter maker), and Dawid Kuperant (tailor) headed the Bund.[73]

In the 1930s, the Bund's executive board consisted of Beniamin Kramarz, chairman (bookkeeper), and Josef Berg, secretary (construction technician).

Tsukunft, which had 75 members, was directed by an Executive Committee, the officers of which were Gecel Lustgarten, chairman (gaiter maker); Sura Sztejnburg, treasurer (seamstress); and Rafał Ruchla, secretary. The head of SKIF, which had 43 members, was Nuha Fajnholc.[74] On 16 January 1932 in the hall of the cinema "Era," Henryk Erlich's lecture "Where We Are Headed" took place.[75] About 300 people took part in the meeting. Several of the listeners stood up and demanded that the chairman of the gathering say a few words about Lenin, [Karl] Liebknecht, and [Rosa] Luxemburg. The organizers refused. Accordingly, the Communists present in the hall (15 people) stood up and shouted "Long live Lenin, Liebknecht, and Luxemburg" and then sang "The Internationale." Then they quieted down, and Henryk Erlich discussed the world economic crisis and an assessment of workers in Poland. He also condemned Piłsudski's policy toward minorities, particularly in regard to Ukrainians.[76]

The Bund also ran the "Liga" Association for Cultural Education. It cooperated closely with the PPS, in which there was a Jewish group of activists headed by Abraham Kadysz in the 1930s. He left for the United States before World War II and stayed there until 1947. He then immigrated to Israel and gave part of his assets to the building of the Siedlce Cultural Center in Acre. This was his homage to his murdered compatriots.

Participation of Jews in the Communist Party of Poland

Many Jews participated in the Communist movement. As a group that was discriminated against and that at the same time strove toward emancipation, it was receptive to this ideology. The Communists were fierce opponents of the newly arisen Polish state, and they strove to liquidate it and build a republic allied to the USSR. Jewish Communists were recruited mostly from the young intelligentsia, which did not have very good prospects in the Poland of that time. It must also be remembered that in 1918–1920 it was still believed that there would be a Bolshevik revolution that would eliminate national discrimination and bring about the universal brotherhood of peoples. Gradually this belief diminished, but it did not lack in followers. The considerable participation of Jews in the Bolshevik revolution, then the role of commissars in strengthening the new regime, and finally their participation in the Communist Party of Poland were exploited by the radical nationalistic circles during the twenty-year [interwar] period to generate and popularize views of the "Judocommune." These views have proponents today as well.

The activity of Communists in Podlasie started in 1919. [77] They did not find many supporters here. The county administrator in his "Report on the Political and Social Situation" from 1 April 1919 to 1 April 1920 remarked that "The Communists are weak and not capable of any significant actions, but this does not in the least preclude the strength of this position in the not-too-distance future, since in certain PPS circles one can note a diversity of concepts, and the more extreme elements are coming closer to communism at a rapid rate."[78]

The situation was similar in the Jewish milieu. During 1919–1920, communizing groups were starting to form in existing Jewish parties. And so, "Kombud" arose in the ranks of the Bund; "Komtsukunft" in the "Tsukunft" Young Workers Organization; and the Jewish Communist Party in Poalei Zion. These groups split from the source parties and first united and then became a part of the Communist Workers Party of Poland.[79] The Siedlce Communists had influence both in the Jewish and in the Polish trade unions of the leather industry (there were two separate unions). There was a several-year lull in Communist activity after the Polish–Bolshevik war.

The KPP [Communist Party of Poland—trans.] renewed its activity in 1923. At that time, two districts, the Siedlce and the Łomża, were united into one, forming the Siedlce–Łomża District Committee. The joining of two districts testified to the small influence the Communists had here. In June 1923, of the total of 363 KPP members in the district, there were 306 Jews and 57 Poles. In later years the proportions evened out, and in 1928 the district organization had 297 members, of which 128 were Poles and 169 were Jews; in 1929 of the total of 370 members, there were 201 Poles and 167 Jews.[80]

Due to the insignificant influence of the Communists in Siedlce, in 1927 the district offices were moved to Międzyrzec Podlaski, retaining the preexisting name. The isolation of the Communists continued in later years, even internally. After the arrests during 1930–1932, Jewish and Polish Communist activists accused each other of betrayal and not abiding by the conspiracy. A split took place between the "Jewish street" and the "Polish street," without interaction between the two. Only in September 1935 was this situation overcome by creating a new District Committee. It consisted of Mejer Lublinerman, secretary; Gerszon Kowieski, technician; Piotr Hok, representative of the "Polish street"; Boruch Zonszajn, representative of the KZMP [Communist Union of Polish Youth—trans.]; Mendel Mokobodzki, representative of the Jewish organization "Pioneer."[81]

The KPP in Siedlce came alive before 1 May. That was the time that fliers were strewn about the city, red flags and banners were hung on electrical and telegraph cables, and Communist slogans were painted on city walls. The anniversary of Lenin's death was also celebrated, with soirees and receptions, as was the anniversary of the Paris Commune, which was on 18 March. This was also the Day of the Political Prisoner and an opportunity to raise funds for this cause. The Communists were not strong enough to have their own May First parade. They mostly tried to join the parades organized by the PPS and the Bund as a group. The socialist activists did not allow such situations to take place. "They [the Communists—author's note] should be moved aside without a fuss and left on the sidelines," proclaimed the District Committee [OK—trans.] of the PPS in Siedlce on 12 April 1926.[82] Other parties took similar positions in regard to the Communists. The Communists gave them cause for this. When in January 1926 Poalei Zion, with the participation of the Bund and the KPP, organized a meeting of the union active membership whose goal was to create a Committee for the Unemployed that would help all unemployed people, Jews as well as Poles, Communist representatives Wolf Ratajewicz and Szyja Słuszny made the implementation of this plan impossible. They accused the Poalei Zion activists of favoring Christian trade unions in allocating unemployment benefits.[83]

A year before the disbanding of the KPP, which took place in 1938, its activity in Siedlce ceased. The contributing factors were the arrests of the leading activists, internal conflicts, and the lack of interest in this ideology among the local population.

There was also a Communist Union of Polish Youth [KZMP—trans.] in Siedlce, in which Jewish youths were also active. The KZMP began its activity in Siedlce in 1922 and focused on trade unions. The Siedlce KZMP had 30 members in December 1928. Its activity intensified before 1 May, on October Revolution Day, or during strikes.

In 1922, within the framework of Sejm elections, the Communist Union of the Proletariat of Cities and Villages registered ticket no. 5 in the Siedlce voting district with two candidates from Siedlce: Karol Wysokiński, age 28, a shoemaker residing at 33 Starowiejska Street; and Abram Wajnapel, age 34, a porter residing at 5 Prospektowa Street. They did not get much support.[84]

There was also a Jewish Communist "Pioneer." It was led by Hersz-Lejb Tenenbaum and Jakub Luzera Słuszny.[85]

Assimilationist Movement

Processes of assimilation, understood as the "process of the adoption by a given group or its individual members of the culture of the other group,"[86] began from the beginning of contact between the two societies, the Jewish and the Polish. Only a small proportion of Jewish society became Polonized by adopting the whole spiritual and religious heritage of Poles. Usually these Jews converted to Catholicism or Protestantism, and sometimes they took on Polish-sounding names or fought for Poland's freedom.

The Jewish social-cultural movement on Polish territory appeared in organizational form as early as the second half of the nineteenth century. In 1907, "Zjednoczenie" [Unity] Academic Society was organized and engaged in rather broad political and cultural activity. In 1913, a camp of so-called Neo-assimilationists arose in Warsaw, and the Party of Independent Jews of Dr. Adolf Gross arose in Kraków. A consolidation of the assimilationist community took place toward the end of World War I. The Union of Poles of the Jewish Faith arose on 23 November 1918 in Lwów. Soon after, Tobiasz Aszkenazy created the Union of Civic Equality of Jewish Poles. This union published the daily *Dzień* [Day] and then *Goniec*

Wieczorny [Evening Messenger] in Lwów. There was a convention of all assimila-tionist oranizations on the territory of Poland In 1920 in Warsaw, and the Federa-tion of Poles of the Jewish Faith was jointly created.

An interesting figure in Siedlce was Adolf Hubert Gancwol-Ganiewski, the son of Maria and Herman. He was born 27 December 1870. Around 1895 he opened a photography studio in Siedlce, which he ran up until August 1942, that is, until his martyr's death in Treblinka. He was a social activist and a righteous man; he partly funded one of the orphanages and constantly took care of it. During a certain time, when he was the manager of the cinema, he would admit orphans for free. Around the year 1928, he converted from the Jewish faith to Lutheranism. It was prob-ably at this time that he separated from his first wife. His second wife was Emilia Lucyna née Gebel, who was a Lutheran. Also during this time he added to his sur-name the Polish-sounding name Ganiewski. He was the secretary of the Circle of Friends of the Polish Academic Community. He photographed the city, the envi-rons; he would set off in a chaise loaded with equipment on longer trips, wandering through the territory of the of Siedlce and Lublin province. He did not limit him-self to taking pictures in his studio. He also took them in the jail, on the street, in the park, in various institutions and schools, observing the everyday life of the resi-dents. During World War II, he was resettled into the ghetto, where he lived with the well-known dentist Gielbfisz. He did not want to take advantage of the oppor-tunity of escaping and hiding. He died consciously along with other Siedlce Jews. After he was taken to Treblinka, his wife Emilia, who, as an Aryan and a Lutheran, was not subject to extermination, followed right after him. She deluded herself into thinking she could free her husband from the camp. She did not know that her hus-band had been sent to the Extermination Camp, not the Work Camp. She did not return from this trip. She was probably shot next to the Treblinka railway station by a gendarme to whom she had turned with a plea for help. Part of Ganiewski's rich heritage has survived to our times. The Regional Museum in Siedlce hold 935 of his glass negatives, and Mariusz Malec made a file, *Photographer Gancwol*. One of the streets in the city is named after him.

Jewish youths were also subject to assimilation, but they did not cut off their ties with Judaism. In the school year 1934–1935, of the 419 students in the B. Prus Public Secondary School for Boys, there were 31 Jews and 2 Poles of the Jewish faith.[87]

In August 1936, the Union of Jewish Participants in Battles for the Independence of Poland (ZŻUWNP) was formed. It had 96 members. On 16 and 22 August 1936, it held two organizational meetings. This was an organization of veterans. Not all its members supported assimilation. There were many Zionists in the Siedlce divi-sion. The last board, elected in 1938, consisted of Henryk Loebel, chairman; Maksy-milian Schleicher, first vice-chairman; Anatol Goldberg, second vice-chairman; A. Brestet, secretary; J. Melber, treasurer; S. Słuszny, member; M. Szampanier, member;

A. Zylberg, member; and N. Plichter, member. Pechranc, Jabłoń, Bresler, Frydman, Alberg, and Finkiel were also active in this union.[88] In December 1935, in response to the anti-Jewish excesses at Lwów University, the Siedlce ZŻUWNP submitted an official protest in this matter to the district administrator. The district administrator sent it to the Lublin provincial administrator. In April 1936, the union organized two lectures in Polish. The first, "If People Knew the Talmud," was given by Tomasz Zaderecki from Lwów. He had an audience of about 600 people. The subject of the lecture should explain this large number of participants. The majority of Siedlce Jews was tied to religion or to the tradition that derived from it, and Poles could listen to a lecture on the Talmud in a language they could understand.[89] The other lecture, titled "Cultural and Military Significance of Polish Jewry," was delivered to an audience of 300 people by Dr. Meir Bałaban from Warsaw.

On 25 September 1936, a bulletin appeared in Polish in Siedlce with the title *Friend of Siedlce*. It was published by ZŻUWNP. In the article "To People of Good Will," the author complained about the practices of the National Democrats in their anti-Jewish campaign. The next article presented the part played by Jews in battles for Poland's independence.[90]

Assimilation and good contacts between the Jewish and the Polish communities were hampered by competition in commerce and crafts. The difficult conditions of existence, the shortage of jobs, and the shortage of sales of goods led to "fighting for customers" and friction. In 1928, there was an incident in Siedlce that had an economic foundation. A farmer from a nearby village was driving along Piłsudski Street with lilacs to sell. At one point, a Jewish teenager ran up to him and took a bunch of lilacs from him. The farmer grabbed him and tried to take the bunch of flowers from him. During the scuffle, about 200 Jews ran up, mostly young people, who tried to snatch the detained thief and beat the farmer. Several Christian passers-by and three policemen came to the aid of the farmer. Since the crowd of Jews was not backing off and was throwing stones at the intervening policemen, a fire hose intended for watering the lawns in that area was used to disperse them. The police arrested four "instigators" without using their weapons. These four were Szymon Goldwaser, Abram Rybak, Abe Czerniewicz, and Nuta Lejban. They were all shoemakers by trade, and the latter two were suspected of belonging to the Union of Young Communists. Marian Gałczyński, the owner of the fruit stand that was located in the area of the incident; Weronika Gerard, a maid by trade; and Józef Gochnio, a farmer from the village of Białki all sustained light beatings. In his report, the district administrator stated that "the whole incident was purely accidental and took this form only because the crowd was composed almost exclusively of teenagers. Moreover, it should be supposed that the aggressiveness of the Jewish crowd was influenced to a certain degree by the fact that the location of the incident, at the intersection of Piłsudski Street and Stary Rynek, was one at which for several years village women had been selling dairy products and eggs, vegetables, fruit, etc., right next to Jewish stores that sell these same products. There is competition then, causing a certain inflammation of relations among the tradespeople."[91]

EDITOR'S NOTE, CHAPTER 5

a. As the rabbis understood "house" to connote the females who are associated with the home, "Beit Ya'akov" was characteristically the name of religious girls' schools.

AUTHOR'S NOTES, CHAPTER 5

1. W. Tyloch, *Judaizm* (Warsaw, 1987), pp. 372–375.
2. Archiwum Akt Nowych w Warszawie (AAN), Ministerstwo Spraw Wewnętrznych. Wydział Narodowościowy (MSW WN), "Żydowskie ugrupowania polityczne w Polsce w dniu 1-go maja 1927," sig. 246, fol. 5.
3. Got(t)lib Jehoszua Heszel (1882–1940 or 1941)—journalist, Zionist activist, representative to the Sejm of the Polish Republic in 1935–1938. He was born in Pińsk, where he received a traditional religious upbringing. He attended university in Berlin, where he received his doctoral degree. He edited Zionist periodicals. He was a member of the Central Committee of the Zionist Organization in Poland from 1916 and was one of the leaders of the Et Livnot faction.
4. APS, KPPPS, sig. 60, p. 383.
5. Organizacja Syjonistyczna w Polsce—informacja o oddziałach 1923–30, Wydz. II Społ-Pol. 1919–1939, UWL, APL, sig. 487, p. 135 (§2 of the Statute of the Zionist Organization in Poland).
6. Ibid., p. 135 ((§2 of the Statute).
7. Ibid., p. 134 (§2 of the Statute).
8. Ibid., pp. 130–135.
9. J. Holzer, "Żydowskie dążenia polityczne w II Rzeczpospolitej," in *Znak*, no. 339–340 (1983): 372; Monografia stronnictwa Politycznego "Org. Syjonistyczna w Polsce," Wydz. II Społ.-Pol. 1919–1939, UWL, APL, sig. 461, p. 85; Organizacja Syjonistyczna—Al Hamiszmar, Wydz. II Społ.-Pol., UWL, APL, sig. 462.
10. J. Holzer, "Żydowskie dążenia polityczne w II Rzeczpospolitej," p. 73; Monografia stronnictwa Politycznego "Org. Syjonistyczna w Polsce," Wydz. II Społ.-Pol. 1919–1939, UWL, APL, sig. 461, p. 85.
11. A. Klugman, *Izrael ziemia świecka* (Warsaw, 2001), pp. 230–240.
12. J. Holzer, "Żydowskie dążenia polityczne w II Rzeczpospolitej," pp. 379–380; Organizacja Syjonistów-Rewizjonistoów "Brit Hazohar"—inf. o oddziałach. Wydz. II Społ.-Pol. 1919–1939, UWL, APL, sig. 492, pp. 15, 20; Monografia Stronnictwa Politycznego "Org. Syjonistyczna w Polsce," Wycz. II Spol.-Pol. UWL, APL, sig. 461, pp. 82–85.

13. Monografia stronnictwa Politycznego "Organizacja Syjonistyczna w Polsce," Wydz. II Społ.-Pol. 1919–1939, UWL, APL, sig. 461, pp. 88–91; Syjoniści—informacja o oddziałach, Wydz. II Społ.-Pol. 1919–1939, UWL, APL, sig. 483, pp. 9, 17, 21, 23.

14. Mapa wpływów politycznych poszczególnych stronnictw politycznych na terenie województwa lubelskiego, Wydz. II Społ.-Pol. 1919–1939, UWL, APL, sig. 196, p. 98.

15. Życie Podlasia, no. 5 (1934).

16. Syjoniści—informacja o oddziałach 1929, Wydz. II Społ.-Pol. 1919–1939, UWL, APL, sig. 483, pp. 35, 52.

17. APS, SPwS 1918–1939, sig. 9, p. 35.

18. A. Bobryk and I. Kochan, *Prawosławie w Siedlcach* (Siedlce, 2007), pp. 137–139. Among the 1,000 followers of Eastern Orthodoxy in Siedlce, aside from the permanent residents of the city, there were Polish soldiers in the military unit stationed there. The originals of letters by and to Hartglas are in the Archiwum Akt Nowych w Warszawie, zespół: Ministerstwo Wyznań Religijnych i Oświecenia Publicznego, sig. 1219.

19. *Nowa Gazeta Podlaska*, no. 40/94/ (1933): 9.

20. Izaak Grünbaum (1879–1970)—Zionist leader, history journalist, lawyer. Representative to the Sejm of the Polish Republic 1919–1933. Co-creator of the National Minorities Bloc. Left for Palestine in 1933. Signatory of the Declaration of Independence of Israel and its first minister of internal affairs.

21. APS, SPwS 1918–1939, sig. 16, fol. 20–21.

22. Chaim Bialik (1873–1934)—reviver of Hebrew poetry, prose writer, translator, publisher. Lived in Palestine from 1924, where he chaired the Hebrew Language Committee and the Hebrew Writers Association.

23. APS, SPwS 1918–1939, sig. 20, fol. 66.

24. APS, SPwS 1918–1939, sig. 25, fol. 152.

25. J. Holzer, "Żydowskie dążenia polityczne w II Rzeczpospolitej," pp. 369–374; Monografia stronnictwa Politycznego Syjonistyczna Partia Pracy Hitachdut, Wydz. II Społ.-Pol. 1919–1939, UWL, APL, sig. 465, pp. 20–29.

26. APS, KPPPS, sig. 59, p. 26.

27. B. Łętocha, A. Messer, and A. Cała, *Żydowskie druki ulotne w II Rzeczpospolitej w zbiorach Biblioteki Narodowej* (Warsaw, 2004), p. 39.

28. J. Holzer, "Żydowskie dążenia polityczne w II Reczpospolitej," pp. 374–375; Monografia Stronnictwa Politycznego pn. Jidysze Socjalistisz Demokratisze Partej—Poalej Cjon in Pojlen—Żydowska Socjalno-Demokratyczna Partia Robotnicza Poalej Syjon w Polsce—Prawica, Wydz. Społ.-Pol. 1919–1939, UWL, APL, sig. 459, pp. 50–55; J. Tomaszewski, *Rzeczpospolita wielu narodów* (Warsaw, 1985), p. 180.

29. APS, KPPPS, sig. 59, p. 35.

30. B. Łętocha, A. Messer, and A. Cała, *Żydowskie druki ulotne w II Rzeczpospolitej w zbiorach Biblioteki Narodowej*, p. 40.

31. Żydowska Socjalno-Demokratyczna Partia Robotnicza "Poalej Syjon w Polsce"—informacje o działalności 1923–1931, Wydz. Społ.-Pol. UWL, APL, sig. 479, p. 8; Monografia Stronnictwa Politycznego pn. "Jidysze Socjalistisz Demokratisze Arbeter

Partaj—Poalej Cjon in Pojlen—Żydowska Socjalno-Demokratyczna Partia Robotnicza Poalej—Sjon w Polsce. Lewica. Wydz. II Społ.-Pol. 1919-1939, UWL, APL, sig. 458, pp. 42, 45, 76; Sprawozdanie starosty siedleckiego o ruchu społecznym za r. 1926, Wydz. II Społ.-Pol. 1919-1939, UWL, APL, sig. 161, pp. 7, 16, 21–22; Holzer, "Żydowskie dążenia polityczne w II Reczpospolitej," pp, 374–375; Tomaszewski, *Rzeczpospolita wielu narodów*, p. 194.

32. Currently the main intellectual center of the Mizrachim in Israel is the religious University Bar Ilan Ramat Gan near Tel Aviv founded in 1855. See Tyloch, *Judaizm*, pp. 270–271; Holzer, "Żydowskie dążenia polityczne w II Reczpospolitej," p. 368; M. Fuks, "Żydzi w Polsce w latach 1918-1945," in *Naród, Kościół, Kultura, Szkice z dziejów Polski*, part 2 (Lublin, 1986), p. 225.

33. Mishnah Brotherhood—engaged in the study of the Mishnah, that is, the collection of books of traditional Jewish law composed of six books, the so-called Orders. The Mishnah was written down around 200 CE.

34. A. Frydman, "Organizacja młodzieży chasydzkiej i 'Młodzieży Mizrachi'," in *Book of Remembrance of the Siedlce Community*, pp. 360–362.

35. Ibid., p. 364; Monografia Stronnictwa Politycznego "Organizacja Syjonistów Ortodoksów 'Mizrachi'," Wydz. II Społ.-Pol. 1919-1939, UWL, APL, sig. 466, p. 79.

36. A. Frydman, "Organizacja młodzieży chasydzkiej i 'Młodzieży Mizrachi'," p. 364.

37. Ibid., p. 365.

38. Ibid., p. 365.

39. APS, KPPPS, sig. 60, pp. 353–380.

40. "Mizrachi"—informacja o oddziałach Wydz. II Społ.-Pol. UWL, APL, sig. 484, pp.3–4; Monografia Stronnictwa Politycznego "Organizacja Syjonistów Ortodoksów Mizrachi," Wydz. II Społ.-Pol. UWL, APL, sig. 466, pp. 72–80.

41. APS, SPwS, sig. 16, fol. 20.

42. D.B. Josef-Pasowski, "Chalucowy ruch młodzieżowy," in *Book of Remembrance of the Siedlce Community*, p. 346.

43. Ibid., p. 346; Sprawozdanie starosty sidleckiego o ruchu społecznym za rok 1926, Wydz. II Społ.-Pol. 1919-1939, UWL, APL, sig. 161, p. 23.

44. Centralna Organizacja Żydów Ortodoksów w Polsce pn. "Szlomej Emunej Israel" (Agudath Israel—Pokój Wiernych Izraelitów—informacja o oddziałach Wydz. II Społ.-Pol. 1919-1939, UWL, APL, sig. 489, p. 40 (citation drawn from an overprint in Polish of the official Agudah document).

45. APS, KPPPS, sig. 59, fol. 3.

46. APS, KPPPS, sig. 60, fol. 362, 386.

47. APS, KPPPS, sig. 60, fol. 385.

48. Meir Szapiro (1887-1934)—rabbi, head of the Polish Agudah from 1922, in 1923-1927 representative to the Sejm of the Polish Republic. His life's work was the creation in 1924 of the Sages of Lublin Yeshiva, renovated in February 2007.

49. APS, SPwS, sig. 8, pp. 2–3.

50. Monografia Stronnictwa Politycznego "Centralna Organizacja Żydów Ortodoksów–"Agudath Israel"—Związek Izraela, Wydz. II Społ.-Pol. 1919-1939, UWL, APL, sig.

485, p. 67; Sprawozdanie starosty siedleckiego o ruchu społecznym za rok 1926, Wydz. II Społ.-Pol. 1919–1939, UW, APL, sig. 16, p. 6; APS, SPwS, sig. 23, fol. 34–35.

51. J. Tomaszewski, *Rzeczpospolita wielu narodów*, p. 168; Fuks, "Żydzi w Polsce w latach 1918–1945," p. 225.

52. Adar—the twelfth lunar month of the Hebrew calendar counting from Passover, or the sixth from the New Year's holidays of Rosh Hashanah. Adar begins in either February or March. It is a joyous month in which Purim, the most cheerful holiday of Judaism, falls. The seventh day of the month of Adar is the anniversary of both the birth and the death of Moses, and the thirteenth is the fast of Esther, right before Purim.

53. Sprawozdanie starosty siedleckiego o ruchu społecznym za rok 1926, Wydz. II Społ.-Pol. 1919–1939, UWL, APL, sig.161, pp. 6, 14–17.

54. APS, SPwS, sig. 23, fol. 95.

55. I. Kaspi, "Early History of the Jews in Siedlce," in *Book of Remembrance of the Siedlce Community*, ed. A. W. Jasny (Buenos Aires, 1956), p. 43.

56. A. Hartglas, *Na pograniczu dwóch światów*, p, 109.

57. Sprawozdanie starosty siedleckiego o ruchu społecznym za rok 1926, Wydz. II Społ.-Pol. 1919–1939, UWL, APL, sig. 161, pp. 7, 14, 21; Monografia Stronnictwa Politycznego "Jidysze Folkisze Partei"—"Folkiści," Wydz. II Społ.-Pol. 1919–1939, UWL, APL, sig. 470, pp. 23–30.

58. APS, KPPPS, sig. 60, p. 395.

59. APS, KPPPS, sig. 62, fol. 37.

60. Noach Pryłucki (1882–1941 or 1942)—organizer of the Folkist party, researcher of the history of Jewish folklore, writer, journalist, poet. From 1922, a representative to the Sejm of the Polish Republic as the only representative of the Folkists. After the start of World War II, he left for Vilnius. In 1941, after these territories were occupied by the German forces, he disappeared without a trace.

61. APS, SPwS 1918–1939, sig. 6, p. 17.

62. APS, SPwS 1918–1939, sig. 7, p. 24.

63. APS, SPwS 1918–1939, sig. 8, p. 7.

64. Berek Joselewicz (1765–1809)—born in Kretinga (Lithuania). From 1788 he lived in Warsaw. In 1794 he organized a Jewish light cavalry regiment and commanded it as a colonel. After the fall of the Kościuszko Uprising, he left for Galicia and in 1798 to Italy, where he joined Dąbrowski's Legions and took part as an officer in the Italian and the Danubian legions. In 1803, assigned to the Hanover Legion in the pay of the French, he fought in the campaign of 1805, at Austerlitz, among others. From 1807, he earned the rank of squadron head of the Fifth Regiment of Rifle Cavalry. He died on 5 May 1809 in a skirmish with the Austrians at Kock. A historic brick building from the last quarter of the nineteenth century has survived on this street in Siedlce (4 B. Joselewicz Street), next to which stands a monument dedicated to the murdered Jewish community. At the corner of this street and Bishop I. Świrski Street is the building that housed Barencwajg's Cheder.

65. M. Madelman, "Żydowska oświata w Siedlcach," in *Book of Remembrance of the*

Siedlce Community, p. 476; AAN, MSW WN, Żydowskie ugrupowania polityczne w Polsce w dniu 1 maja 1927, sig. 246, fol. 9.

66. J. Holzer, "Żydowskie dążenia polityczne w II Reczpospolitej," pp. 366–382; Tomaszewski, *Rzeczpospolita wielu narodów*, pp. 177–179; Fuks, "Żydzi w Polsce w latach 1918–1945," p. 226.

67. G. Lusgarten, "Działalność Bundu w okresie międzywojennym," in *Book of Remembrance of the Siedlce Community*, p. 404.

68. Rewizje i aresztowania członków Ogólnożydowskiego Związku Robotniczego "Bund" w Polsce 1920–21, Wydz. II Społ.-Pol. 1919–1939, UWL, APL, sig. 481, p. 14.

69. Ibid., pp. 16, 22.

70. G. Lusgarten, "Działalność Bundu w okresie międzywojennym," pp. 405–407; Monografia Stronnictwa Politycznego "Bund"—Algemeiner Jidysze Arbeter Bund in Pojlen—Ogólnożydowski Związek Robotniczy "Bund" w Polsce, Wydz. II Społ.-Pol. 1919–1939, UWL, APL, sig. 460, p. 35.

71. APS, KPPPS, sig. 59, p. 39.

72. APS, SPwS 1918–1939, sig. 6, p. 1.

73. Sprawozdanie starosty siedleckiego o ruchu społecznym za rok 1925, Wydz. II Społ. Pol. 1919–1939, UWL, APL, sig.161, pp.17, 21–22.

74. Monografia Stronnictwa Politycznego "Bund"—Algemeiner Jidysze Arbeter Bund in Pojlen—Ogólnożydowski Związek Robotniczy "Bund" w Polsce, Wydz. II Społ.-Pol. 1919–1939, UWL, APL, sig. 460, pp. 28–35.

75. Henryk Erlich (Hersz Wolf)—born in 1882 in Lublin, died in 1942 in an NKVD prison in the Soviet Union; lawyer, Bund leader, editor of several Bund periodicals. In 1939 he was arrested by the Soviet authorities and sentenced to death. He was released as part of the amnesty after the Sikorski–Maisky agreement. He cooperated with the Polish embassy in the USSR. In December 1941 he was arrested again. He committed suicide on 14 May 1942.

76. APS, SPwS 1918–1939, sig. 15, fol. 9.

77. Z. Kaleniecki, "Działalność KPP w Okręgu Siedleckim w latach 1918–1938," in *Społeczeństwo siedleckie w walce o wyzwolenie narodowe i społeczne* (Warsaw, 1981), p. 122.

78. APS, SPwS, sig. 2, p. 3.

79. M. Judenglojbm [*sic*.], "Lewicowy ruch robotniczy w Siedlcach," in *Book of Remembrance of the Siedlce Community*, pp. 400–401.

80. Z. Kaleniecki, "Działalność KPP w Okręgu Siedleckim w latach 1918–1938," pp. 125–127.

81. Z. Kaleniecki, "Działalność KPP w Okręgu Siedleckim w latach 1918–1938," typescript in possession of National Archive in Siedlce (hereafter typescript), p. 501. (There are two works by Z. Kaleniecki bearing the same title: one is published in the book *Społeczeństwo siedleckie w walce o wyzwolenie narodowe i społeczne* [Warsaw, 1981]; the other, a very extensive typescript, is held in the National Archive in Siedlce.)

82. Z. Kaleniecki, "Działalność KPP w Okręgu Siedleckim w latach 1918–1938," p. 153, typescript.

83. Ibid., p. 152.

84. APS, KPPPS, sig. 60, p. 340.

85. Ibid., p. 501.

86. A. Hertz, "Żydzi w kulturze polskiej" (Paris, 1961), p. 133; J. Lichten, "Uwagi o asymilacji i akulturacji Żydów w Polsce 1863–1943," in *Znak*, no. 396–398 (1988): 49.

87. J. Mikulski, "Szkolnictwo średnie w Siedlcach," in *Powiat siedlecki* (Siedlce, 1935), p. 328.

88. *Ziemia Siedlecka*, no. 2 (1938): 3; *Życie Podlasia*, no. 51/86, 52/87 (1935): 4.

89. P. Śmieciuch, "Społeczność żydowska w Siedlcach w latach 1919–1938 w świetle sprawozdań sytuacyjnych starostwa siedleckiego," in *Biuletyn ŻIH*, no. 1 (1992): 83.

90. T. Szczechura, "Materiały bibliograficzne do dziejów zachodniego Podlasia i południowo-wschodniego Mazowsza," in *Prace Archiwalno-Konserwatorskie na Terenie Województwa Siedleckiego* (Siedlce, 1977), p. 143; APS, SPwS 1918–1939, sig. 25, fol. 135.

91. APS, SPwS 1918–1939, sig. 12, p. 61.

CHAPTER 6.

SCHOOLING

In writing about Jewish schooling in Siedlce, I chose as the distinguishing feature the criterion of language. At the outset I would like to explain the language problem of the Eastern European Jews who were called the Ashkenazim.[1] The Ashkenazim in their overwhelming majority used the Yiddish language (also referred to as the Jewish language). This language arose in the middle ages from one of the German dialects among Jews living on the Rhine River.[2]

The other language used by the Jews was Hebrew. It was the language of the elite, a religious and literary language. An attempt to revive it was made in the sixteenth century. It came into common use for good during the Jewish enlightenment (*haskala*) and the birth of the Zionist movement. This took place in the nineteenth and early twentieth centuries.

6.A. Religious schooling with Hebrew and Yiddish

After the age of 4–5, the sons of Orthodox Jews attended cheders, that is, elementary religious schools. In the first years, they studied the Pentateuch of Moses under the direction of *melamdim* (teachers of small children). Some melamdim were assisted by *belfers* (aids) who brought the youngest children to and from the cheder, especially during winter. The study of the Pentateuch generally consisted in the collective reading aloud of particular books [Genesis through Deuteronomy—ed.] in Hebrew and translating them into Yiddish. In this way children became familiar with the beginnings of Jewish history and the Hebrew language.

In the first half of the twentieth century, there was a primary religious school in Siedlce called Talmud-Torah (Study of Torah). The school building was given over for use at the end of August, the beginning of September 1903.[3] It was built by a Jewish entrepreneur of that time, Isroel Grinberg, at a cost of four thousand rubles. The school was blessed by Rabbi Szymon Dow Anolik. The school was attended by boys who were the sons of Orthodox parents. The former teachers of the Talmud-Torah that up until that point was located at 71 Piękna Street probably found employment in the new building. These included Josel Czetwer, who taught the youngest boys; Abraham Ratyniewicz, who was responsible for teaching the Pentateuch of Moses; Baruch Lajbel Strusman, who taught the Gemara (the part of the Talmud that contained [dialectical discussion of the law and—ed.] biblical commentary); and Mosze Mordechaj Kirszenbojm, who delved more deeply into knowledge of the Gemara with the oldest children. At its beginning the school had 60 pupils and was maintained through the voluntary donations of the faithful. The Jewish community council contributed to its upkeep by allocating to it a part of the money brought in by the ritual slaughter of kosher animals.

During the interwar period, the Jewish Orthodox Party Agudah, which took care that all of life conformed to religious dictates, exerted an ideological influence on the school. After Poland gained its independence, the Talmud-Torah was placed under the supervision of the superintendent of schools. Secular elements of study were introduced, such as the Polish language, arithmetic, drawing, history, geography, and the natural sciences.

On average, 300–400 children studied in the school and communicated among themselves in Yiddish. The school day lasted from 8 AM to 7 PM with a one-hour break for lunch. The teaching of secular subjects took a mere two hours a day. The pupils had no summer vacation, and there were also no organized sightseeing trips. As the pupils remember it, "in school, the rabbi ruled with a strap." The school board consisted of N.D. Gliksberg, chair; Israel Gutgeld, Manisz Ridel, Mosze Chaim Lewin, Mosze Zagan, Sander Kantor, Henoch Sztajberg Kałuszyner, Szloma Szmuel Abarbanel, Jehanatan Ajbeszyc, Welwel Orłowski, Jeszajahu Zelikowicz, Eliezer Śliwka, and Josef Czarny. In 1922, at the initiative of Israel Gutgeld, a locksmith's shop was created in the Talmud-Torah, where boys could learn a trade. It only functioned a few years under the tutelage of Josef Berg. The board responsible for the running of the school at that time was not interested in it.

For a certain time, a yeshiva, a Jewish religious university that prepared for taking on the function and office of rabbi, was run in the school. One of the forms of teaching was the analysis by students of rabbinical texts in two-man groups. Much time was also devoted to deliberations about ethics and morality. The Siedlce yeshiva came into being as early as the 1870s and was quartered on Piękna Street in the house of Herszl Śliwka. It was run by Reb Isroel Dragoeiner, who was called Reb Isroelke.[4] He was known for his Orthodox views, among others, he signed a proclamation, "Notes on Faith," which forbade reading secular newspapers. In running the yeshiva, he placed greater weight on the study of the Russian language than on Hebrew. He felt that the Russian language was more useful in contacts with the authorities and residents of the empire. To this end, he brought from Kobryń a respected teacher of Russian, Reb Icchak Tenenbaum. When he took on the function of secretary of the community council and did not have time for lessons in the yeshiva, Reb Isroelke brought in another "Litwak," Szeflan. After the pogrom of

1906, Reb Isroel Dragoeiner left the city, and the new director became Reb Dawid Icchak Międzyrzecki from Radzymin. He was a noted scholar, a Chassid, a follower of the tzadik from Aleksandrów. After the building of the Talmud-Torah school in 1903, the yeshiva was also moved to the new building. It has not been possible to determine when it stopped functioning and was incorporated into the Talmud-Torah. In 1924, efforts were made to reactivate the yeshiva. The school, on the other hand, lasted until the time of World War II.

At the end of 1915, under the German occupation, a school was founded in which Yiddish and Hebrew were used as instructional languages. It was founded by the Brześć Committee that assembled exiles from Brześć and Pińsk who had taken refuge in Siedlce. It consisted of several hundred families. In this school, teachers who were recruited from among the exiles taught. Meals were given to the children. The institution was under the care of the Zionists.[5]

6.B. SECULAR SCHOOLING WITH YIDDISH

In October 1915, the first primary school was founded in which Yiddish was the language of instruction. The school came into existence at the initiative of Fania Radak in cooperation with Cywa Zubrowicz and Rachela Edelsztajn-Berg. Fania Radak was a graduate of the teachers' courses affiliated with the Society for the Dissemination of Education, the director of which was Chaim Fijałkow. Josef Rozenzumen remembered her in the following way: "A 'Litwak' girl arrived here, very likeable, wearing low-healed shoes, and opened a school for Jewish children here in which everything is taught in Yiddish. She speaks Yiddish in such a way that it is a pleasure to listen. I myself teach singing there."[6]

This school taught natural history, arithmetic, history, Polish language, needlework, and singing. It had four grades. It was attended by about 60–70 children, mostly girls. After a certain time it became a private school, in which children paid for their education. Some of the teaching staff was replaced in connection with this change.

In the summer of 1916, a new, six-grade Jewish school was founded. It was attended by about 240 children. It was registered under the private names of the ladies Cywa Zubrowicz, Rojza Tenenbojm, and Mina Gutglik. Aside from the aforementioned, Jakow Tenenbaojm, Ryfka Bursztajn-Mandelman, Dawid Nojmark, Mosze Mandelman, and Josef Zonszajn also taught in this school. The school was free, and the children were enrolled from the poorer spheres. Teachers did not get a salary for teaching; they came mostly from well-off families. If needed, financial aid came from the Jewish Art Society.[7]

In 1917, the Jewish Art Society founded its own school. It was attended by about 80–90 children aged 6–7. The school initially had two grades. The first teachers were Oszer Perelman and Lola Kantorowicz.[8] The official opening took place 31 December 1917, and the teaching staff was joined by Ala Koszer, who later married Oszer Perelman. Singing was taught by Josef Zonszajn, the choir director at the Jewish Art Society.

In May 1918, there was a manifestation of the pupils of all types of Jewish schools. The following schools participated: the school for Brześć and Pińsk homeless children, the Hebrew school, Halbersztat's private school (with Polish as the language of instruction, intended for children from wealthy families), two private cheders run by Hebrew language teachers Goldfarb and Morgensztern, as well as a few Polish city schools for Jewish children (so-called Shabbat schools [szabasówki—trans.]). The parade was composed of pupils, teachers, and athletes and moved out accompanied by the orchestras of Jewish Art and Polish City Schools at 8 AM from the city park and went as far as the Sekuła Woods. About 3,000 children took part in the manifestation. The point of the effort was the consolidation of circles of Jewish youth with the aim of supporting the political aspirations of the Jews, who wanted to form a federal state with the participation of Poles, Jews, and Ukrainians on the territory occupied by the Germans.[9]

After the formation of the Polish state, three boards of education were formed in Siedlce at the beginning of 1919 that directed schooling. They were formed by the political parties. And so there was the Dinezon board of education run by the Folkists,[10] the Medem board of education run by the Bund,[11] and the Borokhov board of education run by Poalei Zion. These boards of education took over the schools and also created orphanages.

The schools and orphanages were supported by party funds. This promising development of schooling was destroyed by the Polish–Bolshevik War. After it, difficult times set in. The Dinezon board of education barely managed to sustain one of the two prewar schools and a preschool during 1921–1926. Because of a lack of funds, a tuition fee was introduced, and the school became subordinated to the Central Jewish School Organization (CISZO), from which it received aid. Dinezon's board of education ran a five- or six-grade school, depending on conditions at a particular time, in which about 200 children studied. The Siedlce authorities impeded the free development of the school. Some classrooms were even requisitioned. In this connection, the Folkists made all kinds of efforts to take back the requisitioned classrooms. This matter was brought up in the Sejm as an example of the restrictive policy of the government in relation to the Jews. Finally, in 1926, the classrooms were returned. In 1921, the teachers in this school were Krusman and his wife, Aharon Sienicki, and H. Borensztajn. In the 1925–1926 school year, the school came under the patronage of the Jewish League for Primary Education[12] and thanks to its aid could continue to function. During this year, Mordechj Giliński "Batko" arrived at this institution after completing the Jewish teachers' college in Vilnius and with his work revitalized the school. In 1925, on the tenth anniversary of the death of Icchak Lejb Perec,[13] the school was named after him and a banner was funded. Thanks to the active battle of the Folkists in the community, in the literal sense, since it sometime came to blows and police intervention, finances managed to be obtained from the community, thanks to which the school did not have any financial problems during 1927–1929. During these years, a full seven-grade school operated and was attended by 250 children. Extra food for the children was also introduced in the classroom (consisting of two rolls and milk or cocoa). In 1928, the tenth anniversary of the school and the regaining of independence by Poland were ceremoniously celebrated. A jubilee exhibit was organized on this occasion. Guests came from Warsaw for these celebrations, among them the leader of the Folkists Noach Pryłucki and the representative of CISZO, Josef Leszczyński. This school lasted until 1933. The economic crisis that encompassed the whole world at the turn of the 1920s and 1930s came to Siedlce as well. The absence of financial aid from educational institutions and the progressing impoverishment of the population made the continued running of the school impossible.

6.C. SECULAR SCHOOLING WITH HEBREW

The beginnings of Hebrew schooling reach back to 1904. It was at that time that a group of Zionists founded the first school in which Hebrew was the language of instruction. It was located on Piękna Street. The teachers in this school were Górewicz, Kapłański, Akiba Goldfarb, and Dawid Morgenstern. There were 180 children who studied in it.[14] In addition, courses in Hebrew for adults were also conducted at that institution. This school existed for several years.

In 1917, a Hebrew-Jewish school was founded by the Zionist M.M. Landau called Daat (Knowledge). It lasted for a short time, however.

After Poland's regaining of independence and the introduction of mandatory schooling for children between the ages of 7 and 14, Dawid Morgenstern and Akiba Goldfarb founded two separate schools taught in Hebrew. Cheders were affiliated with these schools. In 1924, the group Supporters of the Hebrew Language arose in affiliation with Akiba Goldfarb's school, which was located at 22 Warszawska Street. It was formed by Zionist youth aged 16–17. This group organized evening Hebrew language classes for young people from various social strata. Meetings called "question and answer evenings" took place as well as "literary conversations," during which discussions took place exclusively in Hebrew. Lectures on the subject of the Torah and religion were conducted by the well-known Zionist activist and educator Israel Gutgeld. The founders of the group were Sara Kleinlerer, Tonia Barbanel, Mordechaj Gotesdiner, Israel Jon-Tow, Lewi Pasowski, and Dawid Pasowski. Its members gathered in the evening by the drug store on Warszawska Street and demonstratively spoke in Hebrew, attracting thereby the attention of passersby. For them this was a form of demonstrating their views and propagating the idea of Zionism.[15]

In the summer of 1926, a Zionist committee came into existence, composed of Lewi Tenenbojm, Mosze Jon-Tow, Jehoszua Akerman, Fiszel Popowski, Abram Altenberg, and Meir Gutgeld (secretary). The goal of the committee was the founding of a Tarbut (Culture) school. A two-grade school was already formed in the 1926–1927 school year, attended by about 100 children. Their teachers were Josef Okuń (principal), Szalita, Weinen, and Frieden. In following years the school grew considerably and became a seven-grade school. The 1927–1928 school year saw the addition of the teachers Kuszlian and Ihorowicz, and the number of children rose to 200. The school continued to grow the following year. The teaching staff was supplemented by Heler and Mlaszen, and the number of children rose to 250. This school was attended by children from the Protection of Orphans custodial institution. They did not pay for their education, but fees were collected from the remaining pupils. The majority of the school funds were covered, however, by money received from the Jewish community council as well as from party dues. In 1930, changes took place in the management of the institution. Josef Okuń left Siedlce, and Cwi Bokser took his place. In 1931, the school was ceremonially given a blue-and-white banner. In the 1930s, this institution continued to function; during this period it was located at 60 Piłsudski Street. It ran a library, a drama division, and a choir. On 5 May 1934, at the school's initiative, the Holiday of Spring, Lag Baomer, was celebrated. It literally means the Thirty-Third Day of Counting Omer.[16] A parade of about 1,500 people marched down the streets of the city. At the end, those present were addressed in Hebrew by the principal of the Tarbut School, Hersz [Cwi] Bokser. He talked about the significance of the Holiday of Spring and the planting of trees. After him, Lejzor Bernholc spoke and praised the builders of Palestine. He concluded his speech with a shout against Vladimir Jabotinsky. The members of "Brit Trumpeldor" who were gathered at the celebration started to raise loud shouts in honor of Jabotinsky and did not allow any more speeches. Other members of the assembly dispersed to their homes in peace among the general uproar. On the next day, the parade in which about 1,500 young people took part went to the woods located in Skórzec Township. There the young people stayed until evening in a picnic mood.

The last principal of the school was Borenstein. The Tarbut School lasted until the outbreak of World War II. Some of the graduates left for Palestine before the war and thanks to this survived. The task of the school, besides providing primary teaching, was the preparation of settlement recruits for Palestine.[17]

6.D. JEWS IN STATE SCHOOLING WITH POLISH AS THE LANGUAGE OF INSTRUCTION

A portion of Jewish children, independent of the existence of Jewish schools, attended Polish state schools throughout the twenty-year [interwar] period. This applied particularly to the assimilationists. However, after the liquidation in 1933 of the Yiddish-language school, most of its pupils moved to Public School No. 7 at 24 Więzienna Street (currently Świętojańska Street). This building is still in existence today.

Rachela Berg became the principal of this school. At the beginning of the 1933–1934 school year, Jewish pupils en masse left classes on Saturdays. The Jewish community council demanded of the management of this institution and of the school superintendent that pupils be excused from classes on this day so that they might, in accord with the dictates of Judaism, celebrate that day. School authorities did not agree. This caused protests by the Jewish community council, which issued a proclamation, directed primarily at parents, to look after their children and properly celebrate Shabbat along with them. The Zionists also supported the aspirations of the pupils. Those Orthodox students who were older in age would stand in front of the school on Saturdays and try to explain to the Jewish pupils the significance of this day. At the recommendation of the superintendent, the police intervened, intercepting the Orthodox pupils. The dispute ended with the exemption from Saturday school attendance for children of Orthodox parents.[18]

At the same time, the Catholic population of Siedlce started a campaign against teachers of Jewish background employed in public schools. It was particularly vocal in calling for the dismissal of Rachela Berg from her position as principal of the school. This led to a demonstration of Catholics supporting the above demand. A boycott of the school was even threatened in the event that the demands were not met. The pertinent petition was signed by 800 people.[19] State and school authorities strove to soothe the conflict, which they were successful in doing after a certain time.

Jewish schools in Siedlce functioned within the sphere of influence of various parties. Very often, the language used in the school coincided with the political aspirations of the parents whose children attended the relevant institutions. In school, aside from learning, the attempt was made to influence the children politically, bringing up young activists in this way. With this goal, young people's organizations were also formed, both the Zionist Hashomer Hatzair (Young Guard) and Hechalutz Hatzair (Young Pioneer). Yet the political division within Jewish society was not rigid. Some people changed their views; children matured and looked at the world more critically than during their childhood and youth. Jewish young people, after graduating from primary schools, often continued their studies in Polish secondary schools and universities, where they either cemented or changed their previous views.

Author's Notes, Chapter 6

1. Accepted thinking is that as early as the twelfth and thirteenth centuries Jews in Germany were using a clearly changed Germanic language with an admixture of many Hebrew and Romance words. Manuscripts from the fourteenth and fifteenth centuries testify to the existence of a new language. This language subsequently yielded over several centuries to Slavic influences, particularly Polish and Ukrainian. Before World War II, Yiddish was used by about 12 million people worldwide, of whom 3 million were in Poland. The Nazis murdered most Eastern European Jews. Some survived in the United States and in the USSR. Currently, the most well known author who wrote in Yiddish is the American author Isaac Bashevis Singer, who in 1987 won the Nobel Prize in Literature for his creative work. He was born in 1904 in Radzymin near Warsaw; he emigrated from Poland in 1935. [He died in 1991.—ed.] There is another group of Mediterranean Jews called Sephardim, who, aside from Hebrew, also use a language called Ladino. This language arose in the late middle ages in Spain based on Romance dialects, especially Castilian.

2. S. Belis-Legis, "Szkic do autoportretu," in *Literatura na świecie*, no. 12/161 (1984): 3–26; E. Geller, "Jidysz—geneza nazwy i nie tylko," in *Kalendarz Żydowski 1987–1988*, pp. 110–115.

3. Specifically in the month of Elul—the sixth lunar month of the Hebrew calendar, counting from Passover, or the last counting from the New Year (Rosh Hashanah). This month usually starts at the end of August. It is the month that precedes the Day of Reconciliation (Yom Kippur) and is therefore called the time of repentance. During this time, Jews examine their consciences so as to achieve spiritual order.

4. Reb—a courtesy title, emphasizing the erudition of a man. It is the equivalent of the Polish "Pan" [Mr. or Sir—trans.].

5. M. Mandelman, "Yiddish Education in Siedlce," in *Book of Remembrance of the Siedlce Community*, p. 459.

6. Ibid., p. 457.

7. Ibid., p. 459.

8. Ibid., p. 463.

9. Ibid., p. 466.

10. Jakub Dinezon, also Dinesohn (1856–1919)—prose writer, journalist, education activist, founder of many orphanages and schools. He wrote in Yiddish and also translated the works of other authors into this language.

11. Włodzimierz [Vladimir] Medem (1879–1923)—a top leader of the Bund, editor of many socialist periodicals. He studied law at the university in Kiev. He was critical of both Zionism and Marxism.

12. An educational and schooling organization founded by the Jewish Folkist Party in 1922.

13. Icchak Lejbusz Perec [Isaac Leib Peretz] (1852–1915)—born in Zamość, died in Warsaw. An attorney by profession. By defending Poles, he fell afoul of the tsarist authorities and lost his right to practice his profession. At first Perec wrote in Polish,

then in Hebrew, but his greatest achievement is considered to be his introduction of Yiddish into literature. His home became the literary salon of all those who wrote in the Yiddish (Jewish) language. Many writers fell under his influence. Along with Mendele Mojcher Sforim and Sholem Aleichem, he is counted among the Jewish classics. He is the author of *Folk Tales, Tales of the Chassidim, The Golden Chain,* as well as many others.

14. F. Dromi-Popowski, "Hebrew Education in Siedlce," in *Book of Remembrance of the Siedlce Community*, p. 483.

15. F. Dromi-Popowski, "The Group 'Supporters of the Hebrew Language'," in *Book of Remembrance of the Siedlce Community*, pp. 504–505.

16. This is the eighteenth day of the month of Iyar (April–May). An exceptional day of having the nature of a semi-holiday. The days between the holidays of Passover and Shavuot were often times of misfortune and misery for Jews in the past, and thus it is considered a time of mourning and sadness. As tradition states, 24,000 of Rabbi Akiva's students died in antiquity as a result of the plague. The plague subsided only for one day, the thirty-third day of "counting Omer." According to another tradition, it is a day in which God sent manna from heaven during the wandering to the Promised Land. Still others refer to Bar Kokhba's revolt. After many defeats, the rebelling forces scored a significant victory over the Romans on this day. From 1920, the Zionist Organization announced this day as "the day for celebrating the granting of Palestine to the Jews," and in 1928 this day was announced as the day of Jewish sports.

17. F. Dromi-Popowski, "The Group 'Supporters of the Hebrew Language'," pp. 463–502.

18. Działalność antypaństwowa Żydów oraz zajścia antyżydowski 1924–1934, Wydz. II Społ.-Pol. 1919–1939, UWL, APL, sig. 498, pp. 47–49.

19. Ibid., pp. 47–49; *Głos Podlaski*, no. 35, 38 (1934).

CHAPTER 7.

SOCIAL AND CULTURAL ASSOCIATIONS AND CLUBS

7.A. CULTURAL-EDUCATIONAL, WELFARE, AND HEALTH ASSOCIATIONS

Libraries

The Jews had a functioning library as early as the end of the nineteenth century. Its founder and owner was Icchak Lipiec, a bookseller by trade. Icchak Lipiec owned several hundred books that he lent out for a weekly fee. He was a pious Jew, who prayed regularly in the synagogue, but at the same time he "illegally" lent out secular books. His library was doubly concealed: from the tsarist authorities, since he did not have the proper permissions; and from his orthodox confreres, who did not acknowledge the need to read secular books.

The first library was officially registered on 26 July 1900 in the name of Mendel Leibkowicz Miodownik. In was located in Kagan's house on Alejowa Street next to the bookstore. Readers were charged a fee of from 20 to 40 kopeks a month and from 2 to 5 kopeks per book. It was open from 9 AM to 8 PM. In 1911, it contained 1,720 books, of which 850 were in Yiddish, 650 were in Russian, and 220 were in Polish.

Another library was founded in 1901 among the Zionists, who used their own money to acquire books. At first it functioned underground, and the books were housed at Goldwaser's. In March 1904, it was legalized as a private library under the name of the Zionist Mordechaj Meir Landau, the son-in-law of Icchak Nachum Weintraub. It was located on Warszawska Street in Kamiński's house. Readers were charged a fee of 5 kopeks a book. It was open from 8 AM to 9 PM and on Fridays from noon to 3 PM because of Shabbat. In 1911 it had 1,780 books, of which 500 were in Russian, 160 were in Polish, and 1,120 were in Yiddish. It also had collections in French and German. The library was named for Landau after his death. This is how Apolinary Hartglas remembered him:

> I befriended many among them, but especially Mordechaj Meir Landau, whose memory I will revere as long as I live. He was 5 years older than I,

but he had a lung disease and looked almost as old as my father. He was an ardent Zionist; he worked in the direction of promoting the Zionist idea among Siedlce Jews and accomplished much. Wise and sensible, intelligent and well read, and above all of a rare nobility of character, impartial and extremely tactful, he was the one with whom I could easily confer on any social matter. He was a "Litwak" from Brześć on the Bug River, married in Siedlce [to Weintraub's daughter—author's note], he spoke Polish, albeit imperfectly, and he had a gift rare in this kind of Jew: he could identify with the Polish soul and the Polish cause, but at every step emphasizing Jewish separateness, his national pride, and the rights of his nation. And thus Polish society treated this "simple Jew" with all respect and good feeling, while they treated, for example, the assimilationist Dr. [Maurycy—author's note] Stein with clear disregard. I greatly valued and liked Landau, and while speaking at his funeral in 1918, I broke into quite real tears.[1]

Oszer Liwerant was responsible for checking out books. At a certain point, reservations arose as to the proper functioning of the library. It was open inconsistently, the catalogues, if they were compiled at all, were inaccurate, and the person handing out the book had problems finding the appropriate item. The tsarist police tried to control the library; every newly purchased book, legally of course, had to be presented for censorship. Not infrequent were searches of Jewish activists who visited the library. In 1912, the library had 2,500 books. Its work, however, was far from perfect. It was then that the idea arose of annexing it to the Jewish Art Society. This was accomplished in 1912, when the society was undergoing a crisis. A library division was formed consisting of Abraham Huberman, Weluda Frydman, Oszer Liwerant, Dawid Ajzenberg, Mosze Mandelman, and Berl Czarnobroda. The Chassidim joined the Zionists in working on the reorganization of the library. A list was drawn up of all the books, catalogues were compiled, and a reader's fee was introduced. A Polish section was added to the existing Jewish, Hebrew, and Russian sections. It was created by girls from the Bund: Rachela Edelsztajn-Berg, Gołda Halberstat, Terca Cukier, and Bronia Goldberg-Głazowska. Before the outbreak of World War I, there were over 300 readers who were signed up at the library. During the war, the tsarist authorities requisitioned the library building, but the book collection was saved and safely survived the war thanks to a devoted group of supporters of knowledge. After the war, the library renewed its activity, gaining many new readers and expanding its book collection. The new library building was at 66 Warszawska Street, in the offices of the Jewish Art Society. In contrast to the society, the library grew constantly throughout the interwar period. It was destroyed only by the Nazi invasion. In 1926, the twenty-fifth anniversary of its activity was formally celebrated. Famous writers living in Poland were invited to give lectures in Siedlce for this occasion.[2]

"Yiddishe Kunst" (Jewish Art) Literary-Musical Society

Two years after the 1906 pogrom, Jewish society in Siedlce started to shake off its apathy. In August 1908, Hazomir Musical Society came into being, officially registered in 1909, and in 1912 it took the name Jewish Art Literary-Musical Society. The goal of the society was to familiarize Jewish society with music and literature. Members of the first board were Kalman Galicki (chairman), Matitiahu Minc, Icchak Eliahu Cukier, Abraham Zigielkwas (Bund member), Mosze Wołowski (Bund member), Berl Minc, and Josef Rozenzumen (Bund member). In 1910, Icchak Nachum Weintraub (deputy chairman), Jejna Barenbaum, and Icchak Alberg joined the board. The yearly dues in 1912 were 3 rubles for permanent members and 6 rubles for those seeking membership. The society at that time had 150 members. Hazomir, popularly called Zome,[3] was under the influence of the Bund. The society formed a choir, a drama section, and an orchestra. It organized meetings and lectures. It brought lecturers mostly from Warsaw. The tsarist authorities looked unfavorably at the activity of this center of culture. It introduced a censorship of theatrical productions, impeded the organization of meetings and events, and tried several times to close down the society's premises. All of these setbacks were overcome thanks to the unyielding stance of the board, particularly Icchak Nachum Weintraub. Yet Jewish society, which was conservatively disposed, looked with outrage upon the activity of the society, "where cigarettes were smoked on Saturdays, and boys and girls dance together."[4] Within the framework of doing battle with these views, Jakub Tenenbaum wrote a one-act comedy called "Don't Go to the Zome," which was staged many times by the theatrical section of the society.

After regaining Siedlce from the hands of the Red Army in 1920, the military authorities requisitioned the Jewish Art building, and that society moved to a small place at the corner of Długa and Sądowa Streets. The inadequate size of the premises and the general atmosphere were not conducive to carrying on cultural-educational activity. In January 1924, a meeting took place at which a new board was formed: Chaim Goldberg, Menasze Czarnobroda, Jakub Tenenbaum, Moszek Rozenzumen, Moszek Rotbejn, Jankiel Szlechter, Szloma Hochberg, and Abram Gebel. The auditing committee consisted of Berek Czarnobroda, Berek Trybucki, and Jankiel Jabłoń. Starting in 1925, Jewish Art once again energetically began its work. Once a week there were meetings, lectures, concerts, and so forth. The library holdings were enlarged. The board in that year consisted of Mojsze Rotbejn, Mordko Zebrowicz, Mojsze Grabie, as well as Pejsach Kapcan. On 27 February 1925, a lecture was given in the premises of the society by Jankiel Tenenbaum on the subject of party nonaffiliation in social life. The lecture was attended by various party representatives. The lecture was followed by a heated discussion participated in by Lewi Gutgeld and Mozes Grynfarb, who shared Zionist views; Josek Słuszny, a Poalei Zion activist; as well as Pola, a member of the Bund. They all attacked the lecturer, having all come to the conclusion "that a person without party affiliation is not worthy of living on earth."[5]

Jewish Art ceased its activity during a time of crisis in 1933. It was turned into a games and entertainment club.[6]

In April 1935, some of the members left the board of the society. Supplemental elections were called. The disagreements among the activists, however, were very deep. In June 1935 the general meeting of members ended in a brawl. On 6 September 1935, as the result of internal conflicts, the Siedlce district administrator suspended the activity of the Yiddishe Kunst.[7] After a certain time, activity was resumed. On 20 and 21 May 1936, the theatrical section put on two plays: *Ghosts* by Henrik Ibsen and *The Stigma of Race* by Ernst Toller. Both plays were seen by a total of 600 people.

"Tarbut" (Culture) Jewish Educational-Cultural Association

It was founded in Siedlce on 14 April 1922. The goal of the association was the propagation of the Hebrew language as well as Jewish culture and education. The association worked to achieve these goals by founding and supporting shelters for children, preschools, and primary, secondary, and vocational schools; by providing pedagogical courses, courses to raise the skill level of working people, and extension courses. At the head of this society were Lewi Gutgeld, Szyja Celnik, Abram Szalom Engleder, Mejer Tenenbaum, Szyja Cukierman, and Sara Sukiennik. On 29 April 1937, in connection with the holiday of Lag Baomer, an out-of-town trip was organized for the pupils of the Tarbut school. This association was a branch of the Zionist Organization.[8]

Jewish League of People's Education [ŻLOL]

The league came into being in 1924 and carried on cultural-educational work for seven years. Its headquarters were located in the offices of the Jewish Perec School. The chairman of ŻLOL was Menasze Czarnobroda and the secretary was Frydman. The league was a branch of the Jewish Folk Party [i.e., Folkists—ed.]. It organized evening classes in a variety of fields as well as papers and lectures. Polish authorities disbanded this association in 1931.[9]

Yavneh Jewish Cultural-Educational Association[10]

This society came into being in Siedlce in 1934 and had its offices at 8 Szpitalna Street (currently Kochanowski Street). The society had as its aim "the propagation of the Hebrew language, culture, and education among the Jewish people in Poland in the religious-Orthodox spirit."[11] It was hoped that the realization of this goal would be achieved by conducting various kinds of courses, talks, lectures, trips, summer camps, and so forth. The Siedlce division had 30 members and was subordinated to the main offices in Warsaw. The society was a branch of the

Organization of Orthodox Zionists "Mizrachi." The board members were Szloma Pryzant, Dawid Morgensztern, Szmul Landsman, Szmul Jabłkowicz, Mordko-Michel Czarny, Szmul Goldsztejn, Szyja Zelkowicz, Moszko Szymon Mendel, Szoel Ajzenberg, and Mendel Ajzenberg.[12] The association was in existence until 1939.

"Freiheit" (Freedom) Cultural-Educational Society

This society functioned as early as 1919 at 20 Długa Street and ran a drama club under the direction of Jakub Warszawski. It was reregistered in Siedlce on 25 August 1934. The society's offices were at 58 Piłsudski Street. The "Freiheit" Society had as its goal the "propagation of pure science and art among the Jewish masses and the support of physical education."[13] With this aim, it organized courses, talks, lectures, trips, sports clubs, and so forth. The composition of the Siedlce "Freiheit" board of directors was Fajwel Orensztein, Mordko-Boruch Farbsztajn, Dawid Fajgenbaum, Hersz-Abram Wajsman, and Gdale Mocny. On 7 February 1937, a meeting attended by 30 people took place at which a new board was elected. It consisted of Chaim Kamienny, chairman; Chaim Kisielewski, secretary; and Motel Woda, treasurer. The society was a branch of the Right Poalei Zion Party.[14]

"Kultur Liga" (League of Culture) Educational Association

This group was also called the League of Proletarian Culture or the League of Jewish Culture. The association was formed in 1917 in Kiev and was under the influence of the Bund. This organization came into being in Poland thanks to an understanding among leftist circles that cooperated with CISZO (Central Jewish School Organization). Its beginnings went back to 1922, but it was officially registered as an all-Poland organization in 1926. Its foundational assumption was to unite cultural activists of various views and act under the guidance of trade unions. Its goal was the "development and dissemination of Jewish culture of all branches of human creativity, such as literature, art, music, theater, and so forth, and aid in the building of all manner of cultural and educational institutions."[15]

The "Kultur Liga" Association functioned in Siedlce during the 1930s and had 80 members. It was located at 28 Kiliński Street. Its board was made up of Beniamin Kramarz, Hersz Rubinsztejn, Majer Frydman, and Minda Szapiro. The association was a branch of the Bund.[16] It organized a talk by J. Pat from Warsaw on 25 May 1935 titled "Zionism and Socialism," which was attended by 400 people.

League of Aid to Working Palestine

This group is also known as the League of Working Palestine. It was an institution called upon to coordinate the organizations supporting the Zionist labor movement in Palestine. Its beginnings were provided by the Committee for a Working Palestine, which starting in 1923 began forming the Histadrut, the center for trade unions in Palestine. The first convention of the organizations functioning outside

Palestine took place after the Thirteenth World Zionist Congress in 1923. In Poland its development fell to the late 1920s. It was formed from the following parties and organizations: Right Poalei Zion, Hitachdut, Hashomer Hatzair, Hechlutz, and Dror. Its central offices were in Warsaw, with branches in outlying areas. In reality it was a leftist bloc of mutually supporting Zionists groups.

In Siedlce, only the Society of Friends of Working Palestine was active, registered 30 April 1935 with offices at 53 Piłsudski Street. The league initially had 40 members, but in 1937 it already had 70. Szlomo Kamieński and Lejzor Srebrnik were activists. There was great interest in its activity. The meeting called for 8 April 1935, at which the policy goal was presented, was attended by 700 people. The next meeting took place 20 July 1935. Stolarski from Warsaw at that time gave the lecture "Before the Nineteenth Zionist Congress." On 6 August 1935, the society organized a celebration to honor the tenth anniversary of the death of the well-known promoter and social activist Józef Słuszny. The program consisted of speeches and musical compositions. Zamwel Rozenzumen, among others, took the floor. The celebrations gathered together 80 participants. On 8 May 1937, Michel Warszmitel from Warsaw gave a lecture titled "The Problems of Communal Jewish Life in Palestine." In his presentation, which was listened to by about 100 people, he presented an extensive discussion of the issue of the immigration of Jews to Palestine. Then on 29 May 1937, Rozenzumen gave an extensive lecture in Siedlce about Dov Ber Borokhov as an expert in Jewish philology and economics and also discussed Jewish–Arab relations and the role of the British government in Palestine. On 30 June 1937, the Society of Friends of Working Palestine called a meeting at which the organization of a shoemakers union under the aegis of the society was discussed. There were about 200 people present. During the discussion, Boim Liwerant, Srul Garnek, Abram Murawa, and others caused a commotion and called upon those present to refuse to sign up for the emerging union. In this situation, the chairman adjourned the meeting. The supporters of the Bund and the Communists gathered in the courtyard of the property at 53 Piłsudski Street and there continued their stormy debate. As a result, the two sides decided to organize the shoemakers into two separate unions.[17]

Hashomer Hatzair—Young Guard, Scout

This was a leftist Zionist youth organization of a pioneering nature, one of the few Jewish scouting organizations in the Second Republic. It could trace its beginnings to the Austrian partition and a while later started up in the Russian partition as well. It referred to the ethos of the Jewish guards, Hashomer, active in Palestine since 1909. Their goal was to protect Jewish settlers from attacks by Arabs. A founding congress of this organization in Poland was held in Częstochowa in 1917, and the World Federation Hashomer Hatzair was established in Gdańsk in 1924. In accordance with its principles, this was to be a "movement of national renaissance." Its members, called *shomrim*, were obligated to support the Zionist movement, propagate the Hebrew language, and prepare for working the land in Palestine. The full realization of the program was *aliyah*, that is, departure for Palestine and work on *kibbutzim* (settlements, communities). In the first years of its existence, this organization underwent a rapid development. Then it started to evolve ideologically in the direction of Marxism. The highest authority was the congress of members or delegates and the Chief Command. The fundamental organizational units were the *kvutza* (group), *pluga* (company), and *gdud* (battalion). Hashomer Hatzair belonged to the League of Aid to Working Palestine as well as, with the retention of autonomy, to Hechalutz (Pioneer).

Hashomer Hatzair was organized in Siedlce in 1921 by Herszel Słuszny, who ran it for many years. His assistants were Małka Lewin, Jehuda Liwerant, Dawid Jon-Tow, Bunin Czarnobroda, and Josef Kacpan. This organization brought together school children from various environments. It instilled in its members the principles of mutual aid. It organized fund raisers for the purchase of books and school supplies for members who came from impoverished families. The place where they played, met, and paraded was the woods in Roskosz. During vacations, camps were organized in neighboring villages.[18] On 11 June 1932, a meeting of scouts was held from Siedlce, Łuków, Węgrów, and Sokołów Counties. One hundred twenty scouts gathered at 58 Piłsudski Street. They then went to Wólka, where they did sports exercises under the direction of Dorfman, a member of the Chief Command in Warsaw. Other command members, Abram Rowicki and Dawid Rozenbaum, met with a group of 30 candidates for departure to Palestine. From 8 to 16 January 1936, a trip to Domanice was organized in which 55 scouts participated. They were housed in private homes. Sports exercises took place every day.

The board that was elected at the meeting on 13 June 1936 consisted o f Chaim Beagon, chairman; Ber Lederman, vice-chairman; Uszer Trzmielina, treasurer; and Chana Gropman, secretary.[19]

Trumpeldor Association of Jewish Youth—Brit Trumpeldor, Beitar

This association was also called Captain Josef Trumpeldor Scouting Association. From the very beginning, in 1923, this was a Zionist youth organization connected with the Revisionist Zionists and headed by Vladimir Jabotinsky. It referred to scouting models, although it was not recognized by the ZHP [Polish Scouting Organization—trans.]. Its ideological patron was Josef Trumpeldor.[20]

At the head of the national Brit Trumpeldor structure was the Chief Command, to which were subordinated districts and nests, consisting of troops, which in turn were divided into platoons and sections. Members gained the following ranks in turn: private, private-instructor, corporal, patrol leader, section leader, platoon leader, and troop leader. This was a coeducational organization. There were three age groups in troops: 8–13, *kfirim* (lion cubs); 13–18, *tzofim* (scouts), and over 18, *kshishim* (seniors)

Brit Trumpeldor decidedly opposed the idea of class struggle, which led to harsh disputes with leftist Zionist organizations. The main emphasis was placed on educational activity and strict discipline, thus preparing members for participation in Jewish self-defense. The first world congress of this association, which before the outbreak of World War II had about 100 thousand members in 26 countries, was organized in 1931 in Gdańsk. The largest organization was in Poland.

In Siedlce the association was led by Dawid Morgensztern, and its offices were in the house at 10 Asłanowicz Street. It had 40 members in 1932. The board consisted of Uszer Finkielsztejn, chairman; Uszer Sokołowski, secretary; Chil Dugecki, treasurer; Izaak Skała, administrator; and Froim Goldsztejn, member.[21] On 21 July 1935 a lecture was organized titled "Development of Life in Palestine." The lecturer was Jakow Piekar from Warsaw. There were 350 people in the audience. At the invitation of Beitar, Vladimir Jabotinsky came to Siedlce on 21 August 1935. He gave a lecture titled "On the Eve of a New Epoch in the Zionist Movement." As many as 1,000 people came to the meeting with him. The next mass meeting called by Brit Trumpeldor took place on 17 July 1937. It was organized in the courtyard of 20 Kiliński Street as a protest rally against the planned division of Palestine. As many as 1,000 people participated in it. It was lead by Dawid Morgensztern from Siedlce and Menuchim Biegun [Polish name of Menachem Begin—trans.] from Warsaw. A protest resolution was approved, which was to be sent to the League of Nations in Geneva, the British government, and the MSZ [Ministry of Foreign Affairs—trans.] in Warsaw. The members of this association organized a memorial ceremony in the synagogue on 30 May 1938 in honor of Ben Josef, who had died in Palestine.[22] There were about 800 people present. The next meeting dedicated to Ben Josef took place on 6 August 1938 at the Protection of Jewish Orphans building, at which the speaker, Dr. Lipman from the Central Zionist Committee, read a paper titled "Ben Josef's Death and Jabotinsky's Passivity." One hundred fifty people participated in the meeting, mostly young people between the ages of 15 and 25. Referring to the situation in Palestine, Dr. Lipman said, "Marshal Piłsudski won a free Poland with the blood of the legionnaires, not with diplomatic or paper exchanges of platitudes."[23]

"Akiba" Jewish Scouting Organization—Hanoar Haivri "Akiba"

This organization began its activity on 19 March 1935. The scouts' headquarters was located at 30 Kiliński Street. The goal of the organization was "to propagate and practice scouting according to the system of Gen. Baden Powell among Jewish youths" as well as "to raise the mental and physical condition of these same youths."[24]

This organization was officially registered under the condition that it not engage in its activity on school property or recruit its troops from among school children. The leadership consisted of Meir Grynfarb, Pełtyl Celnikier, Mojżesz Międzyrzecki, Jakow Jon-Tow, Stanisław Gilgun, and Natan Belfor. The members of the organization did not have the right to vote; all positions were held by nomination, which was normal practice in scouting. It had 20 members, who paid dues in the amount of 50 grosz a month.[25]

Shortly after its registration, the authorities rescinded agreement for its functioning since the founder of this organization, Dr. Nisan [Natan] Belfor, was suspected of espionage.

"Laboro" (Work) Workers Association of Esperantists, Siedlce Branch

The Workers Association of Esperantists in Siedlce was founded on 18 July 1932. It had its headquarters in the apartment of Szymon Wakierman at 51 Piłsudski Street. The association had as its goal the study of the artificial language Esperanto, which was created by Ludwik Zamenhof.[26] It started out with 50 members but grew considerably in subsequent years. Its board consisted of Dawid Grynfarb (age 44, musician, activist in Left Poalei Zion), Szymon Wakierman (age 22, tailor, activist in Right Poalei Zion), Regina Herszberg (age 22, seamstress, activist in Right Poalei Zion), Josef Pasternak (age 26, sales employee, activists in Communist Union of Polish Youth [KZMP—trans.]), Menachem Morgenstern (age 20, student, activist in Hechalutz—Pioneer), Srul Liwerant (age 27, librarian, Communist), Szyja Zonszejn (age 21, tailor, sympathizer of KZMP), Hersz Czerkiewicz (age 23, gaiter maker, activist in Left Poalei Zion), Izaak Rydel (age 26, office worker, Zionist), and Szymon Rafał (age 22, tailor, activist in Left Poalei Zion). The majority of board members held leftist views.

"Morning Prayer" Workers Physical Education Association

In 1934 the Bund made an attempt to form the "Morning Prayer" Workers Physical Education Association. Those chosen for the board were Noe Blumsztejn, chairman (shoemaker); Beniamin Kramrz, secretary (office worker); Icko Zamieczkowski, treaturer (merchant), Szyja Mejer, vice-chairman (locksmith); Lander Epelbaum, member (shoemaker); Dawid Blumstejn, member (carpenter); and Lejbno Gnajona, member (shoemaker). The authorities did not permit the registration of "Morning Prayer," claiming that the association might fall under the influence of Communism and manifest Communist activity.[27]

Protection of Jewish Orphans

The Protection of Jewish Orphans in Siedlce was a branch of the Central Association for the Care of Jewish Children and Orphans in Warsaw, which went under the acronym CESTONDZ. The goal of the association was the material and moral care for Jewish children and orphans. This goal derived from deep-seated religious dictates. The association was a legal person and was supported by the dues of its members, as well as contributions and donations, income derived from its estate, and through government and self-government grants and subsidies. The association's governing bodies were the General Meeting of Branch Members, the Branch Board, and the Auditing Committee. All elections and resolutions of the General Meeting were passed by a simple majority of votes. The Branch Board consisted of from 3 to 15 members and from 3 to 6 assistants, according to the resolution of the General Meeting. The board was elected for a period of one year and elected from among its members a chairman, secretary, and treasurer.

The Central Association of Care in Warsaw was registered in 1924, and its Siedlce branch was created in 1927. The initiative for the construction of the building for the orphanage came from activists of the local Zionist Organization, which had its headquarters at 26 Kiliński Street. Dawid Rubinstein became the chairman of the committee to construct the home for orphans. He was aided in this endeavor by Uszer Orzeł, Mojżesz Ajzensztat, Szmuel Cukier, and Abram Bresler. The orphanage building was built at 59 Sienkiewicz Street. Currently this building is in the possession of the Podlasie Academy.

The chairman of the construction committee formally transferred the building and the mortgage to the community council on 27 March 1927. The transfer took place with the stipulation that the community council could not change the intended use of the building. The final cost of the home was probably 57,600 zlotys, for that was the security on the mortgage. The construction committee probably could not handle such a large investment, and the religious council had to take over the matter.

During the functioning of the home, the composition of the Board of Directors of the Protection of Orphans was Alter Kamiński, Binem Rotenberg, Dawid Konopny, Srul Cukier, and Jankiel Jon-Tow.

The functioning of the orphanage during the 1930s was described by Ida Jom-Tow:

> We had a large Jewish orphanage in Siedlce. In 1933, when Hitler came to power, he expelled from Germany many Jews who had not been born there. One day, a train filled with Jewish children crossed the border; they were to be housed in over a dozen orphanages. My mother was one of the people who met this train and brought about 14–15 children to our orphanage. The orphanage was collecting money, and once a year it held a large ball in order to collect funds. It also received aid from the Jewish Community Council and from the government. I went there often. The children were well cared for. The home was very clean, and the children had good food, better than in some homes. The children lived there and went to school until they turned 16. It was expected that they would become independent

at that age, but they visited the home on holidays and Shabbat. Once a year my mother would go to Łódź, which was a textile center, and visit factories to obtain fabric for the orphanage. The women sewed sheets, pillowcases, and uniforms for the children out of this cloth.[28]

In September 1939 there were 106 children in the orphanage as well as elderly people needing care. When the city was briefly occupied by the Red Army, these children were evacuated. They were placed in Mińsk, in Belarus, and after the Germans attacked the USSR, they were taken into the depths of the country. Their subsequent fate is unknown.

Association for the Care of Jewish Orphans

The name "Ezrath Yethomim" Society was also used informally, although it was also used in correspondence with the authorities. The association implemented the goal stated in its name and engaged in helping run the orphanage. In 1933 it had about 70 members. In February 1933, the board of directors consisted of Uszer Orzeł, chairman (merchant); Jankiel Jon-Tow (merchant); Aron Jabłoń (merchant); Lejb Wajnsztejn (merchant); Hersz Rozengarten (merchant); and Chaja Tenenbaum. The Auditing Committee consisted of Munysz Rydel (merchant), Jozef Rozenzumen (office worker), and Szyja Cukier (merchant). Sura Szajnberg, Dawid Zonszajn, Szmul Wurman, Szyja Ekierman, Mejer Strzałka, Aron Breszler, and Dawid Rozenberg were vigorous activists in the association.[29] The association organized a concert of religious songs on 6 October 1934 with the participation of E. Kieszkowski from Warsaw. The concert attracted about 120 people, and the income was allocated for statutory goals.

Jewish Committee of the Maritime and Colonial League

This committee came into being in 1934. The Civil Committee consisted of Maksymilian Schleicher, chairman; Uszer Orzeł, vice-chairman; and T. Kramarz, secretary. The committee ran a propaganda campaign with the goal of informing society about the importance of access to the sea for Poland as well as of raising money for the Fund for Protection of the Sea.[30]

Jewish Circle of LOPP (League for Antiaircraft and Antigas Defense)

This circle organized a recitation soiree on 28 March 1937 participated in by Chana Braz from Warsaw. She was listened to by 250 people.

Committee for Aid to Jewish Students—Auxilium Academicum Judaicum

This committee engaged in the activity indicated by its name. On 23 September 1923, it issued a proclamation with the following content:

To the Jewish Population of Siedlce. The Jewish student who arrives from the provinces to study in Warsaw is deprived of a roof over his head. The housing shortage subjects him to physical and spiritual suffering, and more than one student has had to abandon the university bench for this reason. With the aim of relieving this anguish of the Jewish student, a Committee has been formed in Warsaw in whose makeup are Jewish activists who are the most respected and the most dedicated to this cause. This committee has as its goal the building of a home for the Jewish student in Warsaw. Similar committees have been formed in all the cities and towns of Poland where there is need for a healthy Jewish intelligentsia, where a spiritual bond exists with university youths acquiring an education. Full of enthusiasm and dedication, these people are working on the building of a University Hostel in Warsaw, and the broad masses of Jewish society are showing a generosity this time that borders on sacrifice and that is filled with understanding for this sacred civic cause. One can say with all certainty and determination that Polish Jewry will be able to build this house for its student. In connection with this campaign, the [Siedlce] Committee for Aid to Jewish Students has been reorganized and, making aid to and cooperation in the building of a Jewish University Hostel in Warsaw its top mission, is organizing in the very near future a whole series of fundraisers, concerts, and dances, certain that Siedlce will not remain behind other cities and will in equal measure as all the cities in Poland contribute with a generous hand to the building of a roof over the head of the homeless Jewish student.[31]

"Lodging House" Jewish Charitable Society

The only thing that has been established is that on 30 July 1936 it organized a public collection for the statutory goals of the society.

Health Care Society—TOZ

The beginnings of this organization go back to 1912. At that time, the *Obshchestvo Zdravookhraneniya Yevreev* [Russian] was founded in St. Petersburg. Until 1921 the headquarters of the society were located in there, and then they were moved to Berlin. After the First World War, its branches sprang up in various countries, mostly in Europe, and from 1923, in all the larger cities of Poland. TOZ [for *Towarzystwo Ochrony Zdrowia* in Polish—trans.] set itself the goal above all of preventive action, concentrated on preventing the spread of eye diseases, skin diseases, and tuberculosis. It handed out periodical literature and brochures popularizing the foundations of medical knowledge and the principles of hygiene.

The Health Care Society was founded in Siedlce in 1923 on the initiative of Dr. Maksymilian Schleicher, who took on the function of chairman. Members of the society were Sz. Englender (secretary), Jehoszua Ekerman, H. Halbersztat, Henryk

Loebel, Josef Alberg, A. Marki, Lam, Mosze Czarnobroda, and Madl. TOZ provided medical care in all the Jewish schools. It fought against illnesses that were widespread, especially among children, such as scabies, lice, fungal infections, and tuberculosis. It arranged for medical checkups for children and treatment for the sick. Complicated cases were referred to Warsaw clinics, and children with allergies were sent to sanatoriums. The society taught preventive medicine and held camps and day camps for poor children. It owned a health center in the village of Kisielany-Żmichy outside Siedlce. In 1925, a Women's Circle was formed, which arranged for midmorning snacks in Jewish schools. This snack consisted of a roll and a glass of milk or chocolate milk. The Women's Circle cooperated closely with TOZ. The circle included Mrs. Schleicher (the wife of Dr. Schleicher, as chairperson), Estera Zalman, Fela Orzeł, Pua Rabinowicz, Lam, Tabakman, and others.[32] TOZ provided 40 percent of the financing of the Jewish hospital, where in 1932 a gynecological ward was created under the direction of Doctor Henryk Loebel and an internal medicine ward under the supervision of Doctor Głazowski. The activists of TOZ carried on work in preventive medicine, which was intended to inform the people of ways to protect against illness and how to keep one's home clean. With this goal, meetings were held at which local doctors gave talks and medical advice. Well-known doctors from Warsaw were also brought in, such a Dolman and Lewin. The foundations of the Society's budget were membership dues paid by 800 people, as well as income from events and subsidies from the community council and from the central office in Warsaw.

Jewish Tourism Society

This social organization arose in Warsaw in July 1926 at the initiative of Aleksander Dubrowicz and the Organizational Committee. The goal of the society was the awakening of esthetic feelings in Jews, the physical rebirth of the Jewish nation, the exploration of Jewish historical landmarks, and the propagation of interest in folklore. Mention of it was made in Siedlce in 1934.

Alliance of Jewish Women—WIZO (Women's International Zionist Organization)

This was a women's aid organization created by Zionists in London in 1920. Its main goal was the building of an independent Palestine. Autonomous divisions were created in Poland from 1925. It is mentioned in Siedlce in the situational report of the county administrator in 1934.

"Jaffe" (the Joffe Family) Association of Jewish Working Women

This association is only mentioned in the Siedlce district administrative records. Further information is unavailable.

Central Jewish Committee on Emigration to America, Society (Division) in Siedlce

Its headquarters were in the premises of the Mutual Credit Society on Warszawska Street. The board consisted of Józef Turin, Mojżesz Wołowelski, and Nechemja Malin. This society was disbanded by the Siedlce district administration on 20 October 1921. In spite of this, as can be concluded from a police report, it continued to carry on its activity.[33]

B'nai B'rith (Sons of the Covenant) Union of Jewish Humanitarian Associations

This organization was treated by its founders as a kind of religious order. The founders of this religious order wished to unite the divided fragments of Jewish society, basing themselves on the ethical principles of Judaism and on the intellectual values of Jewish culture. This organization was created on 13 October 1843 in the United States. Its guiding motto was "Charity, love, and brotherly harmony." The first lodge in Europe was created in 1882 in Berlin. On Polish territory, the first "B'nai B'rith" lodges arose at the end of the nineteenth century in the Prussian partition (Katowice 1883) and the Austrian partition (Bielsko 1889). Lodges were created in the former Russian partition only after Poland regained its independence (Warsaw 1922). In the early period, the ideology of the order contained ideas convergent with the principles of Masonry. In a later period, the order was connected with the Zionist movement. Its representative in Siedlce was Dr. Henryk Loebel. His name figures in the society's Address Book, which was published in Kraków in 1937.[34] An independent lodge most likely did not arise in Siedlce since it did not have the requisite 20 members. They could have been part of the Warsaw lodge called "Brotherhood," which in 1937 had 118 members. The activity of "B'nai B'rith" in Poland was interrupted by a decree of the president of the republic on 22 November 1938 disbanding Masonic organizations.

In all these associations the governing boards were elected democratically; members had passive and active voting rights. Each association was a branch of a political party, which tried to influence the community and gain supporters through cultural-educational work. The most active society was Jewish Art.

7.B. ATHLETIC CLUBS

The **Jewish Union of the Physical Fitness and Athletics Society** arose in Siedlce in 1921. Its offices were on Długa Street (currently Bishop I. Świrski Street). The goal of the union was to propagate sports among Jewish youth, so a soccer team, **Maccabi**, was formed. The following Zionist activists were members of the board: Hersz Słuszny, Ela Frydman, and Aron Grynberg. In addition to the soccer team, there was also the **Maccabi Athletic Society**, called into being in 1922 by the Zionist

Organization. It was divided into two groups. The first was led by Hersz Słuszny, a pupil at the public secondary school. This group contained about 30 pupils from the upper classes. The second group was led by Leon Halbersztadt and was composed of young people between the ages of 8 and 16. It had about 40 members and was divided into three platoons having the names of Jewish heroes: Eliezer, Bar Kokhba, and Samson.[35] The members of the society trained according to the military model. Poalei Zion also created the **Maccabi Club**, which had 40 members. The club's instructors were Moszek Rowald, Felzenstein, and Abraham Weistman. Athletic training took place on the military field.

During the Second Republic, there were a few more athletic clubs in Siedlce. The best known was the **Jewish Athletic Club "Kadimah" (Forward)**. Dr. Leon Głazowski acted as its chairman, and Anatol Goldberg was the director. Active on the club's board were Natan Halbersztat, Benjamin Bronsztejn, Chlejb Kimdraj, Benjamin Halbersztadt, Jankiel Trzebuski, Tadeusz Kramarz, Dawid Jedwab, Matys Gursztejn, Szmul Nusbaum, and Dr. Henryk Loebel. Kadimah ran the following sections: soccer (this was the best Jewish team in Siedlce), cycling (in 1927 in had about 50 competitors), tennis, table tennis, basketball, and boxing. The number of members could have been as high as about 100 people.

The **Jewish Workers' Athletic Club "Hapoel" (Worker)** was also vigorously active. At first it was a division of the Hechalutz organization, but from 1 September 1933 it became independent and had 150 members. Besides athletic competitions, it also put on theatrical performances, for example, on 8 April 1936 it put on the play *Unser Glojben* [Our Faith] by Sholem Asch; on 2 April 1937 it organized a performance with Jacek Lewi from Warsaw that had an audience of 180. In September 1935, before the Sejm elections, National Party militants threw hand-made petards into the theater. Fortunately, they did not cause any serious damage.[36] In December 1937, the board consisted of Benjamin Czarny, chairman; Mojżesz Zylberman, secretary; and Srul Góra, treasurer; they were all sympathizers or members of Right Poalei Zion. Kadimah and Hapoel were Zionist clubs.

Siedlce also had a soccer team called **Hakoah** [Hebrew for "Power"—ed.] and the popular left-leaning **Star**, whose proper name was **"Stern" (Star) Workers' Physical Education Association**. The players of Star appeared in red shirts, the club's color, which had 50 members. These teams competed among themselves and with other Siedlce teams, both Jewish and Polish, of which there were over a dozen. The cycling division of Kadimah organized bicycle rallies around the country and to Palestine. Sports in Siedlce in those years, especially soccer and cycling, had many followers.

The **"Shomria" (Watch) Jewish Athletic Club** was also mentioned. Further information about it has not been able to be found.

There was also the **"Eva" Women's Athletic Club**. It had at least 25 members. There were three divisions: gymnastics, track and field, and ping-pong. The general meeting of the club took place on 21 January 1933. It was run by [Miss][a] Regina Malin, the chairperson of the meeting. The secretary was [Miss] Hania Tabakman. [Miss] Zalcman gave a report on the activity of the current board. Treasurer Frydberman explained the expenditure of 307 zlotys. The secretary, [Miss] Rapoport, discussed the correspondence with the Alliance of Jewish Women's Athletic Associations. In the discussion that ensued during the course of the meeting, [Miss] Epelbaum proposed more frequent meetings. A new board was elected: [Miss] Hania Tabakman, chairperson; [Miss] Ciwia Zalcsztejn, vice-chairperson; [Miss] Regina Malin, treasurer; [Miss] Ida Cukier, secretary; and Jenta Włodawska, member.[37]

TRANSLATOR'S NOTE, CHAPTER 7

a. In Polish, "daughter of" is indicated by the addition of a suffix, most often "-ówna," to the man's surname, just as "wife of" is indicated with the suffix "-owa." Thus, Malin's daughter's surname would be Malinówna, and his wife's surname would be Malinowa. I have opted to add "[Miss]" or "[Mrs.]," respectively, to the relevant names rather than using the suffix. The use of "Mrs." without brackets indicates the author's use of the Polish equivalent, *pani*. The Polish equivalent of "Miss," *panna*, is not generally used, except in reference to little girls. This suffixation is now considered old fashioned and, from the perspective of gender equality, even insulting.

AUTHOR'S NOTES, CHAPTER 7

1. A. Hartglas, *Na pograniczu dwóch światów*, p. 109.
2. M. Mandelman, "The Library and the 'Jewish Art' Society," in *Book of Remembrance of the Siedlce Community*, pp. 506–508; Kaspi, "Early History of the Jews in Siedlce," pp. 155–156; Kaszyński and Tiliński, *Gorod Sedlec*, p. 119.
3. The abbreviation arose in order to simplify the pronunciation of this work in colloquial speech. So the first letter, 'H', and the last letter, 'r', were dropped.
4. M. Mandelman, "The Library and the 'Jewish Art' Society," p. 507.
5. APS, SPwS, sig. 8, p. 3.
6. Sprawozdanie starosty siedleckiego o ruchu społecznym za rok 1926, Wydz. II Społ.-Pol. 1919–1939, UWL, APL, sig. 161, p. 14; L.P. Maksymiuk, *Konsppiracja w Siedlcach w latach 1907-1914*, typescript of master's thesis in the possession of National Archive in Siedlce, p. 62; APS, Siedlecki Powiatowy Zarząd Żandarmerii, sig. 304, pp. 18, 105, 109, 127–129.
7. APS, SPwS 1918–1939, sig. 23, 26–35.
8. Żydowskie Stowarzyszenie Kulturalno-Oświatowe "Tarbut," Wydz. II Społ.-Pol. 1919–1939, UWL, APL, sig. 1118, pp. 3, 5; APS, SPwS, sig. 27, fol. 51.

9. Stowarzyszenie pn. "Żydowska Liga Oświaty Ludowej," Wydz. II Społ.-Pol. 1919–1939, UWL, APL, sig. 1115, pp. 3, 31–32; T. Moniewski, *Siedlce* (Siedlce, 1929), p. 61.

10. Yavneh—a town in which a well-known Talmudic academy was to be found.

11. Żydowskie Stowarzyszenie Kulturalno-Oświatowe "Jawne," Siedlce branch, Second Social-Political Division 1919–1939, UWL, APL, sig. 1117, p. 2 (Statute point 1).

12. Ibid., pp. 2, 13, 64–66.

13. Stowarzyszenie Kulturalno-Oświatowe "Freiheit," oddział w Siedlcach, Wydz. II Społ.-Pol.1919–1939, UWL, APL, sig. 1116, p. 1 (Statute article 2).

14. Ibid., p. 1–8, 31–32; APS, SPwS 1918–1939, sig. 27, fol. 27.

15. *Polski Słownik Judaistyczny. Dzieje. Kultura. Religia. Ludzie* (Warsaw, 2003), vol. 1, p. 845.

16. Monografia Stronnictwa Politycznego "Bund"—Algemeiner Jidysz Arbeter in Pojlen—Ogólnożydowski Związek Robotniczy Bund w Polsce, sig. 460, p. 35.

17. APS, SPwS, sig. 27, pp. 73–74.

18. Ibid., p. 346; Sprawozdanie starosty siedleckiego o ruchu społecznym za rok 1926, Wydz. II Społ.-Pol. 1919–1939, UWL, APL, sig.161, p. 23.

19. APS, SPwS 1918–1939, sig. 25, fol. 59, 95.

20. Josef Trumpeldor (1880 Pyatigorsk–1920 Tel-Hai)—Zionist leader and organizer of Jewish self-defense in Palestine. After completing a religious school in Rostov and then a Russian school, he studied stomatology. The social concepts of Lev Tolstoy made a deep impression on him. Under his influence, he supported the creation in Palestine of Jewish agricultural communes that could, when needed, provide their own armed defense. In 1902 he began his military service and was sent to the Japanese front. In 1906, he was awarded an officer's rank, in spite of being a Jew, and was distinguished with many medals. Subsequently he started studying law at the university in St. Petersburg. There he gathered a group of people who shared his views, and in 1912 they left together for Palestine. After the outbreak of World War I, he refused to accept Turkish citizenship and was exiled to Egypt. There he tried to form a Jewish Legion as the rudiment of a Jewish armed force. He went to Russia in the summer of 1917 to try to convince the Provisional Government of the need to create Jewish divisions in the Russian army. He was chosen as commissar of matters pertaining to Jewish soldiers. After the outbreak of the October Revolution, he was briefly arrested. Then he worked on behalf of creating a Hechalutz organization in Russia and became its first chairman in 1919. He supported military training for members of the movement and tried to create training and emigration centers. In 1919 he returned to Palestine, where he organized Jewish self-defense in Upper Galilee. That is where he died. He became a national symbol and hero for Zionists of both the right and the left, especially for youth organizations.

21. APS, SPwS 1918–1939, sig. 15, fol. 83.

22. Ben Josef Szlomo (Szulim Tabacznik)—a fighter in Brit Trumpeldor. In his early youth he became connected with revolutionaries and join Beitar. He arrived in Palestine illegally in 1937. The following year he took part in a retaliatory attack on an Arab bus. Even though no one died, he was the only one of the participants in the

action who was sentenced to death. His execution provoked world-wide protests. He became a symbol of the battle for the right of Jews to have their own country and a martyr of the Zionist movement.

23. APS, SPwS 1918–1939, sig. 29, fol 47.
24. Stowarzyszenie Hanoar Haiwri—"Akiba"—Żydowska Organizacja Skautowa "Akiba" w Siedlcach, Wydz. II Społ.-Pol. 1919–1939, UWL, APL, sig. 1133, p. 5 (Statute par. 2).
25. Ibid., sig. 1133, pp. 2–8.
26. Ludwik Zamenhof was born in 1859 in Białystok and died in Warsaw in 1917. He was educated as a doctor. Even as a child, he dreamed of creating a language that everyone could use regardless of their nationality. In one of his letters, he wrote, "I was raised as an idealist, taught that all people are brothers, while on the street and in the yard everything at every step showed me that people do not exist, there are only Russians, Poles, Germans, Jews, and so on. This constantly tormented my childhood soul. [...] Because at that time I believed that adults possessed some kind of all-mighty power, I kept repeating to myself that when I am big, I will without fail eliminate this evil." In July 1887, the first textbook of the Esperanto language appeared in Warsaw under the title *International Language*. The author published it under the pseudonym Dr. Esperanto, which means, "he who is hopeful." Toward the end of the nineteenth century, textbooks for the study of this language appeared in Russia, Romania, Great Britain, and Spain. As years went by, the Esperanto language gained supporters in other countries as well. The First World Congress of Esperantists took place in 1905. From that year congresses are held every year. The years of the Second World War were an exception. German Nazis deemed Esperanto to be an "undesirable language," and Esperantists were arrested and sent to concentration camps.
27. Stowarzyszenie Robotnicze Wychowania Fizycznego "Jutrznia" w Siedlcach, Wydz. II Społ.-Pol. 1919–1939, UWL, APL, sig. 1190, p. 6.
28. I. Jom-Tow (Tenenbaum) [Ida Tenenbaum Yomtov], *The Worst of Times (Najgorszy czas)* (New Orleans, 2002), pp. 38–39.
29. APS, SPwS 1918–1939, sig. 16, fol. 21–22.
30. *Życie Podlasia*, no. 9 (1934).
31. Łętocha B., Messer A., Cała A., "Żydowskie druki ulotne w II Rzeczpospolitej w zbiorach Biblioteki Narodowej," fig. 85A, catalogue entry 339.
32. M. Szleicher, "Działalność TOZ i Koła Kobiecego," in *Book of Remembrance of the Siedlce Community*, pp. 449–453.
33. APS, KPPPS, sig. 58, fol. 151. [This committee was most likely a division of HIAS.—ed.]
34. For more on this subject, see *Archiwum Związku Żydowskich Stowarzyszeń Humanitarnych "B'nei B'rith" w Krakowie (182–1938)*, comp. Bogusława Czajecka (Kraków: Jagiellonian University, 1994).
35. Eljezer/Eleazar/Hebrew Elazar—literally means "God is my help." It is a name that often appears in the Bible. Among others, it was the son of Aaron, who led the Israelites to the Promised Land and then directed the division of the conquered lands. Bar Kokhba—the leader of the Jewish uprising against the Romans in 132–135 CE. The reason for the uprising was Caesar Hadrian's demand to build the city of Aelia

Capitalina on the ruins of Jerusalem with a temple to Jupiter on the spot of the old Holy Temple of Jerusalem, as well as a ban on circumcision. The insurrectionists, in spite of early successes, were defeated, and the Jews were driven out of Jerusalem and Palestine. A time began for them of living in diaspora, dispersion.

Samson—a strongman, hero of many folk tales. As one who was consecrated to God, he was endowed with unusual strength, which resided in his hair. He led an adventurous life. He was betrayed and given over to his enemies by Delilah. The Philistines blinded him and forced him to do heavy labor. Set up to be the laughing stock of the crowds, he took advantage of his strength, which returned when his hair grew out, and destroyed his enemy's temple, perishing with them in its rubble.

36. APS, SPwS 1918–1939, sig. 23, fol. 122.
37. Sprawozdanie starosty siedleckiego o ruchu społecznym za rok 1926, Wydz. II Społ.-Pol. 1919–1939, UWL, APL, sig.161, p. 23; Moniewski, *Siedlce*, p. 67; J. Garbaczewski, "Kolarstwo na Podlasiu," in *Tygodnik Siedlecki*, no. 27 (1988); Relacje mieszkańców Siedlec: Izaaka Halbera i Marii Żyburowej, APS, SPwS 1918–1939, sig. 17, fol. 22.

CHAPTER 8.

INTERNAL SELF-RULE AND THE PRESS

8.A. COMMUNITY COUNCIL—KAHAL

The aspirations and interests of all Jewish parties clashed in the community council. It was a peculiar field of battle. Up to 1926, the Siedlce community council did not have much of an influence on the social life of Jews in Siedlce. The community council building was located next to the synagogue. Up until that year, it was managed by Herszel Tenenbojm (secretary) and Icchak Tenenbojm. Their work consisted of registering newly born children and crossing off the dead from the registry. The community council tax supported the rabbi, who was Gaon Chaim Ginzburg. He held his office in Siedlce from 1908 to 1930. Israel Gutgeld, clerk of the community council, worked toward having that body receive a percentage from kosher butchers. Kosher butchers, however, did not agree to perform their work for a specific wage. They preferred to work independently and to give the community council a small percentage of their proceeds. Kosher butchers performed the slaughter of meat according to strictly defined rules, having as their goal, among other things, the removal of blood, since its consumption is strictly forbidden by religious law. The Burial Society (Chevra Kadisha, literally Holy Society) and the Society of Last Rites (Nosei Hamita, literally Carriers of the Bed [or Bier—ed.]) were also not subordinated to the community council, and members of these societies set their own fees for their services, in this way taking advantage of those who needed their help. The Society of Last Rites fulfilled an important function. Before its founding, the deceased was taken to the cemetery on a wagon. If a wealthy person or a political activist died, he was carried to the cemetery by his friends and acquaintances, and the wagon drove next to them. At the funeral of a poor Jew, the deceased was driven on a wagon, and often he was not accompanied by the ten pious Jews necessary to perform the burial liturgy.

It was for this reason that a group of pious Jews created the Society of Last Rites, so that they might take all the deceased to the cemetery. Members of the board of the Society of Last Rites were Mosz Szmuklarz, Arie Galicki, Icchak Rozengarten,

Mordechaj Górnicki, Berl Srebrnik, Mosze Folszpan, Naftali Kuperszmit, and Rachmil Kewin.[1] The burial of women was handled by a separate committee.

One source of the community council's income was the community council tax. Of the 4,000 Jewish families living in Siedlce, only 360 paid the tax. The council's employees did not want to increase the number of taxpayers because each taxpayer had the right to vote for the community council executive board. The Zionists carried out propaganda campaigns whose goal was to expand the number of taxpayers in order thereby to limit the influence of the Agudah and increase their own.

On 20 November 1925, the community council published an announcement in which the Siedlce rabbinate warned that the fowl sold in some butcher shops and stores might not come from ritual slaughter. Clients should check whether the fowl is provided with a seal from the Jewish Religious Council with the date of slaughter.[2]

It was only in 1926 that elections to the community council were ordered. Men over the age of 21 had the right to vote even if they did not pay taxes. Zionists, the Agudah, Mizrachi, Folkists, and trade workers took part in the elections. The Bund and the Left Poalei Zion boycotted the elections because of a paragraph that barred nonreligious Jews from voting. Every effort was being made to retain the religious character of the community council. In every Chassidic prayer house, and there were several dozen of them in Siedlce, proclamations were hung with an appeal to vote for the Agudah. Of the 20 members of the Community Council Board, the Agudah received 10 seats, that is, 50 percent, and did not receive a majority. The Zionists received 4 seats and the trade workers 4, of whom 3 were Zionist activists and 1 a sympathizer, so for all practical purposes the Zionists had 8 seats, the Folkists had 1 seat, and Mizrachi, 1. The Agudah was represented on the Community Council Board by Jakow Szczerański, Szymon Ridel, Mosze Śliwka, Eliahu Tenenbojm, Sander Kantor, Bunem Huberman, Mosze Zakan, Israel Złotowski, Berisz Gorzałka, and Jakow Cukier; the Zionists, by Icchak Nachum Weintraub, Uszer Orzeł, Mosze Abe Ajzensztadt, and M. Schleicher; the trade workers, by Z.N. Malin, Szmuel Worman, Aharon Marecki, and Berl Srebrnik; the Folkists, by Josef Rozenzumen; and the Mizrachi, by W. Orłowski.[3] Next in order, a 10-member management board had to be elected from the 20 members of the Community Council Board. Since the Mizrachi had no chance of seating their member on the board, it declined to vote, but then it took active part in voting for the chairman. In the board elections, the Agudah received 6 seats and the Zionists and trade workers 4. The Agudah members of the board were Israel Gutgeld, Efraim Halber, Berisz Jakubowicz, Tonia Szyfer, Joel Słuszny, and Oszer-Mosze Nelkienbojm. The Zionists and trade workers were Mosze Goldberg, Jehuda Woda, Natan Hersz Gursztajn, and Fiszel Popowski. At its first meeting, the board decided to elect a chairman. Icchak Nachum Weintraub was the candidate for this position for the Zionists, and Jakow Szczerański, for the Agudah. The Folkist and the Mizrachi supported the Zionist candidate in the voting for chairman, as a result of which the Zionists received 10 votes, the same number as the Agudah. The representative of the authorities present at this meeting supported Jakow Szczerański. The Zionists did not accept this decision. Israel Gutgeld was to take care of the proper functioning of the community council on behalf of the Agudah.

A budget was formulated that took into account only the religious needs of Jews. The Zionists, trade workers, and the Mizrachi delivered lengthy, endless speeches at the meetings of the board in order to prevent the approval of the budget. This situation lasted for several months, paralyzing the normal functioning of the community council. It finally came to blows, which ended with police intervention.[4] The Siedlce county administrator put a stop to this situation by nullifying the previous nomination and demanding new elections. These resulted in the victory of the Zionist representative, Icchak Nachum Weintraub. A new budget was adopted that took into account additional financing of Hebrew language courses, help for immigrants heading for Palestine, support for the Perpetual Fund of Israel [Keren Kayemeth LeIsrael], whose goal was the purchase of land in Palestine for Jews. The needs of the Folkists were also taken into account, that is, additional funding for their school. A certain sum of money was allocated for aid to the Home for Orphans and Seniors. The community council brought the kosher butchers, the Burial Society, and the Society of Last Rites under their control. Only the Women's Committee of the Burial Society remained independent and voluntarily taxed itself for the benefit of the community council. The committee consisted of "soda water" Puria (chairperson), Chana Rybkowska, and Chana Popowska.

After setting its internal matters in order, the community council started its social activity. A Lending Bank was founded thanks to which the needy could get percentage-free loans of up to 200 zlotys. In subsequent years, cooperation between the Zionists and the Agudah went well, until the next election in 1933.[5]

The Executive Committee of the Jewish Religious Community Council approved a two-hour closing of Jewish stores and workshops as a sign of protest against the persecution of Jews in Germany. This strike was combined with the protest meeting in the synagogue. Four hundred people took part.[6]

The next elections for the Community Council Board took place in 1933. This time the Bund took part in them and received 4 seats. The Bund was represented by Josef Rozenzumen, Beniamin Kramarz, Josef Berg, and Jakub Icchak Lajbman.[7] After these elections and the death of Rabbi Ginzburg, the Mizrachi wanted to hand this function over to a progressive rabbi. This was met with sharp opposition by the Agudah, which was interested in retaining its influence in Siedlce. The desire to bring a progressive rabbi to Siedlce caused harsh rivalry between the Agudah and other Jewish groupings. Finally, by a majority of Zionist and Mizrachi votes, Rabbi Zelman Soroczkin, the former rabbi in Łuck, was elected.[8] The election of the rabbi was not acknowledged, and for a long time this important position in the community council was not filled. Internal conflicts led to resignation of the Agudah from the management board and executive committee in 1935 and its boycotting of the opening of the community council. The religious life of the orthodox was confined to individual houses of prayer rather than in the city synagogue.[9]

We can conclude from the list of houses of God[10] active in Siedlce compiled 6 December 1922[11] that the oldest active house of prayer from 1800 functioned uninterruptedly until 1922 and most likely to the extermination of the Jewish community in 1942. Up until the year 1900, there were 7 houses of prayer active in the city, including the synagogue. From 1900 to 1917, another 18 came into being, and between 1918 and 1922, another 7. The combined number of seats in the synagogue, houses of worship, and houses of prayer was 4,352. As many as 32 houses of worship with such a large number of seats testify to the great piety of Siedlce Jews and to the fact that religion determined their lifestyle.

At the end of the 1930s, the community council as the representative of Jewish society started to exhibit ever broader activity. In May 1936, it criticized the management of the cinema Światowid for showing German films. The Siedlce county administrator in his report for November 1938 wrote:

> The most recent proclamations and incidents in Germany are causing fear and depression among Jews. In connection with this, one hears among more reasonable Jews more and more often the view that it is essential to solve their problem on the international arena. In Siedlce, the Jewish Religious Council created a committee for bringing aid to Jews who are Polish citizens displaced from Germany. At the same time, the above-mentioned leaflets were issued. Due to the fact that the tasks of the committee did not correspond to the Polish raison d'être and the formation of the committee itself goes beyond the powers provided for Jew[ish] relig[ious] councils, I disallowed the activity of the committee. The issued leaflets were subject to seizure on the basis of art[icle] 170 of the Criminal Code (here document dated 30 November current year L.B. 10/38). The Executive Board of the Jew[ish] Relig[ious] Counc[il] and Management Board of Right Poalei Zion additionally planned to call for popular protest rallies against the edicts of the Government of the German Reich. Due to the possibility of unwanted demonstrations, I disallowed the above-mentioned rallies.[12]

The actions of the county administrator were undoubtedly the result of the policy that Poland was pursuing at the time. Several months before the attack on Poland, the national authorities were doing their utmost to maintain friendly relations with the Third Reich.

In 1938, the growth in anti-Semitic sentiments in the city was so evident that Stanisław Wąsowski decided to counter these sentiments by printing his own observations titled "Letters from Siedlce" in the newspaper *Ziemia Siedlecka* [In and Around Siedlce]. In one of them he wrote:

> I received a letter with more or less the following content: in its concern for supporting Poles, the Management Board of the Polish Union asks me to take advantage of the services of Polish droshky drivers only, giving thereby a visible and inspiring example of helping one's own. [...] At the bottom was a huge stamp of the Polish Union (of support for the Polish state of ownership in Siedlce)[a] and the signature, as the chairman, of one of the most pleasant and most popular Siedlce attorneys. The Judovorous psychosis never appealed to me, and I believed, and believe, that this whole anti-Semitic drive is a kind of disease or mania that arose against the background of an artificially aroused fear of Jews. If they, the Jews, were not able to deal with us when we were not free, then the current hatred of them threatens us with a certain reduction in culture, in which—alas!— our young people excel. There is apparently something in me that does not allow the hair on my head to rise or my knees to shake at the sight of Mr. Gutgeld or Mr. Rubinsztejn. I cannot find within me that panicky fear of them—although I have at times tried to arouse it in myself artificially... Unfortunately, nothing came of it! I can all the more so not arouse in myself that terrible, elemental hatred of Jewry that fills our national and clerical newspapers.
>
> [...] So this letter took me aback. I remembered that our latest constitution, which is considered the testament of the Great Marshal [Piłsudski—trans.], says nothing of first- or second-class Polish citizens but rather subsumes everyone under one benchmark—citizen of the State. This is one objection, and a cardinal one. Another is a little malicious: Why does the pleasant and likeable chairman of the Polish Union, as an esteemed attorney, not show his own example and stop taking on the defense of Jewish cases?
>
> I know what He and other gentlemen attorneys will say: money plays a role here. And I fully understand. But they are demanding that I completely forget about this money. Of the 53 droshkies in Siedlce, only 14 are Polish. [...] I cannot ride with one constant Polish droshky driver because he might, after all, have a better and more profitable fare, say to Mokobody, to Mordy, to Łosice. And he will go there, and I'll be stuck. Moreover, if I will ride only with one Pole, then in an emergency the Jewish droshkies can refuse to take me (I have already experienced something of this!). Well, and Jewish droshkies are generally cheaper than Polish ones. And on Saturdays, when only Polish droshkies are available, you have to overpay the Polish droshky driver—and almost kiss his hand for him to deign to take you— because he feels that if there are 7 or 8 droshkies (because not all of them

do day trips), then he will get a fare any minute that will pay him 5 zlotys at least.

[...] These are all details and trifles... But if someone else can look to his own advantage in relation to Poles and Jews, then let the physician also look to his own advantage. One cannot be more Catholic than the pope himself! I recall, speaking about the currant battle with the Jews, a certain fact, albeit an isolated one, that was described in his day as an authentic one by the recently departed, unforgettable Franciszek Godlewski.

In the village of Gródek [on the Bug River, Jabłonna Lacka Commune, Sokołów County—author's note], which belonged to him, there was a small Orthodox church, converted from a Uniate church, which in the rather large village of Gródek had one single, authentic Eastern Orthodox parishioner. The rest were Uniates, who, though officially classified as Eastern Orthodox, were fervently devoted to Catholicism. Weddings, christenings, and confessions were conducted in secret by emissary priests usually traveling in peasant garb. (I remember my mother showing me a store in the market square of Sokołów in which such a chaplain lived for a few years, by day a shoemaker soling the shoes of Sokołów townies and by night fulfilling his lofty service. He was betrayed and sent to the depths of Russia, from which he never returned!) And so one evening this kind of priest was to come to Gródek. But the Russian police got wind of something because from morning as many as three guards appeared in the village and started snooping around the whole village. The farmers, seeing that something was not right, went to the old Jew, the leaseholder Lejzor, to take council with him about what to do. The old Jew, born and raised in Gródek, buried in his old age in holy books, advised the farmers to gather at his place, since the police will look for the priest everywhere, but it will never occur to them to look for him in the home of a Jewish Chassid. That is what the farmers did. The priest arrived and in the alcove among holy Jewish books, by the light of a candle placed in a seven-armed candlestick, he performed his duties. The police, however, in spite of the night, noticed women sneaking toward the home of the leaseholder and at that moment broke into the home, where in the alcove they saw a figure in a surplice. But before the guards could make their way through the packed crowd of people to the alcove, the priest had thrown off his surplice, hidden his stole in his pocket, left the house by a side door, and rode away. In the meantime, old Lejzor donned the surplice and in the dark (the candle had been extinguished!) he stood like a white shadow that the guards were approaching. Everything was revealed when the lights were turned on: old Lejzor fell under the blows of the furious guards. Sentenced to five years in prison, he soon died in the Siedlce prison. Thanks to this the priest survived.

Why am I writing this? After all, no one will find such Lejzors today even with an electric flashlight. It would be difficult today to expect any kind of noble reflex from people if you spit in their faces, humiliate them at every step, and treat them like filth… And the Catholic youth and, more importantly, the clergy have forgotten completely the lofty principle: Love thy enemies! Today, when missions are formed, when in every school missionary circles are encouraged and pennies are collected so that some bushman or Zulu can be converted—today the whole area of local proselytism is left fallow, but even more!—the attitude is established that the great and moving slogans of loving one's neighbor are for distant export. And at home what rules is going at each other's throats, guzzling up the blood of people of another race, contempt—and limitless, oceanic hatred. And that is why I brought up the story of Lejzor, in order to turn our gaze away from the present and return to those times when the air fairly trembled with self-sacrifice and when no one asked anyone of their race or their faith. So many reflections were suggested to me by the letter signed by the very likeable and pleasant attorney, long may he live! And may he never lack in Aryan and Semitic cases![13]

8.B. The Jewish Press

The written word was and is of great importance to Jews. Judaism forbids the creation of pictures or sculptures depicting God or the spiritual world. For this reason the word has to replace all this. From age 5 or 6 Jewish boys attended cheders where they learned to read the Torah. Later they became acquainted with other holy books. Secular books as well as newspapers were initially fought against by religious Jews. However, the phenomenon of reading them became so commonplace that it was impossible to counteract it. The first secular newspaper, titled **Antyfanatyzm** [Anti-Fanaticism], appeared as early as 1894. Its editor was Szalom Roczin, a teacher of the Hebrew language in Biała Podlaska. He wrote them by hand in three copies and gave them out to advocates of the Jewish Enlightenment (Haskalah) in Biała Podlaska, Siedlce, and Janów Podlaski. They copied and distributed it, passing it on from hand to hand. In Siedlce, [Miss] Zalcman took care of this. Three issues of this newspaper appeared. Aside from very intense polemics with Chassidim and Orthodox Jews, the columns of this paper contained verses that in a poetic way expressed the vicissitudes and aspirations of local Jews.[14]

In 1922, a professional Jewish paper appeared printed in Yiddish with the title **Shedletser Shtime** (Siedlce Voice). The group that published this paper included J. Grohman, Uszer Liwerant, Lewi Gutgelt and Jontel Goldberg. Only four issues of this paper came out in the form of special issues.[15]

The most popular Jewish newspaper was **Shedletser Vokhenblat** (Siedlce Weekly) published in Yiddish. This was the press organ of the Zionist Organization, and it appeared from 1922 up to the outbreak of war in 1939. The first editor-in-chief was Lewi Gutgeld, up to 31 July 1923; then Goldberg, from 1 August 1923 to 1928; then Uszer Liwerant, from 1928 to 1935. The editorial staff was made up of Lewi Gutgeld, Jakub Tenenbaum, Szymon Rozengarten, Ichiel Grynberg, and Anatol Goldberg. Eisenberg, Weintraub, Minc, Mastbaum, Dr. Kleinwechsler, J. Listek, Pasawski, Friedman, and Srebrnik worked with the paper. The editorial office was at 28 Kiliński Street, and the paper was printed at Wasserman's printing house on Ogrodowa Street. The circulation was as high as 800 copies, a portion of which, about 300 copies, was sent abroad; thanks to this the newspaper had a constant income.[16] This paper was mentioned in the reports of the Ministry of the Interior for 1 May 1927, which confirms the influence that it had.[17] In the beginning of 1936, all Jewish communities took up a campaign in the defense of the threatened ritual slaughter. This campaign was joined by *Shedletser Vokhenblat*, which in issue number 8 of 21 February 1936 published a column titled "Mrs. Prystorowa's Troubles" [Kłopoty Pani Prystorowej]. In it, the author criticized the plan to elimination ritual slaughter, claiming that there are more important matters for parliament to address. According to him, this was unemployment. In the next issue of the newspaper, this subject was taken up again. In the article "Ritual Slaughter" [Ubój rytualny], the author tried to prove statistically that ritual slaughter did not influence the cost of meat, and thus economic considerations cannot be an argument for its elimination.

In 1936, the journalists of *Shedletser Vokhenblat* split. Abraham Frydman and Z. Rozenzumen left the editorial staff. They set up a new weekly, **Shedletser Leben** (Siedlce Life). Its first issue came out 6 October 1936. Rozenzumen was the editor-in-chief. The address of the editorial office and the printing house were the same, 6 Przechodnia Street; Goldberg's printing house Express was located here. In the very first issue, there was an appeal to boycott German films. In connection with this, a prosecution enquiry was launched against the editor-in-chief. The paper came out for two years.[18]

The paper **Dos Noyes Vort** (The New Word) appeared in Yiddish in the first half of 1924. Perhaps this was a special issue because the paper did not continue to be published.[19]

Siedlce socialists in the Bund had their own press organ, the **Shedletser Tribune** (Siedlce Tribune). It appeared for barely two years, that is, from 1928 to 1930. The founder of the newspaper was Lewin, and the publisher was Beniamin Kramarz; it was printed in Yiddish.[20]

Journalists of the Polish press noted that in *Shedletser Vokhenblat* and *Shedletser Trybune*, the whole first page was often taken up with wishes in Polish on the occasion of a wedding or engagement. These texts, in the opinion of the Poles, were not always correct stylistically. This was nonetheless an interesting phenomenon testifying to the penetration of Polish culture into the circle of Jewish society.[21]

Religious Jews congregated in the political party Union of Israel—Agudath Israel, so-called Agudah. From 16 May 1923, Agudah began publication of the weekly *Unzer Veg* (Our Path). The official editor of the paper was Berysz Jakubowicz. The editorial staff consisted of Szalom Jeleń (he ran the paper de facto), Meir Szwarcman, Jehuda Arie Cukier, Aharon Nelkienbojm, Izrael Meir Kleinlener, and Szmuel Ginzberg. In the columns of this weekly, Orthodox Jews expressed their views, conducted campaigns in support of Agudah in elections to the City Council and the Community Council Board, and advocated for the traditional upbringing of children. The Siedlce *Unzer Veg* had readers in Sokołów Podlaski, Biała Podlaska, Międzyrzec, Garwolin, Węgrów, Kock, Stoczek Łukowski, Żelechów, and many other small towns and villages. The weekly printed stories, novellas, poems, and journalistic articles in Yiddish. Among the better-known Jewish journalists publishing in *Unzer Veg* were Rabbi Szimszon Hirsz, Rabbi Meir Zeiman, Rabbi Weinberg, Gedaliahu Bublik, Natan Brinbojm, Rabbi Orsze Rubin, Ajzyk Ber Ekerman, Jehuda Lajba Orlean, and Aleksander Zisze Friedman. The newspaper was supported by the rabbi of Sokołów, Icchak Zelig Morgenstern, who was well known and esteemed in the area; he was the vice-chairman of the all-Polish Agudah and a member of the Executive Committee of the Union of Rabbis in Poland. *Unzer Veg* printed poems by "Awraml" Zonszajn from Międzyrzec. The newspaper had from two to four pages and a circulation of 400. The Chassidic courts and Orthodox Jews in all of Podlasie supported the newspaper, which came out up to 1930.[22] A special issue of *Unzer Veg* came out on 28 February 1936 in defense of ritual slaughter. In this issue, Orthodox Jews called for a one-hour strike on 17 March 1936 from 11 AM to 12 PM.

The Jewish Folk Party, known as the Folkists, affected Jewish society through the press. For a certain time in 1926, that is, during the period of elections to the City Council and the Community Council Board, the Folkists published a weekly *Dos Vort* (The Word). It was edited by a board consisting of Jakow Tenenbojm, Menasze Czarnobroda, and Mosze Mandelman.[23]

On 1 December 1933 the first issue of a new paper, *Unzer Shtime* (Our Voice), appeared, and the second issue appeared on 10 January 1934. The circulation of the second issue was impressive and numbered over 5,000 copies. It was published in Yiddish. Izrael Chaim Ajzenberg figured as the publisher and editor. However, the actual publisher and sponsor of the paper was a certain person in Waraw connected with the top leadership of the Communist Party of Poland [KPP—Kommunistyczna Partia Polski]. In January 1934, at the recommendation of the prosecutor of the Circuit Court in Siedlce, an investigation was started in the case of *Unzer Shtime*. The actual publishers were not discovered, but it was established that this was an effort of the KPP.[24]

The members of the "Yiddishe Kunst" (Jewish Art) Literary-Musical Society published a few issues of the paper *Shedletser Velt* (Siedlce World) around 1935. The editorial staff of this paper wanted to attract people of a variety of political views who wished to develop musical and literary interests within Jewish society.[25]

In January 1927 a group of Siedlce Jews with J. Eisenberg, J. Grynbaum, and J. Tenenbaum at their head began to publish a bimonthly in Yiddish called *Vortslen* (Roots). Only two issues appeared, printed in the printing house of Ch. Rosenblat at 27 Sienkiewicz Street.[26]

Special issues were printed on the occasion of anniversaries of various events or ceremonies. On 15 September 1922, *Shedletser Tsayitung* (Siedlce Newspaper) appeared under the editorship of J. Grohman; the publisher was Uszer Liwerant. *Shedletser Zeitung* had four pages and was published in Yiddish. The second issue was published on 1 October 1922 under the same editorship but with a different title: *Shedletser Vort* (Siedlce Word). The paper had eight pages. On 12 October 1922 the newspaper *Shedletser Tug* (Time of Siedlce) appeared. On 22 October, the newspaper *Simchatenu* (Our Joy) appeared as a special issue, published by graduates of the Hebrew school Tarbut (Culture). The executive editor was H. Szwarc, with editors D.I. Międzyrzecki, Szalom Rejch, Efraim Perle, L. Liberman, and Mordechaj Banak. The paper was published in Hebrew with a circulation of 150 copies and was printed in Wasserman's Printing House in Siedlce at 16 May First Street. The Hebrew school Tarbut published a special issue on 12 February 1932 called *Haboger* (Graduate). The executive editor was also H. Szwarc. The paper was edited by Gitel Morduchowic, Perec Rabic, Szlema Rejch, Ch. Milsztajn, and Małka Ibszyc. The paper was also printed in Hebrew in Wasserman's Printing House and contained six pages.

On 18 March 1932, the special issue *Shedletser Nayes* (Siedlce News) appeared. The editor and publisher was H. Rubinsztejn. It was published in Yiddish in 500 copies and had four pages. It was printed in Wasserman's Publishing House.

In May 1928, the special issue *Unzer Yoyvel* (Our Jubilee) was published by the Hechalutz Organization—Pioneer in Siedlce on the celebration of its tenth anniversary. The editor-in-chief was Abram Kimel, and the editorial board included P. Ben-Dovi, Ch. Suchodolski, A. Kemon, Ada Barg, Szaul Rotsztajn, and Cwi Cynamon. The newspaper was published in Yiddish and printed in Rozenblat's Printing House at 27 Sienkiewicz Street.

On 20 April 1932, the special issue *Unzer Shedletser Nayes* (Our Siedlce News) was published. The editor and publisher was A. Liwerant. It was published in Yiddish in Wasserman's Printing House in 400 copies.[27]

In summing up, it should be stated that the Jewish press in Siedlce, particularly during the twenty-year interwar period, was first and foremost a reflection of the activity of political parties and then of the social life of various groups of the city's residents. On this occasion the conflict that took place in the Joint-Stock Printing

House should be mentioned. On 9 January 1934, the management of the printing house dismissed from their jobs four Jewish workers: Jankiel Zonszajn, Mojżesz Szyfer, Hersz Wiśnia, and Srul Piekarz, who were holding back from work on the basis of personal misunderstandings with the management of the printing house. The next day, a group of about 15 youths broke into the printing house with the known Communist Boruch Stański, who demanded that the dismissed workers be rehired. When the director of the printing house, Pokrzywiński, refused, the arrivals wanted to break into the composing room by force. Fearing the demolition of the composing room, the co-owner of the printing house, Szulim Zalcman, fired three warning shots from a revolver. The assailants then fled. However, on the evening of the same day, "unknown perpetrators" broke six windows in the private home of Zalcman. On 13 January 1934 Boruch Stański was arrested by the police, and on 15 January a large display window of the printing house was broken. In the investigation it was determined that the act was committed by, among others, Jankiel Zonszajn and Lejbko Szejnberg, Communist activists already on record with the police. They were arrested. On 25 January, "unknown perpetrators" pasted obituary notices in Yiddish at various spots around the city, including on Zalcman's house, with the following content: "Death to the dangerous and vile schemer Szulim Zalcman! Because he caused a conflict with his workers in a malicious manner, replaced them with strike-breakers, and provoked the workers by locking them in jail. So we call upon all Siedlce workers to battle against this huckster and scoundrel. We will give him a bloody reckoning! Siedlce workers."[28] On 26 January 1934, the newspaper *Shedletser Vokhenblat* ran a paid announcement presenting the events in Zalcman's printing house. It was placed by the printers dismissed from their jobs.

TRANSLATOR'S NOTE, CHAPTER 8

a. This union, variously known as the "Rozwój" (Development) Society for the Support of Polish Industry and Commerce, or "Rozwój" Society for the Development of Industry, the Trades, and Commerce, or, finally, the Polish Union (Union for the Support of the Polish State of Ownership), was an economic organization founded in 1913 as a branch of the National Democratic Party for the purposes explicit in its name. After achieving a national membership of about 80,000 in 1923, it gradually started to decline.

AUTHOR'S NOTES, CHAPTER 8

1. F. Dromi-Popowski, "Kahal," in *Book of Remembrance of the Siedlce Community*, pp. 414–415.
2. B. Łętocha, A. Messer, and A. Cała, *Żydowskie druki ulotne w II Rzeczpospolitej w zbiorach Biblioteki Narodowej*, p. 72.
3. Ibid., pp. 417–418.
4. M. Mandelman, "Yiddish Education in Siedlce," p. 447.
5. F. Dromi-Popowski, "Kahal," pp. 422–423.
6. P. Śmieciuch, "Społeczność żydowska w Siedlcach w latach 1919–1938," p. 83.
7. G. Lusgarten, "Działalność Bundu w okresie międzywojennym," in *Book of Remembrance of the Siedlce Community*, p. 407.
8. *Nowa Gazeta Podlaska*, no. 51/105/ (1933), p. 7.
9. Wybory rabina w Siedlcach 1933–1936, Wydz. II Społ.-Pol. 1919–1939, UWL, APL, sig.747, p. 23; Budżety i listy składek Gminy Wyznaniowej Żydowskiej w Siedlcach, Wydz. II Społ.-Pol. 1919–1939, UWL, APL, sig. 823, pp. 21–33.
10. The word *bóżnica* (*bożnica*) was used in the Polish language to designate a place dedicated to God. "Synagogue" is a word originating from Greek and designating a "place of meetings." It is a house of worship and liturgy and also a place for studying the Torah and Talmud, a hall for meetings, and the offices of the management board of the community council and the rabbinical court. [Although *synagoga* and *bóżnica* (*bożnica*) are often used synonymously, only *synagoga* is translated as "synagogue" in this book. *Synagoga* as a word is formal and elevated, used by more-educated people or in literature, and is frequently used to refer to large objects in big cities rather than in shtetls. The translation of *bóżnica/bożnica* is more difficult, since it is colloquial and familiar rather than formal. The synagogue in Siedlce was called both *synagoga* and *bóżnica*, for example. In this work, the latter has been translated as "prayer house"; here it is used to refer to places of worship of various sizes, from 10 seats to 1,500, and can thus be referring to anything from a "shtibl" to a "synagogue" and anything in between.—ed. and trans.]
11. See table 2.
12. APS, SPwS 1918–1939, sig. 2975.
13. Stanisław Wąsowski, "Listy z Siedlec," in *Ziemia Siedlecka*, no. 7 (1938): 6 ([Polish] orthography as in original).
14. I. Kaspi, "History of the Jews in Siedlce," pp. 55–56.
15. A. Winter, "Prasa siedlecka w latach 1918–1939," in *Siedlce*, issue 1 (Siedlce 1973), pp. 67–68.
16. APL, UWL, Wydz. Społ-Pol., Ewidencja czasopism żydowskich, sig. 604, fol. 17–18; Moniewski, *Siedlce*, p. 53. Most of the issues of this newspaper are preserved at Hebrew University in Jerusalem. Michael Halber made a microfilm of these newspapers and passed one copy to the Laboratory of the Regional City Library in Siedlce. Warsaw University Library also has certain original copies.

17. AAN, MSW WN, Żydowskie ugurpowania polityczne w Polsce w dniu 1-go maja 1927, sig. 246, fol. 8.
18. A. Winter, "Prasa siedlecka w latach 1918–1939," p. 89.
19. *Gazeta Podlaska*, no. 14 (1924).
20. A. Winter, "Prasa siedlecka w latach 1918–1939," p. 80.
21. *Gazeta Podlaska*, no. 24 (1933).
22. M. Szwarcman, "Ortodoksyjna gazeta *Unzer Weg*," in *Book of Remembrance of the Siedlce Community*, pp. 516–522.
23. M. Mandelman, "Yiddish Education in Siedlce," in *Book of Remembrance of the Siedlce Community*, p. 476.
24. APL, UWL, Wydział Społ.-Pol., sig. 382, p. 6.
25. A. Winter, "Prasa siedlecka w latach 1918–1939," p. 88.
26. I. Kaspi, "History of the Jews in Siedlce," p. 233; T. Szczechura, "Materiały bibliograficzne do dziejów zachodniego Podlasia i południowo-zachodniego Mazowsza," in *Prace Archiwalno-Konserwatorskie na Terenie Województwa Siedleckiego*, issue 1 (1977): 143; D. Grzegorczuk, "Prasa siedlecka w okresie II Rzeczypospolitej," in *Prasa podlaska w XIX–XX wieku. Szkice i materiały*, vol. 1, ed. D. Grzegorczuka and A. Kołodziejczyka (Siedlce 2000), pp. 60–61; D. Grzegorczuk, "Materiały bibliograficzne do historii prasy siedleckiej II Rzeczypospolitej," in *Prasa podlaska w XIX–XX wieku. Szkiece i materiały*, pp. 69–81.
27. *Dokumenty życia społecznego Żydów polskich 1918–1939 w zbiorach Biblioteki Narodowej* (Warsaw 1999), pp. 40–41.
28. APS, SPwS 1918–1939, sig. 21, fol. 4.

CHAPTER 9.

SELF-HELP ORGANIZATIONS

9.A. TRADE UNIONS

After the Polish–Bolshevik War, trade unions started to organize anew. In 1922, two unions, actually federations of unions, were functioning. The first was the **Jewish Branch Union**, which included needle workers, leather workers, butchers, porters, sheet-metal workers, and painters. Its offices were at 7 Piękna Street. In was under the influence of the Bund as well as Communist-inclined Bundists. Two currents clashed at that time among the members of the Bund: the Socialist and the Communist. The union had about 400 members, who paid 400 marks each into a common fund. These monies paid for the office space and the secretary. The rest was known as the strike fund, which was dipped into in the event of a strike. In 1922, needle workers, under the influence of Zionists, and especially Josek Słuszny, left the Branch Union and formed an independent Union of the Needle Branch. The remaining unionists formed the Council of Branch Unions, which consisted of Alter Nauczyciel, chairman (officially he did not belong to any union); Froim Śliwka and Berko Szapiro (both from the Union of the Leather Branch); and Abram Feinapel and Moszko Wysoki (from the Union of the Food-Industry Branch).

The second association was the multibranch **Trade Union of Jews**, which brought together carpenters, locksmiths, and bakers. Its offices were at 24 Piękna Street. It was under the influence of the Zionists. It numbered about 200 members, who paid about 400 marks a week for its activity. At the beginning of the 1920s, the cooperation between the two unions was good.[1]

In subsequent years, the two associations fell apart as the result of political agitation among their members and personal disagreements. The following unions emerged or were formed:

Union of Agricultural Workers in the Food Industry in Poland—Siedlce Division

There were eight founding members, four Jews and four Poles. The management board in 1935 consisted of Józef Alberg, chairman; Symcha Sztajnberg, vice-chairman; Mojżesz Eksztejn, secretary; Abram Rotfarb, treasurer; and members Nuchim Lubliner, Berko Liwak, Józef Jagodziński, and Szmul Winer.

Transportation Workers Trade Union—Siedlce division

Founded in March 1936, it had 30 members. On 12 April 1936, the following management board was elected: Jankiel Lejbman, chairman; Josek Lustigman, secretary; Szmul Lipa, treasurer; as well as Beniamin Węgrowski and Ela Kawecki as members. Abram Wajnapel, Ela Tenenbaum, and Dawid Lejbman were also union activists.

Central Trade Union of the Leather and Allied Industries—Division IV in Siedlce

At the end of 1921, it functioned under the name Labor Union of Workers of the Leather Industry or Union of the Leather Branch. It consisted mostly of gaiter makers and shoemakers. Its offices were located at 7 Piękna Street. The main goal of the union was the battle for an eight-hour workday. The chairman that year was Lewi Altfeder. From 23 to 26 April 1922, the union announced a strike demanding a 30 percent raise for its members. It achieved its goal. On 26 February 1923, the union proclaimed a strike of "mechanized shoemakers," demanding a raise for them. The strike lasted two days. Employers agreed to a wage raise of 50 percent. The strike was led by Moszko Kadysz.[2] It was registered under its proper name on 3 August 1932. The first management board at that time consisted of Szymon Żelechowski, Abram Wajnsztejn, and Josek Rowak. Abram Słuszny, Szmul Winer, Hersz Judka Gutman, Ela Szejbaum, Moszko Mandelman, Chaim Ela Kisieliński, Binem Finfter, Grynberg Motel, Moszek Wajnapel, Abram Szyja Rotman, Wigor Lustigman, Michel Tenenbaum, and Beniamin Kramarz were energetic activists. Bund members, Left Poalei Zion members, and Communists vied for influence in this union. The most spectacular action of this union was the strike announced together with the Christian Trade Union of Workers of the Leather Industry. It started on 29 January 1936. The strike had an economic foundation having to do with raising wages. The announcement of the strike was preceded by many meeting in which workers, unionists, and employer representatives took part. The main contentious issue was the determination of remuneration for seasonal shoemakers. The strike involved 350 people. The meetings called by the strike committee were attended by from 30 to 300 interested people. The organizers and negotiators of the strike were Abram Wajnsztejn, Szymon Dzielkiewicz, and Bolesław Pływak. The representatives of the above-mentioned unions as well as representatives of the Union of Merchants, Siedlce Division, in the presence of the Work Inspector of the 29th District, held four meeting on 10, 12, 16, and 17 February 1936 debating the regulation of prices for the production of footwear. The strike ended on 17 February with the signing of the "Collective Agreement for a Period of Four Months" containing mostly the demands of the workers. The negotiations were supervised on the part of the authorities by vice-administrator L. Walicki. The strikers celebrated their success on 22 February by having a community dance with the participation of 150 people. On 6 June 1936, a management board was elected: Szmul Frydrych, president; Jankiel Cukier, secretary; and Chaim Kisieliński, treasurer. On 23 January 1937, a new board was elected: Moszko Mandelbaum, president; Chaim Kisieliński, secretary; and Binem Finfter, treasurer. The union was under the influence of the Left Poalei Zion. In May 1938, it was suspended by the Polish authorities for Communist activity.

Class Trade Union of the Food Branch

In its initial period it had the name Trade Union of Workers in the Food Industry—Siedlce Branch. Its activists at that time were Moszek Ejbchoren, Szmul Sarnacki, and Srul Sarnacki. This union then changed its name to the Class Trade Union of the Food Branch. There was a rally in the hall of the cinema Lux at the initiative of this union on 20 May 1922. This union was under the influence of Right Poalei Zion. In the presence of 500 people, they reflected on the development of Jewish schooling. The rally was led by Szlome Hochberg, a member of Poalei Zion. The first speaker was Abend, a student of Warsaw University, who pointed out the "lamentable condition of Jewish schooling in Poland." He blamed the Polish government, which had brought about numerous requisitions of school buildings after the Polish–Bolshevik War. In Abend's opinion, Jewish workers should object to this and ask the government to provide assistance, including financial, to Jewish schooling. Tabakman spoke after him, agreeing with the previous speaker, emphasizing at the end that these schools should bring up young people in the socialist spirit so that it would be more informed. Next the floor was taken by Comrade Sender from Warsaw, a member of the Bund. He criticized the preceding speakers, arguing that Jewish workers should join Polish workers and not ask the government for aid in running Jewish schools but rather to demand, having strength in unity and numbers. After him, Arnold and Alter Nauczyciel spoke in the same vein. The rally turned into a political dispute between the Zionists and the Bundists. The dispute was stopped by Josek Słuszny, a member of Poalei Zion, who said that in no case does he agree to the proposal of joining the Jewish proletariat with the Polish and dismissed the rally.[3]

Garment Industry Workers Trade Union—Siedlce Division

In 1921 it was functioning under the name Needle Workers Trade Union in Siedlce or Union of the Needle Branch. Its activists were Chana Handlarz, Boruch Apelbaum, and Chil Gutowski. From 23 to 26 April 1922, it proclaimed a strike, demanding a 30 percent raise for its members. It achieved its goal. On 13 March 1923, the union demanded a raise of at least 35 percent. The employers did not agree, so a strike was called that lasted three days. Sixty workers took part in it.

Employers agreed to a raise of 50 percent but only during the preholiday period; after the holiday of Passover, wages were to return to their previous levels. The strike was led by Josek Słuszny, Chil Kotowski, and Chana Handlarz.[4] In 1923, a section arose as an adjunct to it consisting of the union of bakers, who united during the Passover holiday to defend their interests during the period of baking matzah. Josek Słuszny stood at its head.[5] It took on its proper name in the early 1930s. In October 1932 it had about 150 members. The management board consisted of Judko Rybak, chairman; Szymon Rafał, secretary; and Kielman Kawa, Szulim Rak, Sura Rotsztejn, and Abram Uszer as members. It was registered anew on 2 September 1936 with 34 members. Its activists were Icko Goldberg, Jojne Lipowicz, and Beniamin Kramarz. On 22 March 1934, Tabakman, the owner of a tailor's shop, refused to pay the whole of the insurance premiums for his workers, so the union intervened with the Labor Inspectorate. When this did not help, it called a meeting in the union's premises at 20 Kiliński Street. One hundred people came. A strike was planned, but a policeman present at the meeting explained that their demands were unfounded. At the meeting on 17 October 1936, in the presence of 150 people, a collection was taken up in the amount of 100 zlotys and donated to the cause of the Madrid government. At the next meeting, 24 October 1936, in the presence of 70 people, a new leadership was elected. The management board was made up of Chaim Ajzenberg, chairman; Motel Epelbaum, vice-chairman; Chaim Sokołowski, secretary; and Nusym Rozen, treasurer.

Mutual Aid (Relief) Association of Shoemakers in Siedlce

It arose in 1937 and had 23 members. Its management board consisted of Berko Srebrnik, Abram Krawiec, Abisz Rosjan, Dawid Kogut, Chaim Gruszka, Szymon Grynberg, Motel Garnek, and Gedale Karsz. This association was under the influence of the Bund.

Alliance of Small Merchants

It arose in 1937 and had 43 members. Ela Tenenbaum (merchant), Moszko Bronsztejn, Fajwel Rozenberg, and Chil Mejer Zajdencwajg were on the management board. The Auditing Commission included Moszko Judenglauben, Chil Liberman, and Gdala Nisenbaum. Most of the members were Zionists.

Jewish Construction Workers Union

In March 1935, the management board comprised Jankiel Kapłan, chairman; Jankiel Popiołek, vice-chairman; Zamwel Wajberg, secretary; and Moszko Klain, treasurer. The union had 30–35 members.

Retail and Office Workers Trade Union

This union was active in the 1930s. It had 50 members on 25 October 1936, with a management board consisting of Szlema Czerwoniec, Izaak Jabłkowicki, Chaja Ryza, Estera Stejnberg, and Michał Rydel. The influences of the Bund and Right Poalei Zion clashed in this union.

Central Class Union of Siedlce Shoemakers

In the early 1920s, the attempt was made to create a shoemakers union that would consist of both Jews and Poles. Only 50 people acceded. The authorities did not, however, agree to the registration of the union, fearing that it would implement Communist goals.[6]

Union of Merchants and Industrialists

In 1927, Izrael Gutgeld stood at its head. In that year, before elections to the City Council, a conflict arose between the chairman Gutgeld and the remaining members of the management board, who issued a special communique. It stated that the union has not joined the Agudath Israel bloc. The management board announced that, at the meeting that took place on 22 May, Mr. Gutgeld and Mr. Lichtenpacht received a mandate to initiate a discussion on the subject of creating a unified election bloc, but they were not authorized to join any list.[7]

In the early 1930s, Kazimierz Szymański was chairman. On 2 April 1932, a meeting was organized in the hall of the Jewish Home for Orphans and Seniors with the participation of Walberg, the deputy director of the Chamber of Industry and Commerce in Lublin. About 400 people took part in this meeting, Christians and Jews. The speaker discussed the great significance of consolidating merchants and industrialists, presented the consequences of the global crisis, and called for uniting regardless of religious differences.[8]

Union of Painters and Varnishers

There were two unions with this name, a Polish one and a Jewish one. The two unions consolidated on 13 February 1934. This union detached itself from the Construction Workers Union.

Guild of Sheet-Metal Workers, Locksmiths, Boiler Smiths, and Allied Trades

It was created on 12 August 1934 and had about 50 members.

Trade Union of Jewish Primary School Teachers in Siedlce

It was created in 1925 and had 32 people in its membership. It was headed by Rachela Berg, Estera Śliwkówna, and Rozalia Nengolberg.[9]

Branch Union of Porters

In 1922 it had 120 members and was directed by the porter Wajfeld. It was under the influence of radical Bund activists. It functioned independently only briefly and then became part of the Trade Union of the Leather and Allied Industries.[10]

Branch Union of Butchers

It had 50 members in early 1922. It was under the influence of the Bund. In May 1922, the members of the union now returned to work for their erstwhile "employers and masters" as co-owners. This union was voluntarily dissolved, although members continued to meet for discussions of current matters relating to this trade. The organizer of these meetings was Berko Lubelski.[11]

Regional Council of Trade Unions in Siedlce

It was formed on 15 December 1935. The following Jewish workers' trade unions from Siedlce were in its composition: Garment Industry Trade Union, Leather Industry Trade Union, Hairdressers Trade Union, Trade Union of Workers in the Food Industry, General Retail and Office Workers Trade Union, Transportation Workers Trade Union, Construction Workers Union, as well as the Textile Industry Workers Union from Mordy.

9.B. COOPERATIVES

The cooperative movement among the Jewish population was made up mostly of tradesmen and small merchants. Władysław Rusiński has indicated that in 1926 only 25 percent of Jewish cooperative members in Poland were entrepreneurs. The rest were tradesmen, small merchants, office workers, skilled laborers, and piece workers.[12] The situation in Siedlce was similar. The following cooperatives functioned for a number of years:

General Workers Cooperative

In time it took on a new name: **Jewish Workers Association of Consumers.** In 1922 it had 611 members and had working capital of from 700 thousand to 1 million marks. The management board included Abram Słuszny, chairman; Moszko Kadysz, deputy; Moszko Grabie, member. It was under the influence of the Bund and partly the Zionists. The management board included Abram Wajnapel, Alter Nauczyciel, Josel Słuszny, and Fajga Grynwald. The cooperative carried on intense political action. It took care of political prisoners and their families. It organized night courses for older workers at which the Yiddish language, the Polish language, arithmetic, geography, and economics were taught. The courses took place in the premises at 26 Długa Street. Josek Słuszny and Jakub Groman were involved in conducting these courses and lectures.[13] Its funds were used to finance rural schools functioning in the county and run by the Folkists. On 10 March 1923, a meeting of cooperative members was held in the Community Center that was attended by 40 members. A new makeup of the Chief Council of the Cooperative was elected at it, including Moszko Grabie, Szyja Finkielszwarc, Moszek Orlicki, Zelman Frejlich, Mendel Farbiarz, and Herszek Ofgang, with Chaskiel Frejlich, Mendel Gongolewicz, and Frydrych Berysz as their deputies. The management board included Abram Słuszny, Moszko Kalisz, and Szlama Ajzenberg, with Abram Wajnapel and Dawid Grünberg as deputies.[14]

Folkist Cooperative

In 1922 it had 700 members and working capital of from 2.5 to 4 million marks. It was directed by Izaak Zając. The management board included Josek Jabłoń, Icek Altszuler, and Abram Słuszny (a relative of the Bundist with the same last name). In the beginning of the 1920s, in functioned very efficiently; among other things, it bought up dairy products and eggs in the country and sold it to its members at very affordable prices in unlimited quantities. Goods were also brought from Warsaw, and matzah was sold there at very favorable prices. With the goal of increasing capital, the cooperative organized theatrical performances in which amateurs performed. It ran a Credit Association, thanks to which members of the cooperative could borrow money at a low interest rate for a period of six months.[15] In the Sejm elections, the members voted for Noach Pryłucki.

Jewish Horticultural-Agricultural Cooperative

It had 30 members. After the meeting on 25 June 1932, which took place under the leadership of Berko Zembrowicz; Abram Kimel and Moszko Sokołowski from Siedlce as well as Epsztejn, an agronomist from Warsaw, were the speakers. Herszko Cynamon from Krynica tried to convince the assembled people to organize a fruit-growers cooperative in Siedlce. It was not created due to the objections of a majority of the members.[16]

Author's Notes, Chapter 9

1. APS, KPPPS, sig. 59, fol. 5.
2. Ibid., sig. 61, fol. 9.
3. Ibid., sig. 60, pp. 381–382.
4. Ibid., sig. 61, p. 9.
5. Ibid.
6. APS, KPPPS, sig. 7, pp. 24–25.
7. B. Łętocha, A. Messer, and A. Cała, *Żydowskie druki ulotne w II Rzeczpospolitej w zbiorach Biblioteki Narodowej*, p. 77.

8. APS, SPwS 1918–1939, sig. 16, fol. 71.

9. Związek Żydowskich Nauczycieli Szkół Powszechnych w Siedlcach, Wydz. II Społ.-Pol. 1919–1939, UWL, APL, sig. 1244, p. 8; sig. 1118, p. 50.

10. APS, KPPPS, sig. 59, p. 14.

11. Ibid., sig. 60, p. 353.

12. W. Rusiński, *Zarys historii polskiego ruchu spółdzielczego*, part 2, 1918–1939 (Warsaw 1980), pp. 305–306.

13. APS, KPPPS, sig. 59, p. 42.

14. Ibid., sig. 61, p. 10.

15. Ibid., sig. 59, p. 42.

16. APS, SPwS 1918–1939, sig. 15, fol. 59.

CHAPTER 10.

THE HOLOCAUST

10.A. SIEDLCE DURING THE NAZI OCCUPATION 1939–1944

When on 1 September 1939 the German army crossed the borders of the Second Republic [Poland between the two world wars—ed.], World War II began. Poles offered a fierce resistance. Podlasie, including Siedlce, was not of particular significance. Only the roads and rail lines that traversed this area were important. The German strike, which came out of East Prussia, threatened Podlasie fairly quickly. Stopping the Nazis on the Bug River did not succeed. On 9 September, they broke through the Polish defenses near Brok. The actions of the Modlin Army and the Narew Independent Operational Group were not able to stop the German army.

Siedlce was bombed from the first days of September. Air attacks intensified on 7–9 September. Military barracks, railroad stations, roads, especially Siedlce–Warsaw and Siedlce–Brześć, as well as residential buildings were all attacked.[1] German airplanes fired upon people fleeing along Brzeska Street. Father Józef Księżopolski administered last rites to the dying.[2] On 8 September, in the towns of Marysin and Groszki Stare on the Warsaw–Siedlce Road, airplanes fired upon civilians. At the same time, airplanes bombed and fired at a passenger train at the Sosnowe railroad station. Over a dozen people were wounded and six died.[3] On 12 September, the Siedlce–Brześć Road was again fired upon on the section up to Zbuczyn.

The civilian populations of the city hid from the bombing in cellars and shelters. Some of the residents went to nearby villages, such as Łupiny, or to the fish farm outside the city.[4] Others actively joined in the defense of the city, which consisted mostly of putting out fires and removing the after-effects of bombings. Boy Scout Troop 3 from the Hetman Żółkiewski Secondary School distinguished itself in this defense and later took an active part in the underground.[5]

During the night from 11 to 12 September, the German corps Kempf Panzer Division seized the city, and administrative authority was taken over by the Military Board. The Nazis instituted terror and the death penalty as the basic method

155

of their rule from the very beginning of the occupation. As early as 18 September, they shot 56 people on the road leading to Węgrów.[6]

On 17 September, the Red Army crossed the borders of the Second Republic, in implementation of the secret Ribbentrop–Molotov pact signed on 24 August 1939. On its basis, the Red Army entered the city for several days on 27 September. A portion of the residents took part in a ceremony welcoming the entering Soviet troops. It was organized by the local Communists, both Poles and Jews. It was not a large group and did not have a lot of support among the Polish and Jewish populations. But it was very active. It was the activists from this group that took part, as members of the civil guard, in the preparation and the ceremony of welcoming the occupiers and subsequently in the many acts of repression. The entering Soviet troops were welcomed on Brzeska Street in front of an arc of triumph decorated with red flags, hammer and sickle emblems, and bilingual Polish–Russian banners suited to the occasion. The new occupiers also used terror against the Poles. When they retreated beyond the Bug River, the children from the Jewish Home for Orphans and Seniors as well as local Communist activists went with them.[7]

After the city was taken over again by the Germans, a Provisional City Management Board was constituted, with Mayor Władysław Ślaski at its head. It was composed of Poles and functioned until the end of 1939. The task of the Provisional Board was to return the city to conditions of normal functioning, thus supplying food and necessities as well the rebuilding of municipal enterprises, roads, and public buildings from the damages of war.[8]

In October the occupier instituted a German civil administration. In the General Government [part of occupied Poland that was not annexed to Germany—ed.] that was created, Siedlce County belonged to the Warsaw District, one of four that arose at that time. At the head of the county was the county administrator, who had a broad range of activity and police powers. The administrative apparatus and the police-military forces oversaw the execution of decrees.

The policy of the occupier, in addition to predatory economic exploitation, was aimed at the extermination of the society of the vanquished nation. The occupier consciously strove to break the will to fight in the nation and to destroy society both physically and psychologically. This aim was served by the liquidation of any manifestation of organized social-political, cultural, or scholarly life. The occupier deliberately pushed Polish society into drinking and carried on preventative terror, which was to squelch and thwart all resistance. All the forces at the disposal of the occupier were used in the realization of this endeavor.

The list of crimes committed by the Nazis in Siedlce is long. A detailed list of them is contained in the *Register of Places and Facts of Crimes Committed by the Nazi Occupier on Polish Lands in the Years 1939–1945. Siedlce Voivodship.* This is a publication compiled by the Commission for the Prosecution of Crimes against the Polish Nation—Institute of Remembrance. I will limit myself here to the presentation of several examples of Nazi crimes in Siedlce.

On 27 November 1943, the Nazis shot 10 people. The execution was carried out in front of the wall of the Jewish cemetery near the market hall. The reason for the execution was the accusation of possession of firearms and participation in the resistance movement. Paper bags were placed over the heads of the convicted and their hands were tied behind them with wire. These were Stanisław Cabaj, Bronisław Kondraciuk, Kazimierz Księżopolski, Jerzy Lorkiewicz, Bolesław Ston, Jan Ston, Jan Włodarczyk, Ludwik Zacharczuk, Franciszek Zakrzewski, and Piotr Zakrzewski. Their bodies were taken away in an unknown direction.

On 17 December 1943, another execution was carried out, this time on Piłsudski Street. Again 10 people who were hostages were shot. The reason for the execution, according to the Nazis, was membership in an illegal organization, giving aid to "bandits," possession of weapons, and the hiding of Jews. This was retaliation for the killing of the chief of the local Gestapo, Julius Dube. Those who were executed were Eliasz Bartniczuk, Jan Bartniczuk, Zbigniew Kalinowski, Wiesław Kniaziński, Jerzy Papliński, Jan Perycz, Tadeusz Perycz, Zbigniew Perycz, Franciszek Salka, and Zenon Szmurło. This time as well, the bodies were taken away in an unknown direction.

On 4 July 1944, in retaliation for the murder of the commissar of Siedlce, the gendarmes shot 25 of the people gathered in the marketplace. The names of 11 victims have been established: Józef Bułak, Jan Jóźwik, Zofia Kondracka, Teodor Koziel, Bolesław Kwiatkowski, Zofia Myrcha, Piotr Ostrowski, Danuta Stasiak, Natalia Stasiak, Władysław Skolimowski, and Aleksander Żochowski.

In Siedlce during the entire period of the occupation, according to the *Register of Places and Facts*, the Nazis executed 670 people by shooting, including 298 Poles, 61 Russian prisoners of war, 31 Roma, 26 Jews, and 180 Poles and Jews brought to the city in three trucks.[a]

Polish society reacted to the repressions of the occupier by forming underground organizations. They were formed on the basis of old political parties or social contacts. As early as 4 October 1939, Julian Ochnik started a resistance organization in Siedlce by forming the Service for the Victory of Poland, which was transformed into the Union of Armed Battle [*Związek Walki Zbrojnej* (ZWZ)] and then into the Home Army [*Armia Krajowa* (AK)]. J. Ochnik in his underground efforts relied upon teachers and reservists of the Polish Army, and so on people prepared for this type of work.[9]

The National Armed Forces [*Narodowe Siły Zbrojne* (NSZ)] was another underground organization that had a great deal of influence in Podlasie. The headquarters of the following underground organizations were located in Siedlce: NSZ (XII District), National Military Organization [*Narodowa Organizacja Wojskowa* (NOW)] (IX District), and the Secret Military Organization [*Tajna Organizacja Wojskowa*

(TOW)] (subdistrict). The Peasant Battalions [Bataliony Chłopskie (BCh)] had a great deal of influence in the county. The People's Army [Armia Ludowa (AL)] was also active. These organizations represented all the political movements in the country, from the extreme left to the right. They were differentiated on the basis of the strength of their influence and activity. From 1942, a distinct division emerged between the "London camp" and the "Communists."

The main burden of battle in the county and the city rested with the ZWZ–AK and the BCh. Armed actions concentrated on sabotage and diversion in rail and road transport. It also included the destruction and burning of warehouses and military storehouses, the liquidation of people who cooperated with the occupier and of Nazis who distinguished themselves in their ruthlessness in relation to Poles, and also disarming and the seizure of arms.

Sabotage and diversion took place in various forms. Scouts in the "Grey Ranks" within the framework of "small sabotage" destroyed posters, placards, and decrees of the German authorities, painted over boards written in German. The Fascist flag was torn off the county offices, which were being guarded by German sentries, and a white and red flag was hung on the city hall. In direct actions, several dozen tons of gasoline, over a dozen mechanical vehicles, several large warehouses of straw and fodder, a storehouse of uniforms, a storehouse of the Berg Company, and several tons of resin were destroyed. In requisitioning actions, significant quantities of food products and military equipment, as well as legal tender, were captured. Thanks to disarmament operations, over a dozen weapons were captured.[10]

In April and June 1943, in an all-Poland operation, telephone and telegraph wires were cut on the roads and highways between Siedlce and Sokołów, Siedlce and Mordy, Siedlce and Brześć, Siedlce and Łuków, and Siedlce and Mińsk Mazowiecki.[11] Railway sabotage and diversions developed in Podlasie on a large scale. One of the largest armed operations took place on 7 March 1944, when 7 members of an underground organization were freed.

Alongside armed combat, which had to have a very limited range due to disproportionate repressions, a battle was being waged for national awareness.

As early as 23 December 1939, the occupier issued a decree to suspend school activity in all secondary and preparatory schools. In vocational schools, general education subjects were completely removed, and vocational subjects were reduced to the level of courses in the trades. This fact was reflected even in the names of schools; for example, Private Dressmaking Secondary School for Girls was named Vocational School for Girls levels I and II. By order of the occupying authorities, all libraries in Siedlce and the county were liquidated. The teaching of history and geography was banned in primary schools. The reaction to these actions of the occupier was the organization of secret teaching within the framework of the Secret Organization of Teachers.[12]

The residents of Siedlce became actively involved in saving children displaced from the Zamość region in February 1943. Many orphans found foster families in the city, thereby saving their lives.[13]

Toward the end of July 1944, the troops of the First Belorussian Front of Marshal Konstantin Rokossovsky crossed the Bug River and turned toward Warsaw. The Germans decided to stop the further offensive of the Soviet army in the region of Siedlce and retain the railroad link with Brześć and Małkinia. On the evening of 24 July, the mechanized cavalry group of General V. Kriukov as well as Lieutenant General N. Gusev's 47th Army marched into an attack on Siedlce. Unfortunately, they were unsuccessful. On 26 July the city was surrounded from the east, south, and west. The only route of retreat left to the Germans was in the direction of Sokołów Podlaski. A fierce armored battle took place in the area of Borki on 27 and 28 July. The Totenkopf and Viking German panzer divisions were not able to unblock the city, which was closed off by the Red Army. The battle to capture it lasted until 31 July 1944. An active part in these battles was played by the Red Army, whose soldiers thwarted the blowing up of the city's most important structures, such as the cathedral, railway bridges, and the post office. Among the fallen at that time were Roman Gostkowski, pseudonym "Wesoły" [the Jolly—trans.]; Karol Lewandowski, pseudonym "Miner"; Lucjan Ługowski, pseudonym "Luty" [February or Fierce—trans.]; Jan Ołdakowski, pseudonym "Mętniak" [Muddler—trans.]; Zbigniew Pliszka, pseudonym "Wrak" [Shipwreck—trans.]; and Józef Wołosz, pseudonym "Jog" [Yogi].

There was a prisoner-of-war camp in Siedlce known as Stalag 366. It was set up by the Nazis in June 1941. It was liquidated in July 1944 right before the entry of the Red Army. It was divided into two parts: Teillager A, located in the southern part of the city on so-called Rozkosz in the barracks of the former 9th Light Artillery Regiment and the 22nd Infantry Regiment; and Teillager B, located near the villages of Suchożebry and Wola Suchożebrska (altogether, there were up to 120,000 prisoners of war here). Stalag 366 was intended mostly for Soviet prisoners of war, who occupied it from 1941 to 1944. Aside from the Soviet prisoners of war, the Nazis also imprisoned French prisoners of war in 1942–1943 and Italians in 1944. The number of prisoners of war in the camp (Teillager A) vacillated between 5,000 and 20,000. The highest number was noted in December 1942: 19,459 Soviet and 716 French prisoners of war.[14]

10.B. The Extermination of Siedlce Jews

Just a few days after the Nazis captured the city, that is, on 15 September, they started arresting Jews. After gathering them in the prison, the next day they were led to Węgrów. There in the night about 50 of the arrestees managed to escape from the market square, among them Hercel Kave and his father. The rest were taken in the direction of Ostrołęka. This is how Gedali Niewiadomski remembered the first weeks of occupation in the city:

> The Germans entered Siedlce on 11 September, and already on the third day they started to persecute the Jews. They dragged all the men out of their houses and put them in prison. They were kept for 48 hours without food or drink, 200–300 in a cell;[15] they stripped them of their clothing and beat them. After a few days, the order went out for all the men to gather on the square, for if they found anyone in a house they would shoot him; then they were herded to Węgrów. My father, an elderly man with heart problems, knew that he would not make it to Węgrów and that a German bullet awaited him somewhere outside of the city, where he would not even be buried; but if he were killed in Siedlce, he could count on the fact that the Jews would give him a proper burial. When they were in a narrow street, my father ran into the gate of one of the houses. A German shot at him but missed. On Yom Kippur,[16] the few men who managed to stay in the city prayed in our apartment.
>
> When the Germans entered Siedlce, we hid in the garden. A German walked into our yard and asked a neighbor if she was Jewish. She answered that she was not. They could not tell the difference, but Polish boys and Polish women ran after them and pointed out the Jewish stores, for which they got whatever merchandise they wanted. The Germans took only chocolate, but the Poles took shoes, accessories, manufactured goods; they drove off with wagons full of merchandise. The Germans drove even eighty-year-old Jews to work. When they did not have anything for them to do, they ordered them to stand for hours with their hands up and photographed them. My father was taken to a labor camp in Węgrów. When we found out that the supervisor there takes bribes, my sister Rachela and I went there and bailed him out for ten zlotys. His beard had been pulled out, and he looked like death, that's how they starved and tortured them. One time my mother sent me to the beit-hamidrash with a bowl of food for a madman she took care of. When I got there, I saw that the Germans were throwing out the holy books and tramping on them, and I ran home terrified. Then they settled Jews who had been driven out of other cities into the beit-hamidrash. They begged on the streets and sang in yards; most were from Kalisz. They ate in the kitchen that had been set up for them by the Jewish community council. One day we found out that the Germans are leaving and the Bolsheviks are supposed to arrive. That morning, when we saw the huge Russian tanks, a great joy prevailed in the city. The Jews opened their stores and traded in what they could, because not much was left after the German robbery. In our store we had only cigarettes and a couple of barrels

of herring. The Russian soldiers had a lot of Polish money, they did not haggle, and they bought everything. When we found out that the Russians are leaving Siedlce and anyone who wants to can go with them, my oldest brother took the four of us little ones, and the older siblings stayed with our father. Freight cars stuffed with civilians were attached to the military train.[17]

From the beginning of the occupation, the Germans used their entire propaganda machine to influence Polish society with the aim of rationalizing the murders perpetrated against the Jews. This aim was served, among others, by posters that read "Typhus is one of the most dangerous of diseases, whose course is often fatal. Typhus is very contagious and thus can spread easily and quickly in dangerous epidemics. It is very common in the winter in the General Government, especially among Jews."[18]

On holidays, German soldiers would force their way into the synagogue, beat the praying Jews, tear their liturgical robes off of them, and shoot at those who were trying to escape by jumping out of windows. Josef Rubin died this way on the seventh day of the Holiday of Booths (Sukkot).[19] The Germans robbed Jewish stores and homes from the very beginning. Toward the end of October 1939, soldiers forced their way into the synagogue and the Beit Hamidrash from which they threw out Torah scrolls. In a hate-filled rage they tore them and trampled them.

On the night of 24–25 December 1939, the Nazis set fire to the synagogue. Homeless Jewish refugees found death in its interior. The ruins of the synagogue became the place where Germans committed acts of violence against Jewish people; the gendarme Klemens Wieling, among others, acquired a cruel fame there. At the end of November 1939, the Germans ordered that a Jewish Council—Judenrat—be formed. Its members were Icchak Nachum Weintraub (chairman), Hersz Eisenberg (vice-chairman), Hersz Tenenbaum (secretary, whose responsibility was also to be the liaison with the Gestapo), Dr. Henryk Loebel (health division), M. Czarnobroda (treasurer), M. Rotbejn (work division), attorney Józef Landau (social aid), Abram Altenberg (provision division), L. Grinberg (juristic aid), and R. Leiter (general problems).

The total number of Judenrat members was 25. "Members of the Jewish council were usually well respected Jewish leaders to whom the Nazis gave great authority until such time as they were also deported."[20] The council managed the property and the "work force" of the Jews, compiled "transport lists," that is, lists containing the names of people destined for the death camps. At the beginning of the occupation, the headquarters of the Jewish Council was located in the Jewish Art library building at 69 Piłsudski Street; after the ghetto was closed it was moved to 36 May 1st Street (currently Bishop I. Świrski Street); during the functioning of the "small ghetto," the so-called triangle, it was on the corner of Asłanowicz Street and

November 11th Street in Głuchowski's house; and in the end in a building on "Gęsi Borek" [an area outside Siedlce—trans.]. The Jewish police kept order and wore as an insignia of power caps, clubs, and a special armband with the words "Judische Ordnungdienst." It had about 50 policemen. It was headed by Gewisser. The policemen were also better dressed than the rest of the population. They wore high-top boots, riding breeches, and well-cut cloth jackets or blazers. There was also a Sanitardienst, a Sanitation Service, whose goal was to keep apartments, yards, and streets in Jewish neighborhoods clean. After the formation of the closed ghetto, the functionaries of the Sanitation Service were incorporated into the Health Division of the Jewish Council. Alongside its previous obligations, their members were ordered to quarter more Jews into the ghetto. The functionaries of the Sanitation Service were dressed the same as those in the Service for the Maintenance of Order.[21]

The Work Agency (Arbeitsamt) also functioned within the Judenrat. Its director was Izrael Friedman.

The problem of Jewish councils and participation in them by various social activists was very complicated and painful. Some of the deserving leaders of their community in the interwar period contributed indirectly to the suffering and death of their compatriots. But there were also noble people in the councils who tried to do everything possible to protect their nation. This kind of man was the chairman of the Warsaw Jewish Council, Adam Czerniaków. When he became aware of what the Nazis were aiming at by exploiting the councils, he committed suicide in 1942. In his last letter to his wife, he wrote, "They demand of me that I kill the children of my nation with my own hands. There is nothing left for me but to die."[22] The chairman of the Siedlce Judenrat, Icchak Nachum Weintraub, was already advanced in age. A deserving local social and political activist, he served at the head of the Zionist movement and the religious community council. He kept a chronicle in which he wrote down the more important events in the city as well as the stories told to him by old men. Unfortunately, almost all these writings were destroyed. What survived was only that which he had published in the press during the interwar period. The de facto function of chairman of the Judenrat was fulfilled by Dr. Henryk Loebel, a well-known social activist and member of the B'nai B'rith (Sons of the Covenant) Union of Jewish Humanitarian Associations.

As Emil Karpiński recalled, "people literally fought over positions in the Judenrat and the Jewish police; they gave bribes and used every means possible to get into them."[23] As early as December 1939, the Judenrat received the order to pay a contribution of 20,000 zlotys. From spring to winter 1940, Siedlce Jews were used for soil-improving work on the Liwiec River. Workers divided into groups of 15 did the work under Polish direction. The Germans had supervision over the project as a whole, while the workers were supervised by SS men, who oversaw the progress of the task. About 1,500 Jews left the ghetto every day and went to their assigned jobs.

In April 1940, the Germans registered all Jewish men between the ages of 16 and

60,[24] and in November of that year, they listed all Jews on the streets where they resided most numerously. Two districts were isolated on the territory of Siedlce. District I encompassed the following streets: May 1st (currently Bishop I. Świrski), Orzeszkowa, Kochanowski, Old Square (currently Bohaterów Getta), Browarna, Jatkowa (currently Czerwonego Krzyża), Targowa (currently Czerwonego Krzyża), Asłanowicz, Błonie, and Pusta. A total of 3,958 people resided there—3,589 Jews and 369 Aryans. District II encompassed the following streets: Sienkiewicz, Kiliński, Przejazd (currently an extension of Kiliński), Asz, Kozia (currently this street does not exist), Poprzeczna (currently Esperanto), Pułaski, and Przechodnia (currently an extension of Kiliński). Residents numbered 3,306 Jews and 372 Aryans, a total of 3,678 people. Altogether, according to this list, 6,895 Jews resided in Districts I and II.[25] Districts I and II formed the so-called open ghetto.

In September 1940, Józef Landau, the director of the Division of Social Aid of the Judenrat, presented the very difficult material and food situation of the population in a letter addressed to the central offices of the Jewish Social Self-Aid [Society] in Kraków. He asked specifically to send shoes and clothing for the residents of the center of the city, which had been bombed in September 1939 (to this day, there is a large undeveloped square named after Władysław Sikorski). He also gives a figure of about 1,000 refugees who had arrived in the city already ill and emaciated.[26] In November of that year, the Judenrat received another order to pay a contribution in the amount of 100,000 zlotys. In December 1940, the number of Jews residing in the city numbered 13,000.[27]

At the end of December 1940, a decree of the occupying authorities was issued ordering the wearing of an armband with the Star of David and the word "Jude." The marking of Jewish stores was also ordered. On 30 December, a decree was issued regarding behavior in public places. It required Poles and Jews, under threat of punishment, to behave appropriately toward Germans in public places, "Poles by making way politely, and Jews by clearly making way to the right side of the street or sidewalk, making way on staircases, and so forth, whereas removing of hats is out of the question."[28] The occupiers did not initially differentiate the nationality of the residents of the city in many instances. Situations would often occur when Poles with a so-called Semitic appearance would be punished for not wearing an armband with the Star of David. This occurrence befell Zofia Martyniuk (maiden name Michalik) at the beginning of 1941.[29]

The Germans also decided not to allow Jews to change their religion under the influence of the existing situation. On 21 February 1941, the administrator of the Siedlce diocese Bishop Czesław Sokołowski issued an order directed at the Catholic clergy in which he suspended permission to christen Jews, Moslems, and pagans. He did so under pressure from the authorities of the General Government and the decree of 23 January 1941. The Germans, in order to prevent numerous conversions from Judaism to Catholicism, determined that the decision in this matter would

163

rest with the appropriate county administrator or mayor. The order of the bishop was not very much obeyed, because the authorities of the General Government once again addressed this matter with the Diocese Curia in Siedlce. In a document dated 10 October 1942, they ordered that "adults being christened should be examined for Aryan descent."

On 23 March 1941, an unexplained incident occurred in the vicinity of the burned-down synagogue. As a result of the explosion of a home-made bomb, a German noncommissioned officer was wounded. In retaliation, the Germans conducted searches and arrests on Berek Joselewicz Street and Old Market Square. As a result of these actions, six people were shot and many were wounded. The commander of the SS and the Warsaw District police SS-Gruppenfürer Moder issued an announcement in which he noted that "as a redress for the attack on a member of the German army in Siedlce on 23 March 1941 with the aid of explosive materials, a certain number of arrested people were shot to death."[30] The Judenrat appeased the situation by paying the Germans a contribution in the amount of 100,000 zlotys.

From the report of the Division of Social Welfare of the Judenrat dated 17 June 1941, we find out that this division cared for children, orphans (including 65 residing in the Home for Orphans), the elderly (including 32 residing in the Home for the Elderly), the ill, those unable to work, those without employment or income, prisoners, refugees, the homeless, those whose houses had burned down, and the families of prisoners of war. The hospital, with 50 beds and an internal medicine ward, a maternity ward, and an infectious diseases ward, functioned in an exemplary fashion. Connected to the hospital was an outpatient clinic, in which medical aid was given to 20–25 patients a day. The hospital turned out to be too small, however, because "lately no less than 100 people pass through Siedlce daily; these people stay in Siedlce for several or over a dozen days. These passers-by are given meals and often also monetary relief. These people are usually ill, so very often it becomes necessary to provide these people with medical aid. The hospital is overburdened with patients from these passers-by. Unfortunately, Siedlce has suffered greatly from the passers-by because these people have brought typhus to Siedlce. As a result of the decrees of the Authorities, the Jewish Council has commenced an energetic and costly campaign to eradicate this plague (the establishment of a Jewish epidemic hospital, the activation of a disinfector, mandatory baths in the Jewish bathhouse, sanitary inspections of Jewish residences, and so forth)."[31] Patients were cared for by Jewish doctors Henryk Loebel (residing at 61 Piłsudski Street), Nisan Belfor (2 Floriańska Street), Lejb Głazowski (May 3rd Street), Helena Pfau (54 Sienkiewicz Street), Szol Szwarc (26 Killiński Street), and Szlomo Tenenbaum (5 Kochanowski Street).

The Division of Social Welfare received funds for its activity from the bakers' fees paid by bakers and amounting altogether to 3,000 zlotys a month, fees from the register of named families paid into the Provisions Division and amounting to about 4,000 zlotys a month, allowances from the Main Fund of the Jewish Executive Committee, and also from contributions for welfare goals. These last were a mandatory levy imposed by the Jewish Executive Committee and collected by it compulsorily from Jews residing in Siedlce; they provided 3,000 zlotys a month.[32]

Doctor Henryk Loebel and nurses Edzia Alberg, Dora Goldblat, and Bronka Szaferman provided aid to escaped Soviet prisoners of war, who were hiding in the vicinity of Mokobody. They were also aided by Doctor Lejb Głazowski and Doctor Szol Szwarc. The aid lasted from 4 September to 8 October 1941. While in the village of Pieróg in Skórzec Township, aid was given to escaped Soviet prisoners of war by Doctor Szwarc and medical assistant Józef Alberg, also from the Siedlce ghetto. In the village of Wiśniew outside Siedlce, care for former prisoners of war who were already well was provided by Doctor Nisan Belfor. He also provided "medical protection" in actions of disarming Germans and capturing weapons by the partisans.

On 2 August 1941, the Germans issued a decree on the creation of a closed ghetto. It encompassed almost the entire area of District I. All Poles residing within this area were given time to leave the ghetto up to the day of 6 August 1941 by 8 PM. At the same time, the resettlement of Jews who lived outside its borders into the ghetto was ordered. This affected especially the residents of District II. The deadline for completing the resettlement was designated for the time from 7 to 20 August.[33]

On 1 October 1941, the ghetto was closed. A barbed-wire barrier was erected on the streets that separated the Jewish population from the Aryan. No one was allowed to enter or leave without special permission. After the closing of the ghetto, the population's situation regarding food and health deteriorated rapidly. Over a dozen people died every day. "At the beginning of the occupation, people treated each other with heart, but with the onset of terror, extreme poverty, and all the 'Egyptian plagues,' people's hearts became anesthetized and even degenerated; for a piece of bread or the shadow of hope of saving oneself, many served the Germans and tormented others in various ways. Among others, there were rather large numbers of Jewish policemen and Judenrat functionaries."[34]

After the ghetto was closed, Poles could enter its territory only upon obtaining an appropriate pass for the purpose of picking up goods ordered from Jewish tradesmen earlier. But this lasted for a very short time.[35] In spite of the ban, contact that was now illegal continued between tradesmen in the ghetto, mostly shoemakers, and their trading partners on the Aryan side. They sent orders to the tradesmen and in exchange provided food. The transfer point was a section of Sądowa Street. As a result of a denunciation, the Germans "sealed up" the ghetto. Noach Lasman gave the following description of his week-long stay in the ghetto:

> The narrow streets and sidewalks were so crowded in some places that it was difficult to pass. The whole population of the ghetto must have taken

to the streets. There was, of course, no vehicular traffic. Sometimes I would meet a young man in rags, probably a lone refugee from the Warsaw ghetto. Peddlers stood on street corners and offered passersby cigarettes by the piece, flints for lighters, and pieces of used clothing, which they held in their hands. In one alley, small boys were kicking around a rag ball. Everything put together made a depressing impression, and the lack of space seemed greater than in Łosice. [...] Masza's younger brother, Heniek, came and then her father, a slim man of average height. They both worked at the railway junction in Siedlce, Heniek in servicing railroad tracks, and his father in Reckman's well-known firm as a carpenter. Every morning they went out with work groups and returned in the evening. The father continued to hope that they would open workshops in the ghetto that would make wooden ammunition boxes for the army. Several hundred people worked in the recently activated "sheds" but only in the garment and leather branches. Work in a trade was paid, and the workers received a better allotment of food there. At Reckman's, he worked without pay and was under the constant supervision of Germans, who often tormented the workers.

The men in the family worked for free, so the microscopic food allotments often were not even realized, and black-market products were bought with money obtained by selling things. The Judenrat assumed that the physical safety of the residents of the ghetto was dependent on the level of productivity and so tried to find work for girls, mostly on local landed estates. That was probably the thinking in all the ghettos of the General Government.

[...] Soon after, several hundred thousand zlotys were demanded for setting up a German "Kulturhaus" in an expropriated Jewish house on Pułaski Street; in reality it was simply a brothel for soldiers. Fortunately, Nuremberg legislation did not allow sexual relations with sub-people, so supplying Jewish girls was not demanded. This work was too degrading for German women, so Polish girls were "hired" there.[36]

Lasman also mentioned that there were several cheap cafeterias "in the hallways of houses" on the territory of the Siedlce ghetto, but one could not buy bread there.

In November, Jews from the following villages were resettled into the Siedlce ghetto: Czuryły, Domanice, Krześlin, Niwiski, Skórzec, Skupie, Stara Wieś, Wiśniew, Wodynie, Zbuczyn, Suchożebry, and Żeliszew.[37]

In the winter of 1941–1942, a typhus epidemic broke out. It was an outcome of the terrible conditions that pervaded the ghetto. A large number of people were crammed into a small space, and sanitary conditions worsened because the streets of the ghetto were not provided with a sewer system. As Mojżesz Halbersztadt recalled, "Up to 15 people lived in rooms with an area of 10 square feet. [...] There was not enough room for everyone; people lay outside, in the hallways [...]. The

Gestapo who came into the ghetto would ask ironically if we are receiving letters from our families in Russia around Lake Ladoga, since initially we did not know where the Jewish population was being deported."[38] The possibility of contacts between the Polish and the Jewish populations was cut off, which caused an abrupt worsening in food provision. The only thing that could be acquired without restriction was the *Gazeta Żydowska* [Jewish Newspaper], which was published in Kraków and was intended for Jewish readers. Work camps for Jews outside the borders of the ghetto were praised in it.[39]

In December 1941, the occupiers demanded that the Judenrat provide them with all the fur coats that were in the possession of Jews. Persecutions continued the entire time. The year 1942 was greeted with great concern. The local kabbalists feared it because it was composed of the same numbers as 1492, the year the Jews were expelled from Spain. In January 1942, ten Jews were caught who left the ghetto without permission and tried to peddle in the market square. They were shot trying to escape. On 3 March 1942, the Germans grabbed ten Jews and executed them in Stok Lacki under the pretext that they were evading work. Under German pressure, the Judenrat made an announcement supporting the verdict of the authorities. In June, the Nazis demanded that the Jewish Executive Committee supply a certain number of tradesmen along with their machines. At first the place they had been sent was kept secret. Later it turned out that the place was the camp at Majdanek.[40]

The resettlement into the ghetto of Gypsies (Romas) residing in the county commenced starting on 23 May 1942. They were given a deadline of 15 June 1942 and ordered to wear white armbands with the letter "Z" in lilac on their right sleeves. A Platerów and Sarnaki from 10 to 31 December 1940. These transports included over 500 people and came from lands that were incorporated into the Reich. During 1941, German Gypsies (Sinti) from Köln and its environs, from Hürth among others, were resettled to Siedlce. The number of Gypsies staying in the ghetto is assessed to have been at least 326.[41]

The Jewish population in its majority passively accepted "what fate gave them." Only a few attempted to escape or to fight. In the winter of 1942, the attempt was made to form an underground organization called "Polish Socialists." The representative of this organization, Tadeusz Żelazowski, who came from the vicinity of Węgrów, contacted Dr. Henryk Loebel, who referred him to Emanuel Alberg (Emil Jan Karpiński). Alberg started the effort of gaining collaborators for the organization and distributed the newspaper *Polish Socialists*. The attempt to form the organization ended with the death of Żelazowski, who fell in a battle with the Gestapo outside Węgrów in 1942.[42] Some of those who were braver tried to escape with wounded Italian soldiers on trains that stopped at the train station in Siedlce. Such a successful attempt was made by Hercel Kave along with Liwerant and Nelkienbojm in 1942. They arrived safely in Italy, survived the war, and left for Israel.[43]

On the basis of acquaintance, school, social, family, or political contacts both in the ghetto and outside it, self-defense groups started to form. These groups contacted each other; for example, the group of the Jurzyków brothers from the village Kaczory, tailors by trade, had contact with the group of Goldstejn, a tailor in the Siedlce ghetto. The Jurzyków killed a Pole who together with two Germans robbed sewing materials from the Goldstejn brothers and shoemaking materials from Klejman. The action was carried out 1 November 1939 and reported in the underground publications *Komunikaty Informacyjne* [Informational Communiqués]. A group from Wiśniew and Grabianów, organized by Ksawery Zdunek, a custodian at the Communal Savings Bank, was in contact with the group of Halberstadt, the owner before the war of a radio engineering firm, as well as with the group of Dr. Belfor and [Dr.] Loebel. Dr. Belfor and his wife, Paja, cooperated mainly with Ksawery Zdunek's sister, Organowa, who was a midwife by profession. Zdunek passed on information from radio interceptions and food for the doctors and their families. Halbersztadt, on the other hand, assembled and repaired radio receivers for Zdunek and the BCh [Peasant Battalions]. The group of Władysław Makaruk, a PPS [Polish Socialist Party] activist, had contact with the group of Chaim Mejer, a locksmith by trade, and with Zalcman's group. Makaruk passed on to the Jewish side radio communiques and the underground press, as well as instructions on the formation of underground groups in the system of so-called "fives." Mejer passed on information about the repressions that affected the Jews. He also enabled access to his work group, which worked on the railway, to a member of the underground, who planted a bundle of grenades under the railway track. The grenades exploded in the night on 29 November 1940 without causing much damage. Władysław Makaruk was arrested on 5 April 1941 and this cooperation was broken off. Lucjan Koć, pseudonym "Jarząbek" [Hazel Grouse], the county commander of the BCh, was friends even before the war with Goldberg, the owner of the printing house on Kiliński Street. At the beginning of the occupation, Goldberg printed orders for the Germans and passed on their content to the BCh. He also printed forgeries of the occupiers' forms and documents. In January 1940 Goldberg was even briefly arrested by the Gestapo. His printing house was a contact and informational point for the Jews of Międzyrzec, Radzyń, Sokołów Podlaski, and Węgrów. Wiktor Somla, a youth who was a peasant activist from Stok Lacki, had a group that was in contact with the house painter Zonsztajn. Aside from food, information and communiques were exchanged. Zonsztajn's group was radically opposed to the orders of the Judenrat and the Jewish police, who were intimidated with the help of Somla's members. On 20 November 1939, the members of Somla's group carried out a death sentence on Eugeniusz Szamfarowski, who had been accused of cooperating with the Germans as well as robbing a Jewish property and raping a Jewish woman. Stanisław Cierniak from Wiśniew had contact with the group of Jakub Kramarz and Lejba Krawiec, who were tailors by trade. They had family in the Łuków ghetto and passed on correspondence as well as articles and food through Wiśniew. The group of Antoni Kosieradzki from the village of Mokobody had contact with the Jews in that locality, and in Siedlce with the group of Bracha Zalcman. The simple peasant Antoni Kosieradzki accounted for his help to the Jews in the following way:

> [...] I see the incursion of an age-old enemy—this is none other than the old Teutonic Knights [...]. They will not leave here voluntarily without a fight, so we have to fight with them in some way. In order to win the fight, we have to join with everyone who is against the Krauts and strike where they strike the most. Those are the points where we should organize our counterattack. Since they are hitting the Jews hard, we have to join with the Jews and help them, whether we like Jews or not, whether we have some prejudice or other against them. On one's own, they will defeat us or even smash us, so that we won't even know when. If they find someone else, we will help someone else. But those whom the Germans help, we have to fight with these people. They organized the navy-blue police[b] for their own convenience, so we have to treat these flunkeys as traitors and fight them.[44]

Contacts consisted mainly in organizing supplies for the ghetto and exchanging information, and they lasted until the formation of the so-called closed ghetto. In the middle of 1940, the Polish Armed Organization, of which members of the peasant party were a part, issued a proclamation. In it was written, among other things: "[...] Wherever the need arises, if at all possible, help should be given to citizens of Jewish nationality. The form of the help should be dictated by need on one side and possibility on the other side, with the goal of surviving our common endangerment and our common enslavement. Let us remember that after the annihilation of the Jewish population, the unpredictable occupier will commence with the complete liquidation of Poles."[45] The group of Siedlce Jews who had earlier worked on the estate of Drupie in Skórzec Township in November formed a thirty-strong armed unit. It acted in the forest complex called Jata. This group had occasional contact with other underground units operating on this territory. Only six people from this group lived to see the end of the war: Genowefa Koniak; Necia Goldberg, born Lewin; Szelim Zylbersztajn and his daughter, Miriam, a child of six; Mosze Kawecki; and Ela Gorzeliński. Those who died were Jankiel Gorzeliński, Dawid Figowy, Zofia Zylbersztajn, Regina Gorzelińska, Celina Gorzelińska, Szloma Frejman and his sister and her children, Dawid Gutowski, Regina Gutowska, Mosze Miedziński, Abraham Czysteoko, the tailor Grajoncy and his wife, the two Miller brothers, Szmul Tempeldyner, Adler and his wife and child, and Hanka Kornicka.

Leaving the ghetto without permission was punishable by death. Those who were captured were searched and shot to death in a fanciful way: "Usually between 10 and 11 at night, the convicted were taken to the gates of the ghetto on November 11th Street or Targowa Street. They were ordered to run to the ghetto gates while they were being shot in the back. Every evening the residents of the neighboring houses heard shots. The next day the Jewish police would collect the bodies of those who had been killed."[46]

At the beginning of the occupation, Jewish youths organized a field kitchen where the hungry could eat hot soup. The elderly helped in this work, especially providing financial aid. The donors were Ida Gursztejn, Bronka Jabłoń, Andzia Lewin, Parnas, and the universally known Siedlce photographer Adolf Gancwol-Ganiewski. Another form of resistance was the making of forgeries of the occupier's various forms and documents. This was accomplished in Goldberg's printing house on Kiliński Street.[47]

The contacts of Siedlce Jews with the Jewish leaders of various groupings outside the ghetto, mainly from Warsaw, were maintained among others by Dr. Henryk Loebel, Dorka Krygierowa, [Dr.] Głazowski, Sucharowa, and Jabłoniowa. The contact point was the apartment of Julian Grobelny in Cegłów. He was a PPS activist. All political factions of Jewish society took advantage of this point. The contact point between the county commanders of the Peasant Groups for Independence and Jewish activists in Siedlce was also in Cegłów. Liaisons between them were Ludwik Jarząb, a railway cashier, and Regina Kubalska, a salesclerk at the cooperative there. From May 1940, the road of connection and distribution of all communiques and the press to this place was already well worn. In May of that year, an underground meeting took place in the apartment of Julian Grobelny between Jewish representatives from Siedlce and activists who arrived there from Warsaw. Dr. Henryk Loebel and Dorka Krygierowa came from Siedlce, and Niuta Tejtelbaum and a Jewish socialist who was a friend of Grobelny came from Warsaw. A plan and forms of cooperation were established at this meeting; they were mostly concerned with the resumption of schooling,[48] which was resumed, creating self-teaching groups of several people. In the ghetto, there was, after all, a large group of teachers and young women who were occupied with teaching children within the scope of primary school. This action was supported "on the quiet" by the Judenrat.[49]

The underground site of the Provisional Committee for Aid to Jews (so-called Żegota, which later took on the name of Council for Aid to Jews) operated in Siedlce, whose founder was probably Julian Grobelny (pseudonym "Trojan"), the first chairman of this committee. From the minutes of the committee it follows that between 27 September and 4 December two Jews were moved permanently from Siedlce to Warsaw.[50] The organizers of this site were intermediaries in the transfer of money, food, and medicine to the Siedlce ghetto. Members of the peasant party played a large part in this aid and in the fall of 1941 organized the transfer of a group of Jewish professors from Warsaw to Podlasie.[51] The people of Podlasie helped the Jewish population to the extent that it could, for which the Nazis provided the most severe punishment—death. In October 1943, the Nazis shot to death Tadeusz Perycz and his two sons, Jan and Zbigniew, in the market square of Siedlce for hiding Jews.[52] In the village of Kolonia Wielgorz on the territory of Czuryły Township, the Germans murdered the three-member Domański family: the father, Piotr, who was over 70, and his two sons, Franciszek, age 36, and Antoni, age 31, on the pretext of having hidden three Jews.[53]

Several Jews from Siedlce survived the occupation in a dugout near Międzyrzec thanks to the fact that the monk who accidentally found their hiding place brought them food every day.[54] Jews also hid in the city itself, on the so-called Aryan side. Aurelia Wierzchoń hid two Jewish women: Cypa Orzeł and Danusia Malinowska. Siekierzyński, a resident of Rozkosz, hid Dawid and Ida Jom-Tow. He obtained false papers for them, with which they volunteered "for work" in the Reich as Poles. Thanks to this, they survived the war. Siekierzyński helped other Jews as well, passing on money and information. Regina Kubalska, the chairperson of the People's Union for Podlasie Subdistrict IVa, hid two Jewish women in her one-room apartment at 12a Targowa Street for a long time. Ksawery Zdunek hid a Jewish doctor and his wife for two years. Witold and Maria Kowalski hid Izrael and Rachela Halberstadt; they also helped other Jews. Help was received, among others, by Sara Kruczowa and her son, Cypia Czarnobrodówna, Ita Radoszyńska, Dyna Finkielsztajn-Czarnobrodowa, and Arie Nejman. Many years later, on 19 March 1950, Rachela and Izrael Halbersztadt, in their account given to the Jewish Historical Institute, stated, "[...] We owe our lives to them, and they will forever stay in our memories as models of human virtue. God bless them!"[55] The Sisters of the Sacred Heart from Skórzec took in two Jewish girls, Barbara and Jadwiga Górska (assumed first and last names) for two years. The prioress, Beata Hryniewicz, showed particular concern for the girls. As Barbara Górska recalls, the convent in Skórzec was at the time "the only place where there was love."[56] Jadwiga Budna, whom the Germans resettled from Gdynia to Siedlce, hid a six-person group of Jews, among them Izaak Halber, from November 1942 to July 1944 in her two-room apartment in an attic. She was awarded the medal of Righteous among the Nations of the World by Yad Vashem. It has been possible to establish that other residents of Siedlce and its environs also received this medal: Marianna and Andrzej Zawadka, Antonina Helena Biardzka-Kryńska, Helena Kazimierczak-Gruszka, Bogdan Osiński with his parents and brother, Wacława Jezierska-Radzikowska, Janusz Kowalski, and Genowefa and Aleksander Górzyński. It is also known that the Siedlce doctor Zdzisław Szewczyk helped Jews in hiding by giving them medical aid and passing on medicines.[57]

The AK [Armia Krajowa, Home Army—trans.] did what it could to battle against informers who betrayed Poles hiding Jews to the occupier. In the village of Kolonia Ruda within Bielany Township, Eugenia Gajek, who accused the Karpiński and Rytel families, was shot for such a denunciation. Fortunately, the Jews who were hiding were not found during the raid.[58]

Unfortunately there were also bad examples. There were instances in which the Polish population would denounce Jews who left the ghetto or the work camp in search of food. Most often they were turned over to the navy-blue police or the gendarmerie. Those who were captured usually faced death. There were also instances of criminal murders of Jews by Poles. Such an incident took place in Opole Nowe outside Siedlce, where in March 1944 over a dozen Jews in hiding were murdered, among them Dr. Loebel's son Witold, Roman Głazowski [Dr. Głazowski's son—ed.], Lolka Zalcman, Herszko Cygielstein, Leibko Wiśnia, and Romińska.[59] In Stok Lacki not far from Siedlce, the Jewish family of Josek was murdered; they had lived in this village before the war and owned a store. After the ghetto was formed in Siedlce, they had to move into it. After a certain time, they left the ghetto illegally and were hiding in Stok Lacki in the barn of Ksawery Pasemnik. When on 24 May 1949 an exhumation was conducted in what was customarily called the "stone pit," the bodies of five females were found. All the bodies had broken skulls. Another burial took place in the Jewish cemetery in Siedlce.[60] In the village of Trzciniec in 1943, peasants murdered Szmul and Gieniek Krawiec. They feared that if [the Jews] were arrested, they would give out the names of the farmers who had helped them, as happened in the neighboring village of Jagodne. There an arrested Jew indicated 28 farmers who had helped him. They were arrested by the Germans.

In July 1942, the governor of Warsaw District, Ludwig Fischer, conducted an inspection in Siedlce and met with a representative of the Jewish community in front of the main gate of the ghetto. In his speech he expressed satisfaction that the Jewish people were contributing significantly to furthering the German war effort. He also announced that workshops would be formed in which Jews would find employment. This meeting greatly raised the spirits of the Jews. But these were false hopes. Fischer consciously wanted to calm down the Siedlce Jewish community. Operation Reinhard,[c] the goal of which was the final liquidation of Jews, had already started. Information reached Siedlce about the liquidation of ghettos in other cities, about the deportation of people to the vicinity of Małkinia.

On 20 August 1942, the residents of the ghetto got a serious warning. The Germans demanded the immediate provision of workers who were to unload the railway cars. After they were opened, it turned out that it contained the bodies of women, men, and children who were coming from Radom. The car was part of the "train of death" with which Jews were transported to Treblinka. As a result of a fire, it could not reach its destination. When the workers opened the car, they saw about 100 dead bodies, crowded together and tangled up with each other. All of them had died from a lack of air, from heat, and from the stench of quicklime, which had been spread on the floor of the car. The workers, guarded by SS rifles, had to empty the cars. The dead were taken to the Jewish cemetery, where they were buried. Radom native Heniek Adler saw many Jewish acquaintances among the dead. The Germans circulated the information that these were prisoners being moved to another prison, but no one believed this.[61]

The Jews of Siedlce saw with their own eyes that deportations were taking place. They wondered where. Everyone wanted to believe that it was somewhere east, maybe to Smoleńsk. The word Treblinka was also heard. A mood of uncertainty pervaded the ghetto. Cypora Jabłoń-Zonszajn wrote in her diary, "Then like a bolt out of the blue comes the information that today deportations were taking place in Mińsk Mazowiecki, 40 kilometers from us. We are the next stage, but we still delude ourselves, we hope that this will pass us by, because the local authorities assured us that we are an *arbeitstadt* [a work city—trans.]! Many hands are needed for work. The mood in the city is worsening by the minute. I comfort my dear parents, but at the same time, with tears in my eyes, I look at our joy, my beautiful 11-month-old daughter. Dear God, what will happen to the child, and what harm did she do that she should find herself in such a hell?"[62]

On Saturday, 22 August 1942, in the early hours of the morning, the ghetto was surrounded by the Gestapo from a local outpost, Germans from a border police station in Platerów, the local gendarmerie, Sonderdienst, the Polish navy-blue police, the "deportation group" from Warsaw, and a division of Ukrainians from Trawniki. The action was directed by SS-Obersturmführer Schultz.

Here is the account of an eyewitness:

> People gather in the street, laments and crying can be heard from inside houses, from time to time a man can be seen running past with a package, from time to time a shot is heard, voices are heard—"people, tell us what this means, what's going on?" There is no longer any possibility of leaving the neighborhood. My husband leads us to the police station and from there to the roof of the bathhouse that is next to the station, so that we're close in case they'll honor the families of policemen, as had been the case in Warsaw. I crawl into the attic; I hand my child to a stranger and it cries out "mamma." I'm taking you, little daughter! I try to get comfortable in the attic, asking acquaintances to pull a mattress from the table onto the floor, and try to get my baby to sleep. That is stupid, because now it's okay for her to chatter, better that she sleep later, but who remembers about that! It is 5:30 in the morning. There are more and more people in the attic but none of mine. Why isn't Jakub bringing my parents and Dosia [Danusia—author's note]?[63]

Machine guns are set up on two side of the main entrance to the ghetto. On that day, Jews from Mordy, Łosice, and Sarnaki arrived in Siedlce. The local Jews were all ordered to come to the cemetery next to the burned synagogue by 10 o'clock. Aside from those previously mentioned, the execution of this order was watched over by the Jewish police as well. The action of catching those who were hidden began. There were not many of these because, as Hercel Kave mentioned, "for that you needed courage and a will to live. But apathy was understandable. People who had lived for three years without hope, had been degraded, were now psychologically exhausted without a desire to live."[64] Some, especially those found by Ukrainians, were killed on the spot. The rest were taken to the *Umschlagplatz*. Cypora Jabłoń-Zonszajn noted:

> The hour is 10 o'clock. Individual laments and crying merge into a vast, amorphous wail (we found out later that the Jewish police had received orders, under penalty of death, to empty out all apartments and send people to the rallying point on *Umschlagplatz*). For now we don't know what these horrible, heart-rending shouts mean. Terrified and listening to these incredible sounds, I take care of my child and engage her so that she doesn't cry. For now she is delighted with my breast, which she has not had so much of in a long time, but what will happen later? (Later I feed her *cymbalgina* so that she will sleep a lot.) I don't want to think about anything, because I might go crazy—where are my beloved parents? What is happening to them? Now I pray only that they at least have an easy death (it was not until several weeks later that I found out that unfortunately this, too, was not fated for them). Noon is approaching. From the street could be heard the stomping of the feet of out torturers, constant shots, constant lamentation. Suddenly a terrible pounding shakes the attic. It is the demolition of stores located around our hiding place. In a moment they will come closer to us—God, if only my child doesn't wake up. Unfortunately, the noise is so loud that the child wakes up crying out loud. My companions in misery go wild. A certain woman reaches my child and tries to choke it, but with wild strength I push her away and say that if my child is not to live—all of us can die. To muffle the child's crying, they shove me with her into a wardrobe that is in the attic. I undress the child and give her my breast, sing songs, and distract her however I can. Every minute seems like an age to me. Finally she calms down; she has become accustomed to the noise, which had not yet died down. Sweat is pouring from me in streams; the heat in the attic is incredible—Dosia hands me a lemon, which revives me. I walk the little doll [Rachela—author's note], completely naked (she want to walk), around the whole attic—while sobs shake me incessantly. If only Mommy were with me, how much easier all this would be to bear. She and the child would amuse each other better. Dosia forces a piece of bread and a little water into me (you have to have milk for the child)—how good that she is here! The noise stops (I later found out that the Jewish police purposely broke down the door of the bathhouse to show the Ukrainians that

this is not a residential house, so they moved on—this saved us for now). I leave the child with Dosia on the mattress and go to look through the cracks in the roof to watch the street. A terrifying emptiness, from a distance a loud lament can be heard, the screams of people being killed, and gunshots, incessant gunshots. (We thought that these were shots to scare us, but later it turned out the each gunshot indicated that there was one human life less.)[65]

Those who were gathered on the square and forced to remain seated were plagued by a lack of water, for that day the weather was sunny. A member of the Judenrat, Furman, as someone who spoke German well, got up and headed in the direction of the main gate where the German officer directing the whole operation was standing. He did not manage to reach him. Several shots rang out, and he fell dead. At that moment, those who were manning one of the machine guns set off a volley, killing those who were trying to stand up or who were sitting up straight. Around 11 o'clock, a special division of the *Vernichtungstruppen* [destruction troops—trans.] arrived, composed of Germans and Ukrainians. There was a brief exchange of opinions between the leader of this division and the head of the local *Arbeitsamt*. The former wanted to take all the Jews in the transport, while the latter wanted to keep a certain number of young men and skilled workers. Finally, "around two o'clock in the afternoon, the Germans ordered men between the ages of 15 and 40 to form a column, because those suitable for work would be chosen. From all sides of the cemetery, men dashed to the place where the column was being formed, like wild animals, trampling those left behind. In the end, to the constant beating by the Gestapo, the column formed and started to move slowly forward. The highest ranking member of the Gestapo indicated with a stick who would live and who would die. The one whom he had chosen for work was questioned about his trade and had his hands examined to prevent a nonworker from inadvertently slipping through. Whoever showed some papers or certificates that he was an official of the Judenrat was irrevocably motioned to the left, that is, to death. [...] Those slated for death were accompanied by unmerciful beatings."[66]

That evening, the fire brigade was brought over and told to soak the seated people with water. Cypora Jabłoń-Zonszajn described it this way: "'Water—give me some water'—'drink'—'I feel faint'—'I'm hot'—these shouts merge into a huge shout, a shout of despair of innocent, defenseless people being murdered. A policeman who handed an apple to his mother and a little water is told to sit in the crowd and has his 'insignia' removed. Another ducks a bullet at the last minute after trying to communicate with his wife and child. Shouts of 'Sh'ma Yisrael'—Hear, O Israel—crisscross from all sides. People, why still call for God—rebel! You are going to a certain death anyway! You all know, after all, what Treblinka is! Unfortunately, that strong, essential drive to live prevails. Every one of these unfortunates hopes that maybe he will be chosen for work, maybe he will survive. This is understandable on the one hand, but on the other—not."[67]

Janusz Słodkiewicz remembered:

> The Jews were gathered within the perimeters of the Kirkut [Jewish cemetery—trans.], where they were sitting or lying (one next to the other); they were very tired. However, the rectangle of the walls was closed on the southern side by a stretch of German sentries facing the Jews (most of them were sitting in chairs). In front of these sentries two large containers meant for water were placed (of different sizes, someone among the guards said that one of them was probably from the oil mill because it was "greasy"). Our task was to fill these containers with water. After accomplishing this (we had drained probably half a cistern of water), we were ordered to drive back a bit and stop. The Germans moved back [...]. They signaled and shouted something to the Jews in German. Those poor souls got up in one instant and ran to the containers—scooping out water (the containers were no more than a meter and a half tall) with all kinds of vessels. A terrible crowd of men, women, and children and turmoil resulted. After a certain time (a fair amount of the water must already have been scooped out), they started to tilt the containers, as a result of which they were tipped over and the water poured out on the ground. Then the unfortunates threw themselves into this mud, scooping up water with their hands from the puddles that were quickly drying out, touching their lips to the mud, and so forth. The Germans started to shout for the Jews to return immediately to the Kirkut, and when this didn't help they started to fire into the air and then at people. In the end, the Jews withdrew to the Kirkut, while next to the containers over a dozen figures remained, probably dead (whether they were shot or trampled, I don't know). When people ran to the water, this took place over those lying on the ground in front of them. After regaining control of the situation, the Germans ordered us to drive up from the side of the Square (the western wall of the Kirkut) and pour water over everyone, especially the people who were lying down. I don't remember who in the end took over the hose, got up onto the wall, and started pouring water on the people. This caused a commotion and a throng because everyone was running to the hose not only to get wet but to "catch" water into various vessels, even hats, caps, and even shoes. There were those (made totally desperate) who held money in their hands and waved it around—as if this could assure getting water for money. All this probably lasted about two hours.[68]

Another eyewitness remembered, "Members of the Gestapo were drinking beer at a table set up on the debris of the former synagogue. Around them squatted Jews, one next to another. [...] I saw Dube and other Gestapo members shoot into the crowd of Jews, drinking beer all the while. [...] The bodies of the shot Jews were taken by the Jewish police and driven away in carts [...] to the Jewish cemetery."[69] The history teacher Wasercug was shot on this square, because he was talking to those who were gathered and asking them to maintain some dignity in this final hour. When he was being shot at, he shouted to the Germans, "Your time, too, will come, you miserable vermin!"[70]

During this whole time, the Germans were shooting Jews in the Jewish cemetery by Szkolna Street. One of the eyewitnesses remembered those days in the following way:

> When we drove into the courtyard of the prison, I noticed a group of Jews there—men. They were well dressed; they were even wearing fur coats. [...] A Gestapo member announced to the Jews who were gathered in the courtyard that they will travel to the east and will work there, that they are in no danger. Then these Jews were ordered to get into the car that was being driven by Domański. [...] The Gestapo member got into the cab of the car. I was standing on the running board of the car. We drove to the Jewish cemetery. There I saw many dug holes as well as a lot of bodies of people of Jewish descent. These were bodies of men, women, and children. The group of Jews who had been driven to the cemetery by us was placed in three rows in such a way that the first tow was standing against the wall, those in the second row were kneeling, and the Jews in the third row were either half reclining or sitting down. One got the impression that this group had been arranged for taking a photograph. These Jews were fired at with machine guns manned by three Gestapo members and four functionaries of the *Sonderdienst* [Special Services—trans.] [...], these same Gestapo members and *Sonderdienst* functionaries later finished off those Jews who were lying on the ground with their pistols. [...] We drove a group of women of Jewish descent, numbering thirty some people, from the prison to the Jewish cemetery. All the Jewish women driven to the Jewish cemetery were shot against the cemetery wall by the same perpetrators. While they were being shot, the women, unlike the men, shouted aloud, lamented, and even offered resistance.[71]

Residents of the city whom the Nazis had themselves acknowledged as Jews were also shot to death at this cemetery. Marcin Hora, the commander of the fire brigade, described this in the following way: "I personally saw 180 people, brought in three trucks, shot to death at the local Kirkut in August 1941 [1942—author's note]. These were men and women. Apparently they were accused of being third-generation Jews. Among them were wives of former high-ranking officials and Polish military men. Almost every one of those who were shot had a prayer book and other objects for the practice of the Roman Catholic religion on them."[72] Here also, on

13 May 1943, the final Siedlce Jews who until that time had been working in various labor groups were executed. Twenty Polish policemen assisted.[73]

In the meantime, the liquidation action continued. Cypora Jabłoń-Zonszajn noted, "It is dawn—poor dolly wakes and whimpers with hunger. My breasts are empty and so bitten up that every touch brings me terrible pain—but I control myself as best I can—just so the child is calm. I give her a piece of cracker, pour juice on it, juice Mommy had given me at the last moment, and pour a little raw water on my hand. The doll drinks greedily, and when she's done, bites my hand— she wants more. Dear God, how can one stand it to watch this torment of a child! It is quiet until 10—then the orgies begin again, again the terrible lamentation, again the shooting. The orgy of 'resettlement' was started again."[74]

On Sunday, 23 August, about 10,000 Jews were loaded onto freight cars and taken to the nearby death camp in Treblinka. Floriańska Street, along which the column walked to the train station, was lined with corpses. Ela Kaselbrener, who was 62 years old, was not noticed as he separated himself from the group walking toward the train ramp. He knelt before a cross on the corner of May 3rd Street and Floriańska. The escorting SS men did not pay attention to him. Before the war, Ela Kaselbrener had a mill in Siedlce, and most likely local millers hid him and aided him. He survived the war.[75] A Home Army photographer took several photographs of the marching column from a hiding place in order to document in this way the extermination of Siedlce Jews. These photographs are in the possession of the Regional Museum in Siedlce.[76] Photographs of people being loaded onto freight cars, taken by Hubert Pfoch, a Wehrmacht soldier passing through Siedlce on his way to the eastern front, have also survived.[77] This is how Noach Lasman described the moment of the loading: "Someone started shouting 'wasser, wasser— water, water.' Everyone took up that cry. Those in other freight cars also took it up, and several thousand people were chanting 'wasser, wasser.' Suddenly, the sound of an automatic weapon was heard inside the freight car. That was how the soldiers had decided to calm the people down. One of the murderers was placed up on the ramp; he stuck the barrel of his rifle into a small window and fired blindly into the crowd. Screams of pain and shouts of the dying and the severely wounded replaced the word 'wasser'."[78]

The action of searching out people in hiding continued the whole time. Cypora Jabłoń-Zonszajn noted:

> The Ukrainians are having a good time with the *Sonderdienst*. They broke down a store (the bakery of a baker at 2 Jatkowa Street), they took out over a dozen people hiding there and shot them to death. We hear in turn shots and the shouts of those being murdered; a few moments of silence, steps, and the beautiful choral singing of the song "Volga." I look with horror at Dosia. "Volga," that beautiful, sentimental "Volga" here, during

such bestial murders of defenseless people, mostly women and children? How much sadism and cruelty these people have within them! [...] It is 4 o'clock in the afternoon. The shots do not stop even for a moment, nor do the laments and sobs. The child is asleep, so I stand by the roof and watch the street. A wagon drives by piled high with corpses—they are being led by our policemen. They look terrible—pale, exhausted, dripping with sweat. I marvel at their activity: to take part in such actions and not go crazy when you are seeing those closest to you being murdered! (I later found out that thanks to their actions hundreds of people were saved.) The scene changes in one second. Some Ukrainian or Lithuanian (the same devil) is leading a couple with a child. The child is crying with fear and cannot walk. The escort pushes it with a kick, and when that doesn't help, he starts to beat it with the butt of his rifle. Then the unfortunate father with his last remaining strength throws himself at the perpetrator and slaps him once and again. Within a split second three shots are heard, and three corpses are lying on the street, while the perpetrator walks on whistling merrily. I stand at my observation point frozen with horror, but I'm glad that the "pure-blooded Aryan" felt the dirty hand of a louse-ridden unfortunate Jew on his face. Would there were as many such cases as possible. Tears fall from my eyes without stopping—were my dear old ones beaten? My dear ones, how could I have abandoned you! Have you forgiven me that? But I did it for your beloved granddaughter![79]

On 24 August the personnel and patients in the Jewish hospital on May 1st Street (currently the building of the First Aid Squad on Bishop I. Świrski Street) were murdered, altogether about 100 people. All the patients were shot in their beds; also murdered were over a dozen newborns. The hospital personnel, doctors, nurses, and medical assistants, were shot to death in the hospital courtyard. Among those murdered was Dr. Henryk Loebel.[d] Albert Fabisch was in charge of liquidating the hospital.[80] Miraculously, R. Landau [Estara Rosa; see editor's note e—ed.] survived; she dug herself out from under the corpses after the massacre and the departure of the Germans. It was evening when the freight cars were drawn up and took 5–6 thousand people. They may have arrived at the death camp in Treblinka the following day, because the crew did not murder deportees at dusk.

Two days later, that is, 26 August, a group of 29 women was shot to death at the cemetery; they had earlier worked at sorting the clothing of those who were murdered. The night before the execution, Estera Spektor managed to escape from the makeshift prison.[e]

After the liquidation of the ghetto on 27 August, the Nazis made the following announcement: "As a result of the resettlement of the Jews, apartments and workplaces have become vacant in the cities of Siedlce, Łosice, and Mordy. The possibility of creating a life-long living in the above-mentioned cities is currently opening up for ambitious and brave people, in particular specialists in all trades."[81]

The example of the liquidation of the ghetto in Siedlce was included in the report of the united underground organization of the Warsaw ghetto to the Polish government in London and the allied governments dated 15 November 1942. The report was delivered to the Polish government-in-exile by courier Jan Karski. After the liquidation, a so-called cleansing began, that is, the search for hidden Jews. And so, in the bakery on Targowa Street belonging to Jankiel Piekarz, a *Sonderdienst* patrol under the command of *Volksdeutsche* Backenstoss discovered a group of 30 people. The whole family of the baker and several of his neighbors were hiding there. They had been sitting there for five days. Backenstoss, after discovering their hiding place, opened fire with his machine gun and killed everyone on the spot. Those who died in this group, among others, were Haskiel Trzebucki and his fiancée, Franka Piekarz, as well as the family of Jankiel Dekiel. The entire Lewin family was discovered in the attic of a house on Asłanowicz Street. They were led to the cemetery and shot to death. Kuba miraculously survived—his fatally shot mother covered him with her body while falling down. Kuba stayed that way for several hours and at dawn ran away from the cemetery. He hid thanks to the help of his friends and obtained forged documents. Fifty people were discovered on the territory of the Jewish bathhouse and killed; twenty people, including the family of Efraim Celnik, [were killed] in the offices of the Judenrat. During the "cleansing" operation, about 200 people were found and murdered, among others, Przeździecki and Goldblat. The corpses were collected by groups of Jews, who themselves pulled a two-wheeled cart they called an Arba.[f] They pulled it to the gates of the ghetto and transferred the bodies onto horse-drawn wagons driven by Poles. They were the ones who took the bodies to the Jewish cemetery.

Out of about 600 people chosen earlier, the so-called small ghetto was formed, called the *Drayek* [Yiddish for "triangle"—trans.]. It was located in the triangle of Sokołowska, Asłanowicz, and November 11th Streets. These people were used for "clean-up work" after the liquidation of the ghetto. In the following days, after receiving assurances of personal safety by the German authorities, about 1,500 Jews reported to the small ghetto. Some of them had been hiding on the territory of the ghetto and others in the close vicinity. A new Judenrat was formed, headed by Hersz Ajzenberg and two members, Mosze Rotbejn (director of the employment office) and Anatol Goldberg (director of food provision). An out-patient clinic was formed, the director of which was the only surviving Jewish doctor, Balfor. A police force was also created that occupied a separate little house and functioned as sentries and for the maintenance of order. Rubinstein became its commander, and after him this function was taken over by Abraham Gessler.

"The Germans left the small ghetto as bait. People started flocking to it, seeing that mass murders were no longer taking place and succumbing to the rumors that the worst has over and that somehow one can survive. Life has its laws, and stalls with food and used articles opened up on the territory of the small ghetto. People peddled whatever they could through the wires. For rags, footwear, dishes, and God knows what, you could get bread, potatoes, and at least some bit to east."[82] The number of people crowded into the small ghetto is estimated at 1,500–3,000. Not only Siedlce Jews were there but also escapees from other towns wandering around the area as well as Gypsies. Conditions in the ghetto were awful, with an insufficiency of water constantly being experienced. Some of those settled in the ghetto collected abandoned property, which was then sorted. The better things were sent to Germany for victims of bombings, the rest was sold to the Polish population.

The functioning of the "Jewish residential district" in Siedlce was confirmed by the decree dated 28 October 1942 issued by Krüger, the chief of the SS and of the police of the General Government. Cypora Jabłoń-Zonszajn wrote, "We are sitting in horrible conditions in a dirty, louse-ridden neighborhood filled with Gypsies, who have become our heirs—in a neighborhood in which death constantly hangs in the air. The mood is almost incessantly panicked. Every day new people arrive, fugitives from wagons from other cities: Łuków, Węgrów, Międzyrzec, Kałuszyn, Sokołów Podlaski, and many, many more. Every day we hear that in one place the operation was repeated a second time, in another a third time! Why are they not moving us yet? This time, however, we have no illusions. We know that this will not pass us by."[83] Jews and Poles were aware of the hopeless situation. After many years, Czesław Ulko, in characterizing that time, said, "I was walking to work after lunch. I saw a Jew I knew, the shopkeeper's son Jankiel Zybersztein from Kazimierz Street, sweeping the street by the county offices. I said to him, 'Jankiel flee because they'll kill you.' Then he said, 'Okay, but where?' Only later did I reflect on the aptness of his answer."[84]

Wiktoria Śliwowska noted an incident from the environs of Siedlce, where a young boy had escaped from the ghetto and was trying to survive, living in such a way as not to be noticed by anyone:

> Hunger was becoming worse and worse in Warsaw for the average resident. To say nothing of the closed ghetto. When I was ten years old, I went for the first time to a village outside Siedlce. I went there several times during the war, where by working very hard I could eat my fill of potatoes and milk. From time to time, something better would come up, such as fruit in the summer. One time, I'm standing under a tree, looking for the ripest cherries. And there were many cherry trees there covered with fruit. Suddenly, a Jewish boy, a little older than I, appears noiselessly in front of me and shows me how to eat cherries so that no one can tell whether a person or a bird ate it. He took a ripe cherry into his mouth in such a way that the fruit stayed in his mouth but the pit was left attached to the stem.

I do the same, turn around, and he's gone. The next day toward evening, he appeared unexpectedly in front of me and handed me some wild berries on a large leaf. I understood that very early in the morning he goes into the woods with the cows of the farmer who is hiding him. The Germans at that time had conducted several roundups in the village at night. At first I did not understand but later it became clear to me why every time I saw him, even on a sweltering day, he was wearing his coat. I understood that he always wanted to be ready to run and have all his belongings with him. I found out from my brother, who sometime visited me from Warsaw, that the name of my acquaintance was Abram. I also understood that he often observed me, he knew me, and he heard my conversations with others; that he himself, in hiding, trusted me and appeared to me, seeking out contact with people. Unfortunately, I don't know whether by some miracle he survived. I fear not.[85]

The first order given to the new Judenrat by the German authorities was the command to pay the fire department for pouring water on people during the resettlement. A guard stood at the gate of the small ghetto consisting of two Jewish policemen and one Polish navy-blue policeman. The ghetto received a daily ration of bread, which came to 250 grams per person. It was also permitted to bring in candles, matches, coffee, and chamomile.[86]

A group of Chassidim, followers of the tzadik from Radzyń, ended up in the ghetto. They differed from the rest of the residents not only in their traditional garb but also in their behavior. They helped each other and considered their most important task to be the gathering of holy books, in which no one was interested. They helped believers celebrate Rosh Hashanah (New Year)[87] and Yom Kippur (Day of Judgment).[88] The Chassidim formed "an island amidst the sea of inhuman behavior," where stripping corpses of everything that could still be useful was considered something normal. This is how Noach Lasman described those days: "The general public in Siedlce was resigned. No escape from the trap could be seen. People were starving, exhausted, ragged, sleepy, overworked, and they awaited death as a salvation. The resignation was all the deeper since even a kind word could not be heard from anywhere. Without someone's help or kindness from the outside, you couldn't even dream of surviving. For those who had jumped out of the trains of death, the ghetto in Siedlce was now the closest place of refuge. The autumn rains chased people from the fields, and camp managers got rid of those who could not work by sending them 'home'."[89]

Over a dozen children were staying "illegally" in hiding in the small ghetto. All the residents were taken outside the city on 25 November 1942 to what was called Gęsi Borek [goose woods—trans.] (the B. Limanowski colony). The pretext was supposed to be the threat of an outbreak of a typhus epidemic, which could have infected the rest of the city. The displaced people were allowed to bring with them only what they could carry. The sick and the old were allowed to be driven in carts. The pretense was that the settlement there of Jews who survived the liquidation was of a permanent nature. All the members of the Jewish Executive Committee were given passes allowing them to stay in the city for a period of three months. Ida Jom-Tow wrote, "Not far from Gęsi Borek was a glassworks, in which several dozen Jews worked. They lived close to the glassworks. Things that were smuggled from the ghetto were also brought to them. During the last two days of the functioning of the small ghetto, several wagonloads of goods managed to be brought. The Gestapo and the gendarmerie 'turned a blind eye' and pretended not to see what the Jews were moving. Naïve people were happy that they had managed to trick the Germans. On the last day before the move to the new ghetto, several dozen people were secretly taken to the glassworks, among them the old and the sick. They were hidden in the neighboring barn."[90]

One of the blocks of this ghetto was occupied earlier by Gypsies. After three days, on 28 November, the Nazis liquidated this ghetto.[91] The area was surrounded during the night. In the morning people were driven out of the houses, positioned in a column of five people, and herded to the train station, where freight cars were already waiting. Some of the marchers were preparing for death in prayerful moods and clothing. At the head of the procession walked the aged Icchak Nachum Weintraub. People already knew what awaited them. "As soon as the train moved, people in many cars started energetically breaking openings. The well-known Siedlce master locksmith Szymka Wilk had taken his tools with him and could use them to open the locked car. When the train was at full speed, Wilk opened his car and a large number of people sentenced to death jumped out. Many also escaped from the car that contained the Jewish police. But many were shot on the spot or captured."[92]

This is how Samuel Willenberg, a prisoner of the death camp, described the arrival of this transport to Treblinka: "Mitte shouted for the freight cars to be opened. A child's hand slid out of a crack in the door. Suddenly we saw that all the cars were filled with corpses. Intertwined bodies of adults and children. Stripped and completely naked. One solid mass of human bodies with signs of beating and bullet holes."[93]

10.C. Labor Camps for Jews

Labor camps for Jewish should also be mentioned. These camps had as their goal the destruction of the Jewish nation through hard physical labor. There were several camps within the city limits in which only Jews worked.

Camp I—Military Provision depot No. 6 (A.V.L.)

This camp was set up in the beginning of 1940 and closed down in 1942. It was located in military barracks. The area of the camp was about 5 square kilometers. The prisoners were housed in a two-story brick building on the site of the old barracks of the 22nd infantry regiment. On the average, about 100 people worked in it. Altogether, about 5,000 Jews went through this camp. The prisoners worked on the territory of the camp in unloading freight cars containing food. During the liquidation of the camp, the prisoners were settled in the small ghetto.[94]

Camp II—Reckmann Construction Company

The name comes from the last name of the owner, Richard Reckmann. It was established in the fall of 1941 and liquidated in March 1943. It was located in the depot and two barracks next to the train tracks. The camp encompassed about 5 square kilometers. On the average, about 500 people stayed in it. Altogether, 15,000 Jews went through the camp. The prisoners worked in the Reckmann company building tracks and in the railway workshops, as well as on construction sites. There was an epidemic of typhus and dysentery in the camp. There was an infirmary. For their heavy, almost superhuman work, the prisoners received 200 grams of bread, half a liter of black coffee, and one liter of soup made of chestnut puree, rutabaga, or beets. Many Jews were shot to death by the Nazis; many died as a result of beatings. There were instances of burying prisoners "alive" on the construction site. The seriously ill were sent back to the ghetto. The camp was essentially intended to destroy the people who worked there. The testimony of Srul Mejer, a prisoner of this camp, attests to this: "A dentist from Siedlce, a Litwak, was shot by one of the Germans guarding us for walking slowly to work."[95] An eighty-year-old ritual butcher was beaten and trampled on by the German guards because he was not able to unload coal. Severely beaten, he soon died. When the camp was liquidated, almost all the prisoners were shot to death. Three people managed to survive: Srul Krawiec, Izaak Rafał, and Motl Orlański.[96] The barracks burned down during the battle for the city in July 1944.

Camp III—Kisgrube (Gravel Pit) German Construction Inspectorate No. 8

It was established in the fall of 1941 and liquidated on 14 May 1943. It was located behind the Siedlce–Łuków railroad track by the Łuków road. It occupied an area of about 2 square kilometers. About 300 people on average stayed in it and lived in two wooden barracks and railway cars. The prisoners worked in the gravel pit, where the norm was loading 150–200 wagons of sand a day. Food consisted of 250 grams of bread and 1 liter of soup. The director of the camp was inspector Hoppe. There were instances of deaths due to beatings as well as during loading work. During the liquidation of the camp, some of the prisoners died in buildings that were set on fire by the Nazis, and the rest were shot to death at the Jewish cemetery. The only survivor was Leon Kapłan.[97]

Camp IV—Wolfer und Göbel Road Construction Company

It was established in the fall of 1941 and liquidated in October 1942. It was located on Brzeska Street. About 2,000 people on average stayed there, including about 100 from Łosice. The prisoners lived in ten wooden barracks. The director was a certain Wasilewski, a Volksdeutsche. The leader of the Jewish police was Mosze Hubermann. Altogether, 20,000 Jews went through the camp. The prisoners doing roadwork in the Wolfer und Göbel Company labored, among other things, on the roads and railroad tracks between Siedlce and Brześć and Siedlce and Warsaw. This company acted within the framework of the Todt Organization. A dysentery epidemic raged in the camp. During the liquidation of the camp, the prisoners were settled in the small ghetto.[98]

Camp V—Bauzug [Work Train]

It was located next to the railroad station. The camp was occupied permanently by about 100 prisoners, who lived in train cars. These prisoners worked on repairing train tracks on the Siedlce–Brześć line on the Bug River. The director of Bauzug was Walter, a railway man from Wuppertal.

Camp VI—German Construction Inspectorate

It was located in a barrack connected to the Railway Houses. It functioned from 1942 to 14 May 1943. It was occupied by 60 people, who were engaged in unloading construction material. The director of the camp was the German Schefner.[99]

In addition to the above-mentioned camps, Jewish units of about 30 people worked on the territory of the Agricultural Syndicate, about 60 worked in the glassworks located in Gęsi Borek, and about 100 people worked at the military airport located in Nowe Siedlce.

The number of Jews who passed through the Siedlce labor camps should not be connected only with local Jews. Jews from neighboring cities, towns, and villages could be found in the labor camps, as well as those displaced for other localities. Altogether, 17,000 Jews died in Siedlce or were removed to Treblinka. They came not only from Siedlce but also from ghettos in Łosice (from Łosice, Huszlew, Olszanka, and Świniary), Sarnaki (from Sarnaki, Górki, Kornica, and Łysów), and Mordy (Mordy, Krzesk-Królowa Niwy, Przesmyki, Stok Ruski, and Tarków). Only a small number managed to hide, but even they continued to be in danger. The Siedlce dentist Stanisław Gilgun died during the Warsaw Uprising. Antoni and Stanisław Górka, hiding in Warsaw, were discovered and tortured to death in a Gestapo prison.

In 1944, the Germans tried to wipe out the traces of their crimes. [Wilhelm] Koppe, the Superior Commander of the SS and Police in the General Government, issued an order to the commanders of the Security Police and SD [security service—trans.] in specific districts to form "special 1005 units" (*Sonderkommando 1005*). They were given the order to exhume and burn the bodies of Jews murdered in the General Government so that the Red Army would not be able to find traces of the extermination of the population in occupied territories. In the Warsaw district, this operation was directed by Kurt Nicolaus. He had at his disposition several functionaries of the Warsaw security police, a commando unit of the [Jewish] police service, numbering 60 people, as well as a Jewish labor group from the Łódź ghetto. As he himself testified, "special unit 1005" under his command exhumed and burned hundreds of bodies in the regions of Siedlce, Sokołów Podlaski, and Węgrów alone.[100] The "clean-up" procedure took place in the following manner: the German police would surround an area, a Jewish commando unit would dig up the bodies, place them on wooden or steel grills, pour gasoline on them, and burn them to ashes. The human ashes were then poured into the former places of burial, and the whole thing was covered with soil. During this operation, the stench of burning bodies drifted over the city for several days.[101]

EDITOR'S NOTES, CHAPTER 10

a. The number of executed Jews cited here does not include those executed during and after the liquidation of the ghetto.

b. The navy-blue police (Polish: *Granatowa policja*)—the popular name of the Polish police in the German-occupied area of the General Government during the Second World War. The official name of the organization was Polish Police of the General Government (German: *Polnische Polizei im Generalgouvernement*; Polish: *Policja Polska Generalnego Gubernatorstwa*).

c. Operation Reinhard (German: *Aktion Reinhard* or *Einsatz Reinhard*)—the code name given to the Nazi plan to murder Polish Jews in the General Government. The operation marked the most deadly phase of the Holocaust with the introduction of extermination camps.

d. Melech Fainzilber, in *Oif di khurbot fun main haim (khurban Shedlets)* [On the Ruins of My House (the Extermination of Siedlce)] (Tel Aviv, 1952), provides the following list of executed hospital personnel and their family members:

Dr. Henryk Loebel, Hospital Director, Gynecology;

Dr. Loebel's wife;

Dr. Leon Głazowski, Internal Diseases;

Dr. Głazowski's wife;

Dr. Szaul Szwarc, Infection Diseases;

Dr. Szwarc's wife;

Dr. Szloma Tenenbaum, Infection Diseases;

Josef Alberg, Medical Assistant;

Jakub Tenenbaum, Medical Assistant;

Fela (Fejga) Friedman, Nurse;

Sara Rabinowicz, Nurse;

Edzia Alberg, Nurse;

Rywka Barg, Nurse;

Cesia Temkin, youth, hospital employee;

Dwora (Dorka) Goldblat, Nurse;

Bronka Szaferman, Nurse;

Mrs. Epsztein, Nurse, from Łódź;

Estera Zalcman (mother of lab technician Lola Zalcman, who escaped execution);

Rachela (Ela) Zalcman, Lola's younger sister

Berl Czarnobroda;

Berl Czarnobroda's wife;

Mrs. Lewin-Ajzensztadt;

Ewa Grinszpan;

Dr. Nisan Belfor, a surgeon at the hospital, was out of town at the time of the execution. He organized a hospital in the small ghetto and committed suicide before its liquidation;

Dr. Helena Pfau, another doctor associated with the hospital, committed suicide on Umschlagplatz by taking cyanide before the liquidation of the hospital.

e. List of women executed at the Jewish cemetery on 26 August 1942 according to Fainzilber in *Oif di khurbot fun main haim*:

Estera Rosa Landau;

Sara Jabłkowicz;

Chana Piekarz;

[Mrs.] Stołowy;

[Mrs.] Stołowy, sister;

Sara Waksztajn;

[Mrs.] Ferster-Wajman;

Sara Gelbisz;

Jenta Lederhendler;

Golda Goldring;

Chawa Felzensztajn;

[Mrs.] Felzensztajn-Miodownik;

Chana Kramarz;

Gitel Kramarz;

[Mrs.] Bronsztajn;

Sara Grynwald;

[Mrs.] Suchodolski (wife of Nachman);

Bracha Radoszyńska-Nojman;

Rachela Cukerman;

Rywka Felzensztajn;

Rachela Kon;

Sara Klajnlerer;

Rachela Ajnemer;

Towa Epelblat;

Estera Kisielińska;

Niunia Felzensztajn;

Perla Rybak;

[Mrs.] Kornicka.

Estera Spektor was with the group of 30 women jailed before the execution, but she escaped. The name of one woman is not included in the list of the 29 who were executed.

f. Arba—Talmudic term referring to a barge or wagon for transporting produce. Not to be confused with the more common *arba*, meaning "four."

Author's Notes, Chapter 10

1. S. Lewandowska, *Ruch oporu na Podlasiu* (Warsaw, 1976), pp. 35–36.
2. Okręgowa Komisja Badania Zbrodni Niemieckich (OKBZN) w Siedlcach, sig. 26, p. 30.
3. S. Lewandowska, *Ruch oporu na Podlasiu*, pp. 35–36.
4. A. Zawadzka, *Szkoła siedlecka w okresie okupacji hitlerowskiej 1939–1944* (Warsaw, 1986), p. 63.
5. H. Piskunowicz, "Siedlce o okresie okupacji hitlerowskiej w latach 1939–1944," in *Społeczeństwo siedleckie w walce o wyzwolenie narodowe i społeczne*, ed. J.R. Szaflik (Warsaw, 1981), p. 253.
6. *Rejestr miejsc i faktów zbrodni popełnionych przez okupanta hitlerowskiego na ziemiach polskich w latach 1939–1945. Województwo siedleckie* (Warsaw, 1985), p. 235.
7. "I left my gas mask in Israel and came to Siedlce," author's interview with Henryk Rajze published in *Kurier Siedlecki*, no. 2 (14 March 1991).
8. For more on this subject, see J. Kuligowski, "Tymczasowy Zarząd Miejski w Siedlcach w świetle protokołów posiedzeń," in *Prace Archiwalno-Konserwatorskie na Terenie Województwa Siedleckiego*, no. 6 (1989): 88.
9. J. Ochnik, *Rozkaz konspiracja* (Warsaw, 1995), p. 43.
10. H. Piskunowicz, "Siedlce o okresie okupacji hitlerowskij w latach 1939–1944," p. 265.
11. S. Lewandowska, *Kalendarium ważniejszych działań bojowo-dywersyjnych* (Warsaw, 1972), p. 411.
12. A. Zawadzka, *Szkoła siedlecka w okresie okupacji hitlerowskiej 1939–1944*. This

phenomenon is also described in *Działalność Tajnej Organizacji Nauczycielskiej na terenie obecnego woj. siedleckiego w latach 1939-1944* (Siedlce, 1992), published by the District Historical Commission in Siedlce affiliated with the Polish Teachers Union.

13. B. Kozaczyńska, *Losy dzieci z Zamojszczyzny wysiedlonych do powiatu siedleckiego w latach 1943-1945* (Siedlce, 2006).

14. For more information, see E. Kopówka, *Stalag 366 Siedlce* (Siedlce, 2004); *Obozy hitlerowskie na ziemiach polskich 1939-1945. Informator encykopedyczny* (Warsaw, 1979), pp. 447-448.

15. There should be 20-30.

16. Yom Kippur—Day of Atonement or Day of Judgment, the most solemn Jewish holiday, falling on the tenth day of Tishri (September–October). This is a day of the forgiveness of sins by God both for individual people and for the whole nation. Fasting and mortification are mandatory on this day.

17. H. Grynberg, *Dzieci Syjonu* (Warsaw, 1994), pp. 24-25 (based on the testimony of Gedali Niewiadomski, age 13, from Siedlce).

18. APS, Zbiór afiszy okupacyjnych powiatu siedleckiego.

19. The Holiday of Booths (the Feast of Tabernacles, or Sukkot)—commemorating the times in which the sons of Israel lived in the desert after the exodus from Egyptian slavery. It starts on the fifteenth day of the month of Tishri (September–October) and lasts seven days. On this holiday it is customary to sleep and take meals in structures built especially for this purpose next to your house. On the seventh day of this holiday, called Hoshana Rabbah, that is, on the day when that tragedy took place, prayers are said in the synagogue, and the podium (bima) from which the Torah is read is circled seven times. On the night of that day, Jews stay in the synagogue in prayer and in studying the Torah.

20. H. Arendt, *Eichmann w Jerozolimie* (Kraków, 1987), p. 151.

21. Jewish Historical Institute in Warsaw (ŻIH), Group: Social Courts. Halbersztadt Szmul, sig. 313/41.

22. M. Fuks, *Adama Czerniakowa dziennik getta warszawskiego 6 IX 1939-23 VII 1942* (Warsaw, 1983), p. 306.

23. E. Karpiński, "Wspomnienia z okresu okupacji," in *Biuletyn Żydowskiego Instytutu Historycznego* (ŻIH), no. 149 (1989): 66.

24. "Daty żydowskiej martyrologii w Siedlcach," in *Book of Remembrance of the Siedlce Community*, p. 706.

25. APS, AMS, sig. 2364, 2368 (Numerical list of Aryan and Jewish population in the neighborhoods of the "Jewish Ghetto on the territory of the city of Siedlce"). This number seems underestimated. See table 4.

26. B. Engelking, "Życie codzienne Żydów w miasteczkach dystryktu warszawskiego," in *Prowincja noc. Życie i zagłada Żydów w dystrykcie warszawskim*, ed. B. Engelking, J. Leociak, D. Libionka (Warsaw, 2007), p. 150.

27. T. Brustin-Berenstein, "Deportacje i zagłada skupisk żydowskich w Dystrykcie Warszawskim," in *Biuletyn ŻIH*, no. 1/3 (1952): 122.

28. APS, Zbiór afiszy okupacyjnych powiatu siedleckiego (Order of 30 December 1940).

29. Z. Martyniuk, *Moje Siedlce. Wspomnienia z młodości* (Siedlce, 2007), p. 113.
30. Ossoliński National Institute in Wrocław (ZN Ossolińskich), Lucjan Koć, *Pomoc i współpraca z ludnością żydowską ludności wiejskiej powiatu siedleckiego z uwzględnieniem sytuacji zagadnień żydowskich na innych powiatach Podlasia— w okresie okupacji hitlerowskiej w Polsce*, p. 120 (microfilm). According to Lucjan Koć, this was a German provocation. A drunken soldier either threw or accidentally dropped a grenade. "Daty żydowskiej martyrologii w Siedlcach," in *Book of Remembrance of the Siedlce Community*, p. 706—the author describes this incident as a German provocation. Wanda Więch-Tchórzeska ("Źródła do dziejów okupacji hitlerowskiej na Podlasiu południowo-zachodnim," in *Podlacie w czasie II wojny światowej* [Siedlce, 1997], p. 37) maintains that this was an action of the Polish resistance movement. This event could also have been a Jewish self-defense action.
31. Archiwum Państwowe w Krakowie, Izba Zdrowia GG, sig. 250, p. 46.
32. Ibid.
33. APS, Zbiór afiszy okupacyjnych powiatu siedleckiego (Announcement no. 1 of 2 August 1941); also described in W. Ważniewski, *Na przedpolach stolicy 1939–1945* (Warsaw, 1974), p. 124.
34. E. Karpiński, "Wspomnienia z okresu okupacji," p. 68. The author was given similar information by Ms. Renia Pancerowa.
35. Z. Martyniuk, *Moje Siedlce. Wspomnienia z młodości*, p. 116.
36. N. Lasman, *Szosa*, fol. 3 (A fragment of a typescript made available by the author. The book was written in Polish but has unfortunately not appeared in that language. It was translated into Hebrew and German under the title *Die Straße* and published in Israel and Germany in 1999. The author was in the labor camp next to Brzeska Street. The task of the prisoners was to keep the so-called Brześć Highway in good condition.)
37. APS, Zbiór afiszy okupacyjnych powiatu siedleckiego (Order of 25 November 1941).
38. IPN, Ankieta Sądów Grodzkich (ASG), sig. 49, fol. 161.
39. N. Lasman, *Pięćdziesiąt kilometrów od Treblinki* (Warsaw, 1984), p. 7.
40. "Daty żydowskiej martyrologii w Siedlcach," in *Book of Remembrance of the Siedlce Community*, p. 707.
41. APS, Zbiór afiszy okupacyjnych powiatu siedleckiego (Order no. A67//42 of 23 May 1942); M. Zimmerman, *Rassenutopie und Genozid, die nationalsozialistische Lösung der Zigeunerfrage*, pp. 278–283; letter of the curate of the cathedral parish to the canon of the Siedlce deanery dated 19 August 1942; J. Kuligowski, "Liczebność mieszkańców Siedlec, stan z dnia 1 X 1940," in *Prace Archiwalno-Konserwatorskie na Terenie Województwa Siedleckiego*, no. 10 (1997): 212.
42. E. Karpiński, "Wspomnienia z okresu okupacji," p. 66. "Polish Socialists" were also active in the Żoliborz district in Warsaw. Most likely Tadeusz Żelazowski had contact with them.
43. H. Kave's account to the author; H. Kave, "Przeżyłem wysiedlenie siedleckich Żydów," in *Book of Remembrance of the Siedlce Community*, p. 637.

44. L. Koć, *Pomoc i współpraca z ludnością żydowską ludności wiejskiej powiatu siedleckiego*, pp. 52–53 (microfilm).

45. L. Koć, *Pomoc i współpraca z ludnością żydowską ludności wiejskiej powiatu siedleckiego*, sig. 301/6517.

46. I. Jom-Tow (Tenenbaum), "Zagłada Siedlec," in *Book of Remembrance of the Siedlce Community*, p. 649.

47. S. Lewandowska *Ruch oporu na Podlasiu*, p. 66.

48. Ibid., p. 258.

49. N. Lasman, *Szosa*, p. 7 (typescript, fragments sent to the author).

50. A.K. Kunert, comp., *"Żegota" Rada Pomocy Żydom 1942–1945* ["Żegota" Council to Aid Jews] (Warsaw, 2002), p. 73.

51. H. Piskunowicz, "Siedlce w okresie okupacji hitlerowskij w latach 1939–1944," p. 203.

52. *Rejestr miejsc i faktów zbrodni popełnionych przez okupanta hitlerowskiego na ziemiach polskich w latach 1939–1945. Województwo siedleckie*, p. 240.

53. An account given to the author by the priest Wincenty Płudowski.

54. S. Lewandowska *Ruch oporu na Podlasiu*, p. 253.

55. ŻIH, Halberstadt Israel and Rachela, sig. 301/6436.

56. Interview with Barbara Górska taped in 2000 in Tel Aviv commissioned by the Ministry of Culture and Art. Screenwriter and director, Jacek Jędrzejewicz; producer, Jarosław Sokołów; cinematographer, Marcin Koszałka. See appendix X.

57. A copy of Izaak Halber's *Declaration* is in the author's possession.

58. W. Grzymała, *Wspomnienia* [Memoir] (Białystok, 1982–1985), p. 28. Typescript made available to the author by Zbigniew Wąsowski.

59. Muzeum Walki i Męczeństwa w Treblince. Video account of Bogdan Osiński.

60. PN, SWMW 89 (1949–1951), fol. 227

61. I. Jom-Tow (Tenenbaum), "Zagłada Siedlce," p, 650.

62. IPN, *Pamiętnik Cypory Jabłoń-Zonszajn ur. w 1915 r. i zamieszkałej w Siedlcach do 1942 r.*, p. 1. A xerographic copy of the typescript is in the possession of the author. This diary was published by Agata Dąbrowska in *Szkice Podlaskie*, no. 9 (2001): 228–244. "The Fate of Zofia Olszakowska-Glazer, Her Friend Cypora Jabłoń-Zonstein and Her Daughter Rachela," which can be found on the internet site www.ceo.org.pl, was prepared by the young people in Secondary School No. 94 in Warsaw. Some very interesting photographs are also placed there. See also *Bunt Młodych Duchem* [Revolt of the Young at Heart], no. 5 (2007): 7–8. [Agata Dąbrowska's article, in Polish, including Cypora's diary, can be found on the web at http://mazowsze.hist.pl/33/Szkice_Podlaskie/699/2001/24747/.—trans.]

63. IPN, *Pamiętnik Cypory Jabłoń-Zonszajn*, p. 2.

64. H. Kave, "Przyżyłem wysiedlenie siedleckich Żydów," p. 635.

65. IPN, *Pamiętnik Cypory Jabłoń-Zonszajn*, pp. 3–4.

66. E. Karpiński, "Wspomnienia z okresu okupacji," p. 70.

67. IPN, *Pamiętnik Cypory Jabłoń-Zonszajn*, p. 7.

68. A. Celiński and R. Dmowski, *Zarys dziejów ochrony przeciwpożarowej w mieście*

Siedlce (Siedlce, 2007), p. 89. Photographs of the people gathered at the cemetery taken by Fritz Hoeft have survived. See photographs no. 114–116.

69. M.T. Frankowski and J. Staszewski, "Musimy Żydów zniszczyć" [We Must Destroy the Jews], in *Tygodnik Siedlecki*, no. 36 (1986): 5.

70. "Daty żydowskiej martyrologii w Siedlcach," in *Book of Remembrance of the Siedlce Community*, p. 708.

71. Ibid., p. 5.

72. IPN, OKBZN Siedlce, sig. 44, fol. 4. Jan Michalak also mentions this in his account (Museum of Struggle and Martyrdom in Treblinka. Videocassette, account of J. Michalak).

73. D. Libionka, "Polska konspiracja wobec eksterminacji Żydów w dystrykcie warszawskim," in *Prowincja noc*, p. 468.

74. IPN, *Pamiętnik Cypory Jabłoń-Zonszajn*, pp. 4–5.

75. Ela Kaselbrener changed his religion from Judaism to Roman Catholicism on 3 October 1944 in the parish of St. Stanisław in Siedlce. His godparents were Franciszek Maksymiuk and Maria Moskwiak. Then on 30 December 1944 he married Helena Arak, who was 47 years old at the time. In 1947 he changed his name to Aleksander Szczepański. He died on 20 January 1967 and was buried in the cemetery on Janowska Street. To this day, a small shrine stands on his former property at 46 Brzeska Street as thanks for saving his life.

76. See photographs no. 117–121.

77. See photographs no. 122–125.

78. N. Lasman, *Piędziesiąt kilometrów od Treblinki*, p. 23; information about the liquidation of the ghetto in Siedlce was sent by L. Berezowski (Leon Feiner) in the document "Do p. Zygielbojma, członka Rady Narodowej RP w Londynie" [To Mr. Zygielbojm, Member of the National Council of the Polish Republic in London], Sikorski Historical Institute, ref. S.P.P., file 15, item 107.

79. IPN, *Pamiętnik Cypory Jabłoń-Zonszajn*, pp. 5–6.

80. In the spring of 1943, the Special Military Court of Warsaw Territory with a branch in Siedlce issued a death sentence against Albert Fabisch for his bestial liquidation of Jews. The order to carry out the sentence was given by the commander of the Home Army, Siedlce Territory, Major Marian Zawarczyński "Ziemowit." Fabisch was kille 4 July 1944. See M. Bulik, *Mój udział w akcjach zbrojnych w czasie okupacji hitlerowskiej w Siedlcach* [My Participation in Armed Operations during the Nazi Occupation in Siedlce] (Siedlce, 2005).

81. APS, Zbiór afiszy okupacyjnych powiatu siedleckiego (No. 894/42 of 27 August 1942).

82. E. Karpiński, "Wspomnienia z okresu okupacji," p. 74.

83. IPN, *Pamiętnik Cypory Jabłoń-Zonszajn*, p. 11. Cypora Jabłoń gave her daughter, Rachela, to her friend Irena Zawadzka and took poison. Rachela managed to be saved thanks to the help of Irena Zawadzka and Zofia Olszakowska. Forged documents were prepared for her under the name Marianna Tymińska. After the war she was sent to Israel, where Cypora's older brother, who had gone there before the war, lived. Rachela took up residence with him on a kibbutz. She later married, had two

sons, and took up residence in the United States. She came to Poland for the first time in the 1980s. She died in 2002. Zofia Olszakowska-Glazer and Irena Zawadzka were awarded with the Righteous Among the Nations of the World medal. Dosia (Danusia), Cypora's friend, survived the war thanks to her Aryan looks and forged documents obtained for her by Zofia Olszakowska. After the war, she took up residence in Israel.

84. Account of Czesław Ulko of 2 January 1999, in the author's possession.

85. W. Śliwowska, comp., *Czarny rok... czarne lata* [Black Year... Black Summer] (Warsaw, 1996), p. 81.

86. N. Lasman, *Piędziesiąt kilometrów od Treblinki*, pp. 55, 65, 71, 83.

87. Rosh Hashannah is celebrated the first and second day of Tishri (September–October). On Rosh Hashannah, God is acknowledged as the King of the Universe, who judges all his creatures and joins justice with mercy. In Poland, it was also know by the name of Holiday of Trumpets.

88. On Yom Kippur, man searches for God through repentance. These are the two most holy days of the Jewish religious calendar.

89. N. Lasman, *Piędziesiąt kilometrów od Treblinki*, p. 91.

90. I. Jom-Tow (Tenenbaum), "Zagłada Siedlec," pp. 666–667.

91. W. Sobczyk, "Założenia projektowe na zagospodarowanie terenu cmentarza–pomnika męczeństwa Narodu Żydowskiego w Siedlcach," Biuro Badań i Dokumentacji Zabytków w Siedlcach, p. 23.

92. I. Jom-Tow (Tenenbaum), "Zagłada Siedlec," pp. 670–671.

93. S. Willenberg, *Bunt w Treblince* (Warsaw, 1991), p. 23. The author of this book estimates this transport at 6,000–7,000 people. These numbers seem to be overestimated.

94. IPN, ASG, sig. 49, fol. 155.

95. IPN, ASG, sig. 49, fol. 158.

96. IPN, ASG, sig. 49, fol. 154.

97. IPN, ASG, sig. 49, fol. 153, 158.

98. IPN, ASG, sig. 49, fol. 151. E. Weinstein, *17 dni w Treblince* (Łosice, 2008), p. 55.

99. IPN, ASG, sig. 49, fol. 151.

100. J.A. Młynarczyk, "'Akcja Reinhard' w gettach prowincjonalnych dystryktu warszawskiego 1942-1943" ["Operation Reinhard" in the Provincial Ghettos of Warsaw District 1942-1943], in *Prowincja noc*, p. 74.

101. W. Sobczyk, *Założenia projektowe na zagospodarowanie terenu cmentarza–pomnika męczeństwa Narodu Żydowskiego w Siedlcach*, p. 4. J. Goldman claims that these were Romanian Jews. The authors of the book *Dokumenty i materiały do dziejów okupacji niemieckiej w Polsce* (vol. 2, *Akcje i "wysiedlenie,"* part 1, comp. Dr. Józef Kernisz [Warsaw–Łódź–Kraków, 1946], p. LXV] claim that the clean-up operation was conducted with the aid of a 40-member group of Jews from Białystok.

CHAPTER 11

AFTER THE WAR

After the Germans were driven out of the city, some of the surviving Jews returned to their homes. Within the territory of Siedlce County, there were barely about 200 in October 1944.[1] Some of them entered into the structures of the newly organized Communist authorities, occupying prominent positions in the party apparatus and in the Public Security Service.[2a] They also tried to rebuild religious life. On 20 December 1944, the county administrator confirmed Aria Lejb Nejman in the position of rabbi in Siedlce. Nejman was a graduate of the rabbinical college in Brześć and the last rabbi in Siedlce. The Homeland Association of Siedlce Jews numbered 450 people throughout all of Poland. Aside from Siedlce, they lived in Legnica (73 people), Dzierżoniów, Łódź, Strzegom, Szczecin, Wałbrzych-Boguszów, Warsaw, Wrocław, and Ziembice. A committee existed at that time, with a management board consisting of Chaim Rajze, director; Jankiel (Jontel) Goldman, chairman; A. Frydman, secretary; Artur Kupfersztein, secretary; Symcha Lew, secretary; Perelman; S. Nusbaum, secretary; F. Morgensztern, secretary's aid; Ch. Kramarz, cook; and J. Wajnapel, custodian.[3] The offices of the committee were first located at 5 Browarna Street and later at 41 Pułaski Street.

The majority of the surviving Jews, however, gradually left the city. The first such collective departure took place in March 1945 after clashes between liberation units and the functionaries of the new authorities intensified.[b] In Siedlce at that time a policeman of Jewish descent by the name of Orzeł was killed, and lieutenant Pszenica, buried in the Jewish cemetery in Siedlce, was killed outside Kałuszyn.[4]

In 1946, at the initiative of and thanks to the insistence of Jontel Goldman, 90 bodies were exhumed and laid to rest in the cemetery. A memorial tablet was placed in this spot in three languages: Hebrew, Yiddish, and Polish. Its text is as follows: "Here rest the remains of Jews murdered and burned by the barbaric Nazis in Siedlce and its environs in the years 1942–1943 exhumed from the place of their extermination by the Jewish Committee on the fourth anniversary of the liquidation of the ghetto. We pay homage to their martyr's death. The Jewish community in Siedlce on 22.08.1946." The monument has been vandalized, and the above text is no longer readable. The next action of this kind, encompassing all of Siedlce

County, took place in 1948. At that time 37 bodies were exhumed from territories belonging to the Siedlce railroad: 18 people murdered in Krzymosze, 18 murdered in Opole, and the remains of Jakub Sosnowicz, murdered in 1943 and buried in Siedlce on Partyzantów Street.[5]

In 1945, the majority of Siedlce Jews went to Łódź and later left for Israel or other countries. In the 1950s, however, the Jewish community was organized enough to propose to the authorities a change in the name of Tylna Street to Szalom Asz Street, a Jewish writer who died in 1957. This is one of the oldest streets in the city, and it ran along the backs of inns, which formed the western frontage of the main market square. It was originally called Koźla Street, and that is what it was listed as in the inventory of Siedlce property from the eighteenth century. On a map of the city from 1820, it appears as Szeroka Street. Later, around the middle of the nineteenth century, it was called Tylna Street. This name remained until the twenty-year interwar period.[6]

Another street was given the name Bohaterów Getta Street. This is one of the oldest streets in the city. It originally bore the name Koński Rynek [Horse Square—trans.], then, until the postwar period, Stary Rynek [Old Market Square—trans.]. The decree giving the street its current name has not been preserved. During the German occupation, this street was part of the ghetto. Historic brick buildings are located on it from the nineteenth century (no. 2), from the turn of the nineteenth and twentieth centuries (nos. 5, 7, and 9), and from the beginning of the twentieth century (nos. 11 and 13).[7]

In 1950, Jontel Goldman, a Siedlce bricklayer, commenced efforts aimed at cleaning up the cemetery and the building of two monuments memorializing the annihilation of local Jews. One was placed in 1953 in the location of the first cemetery, where on 22 August 1942 the Germans began the action of deporting Jews to Treblinka. This monument was moved in 1982 in connection with the construction of the PKO [General Savings Bank—trans.] building. Currently it is located on Berek Joselewicz Street. The text on the panel reads [in Polish and Yiddish—ed.], "A place sanctified by the blood of 17,000 Jews, victims of Nazi genocide." The second monument was to be placed in the cemetery on Szkolna Street. In connection with this project, gravestones, which the Nazis had used as curbstones, were removed from Siedlce streets in 1958 and placed in the cemetery. The year 1961 saw the creation of the Jewish Cemetery Inspectional Commission, which, after a thorough tour of the area, concluded the following:

1. The area of the cemetery must be put in order:
(a) paths need to laid out, graves need to be marked, graves need to be put in order by arranging gravestones, planting flowers, and so forth. Special memorial tablets need to be placed on 18 mass graves that are 5 meters and 10 meters long;

(b) a pyramidal monument needs to be formed out of 2,000 gravestone tablets;

(c) tablets need to be placed where people were shot to death against the cemetery wall (bullets can be seen imbedded in the cemetery wall). Cover them with glass and create inscriptions. In one place 29 women were shot to death (their names are known);

(d) secure the wall surrounding the Jewish Cemetery (the wall is crumbling);

(e) secure the entrance gate, which has moldered;

(f) in 1942, a transport of deportees from Radom were brought here (this tomb must be put in order);

(g) bushes, flowers, and so forth need to be planted on the territory of the cemetery.

At the same time, the commission stated that this cemetery, which is essentially not a cemetery but a place consecrated to the blood of innocently murdered citizens of Jewish nationality, must be put in order and secured.[8]

In order to effect the recommendations of the commission, the Siedlce Committee for the Protection of Jewish Cemeteries and Places of Execution in Siedlce, Mordy, Łosice, Sokołów Podlaski, and Węgrów was formed on 12 November 1962. The committee was composed of Jontel Goldman, chairman; Bronisława Szlezinger, vice-chair; Henryk Rajze, secretary; Goldfarb and Mieczysława Krawczyk, members. Witold Sobczyk drafted the initial design and cost estimate layout, and Rappaport designed the monument. This monument was to be a pyramid made of gravestone taken up from streets, and on it was to be the figure of Rachel crying over her children. The historical part of the design layout was executed by Jontel Goldman. This draft contains very valuable photographic material depicting everyday life in the Siedlce ghetto, as well as the moment when the ghetto was liquidated. Some of the photographs were taken from hiding. The project was never implemented since the city authorities came up with other plans that greatly diminished the size of the cemetery. Part of the terrain was planned for widening the road and building one-family homes. The Committee for the Protection of Jewish Cemeteries protested vehemently. There was even a dispute between the Siedlce Committee for Protection and the Main Management Board of the Social-Cultural Society of Jews in Poland [TSKŻ]. The society was accused of failing to give the cemetery adequate protection. In answer, the Main Management Board of the TSKŻ delegalized the Siedlce Committee for Protection. As a result of this dispute, no plan was executed.[9] The consequence of these disagreements was that at the present time it is impossible to determine the place along the cemetery wall where the executions took place, and the names of the 29 women shot to death in this spot have been forgotten.[c] The tomb of the Radom Jews has also fallen into oblivion.

The last burial in this cemetery took place in 1962. The next plans for putting the cemetery in order arose. A detailed plan to develop the spacious City Center–West area in Siedlce was accepted in 1972. It provided for a two-meter widening of Spokojna Street in the direction of the cemetery. An area of 800 square meters was to be set aside for a lapidarium, while the rest was intended for multi-family housing. Construction, however, was not begun. Another attempt to put the cemetery in order was made in 1980. Another technical design was authored by Beata Michasiuk and prepared by the Union of the Jewish Faith. The project was not executed due to a lack of funds for this goal. In 1983, a new design was prepared, which in turn was not accepted by the Religious Union of the Jewish Faith. Then, in 1987, the Social Committee for Putting the Cemetery in Order was created. The next design, partially executed, was prepared by Engineer Ratajski. Within the framework of the undertaken tasks, the wall was fixed; a new, metal gate was made; the grounds were cleaned up, clearing out unnecessary forestation; and overturned tombstones were righted.[10] The only curious thing is that, given the existence of so many designs, another one was prepared. In evaluating these actions, one can only conclude that more time was devoted to debating the designs of the cemetery than to working on putting it in order. In 1993, the cemetery was listed in the registry of historical landmarks. In recent years it has suffered significant damage.

The departure of Siedlce Jews from the city and the country took place after 1968. The Communist authorities of the time instituted an anti-Semitic campaign as a result of which over a dozen people left Siedlce, headed mostly for Israel.[d]

In the beginning of the 1990s, after democracy was restored in Poland, some young people discovered their Jewish roots. Their number is estimated at over a dozen. They belong to the Jewish Religious Council in Warsaw, and they treat their faith very personally.

In the first years of the twenty-first century, the Jewish Religious Council in Warsaw regained several developed lots in the city. These were the buildings of the Jewish hospital, the mikveh–bathhouse, and the butchers' prayer house. All the buildings were dismantled, and the lots were sold. Residential houses were built on all these lots. The fact that this area had a Jewish history spanning several centuries was not memorialized. The only place remaining in the possession of the Jewish Religious Council in Warsaw connected with the history of Siedlce Jews is the cemetery on Szkolna Street. Clean-up work was carried out on its territory in 2008 consisting of the removal of superfluous trees.

In 2000, the first organized group of Siedlce Jews living in various foreign countries came to Siedlce, headed by its chairman, Hercel Kave. They met with the then-mayor of the city, Mirosław Symanowicz. The next Siedlce homeland association from Israel arrived in 2006, headed by its chairman, Israel Zylberstein. They also met with Mayor Mirosław Symanowicz. Then a group of Israeli youths from Bat Yam came in 2007. They met with the mayor of the city, Wojciech Kudelski, and a group of Polish youths from the Saint Queen Jadwiga Second General Preparatory

High School. The young people toured the city and paid tribute to the Jews murdered during World War II. This was how the symbolical return of Siedlce Jews to their city took place—now only in the emotional sphere. The next group of young Israelis came to Siedlce on 19 March 2009. They met with representatives of the city's authorities and the young people of the B. Prus First General Preparatory High School. The meeting took place in the Jewish cemetery, where tribute was paid to those who were murdered.

EDITORS' AND TRANSLATOR'S NOTES, CHAPTER 11

a. This is true of the country's central organs but less so of the local situation in Siedlce. According to Wiesław Charczuk in „*Najpierw popili sobie w urzędzie…*" *Zbrodnia ludobójstwa komunistycznego aparatu bezpieczeństwa na członkach opozycji antykomunistycznej w Siedlcach 12–13 kwietnia 1945* ["First They Had a Few Drinks at the Office…" The Crime Murder by the Communist Security Agency Perpetrated against the Anticommunist Opposition in Siedlce on 12–13 April 1945] (Siedlce, 2011), pp. 54–62, out of 98 functionaries of local security-services staff in 1945, 12 were of Jewish nationality, none of them in a commander or deputy commander position. Out of these 12, 3 people were previous residents who returned to town. One person, a prewar trade union and Communist activist, filled a managerial position that may be considered prominent.

b. This statement by the author merits elaboration. The "liberation units" were mostly right-wing underground organizations that continued their fight for Polish liberation in mid-1945 by concentrating on the Soviet threat after the Nazis began to withdraw; they also targeted Jewish survivors, who were considered Soviet allies. These post–World War II clashes between the right and the left have their origins in pre–World War II perceptions.

In the interwar period, there was a strong tendency, especially among modernizing (non-Orthodox) Jews, to conceive of liberation in terms of an international socialist revolution. This conception was strongest in the Bund. That said, the predominant sentiment in the Bund was anti-Leninist and, after the Bolshevik Revolution, anti-Soviet; an important minority, however, were pro-Lenin and pro-Soviet. In the early stages of the Russian Revolution, when its course and international stance were still up for grabs, there were hopes even among the moderate Jewish leftists that Soviet policy might be something they could agree with; however, with the rise of Stalin, these hopes were disappointed. After the 1920s, affiliation with the Bund declined; the main beneficiaries of this tendency were probably the Zionists.

It was natural, under these circumstances, for the Polish right to be oblivious to the gradations among the Jewish left and to lump all Jewish leftists (including the Bund and the anti-Stalinists among them, and maybe even the Zionists) with the Communists. This lack of differentiation becomes apparent if one examines the types of organizations that were banned before the war because of the fear that they were likely to promote Communism (see chapter 9). To the extent that the Polish right influenced Polish state policy, the sense of alienation among Jews generally increased and both their leftist and their Zionist sympathies were reinforced, each of which were predicated on the notion of looking elsewhere for answers since acceptance by the Poles did not seem to be forthcoming. To the extent that Jews adopted this attitude, it in turn reinforced the Polish right's perception of them as an alien group within Poland.

Against this background, the participation of a small minority of surviving Polish Jews in the Communist regime after World War II could naturally be perceived by the Polish right and a significant part of the Polish center as repeating the pattern of Jewish leftist deviation from the national consensus.

The discourse in Poland has been very charged since the fall of Communism with regard to the relations of Polish society as a whole to Jews during the Holocaust and immediately after the war. A balanced view is very difficult to come by, and this book is not the place to enter into that heated discussion. The reader may wish to start by looking at Dr. A.J. Prazmowska's review of Jan Gross's *Fear: Anti-Semitism in Poland after Auschwitz: An Essay in Historical Interpretation* (http://www.history.ac.uk/reviews/review/627) for a sober presentation of the issues raised in Gross's controversial book.

c. The list is presented in Editor's Note e in Chapter 10.

d. Seven people can be identified, and a few more are estimated according to unofficial data.

AUTHOR'S NOTES, CHAPTER 11

1. N. Lasman, *Wspomnienia z Polski 1 sierpnia 1944–30 kwietnia 1957* (Warsaw, 1997), pp. 15, 51.

2. John Sack, in his book *Oko za oko* (Gliwice, 1995), tries to answer the question of why this was the case.

3. A. Skibińska, "Powroty ocalałych," in *Prowincja noc*, p. 594.

4. W. Grzymała, *Wspomnienia* (Białystok, 1982–1985), p. 62. Typescript made available to the author by Zbigniew Wąsowski; Sobczyk, *Założenia projektowe na zagospodarowanie terenu cmentarza–pomnika męczeństwa Narodu Żydowskiego w Siedlcach* (photographs with caption no. 22).

5. W. Sobczyk, *Założenia projektowe na zagospodarowanie terenu cmentarza–pomnika męczeństwas Narodu Żydowskiego w Siedlcach*, pp. 24–29.

6. Szalom Asz [Sholem Asch] (1880–1957)—Jewish writer, father of the American author Nathan Asch. Born 1 January 1880 in Kutno. He debuted with a short story on a biblical theme in Polish. His acquaintance with S[tanisław] Witkiewicz and S[tefan] Żeromski had a significant influence on the development of his talent; he also corresponded with [Eliza] Orzeszkowa, [Bolesław] Prus, [Władysław] Orkan,

and [Andrzej] Niemojewski. [These were among the most notable Polish writers of the time.—trans.] He started writing exclusively in Yiddish early, gaining fame with his novel *Shtetl* (1904) and a volume of short stories. In 1914 he left for the United States, where he wrote the satirical novel *Onkel Moses* (1923) and a novel about Jewish immigrants, *Ameryka* (1926). He is also the author of a number of novels and short stories with historical and social themes: *The Mother* (1925), *Motke the Thief* (1925), the trilogy *Before the Flood*, as well as plays. After the Second World War, he wrote "Triumphant March," an elegy dedicated to the exterminated Jews. He spent his last years in Israel. His works belong to the classics of Yiddish literature, and his plays contributed to the development of the Yiddish theater. A group of historic inns from the turn of the eighteenth and nineteenth centuries is located on this street.

7. U. Głowacka-Maksymiuk, *Ulice Siedlec. Historia. Patroni. Zabytki* (Siedlce, 1997).
8. Minutes in the author's possession.
9. Materials in the author's possession, provided by J. Goldman.
10. Materials in the possession of the Department of Social Issues of the Provincial Office in Siedlce.

CONCLUSION

Jews were present in Siedlce essentially from the moment it received the rights of a city (1547). Until 1804, the city was in private hands. Individual owners brought Jews in and allowed them to settle. They felt that the city would be able to develop thanks to this. And indeed, that was the case. The Jews were engaged mostly in the trades and commerce. But areas such a medicine, construction, or transport were also their domain. The Jewish population was dominant in Siedlce in the nineteenth century, comprising about 70 percent of residents. The Yiddish language was heard more than Polish in certain quarters of the city. Many Jews participated in the uprisings of the Poles against the Russian partitioner in 1830 and 1863. They were an important provision and logistic base in these actions. They sometimes fought with weapons in their hands.

In addition to the material development of the city, figures such as Jehuda He-Chasid, Rabbi Benjamin Dow Anolik, and Rabbi Meisels contributed to the spiritual growth of Jews. Their attachment to religion and tradition had a decisive significance in the lives of many of the city's residents. Until recently, the Jewish hospital building was a symbol of the battle for faith and tradition. It was built using monies that were earmarked for penalties place on Orthodox Jews for not wanting to "Europeanize," that is, they did not cut off their sidelocks or beards and continued to wear their gabardines. Unfortunately, the hospital was demolished before our very eyes in the beginning of the twenty-first century. A structure that was inextricably tied to Jewish history disappeared from the landscape of the city.

From the beginning of the twentieth century, two groupings clashed: Orthodox Jews, with their attachment to religion and tradition; and the Bundists, with their faith in socialism. Later, Zionists were added, and they battled sharply against both groupings and dreamed of a Jewish state in Palestine. The pogrom that was staged by the tsarist troops in 1906 put a stop to the political life that had been developing vigorously. The Jews closed themselves up in their homes, prayer houses, schools, societies, or friendship and neighborhood groups. They joined a very active political life anew only in 1915 under the German occupation. The Bolshevik invasion in 1920 and the attitudes of certain Jews also brought about a mutual lack of trust between the two societies, each accusing the other of ill will. In the twenty-year interwar period, a number of parties as well as several dozen societies and labor unions were active in the city. In the 1930s, the Zionists gained ever greater significance, contributed to by the economic crisis and the lack of prospects in Poland.

The period of the Second World War brought the almost total annihilation of the Jewish community of the city: 12,500 people were loaded onto freight cars and sent to the death camp in Treblinka. Besides people, the Nazis also destroyed the material traces of the Jewish presence. The city's synagogue was burned down as early as December 1939. The two oldest cemeteries were completely destroyed, and the newest one, on what was at that time Szkolna Street, was partially destroyed. The Germans burned down the building and all the documents stored by the Jewish Religious Council. At that time, the chronicles of various religious brotherhoods containing valuable material went up in flames. The remaining documents were lost in the ghetto or were burned in Treblinka. What little material survived is now found in the National Archive and Registrar's Office in Siedlce.

Jewish society did not rebuild in Siedlce after the war. As a result of the complicated political situation, Jews emigrated to the United States, Israel, or other countries. Currently, aside from the modest memorial on Berek Joselewicz Street, there are no clear traces of the Jewish heritage in the city. Yet they set the tone for this city together with the Poles in the nineteenth and twentieth centuries. Today, unfortunately, very few still remember.

This book does not exhaust the studies dealing with the Jewish population in Siedlce. Articles and books about the Jews in neighboring cities, such a Sokołów, Węgrów, Mordy, Łosice, and Łuków, are making an appearance. The Siedlce Jews had very good contacts with the residents of these cities. An analysis should be made of what connected the local Jews with the residents of those cities and what differentiated them. To what extent was so-called Jewish solidarity proven correct in difficult moments, or to what extent was this a myth that survives among Polish society.

The person who, along with Professor Zofia Chyra-Rolicz, supported me in my research was Michael Halber. I therefore decided to include in this book the "Additional Bibliography" put together by him. This is a guideline for people who do not know Polish and for researchers who would like to delve deeper into my findings to date. Some of the entries there have now been translated into Polish, such as Eddie Weinstein's *17 Days in Treblinka* (Łosice, 2008), while others, such as Noach Lasman's *The Road* [Szosa], have been translated into Hebrew and German but have not been printed in the language in which they came into being, that is, in Polish. [Lasman's *Szosa* has now been published in Polish (Poznań: OPAL, 2006) and is available online as a PDF manuscript.—trans.] Still others, such as Małgorzata Niezabitowska's *Remnants: The Last Jews of Poland* [*Ostatni. Współcześni Żydzi polscy*], are a translation of the Polish edition into English and German.

Finally, one must reflect: Did the city's Christian society, seeing the extermination of the Jews, realize what was happening? Were the following generations of Poles living in this city aware of this tragedy? The answers to these questions are difficult, and surveys should be conducted among the residents for this purpose. From my observations and experience I conclude that barely a part of the residents had or have such awareness; the majority, however, did not and does not. I hope that this book will contribute to the first group's becoming the majority.

APPENDIX 1.
MICHAŁ KAZIMIERZ OGIŃSKI'S LETTER TO RABBI ABRAHAM FRĘKLIN FROM 1797

[The Polish text renders the contents of the letter in eighteenth century Polish, for that is the language of the original. For the sake of clarity, this translation is given in modern English.—trans.]

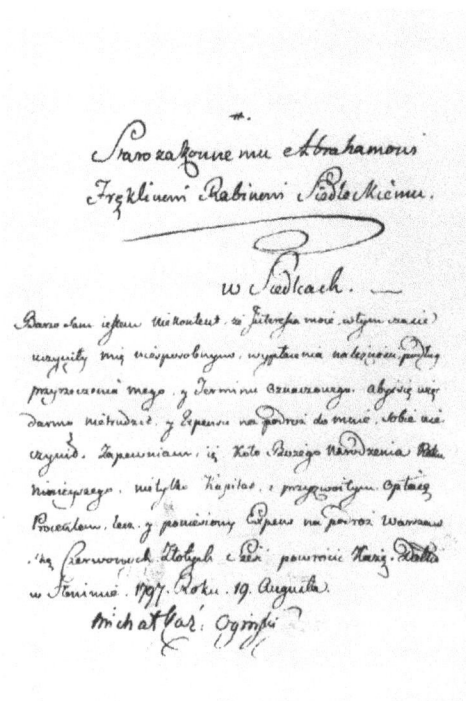

To the Orthodox Abraham Fręklin, the Siedlce Rabbi

in Siedlce—

I am myself discontented with the fact that my interests have made it impossible for me to pay the charge according to my promise and within the indicated timeframe; therefore, do not trouble yourself in vain and do not incur the expense of traveling to me. I assure you that around Christmas of this year I will cover the cost not only of the capital, with a decent interest payment, but I will order that the expenses incurred in the Warsaw journey of six red zlotys be reimbursed. Dated 19 August 1797 in Słonim.

Michał Kaź: Ogiński

Source: D. Michalec, *Aleksandra Ogińska I jej czasy* (Siedlce, 1999), pp. 58, 156.

APPENDIX 2.
LIST OF VICTIMS OF THE 1906 POGROM IN SIEDLCE

1. Borycz Jan (Christian)
2. Bursztain Bluma, age 40
3. Cencel Stanisław, age 45
4. Diament Zalman Mosze, age 45
5. Feder Szalom Dow, age 76
6. Gersz Szyja, age 22
7. Goldberg Mordka, age 30
8. Goldstein Josef, age 30
9. Izrael Abram, age 25
10. Liberman Jakow Chaim, age 30
11. Libhaber Chana, age 52
12. Liuk Hanna, age 50
13. Lipszyc Jehuda, age 18
14. Macieliński Dow, age 25
15. Milczak Abraham, age 19
16. Miller Josef Mordechaj, age 40
17. Rafał Abraham, age 22
18. Ratyniewicz Szraga, age 32
19. Rozen Jehoszua, age 3
20. Słuszny Nachum, age 18
21. Solarz Meir, age 18
22. Solarz Sara, age 70
23. Stachowski Jehoszua, age 19
24. Stachowski—child
25. Szklarz Dow, age 30
26. Szklarz Berek, age 40
27. Szreder Szmul Berek, age 65
28. Świecący Kamień Hanna, age 18
29. Tajblum Mendel, age 34
30. Tajgenbojm Debora, age 17
31. Winberg Icchak, age 45
32. Winsztain Szajdla, age 34
33. Wolf Meir
34. Zonszein Gabriel, age 20

Source: Archiwum Państwowe w Siedlcach, Siedlecki Gubernialny Zarząd Żandarmerii, sig. 158, p. 28; Kaspi, "History of the Jews in Siedlce," in *Book of Remembrance of the Siedlce Community* (Buenos Aires, 1956), pp. 112–113.

APPENDIX 3.
LIST OF THE OLDEST SURNAMES OF JEWISH FAMILIES IN SIEDLCE FROM THE EIGHTEENTH CENTURY

[The names are given here in the order in which they appear in the Polish original.—trans.]

Anyż, Altan, Ajzenberg, Aronowicz, Arman, Ajzakowicz, Ajzensztadt, Angelczyk, Akierman, Agresbaum, Amsterdamski,

Baran, Blumsztejn, Berenbaum, Bobek, Blady, Białyłew, Białepole, Bromberg, Brukarz, Brzezina, Białytist, Białobroda, Biały, Bursztyn, Bachrach, Brener, Bronstejn, Boruchowicz, Borensztejn,

Cukiersztejn, Cynamon, Cynowagóra, Celnikier, Cybula, Cerenfeld, Cybulski, Cymbalista, Cymerman, Celnik, Cik, Całkowicz, Cukier, Cukierfeld, Cygielsztejn, Cwangman, Ciszyński, Ciemny, Cacko,

Drewno, Drewniany, Drzewo, Dudaszek, Dobreserce, Dua, Dozorca, Dąb, Dąbrowa, Damski, Dawidowicz, Dajen, Delman, Dolina, Dobryrybak, Dobrowolny, Dobrzyński, Dobrezłoto, Drogikamień, Dystelman, Dziewulski,

Eplewicz, Epelbaum, Edelman, Edelsztejn, Edelbaum, Elfant, Erlich, Esseryk, Elman,

Farbiarz, Fajnholc, Fejganbaum, Fajnsztadt, Fajer, Fajn, Fajwełowicz, Feldman, Felszer, Federman, Frydman, Figowy, Finkelsztejn, Firsztenberg, Fiszman, Fisz, Forman, Fogelfeld, Frajman, Frymerman, Frydrych,

Gałąska, Garncarz, Gaik, Grający, Garbarz, Grynberg, Galicki, Gertner, Głownia, Goldshmidt, Goldman, Goldwirt, Goldsztejn, Goldfeder, Gildblat, Goldfarb, Groch, Grzywacz, Gryner, Grynszpan, Gruszka, Grzebieniarz, Gurfinkiel, Guterman, Gutgold, Gutszmidt,

Handlarz, Herszkowicz, Himelsztajn, Husyd, Herszenzon,

Izraelski, Ickowicz, Iserowicz,

Jubiler, Judkowic, Jungerman, Jabłko, Jabłonka, Jabłoń, Jasnagwiazda, Jasnagóra, Jadowski, Jakóbowski, Janklowicz, Jawerbaum, Jerzmowski, Jedwab, Jadło,

Kapłan, Kawe, Karsz, Kamienny, Kapura, Kamiński, Kanarek, Kant, Kafowicz, Kahan, Kania, Kadysz, Kamień, Kawecki, Kapelusznik, Kenigsberg, Kelmanowicz, Kejzman, Kopytowski, Korona, Konewka, Koński, Konopny, Kowal, Kozienicki, Kon, Kogen, Kotuński, Kamar, Kornicki,

Laska, Las, Laufman, Laksfisz, Lewin, Lew, Lewit, Lejbowicz, Lewita, Lebengilk, Liwerant, Lis, Linka, Lipiec, Lipecki, Lichtenberg, Libfrajd, Litmanowicz, Lipszyc, Lubelczyk, Lubelski, Leśniczy, Lonka,

Łęczycki, Ławnicki, Łazowski, Łosicki, Łagowski, Ławecki,

Markusfeld, Makobodski, Mendelson, Mocny, Mrożnicki, Miedziany, Minc, Matysowicz, Mandelbaum, Międzyrzecki, Mąciarz, Młynarz, Murawa, Malin, Moszkowicz, Mandelcwajg, Makówka, Mydlarz, Milgrom, Mączny, Miler, Masło, Marchewka, Mróz, Mosiążnik, Mordski, Miły, Morgenstejn, Majorowicz, Mordkowicz, Morgensztern, Mak, Miska, Manna,

Nejman, Niski, Nerkowagóra, Niebieskikamień, Nadworny, Nusbaum, Nauczyciel, Niwka, Niebieskafarba, Nisenholc, Niebieski, Nutkowic, Nuchymowicz, Niemieckafarba, Norman, Nelkenbaum, Nowack, Niewczyński, Nusynowicz,

Ogórek, Orzeł, Orzechowicz, Ogrodnik, Ospały, Osiński, Orensztejn, Opolski, Ogórkowedrzewo, Orzech, Osina,

Rynecki, Rubinsztejn, Rafał, Rubinkowy, Różowagóra, Rak, Rozenbaum, Ryba, Rybak, Rowek, Rychter, Rajzman, Rozenberg, Różowykwiat, Rydel, Rakowski, Rozenwaser, Robak, Rzetelny, Rozenblit, Rodzącedrzewo, Rogowykamień, Ryza, Rozengarten, Rogowicz, Rossenberg, Rozenfeld, Rozen,

Stołowy, Skórnik, Srebrnykamień, Światły, Silny, Srebrnykąt, Świecącykamień, Srebrnagóra, Suchożebrski, Szklarz, Sokołowski, Sukiennik, Sercha, Segal, Safirsztejn, Srebrnik, Smoła, Słuszny, Salamander, Senderowicz, Skórzecki, Sobol, Szafir, Solarz, Sektor, Szielman, Szmulowicz, Szenkman, Szmuklarz, Szumacher, Szwarc, Szczupak, Szczecina,

Tabak, Tenenbaum, Tabakman, Tykocki, Tejblum, Tejtelblum, Tejwes, Tęcza, Topor, Trzmielina, Towjowicz, Turban, Tajer, Twardagóra,

Ubogi, Uczony, Uberman, Ujrzanowski, Urman, Uczeń, Urwicz, Unger, Urch, Uterhaus,

Wilk, Wysoki, Wyrobnik, Wodnykamień, Wynograd, Wajnsztejn, Wrona, Węgrowski, Wyszkowski, Waksman, Wiernik, Wróbel, Wólfowicz, Wesoły, Włodawski, Woskowy, Wielki, Wolnicki, Winogron, Wajnszelbaum,

Zielonofarba, Złotykamień, Zając, Zonszejn, Złotowaga, Zylbersztejn, Zuck, Zysmanowicz, Zysman, Złotagóra, Zielechowski, Żelaznagóra, Zręczny, Żelazny, Zbuczyński, Żebrak, Zalcman, Zylberman, Zanwelew[i]cz, Złotabroda, Zys, Zylberberg, Zylberfuden, Zebrowicz, Zynger.

Source: *Shedletser Wochenblat*, no. 19 (1937).

TRANSLATOR'S NOTE: Among the surnames in this list, there are those that are quite Polish sounding: "Jerzmowski," "Ciszyński," "Dziewulski," "Niewczyński," "Kawecki," "Sokołowski," "Dobrowolny," and so on. Some clearly have a Jewish reference, many with the "-owicz" suffix that means "son of": "Ickowicz," "Izraelski," "Lewin," "Dawidowicz," "Matysowicz," "Kahan," "Manna," "Aronowicz," "Janklowicz," and others. Some are adjectives: "Zręczny" [skillful], "Konopny" [hempen], "Blady" [pale], "Drewniany" [wooden], "Ciemny" [dark], "Kamienny" [stone], "Niski" [short], "Uczony" [learned], "Niebieski" [blue], and so forth. Others name professions: "Celnik" [customs official], "Farbiarz" [dyer], "Jubiler" [jeweler], "Kapłan" [priest], "Kapelusznik" [hatter], "Ogrodnik" [gardener], "Handlarz" [merchant], "Nauczyciel" [teacher], and so forth. Still others are the names of fruits, animals, birds, or objects: "Baran" [sheep], "Cacko" [bauble], "Drewno" [wood], "Gałązka" [branch], "Konewka" [watering can], "Lis" [fox], "Smoła" [tar], "Masło" [butter], "Ogórek" [cucumber], "Korona" [crown], "Szczupak" [pike], "Gruszka" [pear], "Wilk" [wolf], "Zając" [hare], "Rak" [crayfish], "Tęcza" [rainbow], "Marchewka" [carrot], and others. Many are compounds: "Białylew" [white lion], "Cynowagóra" [tin mountain], "Jasnagwiazda" [bright star], "Niebieskikamień" [blue stone], "Ogórkowedrzewo" [cucumber tree (!)], "Srebrnykąt" [silver corner], "Złotabroda" [gold beard], "Rodzącedrzewo" [fertile tree], and others. Some of these compounds are clearly direct translations from German (such as "Białepole" = Weissfeld = white field), and some even have both a translated form and a Polonized spelling of the German surname: the German Eisenberg is both Żelaznagóra and Ajzenberg, the German Gutgold is both Dobrezłoto and Gutgold, the German Goldstein is both Złotykamień and Goldsztejn, Rozenberg is both Różowagóra and Rozenberg, and so forth. There are even combinations of Polish and German spellings: "Cukierfeld" = Polish "cukier" [sugar, although phonetically similar to the German *Zucker*] and German "feld" [field]. The diversity in these surnames gives a vivid picture of the nature of the Jewish community, its background, its professions and trades, its appearance, and in many cases its distinctiveness from or similarity to the surrounding Polish community.

APPENDIX 4.
LIST OF DROSHKY DRIVERS IN THE CITY OF SIEDLCE AS OF 19 OCTOBER 1919

1. Lew Lejbko
2. Pięknedrzewo Moszko
3. Lew Moszko
4. Liberman Berko
5. Kopyść Karol
6. Bursztyn Aron
7. Lew Szapsia
8. Staręga Antoni
9. Szmielina Jankiel
10. Bibersztajn Bjuma
11. Bursztyn Szaja
12. Lewin Gecel
13. Jerzymowski Icko Abram
14. Sikorski Franciszek
15. Gruszka Herszko
16. Dębowicz Szlama
17. Federman Abram
18. Staręga Jan
19. Bursztyn Moszko
20. Bursztyn Lejbko

Source: Archiwum Państwowe w Siedlcach, Komenda Powiatowej Policji Państwowej w Siedlcach, sig. 116.

Out of 20 droshky drivers, 16 were Jews. They mostly drove their own vehicles. The surname Szmielina appears in other records as Trzmielina. Worthy of attention is the Polonized entry of the surname Pięknedrzewo [beautiful tree—trans.] and also the entry Dębowicz Szlama—a Polish-sounding surname and a Jewish first name.

APPENDIX 5.
MAP OF THE GHETTO IN SIEDLCE

[The meanings of street names, when not names of people, are given in brackets. Current street names are given in parentheses and italics. Designations that are not street names are given in translation only.—trans.]

1. Map of Ghetto
2. SOKOŁOWSKA [Sokołów] Street
3. BŁONIE [Commons] (*Osiedlowa [Housing Development] Street*)
4. SMALL WICKET, only for Gestapo, place of executions
5. TYLNA [Back] Street (*Commons*)
6. GATE
7. GATE
8. ASŁANOWICZ Street
9. SMALL GHETTO "Triangle"
10. BROWARNA [Brewery] Street
11. TARGOWA [Market] Street (*Czerwonego Krzyża [Red Cross] Street*)
12. TYLNA [Back] Street (*Pusta [Empty] Street*)

13. CMENTARNA [Cemetery] Street
14. NOVEMBER 11TH Street
15. MAŁA [Small] Street
16. JUDENRAT
17. HOSPITAL
18. KATEDRALNA [Cathedral] Street
19. GATE
20. SZPITALNA [Hospital] Street (*Kochanowski Street*)
21. STARY RYNEK [Old Square] (*Bohaterów Getta [Heroes of the Ghetto]Street*)
22. MAY 1ST Street (*Bishop Świrski Street*)
23. STARY RYNEK [Old Square]
24. JOSELEWICZ Street
25. MYLNA [Mistaken] Street
26. ORZESZKOWA Street
27. JADOWA [Venomous] Street (*Sądowa [Court] Street*)
28. WOJSKOWA [Military] Street
29. PIŁSUDSKI Street
30. MONUMENT
31. GATE
32. UMSCHLAGPLATZ (square for deportations).

Source: Determinations of the author on the basis of material from Beit Lohamei Hagetaot in Israel.

APPENDIX 6.

TEACHERS OF JEWISH NATIONALITY CONNECTED WITH SIEDLCE WHO WERE MURDERED OR MISSING DURING WORLD WAR II

1. Altman Efroim, teacher at Primary School No. 1 in Siedlce, shot to death in Siedlce ghetto.
2. Barg Rachela, teacher at Primary School No. 7 in Siedlce, murdered in Siedlce ghetto.
3. Felsenstein Sara, teacher in Łosice, missing in Siedlce ghetto.
4. Kafebaum Ita, teacher in Mordy, killed.
5. Landau Estera [Rosa], teacher at Primary School No. 7 in Siedlce, murdered in Siedlce ghetto [one the 29 women executed at the cemetery—ed.].
6. Neugoldberg Lija, teacher at Primary School No. 5 in Siedlce, murdered in Siedlce ghetto.

7. Reichner-Wasserman Estera, teacher at Królowa Jadwiga Secondary and Pre-paratory High School in Siedlce, died in unknown circumstances.
8. Rotbaum Abraham, teacher at B. Prus Secondary and Preparatory High School in Siedlce, died in 1943 in Warsaw ghetto.
9. Skorecka-Parnasowa Rojza, teacher in Mordy, murdered in Siedlce ghetto.
10. Szaferman Moszek, teacher at Primary School No. 7 in Siedlce, murdered in Siedlce ghetto.
11. Szwarc Estera, teacher at Primary School No. 6 in Siedlce, died in Siedlce ghetto.
12. Wassercug Abraham, teacher at Primary School No. 6 in Siedlce, murdered in Siedlce ghetto.

Source: *Działalność Tajnej Organizacji Nauczycielskiej na terenie obecnego woj. Siedleck-iego w latach 1939–1944* (Siedlce, 1992), p. 175. [The plaque in memory of Siedlce teachers who perished during WWII includes many of these names; see http://www.siedlce-zwied-zanie.pl/pomnik012.htm.—ed.]

Appendix 7.
Assurance in Place of an Oath

Document from the time of World War II that one is not a Jew. Whom the German occupiers considered a Jew is clearly stated in the text.

Translation:
Assurance in Place of an Oath.
I.

After careful examination, I know of no circumstances that would justify the assumption that I am a Jew in accordance with §§ 1 and 2 of the decree on the meaning of the concept "Jew" in the General Government dated 24.7.1940 (Depart. of Decr. of the G.G. I, p. 231).

The content of referenced §§ 1 and 2 is as follows:

§ 1. To the extent that the concept "Jew" is in use in the legal and administrative regulations of the General Government, this should be understood as,

1. who is a Jew or is considered a Jew on the basis of the regulations of the German Reich;

2. who as a former Polish citizen or as a stateless person according to § 2 of this regulation is a Jew or is considered a Jew;

§ 2. A Jew is a person who by race is descended from at least three grandfathers and grandmothers who, in the full meaning of this word, are Jews.

A person is considered a Jew who, according to race, is descended from two grandfathers and grandmothers who, in the full meaning of this word, are Jews,

a. if he belonged to a Jewish religious community on 1 September 1939 or was later accepted into it,

b. if, from the moment this regulation went into effect, he was joined in marriage to a person of Jewish descent or later became joined in marriage to such a person,

c. if he is descended from a Jew due to an extramarital affair as understood by excerpt 1. and was born after 31 May 1941.

A Jew in the full meaning of this word is considered to be that grandfather or grandmother who belonged to a Jewish religious community.

I have been informed that I am subject to punishment according to § 156 of the criminal statute for the German Reich dated 15.5.1871 (Rgbl. S. 127) for giving a false assurance in place of an oath.

Eigenhändige Unterschrift
Handwritten signature

_____

Source: From the author's collection.

APPENDIX 8.
FRITZ HOEFT'S INFORMATION ON THE SUBJECT
OF TAKING PHOTOGRAPHS
DURING THE LIQUIDATION OF THE GHETTO

Fri[.....]
Lei[.....] Leica-Foto
Nuss[.....] Nussdorf/In[.....] nbein.
b. Rosenhei[.....]

398/361

München 24. August 1946.

dem

Bericht zu dem Historischen Komitee übergebenen Leicafilm.

In meiner Tätigkeit als Obertruppführer der Organisation
Trott ,Kraftstoffeinsatz Centrale Berlin,machte ich im August
1942 eine Dienstreise zwecks Inspektion der im Generalgouvernement
gelegenen Tankstellen der O.T. .

Bei meiner Durchreise durch Siedlce(150 km östlichWarschau)
übernachtete ich in der Roten Kreuz Baracke am Bahnhof.Fast die ganze
Nacht hiendurch hörte man einzelne Gewehrschüsse,die mich veranlasten
schon um 5 uhr Früh aufzustehen und einen Spaziergang durch die Stadt
zu machen. Auf dem Wege zum Marktplatz fand ich in Abständen von ca.
100 m tote Juden auf der Erde liegen.Meist waren es Ältere,Männer und
Frauen.Eine alte Jüdin konnte ich leider nur fotografieren,da ich nur
dort am Bahndamm ca. 100 m vom Bahnhof entfernt unbeobachtet war.
Als ich mich weiter dem Stadtkern näherte kam ich an einen Kordon
von polnischer Polizei den ich in deutsche O.T. Uniform mühelos
durchschritt.Auf iena Platz in der Stadtmitte der wiederum von SS
abgesperrt war,sah ich 12.000 Juden mit ihren Bündeln auf der Erde
hocken.Es war Befehl ergangen nicht den Kopf zu heben,so dass die
Juden(es war 10 oder 11 uhr geworden),in der an dem Tage herrschenden
glühenden Hitze zusammengekauert auf der Erde sitzen mussten.So bald
eine Person,ob Kind ob Erwachsener den Kopf erhob legte einer
der 3 SS Männer,die in 20 m Entfernung der Menge der Juden auf Stühlen
sassen und von denen 2 mit Infantriegewehren und einer mit Maschinen-
pistole ausgerüstet waren,an,und schoss den betreffenden Juden nieder.
Da ich mit meiner Leica umgehängt betreten hatte,sagte der eine SS
Mann ein Unterscharführer,zu mir ich könnte zwar Aufnahmen machen,
aber es wäre doch sicher nicht erwünscht,wenn diese Aufnahme in die
Presse käme.Ich machte nunmehr ca. 10 Aufnahmen,die ich dem oben er-
wähnten Komittee übergeben habe.

215

- 2 -

Als ich einige Stunden später am Güterbahnhof verbei kam.
sah ich die Juden auf einer Strasse neben der Bahn angetreten, auf
den Abtransport wartend. SS Leute liefen mit Hundepeitschen bewaffnet
die Reihen auf und nieder und schlugen wahllos auf die in der Hitze
stehenden Juden ein. Auch hievon habe ich einige Aufnahmen.

Einige Tage vorher hatte ich bei der Inspection des O.T. Kraftstof
lagers Ujasd bei Tomaschov dass dortige Getto besichtigt. Ich habe
dort sogar Bekannte Berliner jüdische Familien wiedergesehen, die dort
unter den primitivsten Verhältnissen hausten. Einige Aufnahme von
jüdischen Lagerpolizisten, verhungerten und zerlumpten Kindern und
der Prozesur des Haarschneidens in der Entlausungbaracke habe ich
ebenfalls den Kommitée übergeben.

Ich versichere an Eides statt, dass ich diesem Bericht weder etwas
hinzugefügt habe und meine Angaben den Tatsachen entsprechen.

Source: Yad Vashem archive in Israel.

TRANSLATION:

Munich, 24 August 1946

Fritz Hoeft
Leica Photo
Nussdorf/Inn
k. Rosenheim

(company stamp)

Information concerning the Leica film handed over to the Historical Committee
In my work as a higher commander of the Trott Organization [reference is to
the Todt Organization[1]—author's note], the Center for the Use of Fuels in Berlin,
I was on a business trip in the General Government in August 1942 in order to
inspect the gasoline stations located there.

While traveling through Siedlce (150 kilometers east of Warsaw), I put up in the
barracks of the Red Cross at the railroad station. Almost all night one could hear
individual gun shots, which forced me to rise at 5 in the morning and take a walk
through the city. On my way to the market square, I saw dead Jews lying about 100

meters apart. Most often these were elderly men and women. I could photograph only one elderly Jewish woman because I could be undetected on the embankment at a distance of about 100 meters from the station. When I approached the center of the city, I walked past a cordon of Polish police, because, being in the uniform of the German Trott Organization, I could move about without a problem. The square in the center of the city was surrounded by the SS, and I saw 12,000 Jews there who had squatted on the ground with their bundles. A command was given that they may not raise their heads, so they had to sit hunched on the ground in the terrible heat of that day (it was already 10 or 11). If some person, no matter whether a child or an adult, raised his head, then one of the SS men, who were sitting in chairs 20 meters away from the crowd and were armed, two with infantry weapons and one with a machine gun, would shoot at the Jew. Since I had my Leica camera hung over my shoulder, one of the SS men, he could have been a non-commissioned officer, told me that I could take pictures, but that it would not be desirable for them to find their way into the press. I took about 10 pictures, which I handed over to the above-mentioned committee. When after several hours I was walking past the freight station, I saw Jews on one street next to the station as they waited to be loaded. The SS men were running along the rows armed with whips, and they were randomly beating the Jews standing in the heat. I also have several pictures from that spot.

A few days earlier, during my inspection of fuel depots in [the town of] Ujazd next to Tomaszów, I visited the ghetto there. There I even saw a Berlin family of Jews I knew, who were living there in primitive conditions. I also handed over to the committee a few pictures of the Jewish police, starving people, and abandoned children, as well as the process of delousing.

I testify under oath that everything corresponds to the truth and that I have added nothing.

Fritz Hoeft
Nussdorf/Inn
(—) signature

APPENDIX 9.
INTERVIEW WITH HUBERT PFOCH

Hubert Pfoch, geboren 1920, war während des Krieges Soldat und danach Funktionär der Sozialdemokratischen Partei Österreichs. Nach dem Krieg engagierte er sich sehr für den Wiederaufbau Wiens; zeitweilig war er Präsident des Wiener Landtages.

Herr Pfoch, als junger Soldat der Wehrmacht haben Sie einmal einen Deportationszug gesehen. Was haben Sie da beobachtet?

Ja, ich bin damals mit hundert anderen Soldaten von Wien an die Front nach Rußland abkommandiert worden. Und am 22. und 23. August 1942 bin ich in Siedlce oder Sielce in Polen einem Transport begegnet und habe mit angesehen, wie die deutsche Polizei, SS, aber wie sich später herausgestellt hat, ukrainische Hilfswillige...

In SS-Uniform?

In SS-Uniform... in ganz grausamer Weise Hunderte Juden, die zuerst auf einem Perron saßen, in die Waggons hineingeprügelt haben, mit Schlagen und Stoßen, mit Schießen und Schreien.

Haben Sie auch einen Mordfall erlebt?

Ja. Zuerst habe ich noch probiert, unseren Zugkommandanten zu einer Intervention zu überreden – unter dem Vorwand, wir seien deutsche Soldaten, sogenannte Front, und unsere Kampfmoral würde ja nicht gerade gestärkt, wenn man Zeuge solcher Grausamkeiten würde. Ein SS-Offizier, es war aber ein Deutscher oder ein Österreicher mit einem Wolfshund, hat uns beteuert, wir sollten schauen, daß wir wegkommen, sonst ließe er einen Waggon anhängen und wir könnten uns Treblinka von innen anschauen.

Sie haben doch den Mord an einer Mutter und einem Kind gesehen.

Ja, ich habe mit anschauen müssen, wie ein ukrainischer Hilfswilliger eine junge Frau mit Kind, die sich zu Boden geworfen hat, so gerichtet hat, daß der Kopf des Kindes auf dem Kopf der Mutter lag, und mit einem Schuß beide tötete.

Und er hat gelacht dabei...

Ich habe dann versucht, das zu dokumentieren. Und ich habe ja im Krieg immer auch ein Tagebuch geführt. Das besitze ich noch. Ich habe mir vom Waggon meinen Fotoapparat geholt und habe unter großer Gefahr vier Aufnahmen von diesen Szenen gemacht.

Ich habe sie auch damals dem Staatsanwalt im Prozeß gegen die Lagermannschaft von Treblinka zur Verfügung gestellt, und sie sind 1965 mit als Material, als Zeugenmaterial, verwendet worden.

(Abb. 1) Das ist der Perron des Bahnhofes von Sielce [Siedlce], und hier sind Angehörige von jüdischen Hilfstruppen, die schon mehrmals in diesen Autos gekommen sind, um die Toten abzutransportieren, die in der Nacht von ukrainischen Hilfswilligen erschossen wurden. Sooft einer aufgestanden ist, hat er auf die Gruppe geschossen, und es hat eine große Zahl von Toten gegeben oder Erschöpften, die von diesen Leuten wie Mehlsäcke auf das Auto geworfen worden sind. Bei der

Verladeszene habe ich dann dieses Bild fotografiert (Abb. 2), nachdem die Soldaten, die mit mir unterwegs nach Rußland waren, zu dem Transport hingegangen sind. Dort lagen die, die nicht schnell genug gelaufen und von der SS erschossen worden sind. Hier sieht man zwei dieser Toten. Der eine Mann hat einen Gehirnaustritt gehabt und über den ist der Waggon drübergefahren und hat ihm die Hand abgedrückt. Und dann gibt es noch diese schreckliche Szene (Abb. 3), wo die Gruppen für den Transport in den Waggon hineingeprügelt werden, und zwar auch so, daß die Familien zerrissen wurden. Der Vater in einem Waggon, Mutter und Kind woanders, und man sieht ja die Ärmlichkeit dieser Leute, die angeblich aus dem Warschauer Ghetto gekommen sind und nach Treblinka in dieses Vernichtungslager gebracht worden sind, wie ich spater erfahren habe. (Abb. 4) Dieser Soldat, ein Ukrainerder, der dann diese Mordszene mit Frau und Kind gemacht hat – und andere haben mit ihren Gewehrkolben so reingeschlagen, daß die Kolben gebrochen sind und sie nur mehr den Lauf mit dem Schloß in der Hand gehabt haben. Rechts im Bild sieht man noch einige Deutsche, die das mit anschauen, aber natürlich nichts dagegen tun konnten. Ich habe das alles notiert, also zum Zeitpunkt des Geschehens.

Mir war schrecklich übel. Aus dem Lager in Trehlinka, wo wir vorbeigefahren sind, ist ein penetranter Leichengeruch in der Luft gewesen, und ich habe mich bei der ersten Station hingesetzt, und das alles, was ich gesehen habe, aufgeschrieben und dokumentiert, wie ich auch sonst immer wahrend der Kriegsgeschehen liier Eintragungen gemacht habe – wo wir uns aurhalten, wer verwundet, wer gefallen ist. Und ich habe auch politische Kommentare in das Tagebuch mit entsprechender Vorsicht aufgenommen.

Source: Michel Alexandre, *Der Judenmord. Deutsche und Österreicher berichten* [(Cologne, 1998)], pp. 33–36.

TRANSLATION [from the Polish—trans.]:

Hubert Pfoch, born in 1920, was a soldier during the war and then an activist of the Social-Democratic Party of Austria. After the war he was very involved in the rebuilding of Vienna; for a time he was also the chairman of the Viennese *Landtag* [Parliament].

Mr. Pfoch, as a young soldier of the Wehrmacht you saw the deportation train. What exactly did you see?

Yes, at that time I was sent from Vienna to the eastern front. From 22 to 23 August 1942 I encountered in the town of Siedlce or Sielce in Poland a transport and I saw the German police, the SS, or, as it later turned out, Ukrainian helpers...

In SS uniforms?
In SS uniforms… drive hundreds of Jews, who had been sitting on the platform, into freight cars in a very brutal way, with beating, shooting, and shouting.

Did you witness the killing?
Yes, first I still tried to convince the commander of the transport to intervene. I used the pretext that we are German front-line soldiers, and morale would not be strengthened by being witnesses to such cruelty. The SS officer, he was either a German or an Austrian with a German Shepherd dog, assured us that if we refused to be witnesses to the killing, he would order another car to be attached to the transport, and we would be able to have a view of Treblinka from the inside.

Did you see the killing of a mother and child?
I had to watch as a Ukrainian helper picked up a young woman and child, who had earlier thrown themselves onto the ground, and stood them up in such a way that the child's head was resting on its mother head, and he killed them both with one shot.

And he was laughing…
I tried to document all of this. And during the war I also kept a diary, which I still have. I also pulled my camera out of the train car and, being in great danger, took four pictures of those events.

I was also as the disposition of the prosecutor during the trial against the staff of the camp in Treblinka in 1965. My pictures were used as evidentiary material. This is the platform of the train station in the town of Sieice [*sic*], and here are the members of the Jewish auxiliary units, who often came in these cars to take away the bodies of those who had been shot to death during the night by the Ukrainian helpers. As soon as one of the reclining people rose, the Ukrainians would shoot at the whole group. There were a lot of dead and exhausted people, who were thrown onto trucks like sacks of flour. I photographed a loading scene [see photograph 125—author's note] while the soldiers who were with me going to Russia were walking toward the [military] transport. Lying on the ground were those who couldn't run fast enough and so were shot to death by the SS. Here we see two of those who were killed. You can see the brains leaking out of one of them; moreover, a passing train cut off his hand [see photograph 124—author's note]. Then there is this terrible scene [see photograph 122—author's note] in which we see a group of people being driven into a freight car in such a way that families were separated. The father into one car and the mother and child into another; and we can also see the misery of these people, who were supposedly from the Warsaw ghetto and were taken to the death camp in Treblinka, as I later found out. This soldier [see photograph 123—author's note], a Ukrainian, who was the perpetrator of the killing of the mother and child, and others were hitting so hard with the butts of their rifles that these would crack. On the right we can see several Germans, who see this but of course can do nothing. I noted all this as it happened.

I felt terribly ill. An intense stench of bodies was being exuded from the camp in Treblinka, past which we were riding. I sat down at the first station and wrote down what I had seen. I took quite thorough notes from the time of the war—where we stopped, who was injured, who died. I also wrote down political commentary in my diary, with appropriate caution.

APPENDIX 10.

THE ACCOUNT OF SISTER OF THE SACRED HEART BENEDYKTA (APOLONIA KRET) WRITTEN DOWN BY PIOTR KOMAR (SKÓRZEC, 02.06.2008)

In looking through the convent chronicle with Sister Benedykta, I found an entry dedicated to Barbara Piechotka. It related that it was a commander of the navy-blue police that asked the Sisters of the Sacred Heart to take into their care one of two girls he found in the woods. The older one was taken by a local farmer's wife to work, while the younger one was to be taken care of by the sisters. As we can conclude from the entry in the chronicle, the girl was about 4 years old, was sick, and was terribly neglected.

Yet Sister Benedykta asserts that it happened differently. In spite of her advanced age (90 years old), she remembers those times fairly well. It was 1944. According to the sister, one of the nuns once went to the local, Skórzec, township offices in order to take care of some clerical matters; as far as she remembers, it was December and there was snow on the ground [an error either in the month or the year, since in December 1944 the Red Army was already in this area—author's note]. While she was in the township offices, a farmer burst in and started to shout that he had been left an orphan who was louse ridden, neglected, and on top of that sick. When she returned to the convent, the sister immediately told this whole incident to the mother superior, who ordered the farmer to be found immediately and the child to be taken from him and brought without delay to the convent. It was painful to look at the child; it had lice everywhere. The sisters cleaned her up and dressed her in new clothes because the others were only worth burning. As the sister says, she swept the lice from her cut hair with a broom since they were scampering away from the flames that were coming out of the oven. Then the sisters rubbed the girl with an ointment for over a dozen days until all the lice were gone.

She was a very nice child who loved to sing love songs and who was in fact about 4 when she was found. During the first stage of her upbringing, no one, not even the mother superior, knew that she was Jewish. Taking into account that at that time, if it had come out, it would have meant death.

Sister Stanisława, along with the local priest, prepared her and her older sister, Jadzia, for First Holy Communion. The sister let the girls know that in order to take First Holy Communion they have to be christened. To which both in unison answered that they were Catholics and both had been christened in Warsaw. It was after the fact that Sister Stanisława went to Warsaw to check if they were indeed telling the truth, and that's when it all came out. These people didn't exist; they had themselves adopted the name Górska, and they had made up the whole story of the christening. They claimed that that's what their parents had taught them. They also said there had been three of them, but they didn't know the fate of their sister; they didn't know who had taken her. They also admitted to the worst for those times: that they were Jewish. Their parents and brother had died during the escape from the Warsaw ghetto. The girls had escaped from the ghetto and walked as far as Czerniejew, from which an unknown man had driven them in his wagon to Skórzec.

Sister Stanisława thought through the whole situation and decided to christen the girls. First she went to the local priest, who along with her had been preparing the girls for First Holy Communion. The priest, outraged by the whole thing, yelled at her that he would not christen the girls. No one at the convent knew about the whole matter yet. After this, the sister, under the pretext that she was taking them to the doctor—claiming that one of the girls has a polyps in her nose—rode with the girls on horseback to the Kotuń priest, who christened them. Considering the times then, he did not write up a certificate of christening for the girls, undoubtedly in fear of punishment, even by death.

Only after the fact did the convent sisters find out about the true ancestry of the girls. This did not, however, change their attitude toward them. They continued their upbringing. The girls were accompanied to and from school, since there was a fear that the Jews would kidnap the girls. After a time, the Jews indeed came for the girls in a horse-drawn droshky, as Sister Benedykta recalls. They said that, through kindness or by force, they would still take the girls. They wanted to pay the mother superior for taking care of them, but she pushed the money aside, stating that it was not for this that she had raised the girls. The year was 1946, but the sister was not entirely sure.

After the girls had been taken, the mother superior could not rest, since she had heard rumors of trade in children. Only when Basia sent a letter from Zabrze that she calmed down and sighed with relief. She wrote in it that all her things were taken when she was leaving for Israel.

Until this day, Basia keeps in touch with the convent, not only by mail but also visiting the convent in person. She visited the convent for the last time in 2002, as the entry of 12.09.2002 in the chronicle testifies. She at that time came to Poland with an attorney, who went with her even to Kotuń in order to find her certificate of christening. However, there was none, since as I already mentioned above, the priest had not issued one out of fear for his own life. She did not hide her disappointment over this fact, since, as she said, a Polish citizenship was important to her, for reasons not further clarified.

Basia more than once invited the sisters to Tel Aviv, where she now lives. Some of them accepted her invitation, and she, of course, covered all the travel costs. She sent packages and Christmas cards. As Sister Benedykta recalls, she even sent 50 dollars several times. The point was not about the money itself, the sister states emotionally, but about the very fact of remembering. Sister Benedykta was awarded a medal. As she says with a smile, "Smashing those lice was worth it."

Basia's fate after being taken from Skórzec varied. She finished her studies, was a Hebrew language teacher, got married, and changed her real name, Faktor, to Piechotka. Then she was divorced; as she stated, she was too delicate for her husband. Now she is retired. She even wrote several books about her time in Poland. She wrote about her story, representing the Poles in "too rosy a light," which was the reason the books were not accepted for publication.[a] She considers the years spent in Skórzec as the happiest in her life.

At this point it is worth mentioning that the headquarters of the Gestapo, where people were tortured and many died, was also located in the convent of the Sisters of the Sacred Heart. The sisters also helped many orphans from the Zamość region.

EDITOR'S NOTE, APPENDIX 10

a. It is difficult to say with any certainty why Basia's books were not published.

APPENDIX 11.
AGNIESZKA BUDNA "JADZIA"

She was born in 1909 or 1916 in Aleksandrów Kujawski, in a Catholic family. She lived in Gdynia until the war. After the occupation of the city by the Germans, she was displaced as a Pole. She spent several weeks in a transition camp in Częstochowa. Then, at the end of September 1939, she ended up in Siedlce via Warsaw with Helena Górska and her two children. The German Labor Office referred her to the Siedlce

Criminal Police Department, Kripo, as a cleaning lady. At that time, the department was headed by an officer named Zulauf. The station was still being set up at the time, and the painting and carpentry work was being done by Jewish workers. Budna became acquainted with and befriended them. When the first liquidation of the ghetto took place, that is, 22–24 August 1942, the Germans still left Jewish labor detachments behind. When they started preparations for complete liquidation, Budna, in October 1942, hid six people: Motl Galicki; Lipa Galicki, Motl's teen-aged brother, whom she brought from the camp on the so-called Bauzug train; the Halber brothers, Izaak, who escaped from a labor detachment at the airport, and Abraham, employed as a mechanic at Kripo; Melech, who escaped from a transport to Treblinka; and Dawid Grünberg. Budna took up residence with the fugitives in a modest two-room apartment in the garret at 43 May 1st Street (currently Bishop I. Świrski Steet; the building from that time has been partially rebuilt). The apartment contained an alcove used as a storeroom for coal, wood, and potatoes. This space had a double wall, behind which the fugitives could hide when necessary. There was very little space there, and they only went there in the event of a threat; otherwise they spent the whole time in the room. While "Jadzia" was at work, there had to be absolute silence in the room. Love developed between Budna and Motl Galicki. Motl always impatiently awaited "Jadzia's" return, and opened the door for her. A neighbor noticed this, and pointing at "Jadzia" in the market square accused her of hiding a Jew. Budna reacted decisively with a denial. She called her a vicious gossip, explaining that this was not a Jew but her man. In order to remove suspicion from herself, she invited Commander Zulauf and several policemen for dinner the next day. A roast goose and some alcohol created the right atmosphere. The Germans were loud, which all the neighbors noticed. That removed suspicion form "Jadzia," who bought three rabbits and kept them in the storeroom. Any knocking sounds in the apartment during the tenant's absence could be explained in this way.

And so all lived to see the arrival of the Red Army, after which Agnieszka Budna and Motl Galicki were officially married. In September 1945 they had a daughter whom they named Bela. They left for Munich with her husband's family. They soon returned, however. Motl died in January 1946, and Agnieszka returned to Gdynia. Then she worked in a hat cooperative in Legnica. Here she met Szymon Widerschal, whom she married. Unfortunately, her daughter, Bela, fell under a train and died. This was a horrible event for the mother, who blamed other children for the accident. She left for Israel in 1958 with her husband, and in 1987, at the application of Izaak Halber, she was awarded the title of Righteous among the Nations of the World. Her photograph along with an interview appeared in the prestigious album *Rescuers: Portraits of Moral Courage in the Holocaust* by Gay Block and Malka Drucker. She died in Israel in 2004.

Source: Yad Vashem in Jerusalem, Testimony of Agnieszka Widerschal, sig. 2222/119–/

(03.2555); W. Stefanoff, "Jedna na milion," in *Gazeta Stołeczna*, 30.10–01.11.1993; from the recollections of Izaak Halber and his letter to Yad Vashem in Jerusalem dated 10 March 1986, in the author's possession.

APPENDIX 12.

LETTER FROM THE CHAIRMAN OF THE UNION OF SIEDLCE JEWS IN THE UNITED STATES TO THE COUNTY ADMINISTRATOR IN SIEDLCE WITH THANKS FOR HELP DURING THE EXHUMATION OF JEWS MURDERED BY THE GERMANS DURING WORLD WAR II

Source: Archiwum Państwowe w Siedlcach.

TRANSLATION:

To the County Offices in Siedlce

Union of Siedlce Jews in Cleveland, Ohio, USA
Siedlce Relief Society
7543 Broadway Ave., Cleveland, Ohio

We hereby have the honor of expressing our sincerest thanks to the County Offices in Siedlce for the disinterested help offered to our compatriots remaining in Siedlce during the exhumation and provisions of last rites to the dear remains of our martyrs.—God bless you!

[STAMP]Siedlce Relief Society
Cleveland, Ohio

[STAMP]Siedlce County Offices
In [ILLEGIBLE]
22 V 1948
No. [ILLEGIBLE]

[HANDWRITTEN]Chairman J. Gongolewicz
[HANDWRITTEN]/J. Gągolewicz/

APPENDIX 13.

STATEMENT CONCERNING THE POLICY OF LOCAL AUTHORITIES REGARDING THE PROTECTION OF LANDMARKS AND RESPECT FOR PLACES OF NATIONAL REMEMBRANCE IN SIEDLCE

Reprehensible events have taken place in Siedlce in recent years regarding the protection of landmarks and places of national remembrance. They have shaken public opinion. They consist of the following:
— the demolition of nineteenth-century buildings and wooden houses in the center of the city;
— the removal of the landmark memorializing the historical place of execution of Poles during World War II as well as the stone and tablet in honor of the Home Army on Piłsudski Street;
— the demolition of the Jewish prayer house on Asłanowicz Street;
— the demolition of the Jewish hospital on Armia Krajowa Street;

—the destruction of the historic nature of Duchess Aleksandra Ogińska's seventeenth-century park;

—the destruction of the historic nature of several Siedlce streets.

In 1995, an opinion titled "Siedlce. A Study in Cultural Significance" was commissioned by the Siedlce City Offices in the matter of preparing detailed plans for the spatial development of Siedlce. On several hundred pages, the authors describe the urban value of historic buildings and present concrete recommendations about putting them under conservation protection. In spite of the opinion of specialists, many buildings and places important for the history of Siedlce are disappearing from the panorama of the city. Local authorities are ignoring the recommendations of experts.

The most disturbing recent example of the destruction of buildings important to the cultural space of the city and arousing protests among sympathizers of Siedlce is this year's demolition of the building of the old Jewish Hospital on Armia Krajowa Street. This building had an over 130-year-long history and was one of the few Jewish structures that survived the Second World War. In the professional literature it was noted as a landmark and as a unique building. It also existed as a landmark in the consciousness of Siedlce natives. As a religious hospital, it was exceptional on a national scale. It was probably the only surviving Jewish hospital in Poland. The property of the hospital was bordered by the old Jewish cemetery, destroyed only during World War II. According to some sources, it also included the hospital property.

In 1906, the hospital was one of the main places in which the tsarist pogrom of the Jews took place. It went down in history as the "great Siedlce pogrom." People were murdered in the shelled building, in which the wounded were hospitalized. Many were killed on their way to the hospital. The Russian extermination of the Siedlce Jews was reported on in the largest newspapers in Europe and the United States: *Time, Die Welt, Arar, Berliner Tageblat, Der Neuer Weg, Forwerts*, and many others. The pogrom outraged the opinion of the whole world. Half of the population of Siedlce before the war was of the Jewish faith, and 17,000 Jews were murdered in the city's ghetto during the Nazi occupation. Now the last reminders of them are being liquidated.

Those who have an interest in the history of Siedlce as well as in the development in Poland of research on the history of local societies are outraged by the liquidation of reminders and proof of the 400-year-long presence of Jews in Podlasie. A federative understanding of culture, one of the fundamental characteristics of which is openness, requires us to take care of the history of our society in its multinational dimension. Father J. Bocheński, a Polish-Swiss philosopher, once said about this openness, "The idea of a homogeneous state [...] is in direct opposition to the ideology of classical Poland. In Poland, everyone had a place."

The liquidation of the building of the Jewish Hospital is also the destruction of the legacy of Polish culture, an open and multifaceted culture. Jewish culture is not something that is isolated from and indifferent to our culture but is its historical element that derives from the tolerance that is rooted in our history. Those signed below express their surprise at the transfer to a private investor of the building, reclaimed by the Jewish Council in the 1990s, that was the last of the places of martyrdom of the Jewish nation from the times of the tsarist holocaust preserved in Siedlce.

In light of the above-mentioned facts, those who love Siedlce are expressing their disapprobation of the policy of the local authorities concerning the preservation of landmarks as well as respect for places of martyrdom of the Polish nation leading to a loss of the architectural and historical identity of the city. They are expressing their indignation at the institution responsible for the preservation of the Polish cultural tradition. They are proposing that immediate steps be taken to protect all structures that are unique in Siedlce architecture from liquidation and well as the initiation of procedures for the bestowal of the legal status of landmarks of art to buildings that are important for the architectural tradition and history of Siedlce. They are also proposing that particular protection be given to places of national remembrance. These places are designated by history for all time.

[Following are the signatures of 246 residents of Siedlce—author's note.]

Source: Text of the "Statement" in the author's possession.

APPENDIX 14.

MAP OF THE CENTER OF THE CITY

Marked sites:

① Jewish cemetery.
② Building of the former Talmud-Torah religious school.
③ Monument memorializing the extermination of the Jewish community.
④ Ramp by which Jews were loaded onto freight cars.
⑤ Prison.
− − − − − The final road of Siedlce Jews

Source: Drawn by the author.

APPENDIX 15.
ANNE SAFRAN—"WANDERING AROUND SIEDLCE"

I wander around Siedlce seeking a face I may know.
Here's Jatkowa Street, there Długa... But no, you I don't recall!
My grandfather's house destroyed, the deep well boarded up...
How everything has been washed away by bloody, cruel years!

In the city park I hear weeping trees.
The stream by the hillside—why's it bubbling so noisily now?
Where are my friends, those who were cheerful and fair?
I feel their shades surrounding me...

Siedlce, 1962.

Source: Fragment from the collection *Will to Live* (New York, 1968). Translated from Yiddish into Polish by Michael Halber.

APPENDIX 16.
STORIES BY BRACHA KAHAN (BEATRICE STOLOVY)

The Jewish stories written in Yiddish by Bracha Kahan (Stolovy) were translated for the first time into Polish by Maria Halber and edited by Edward Kopówka in consultation with Michael Halber.

Bracha Kahan was born in Siedlce in 1899. Her father, Abraham Hersz Kahan, was a butcher, the co-owner of a butcher shop. Her mother, Rojza née Osina, was occupied with raising five children: Bracha, Chana (Anna), Chaim Lejb, and Sara. The family lived at 8 Jatkowa Street.

Bracha's formal education was limited to three grades of the Russian public school, which was free. Her parents were financially unable to provide further education for their daughter, although her mother had ambitions to give her children an education. Bracha received private lessons in Polish and Yiddish. In 1915–1916, she took part in the classes of the drama section of the Yiddishe Kunst club (the so-called Hazomir) and attended classes in Hebrew. She immigrated to America in 1916 with her sister Anna, who was two years younger than she.

After arriving in the United States, Bracha worked hard in New York confectionary workshops, studying the English language at night. Some of the money she earned she sent back to Siedlce to her family, whose financial circumstances were dire. In 1920, her parents and the rest of her siblings immigrated to America. In that same year, Bracha married Izaak Stolovy, who had emigrated from Siedlce to Chicago a few years previously. Two children were born of this union: Alexander and Edith, who later took the name Semiatin.

Bracha Stolovy published poems in the Jewish press in the United States (*Der Tog* and *Forverts*). She also published three books in Yiddish: *Mayn velt* (My world), 1952; *Verter un verlekh fun yidishn folklor* (Proverbs and sayings from Jewish folklore), 1976; and *Fun fargengene teg* (From bygone days), 1978. This last publication contains mostly poems and recollections. Bracha Stolovy died in 1983.

"The Wench"

Long, long ago, in my Polish city of Siedlce, where I was born and raised, one often saw people who were not in their right minds running around the streets. At that time these people were not placed in institutions, as they are now. They walked around freely, as long as they did no one any harm. I have not forgotten those characters, which have engraved themselves in my memory, even though I came here as a young girl.[2] The demented paupers wandering about the streets were sick, ragged, and hungry. No one took an interest in them. Only the children noticed them, ran after them, taunted them, and teased them. We all know how cruel children can be in relation to handicapped people if the proper attitude toward them is not explained to them. One of these unfortunate figures was "The Wench." That's what they called her. No one knew her real name. It was said in the city that she had come from afar and from a pious family. She went mad because her parents forced her to marry someone they had sought out themselves and did not allow her to marry her beloved, who was a tailor. Every spring "The Wench" would appear on the streets of the city. She was a tall, slim woman with beautiful eyes. She walked around clad in a black shawl. In her arms she carried a child wrapped in rags. She talked to herself, constantly rocked the child, comforted it, and kissed it constantly. And so she wandered about with the child for days and weeks. And then one day, a terrible scream was heard throughout the city: "Where is my child!" she called in a terrible voice. "Help! Give me back my child!"

No one even looked at her. No one was interested in the woman's fate. Just as before, when she was walking around with the child. Everyone was indifferent to her screams. Only the rascals ran after her and mimicked her.

"You want a child? Here!" they yelled and pelted her with stones and rag balls.[3]

In the city they said that "The Wench" lived in the ruins outside town in the winter. She was kept by irresponsible youths,[4] who took advantage of her in exchange for food. No one in the city wanted to look after her. Everyone said, "Let someone else take care of her."

And so it was repeated from year to year. Until the following spring. With its arrival, "The Wench" would again appear on the streets with a newborn child wrapped in rags in her arms.

"Candies, Chocolates, Jellies"

When I recall the shops in the old days in Siedlce, A. Liessin's peom "Der Kramer" (The shopkeeper)[5] immediately comes to mind. In it, the poet so authentically described that life, that hunger, that cold, and those meager earnings. He showed how a poor shopkeeper, waiting hopelessly for a customer to whom he could sell a herring for two kopecks, would become engrossed in the meantime in musings about the Holy Land and the Messiah. This poem reminds me of the story of a little stall belonging to my relative in Siedlce. Her husband was a room painter and a good craftsman. He painted the walls for rich customers, and his favorite theme was beautiful green meadows, trees, and even birds. In spite of his honest labor, he could not earn enough for bread and rent. His wife, our relative, decided to open a stall. She borrowed a few rubles and made a special box with compartments according to her own concept. She put into it candies, chocolates, jellies, and other goodies. She also bought a few seltzer siphons, and she displayed all this, along with a few colorful glasses, in one of the windows of her apartment, which was located facing the street. And so she became a merchant! One day passed, then another, a third, and no one came to make a purchase. The saleswoman was forced to leave her stall to buy some potatoes and kasha herself.

"And what if a customer comes and I'm not here?" she thought. And she had a brilliant idea: "I'll engage my six-year-old sister, who is being raised in my home."

As she thought, so she did.

"Esther," she called. "I'm going shopping, and you pay attention to the children and the stall. I'll show you how to open this box if a customer should come. Remember, you must take a kopeck for each piece, a two-kopeck coin for two pieces, and don't forget to close the box right away and put it back in the window.

"Yes," Esther nodded her pretty little head.

My relative obviously forgot that you don't send the cat for milk. Little Esther could not resist opening the box. At first she only wanted to have a look at all these delicious treats. But she could not resist, took a candy into her hand, and carefully bit off a piece from one side. She also took a chocolate and delicately nibbled on it. She placed the nibbled-on sweets back into the box in such a way that no one would notice. Then my relative came back home, checked that the box was closed, and calmly started to prepare dinner. Little Esther watched the stall every time my relative had to leave the house. And she always nibbled on a piece of the goody. This lasted until a customer came and bought a few candies. When my relative counted out the candies, she noticed a misfortune. All the sweets had been nibbled on at one side. I can imagine what a scolding little Esther got. I well remember the frightened eyes of the six-year-old "big girl" when our relative brought her to my mother for judgment.

"I don't want to see her in my house anymore," she said. "She has brought misfortune to me. If she had taken a few chocolates, I could understand. But she nibbled off a piece of all the sweets. How can I sell them now?"

My mother gave Esther a proper talking to and my relative a few guldens, and the trial ended there…

"Great-Grandmother Matl"

My maternal great-grandmother lived to be almost 100. She outlived all her children. I have remembered her as a slim, tall, straight-backed woman dressed in a black silk dress. She wore a bonnet[6] on her head that matched her dress and was decorated with silk flowers and velvet bows. She never wore glasses, although her vision was poor in the last years of her life. She often visited her daughter Rojza, my mother, who was brought up in her home until her wedding.[7] Grandma Matl, as we all called her, was perfect in everything: dressing, cooking, as well as running a home, which was a rarity in those times, that is, in 1910. She never ate roasted or cooked food prepared by another's hands. She cooked and baked herself until the last days of her life. She did not trust another's hands.[8] I remember her cleanly maintained apartment, a living room and kitchen. I was then 9 years old,[9] and Mother would send me to her to invite her for the holidays. I would run the two streets to her house, cheerful and glad, for I knew that Grandma would treat me to home-baked cookies.

To this day I remember the impression her little apartment had on me. The first thing that struck you after entering the room was her bed, which shone with cleanliness and whiteness. It was covered by a hand-made bed-spread. Two big, down pillows lay on it in embroidered white pillowcases. The table was also set with an embroidered tablecloth. There was always a carafe of wine and challah in the room as well as silver candlesticks with candles ready to light when Shabbat came.

Grandma offered me her cookies, as usual, waited until I ate them, then, elegantly dressed, followed me to our house.

Once my mother sent me to Grandma's to bring her to a Siedlce photographer. She very much wanted to have her picture. I knew that very pious Jews did not allow themselves to be photographed because they considered this a sin: "Man," they would say, "was created in the image of God."[10]

I walked and wondered if Grandma would allow herself to be photographed. When I arrived, I politely asked, "Grandma Matl, do you want to be photographed?"

"Why not?" she answered. "Let all my children, grandchildren, and great-grandchildren have my photograph. When they look at my picture, then they will not forget me."

Mother was already waiting for us at the photographer's studio to bring Grandma Matl inside. Grandma hesitated a moment: "Wait, Rojzele," she said. "I think my collar is not even. One corner is longer, and the other is shorter," Grandma said.

"It's even, it's even, everything is fine," Mother answered.

And the photographer took Grandma's picture.

When I now look at Grandma's picture, I see with surprise that, indeed, one corner of her collar is shorter than the other.

Written May 1977.

[Editor's Note: The photograph described in this story is reproduced as Photograph 52A in the photographs section.]

"Skheda"

I spent my childhood years in the *skheda*.[11] That's what my mother and father would call our apartment, which our grandfather, rest his soul, left to his children as an inheritance. This was a small wooden house with four tiny apartments and three little stalls. The seven siblings split this among them after our grandfather's death. Some got apartments, others stalls. When I got older and was 6,[12] the *skheda* got too tight for us because of the arrival of several siblings. These three cramped little rooms became filled with additional beds, little beds, and cradles. My father decided to move to a larger apartment and to rent our part of the *skheda*. He calculated that, although it will be hard for him to pay rent, at least the family would not suffer by living in such a cramped space.

"We will live like human beings," he said. "When I get the rent for the *skheda*, I'll add a few rubles, and we'll manage somehow."

This idea was a good one, but anxiety crept in at the very beginning. The man who had rented the apartment, a cheder teacher, a poor beggar, did not have the money for the rent in the very first quarter. In those times, rent was paid quarterly, that is, for three months. The tenant came to my father, made excuses, and asked my father to wait a little.

"As soon as I get the tuition money from a few tenement-house owners whose sons I teach, I'll immediately bring it with thanks," he said.

But he didn't have it to pay in the second quarter either, and he didn't even come to make excuses. My mother started to nag my father, claiming that this so-called teacher would bring us grief. She had hoped that the rent from this apartment would buy new shoes for the children since they were walking around in shoes with torn soles. But my father justified the tenant. "But he's a pauper. As soon as he gets the money, he'll bring it to us. Don't worry, he's a decent Jew. Trust me."

And that was the first time we children heard our parents arguing. We marveled. What could have happened?

"What is he thinking!" my mother yelled and started to cry. "We have to get the apartment back. My children are dearer to me than this tenant. Let the rich Jews in the city support him. Go to him again and tell him you need the apartment back for yourself and he should just move out."

My father came to the conclusion that my mother was right, and with a heavy heart he went to his tenant. This was before Sukkot. Cold winds were already blowing, and a light rain was falling. Mother sat and waited for the money that my father was supposed to bring. The thought out loud, "Bruchele needs a new coat because she has started going to school. Chana should get a new dress because she's grown out of the old one. The boys need new shoes and yarmulkes for when they go to the synagogue."

My father returned. He didn't say anything. He took the Talmud book[13] and immersed himself in contemplation. My mother tried to talk to him a few times, but my father didn't listen to her at all and just "mumbled" verses. At a certain point, my mother lost her patience. "You went to take care of something," she said loudly. "Tell me what you accomplished," she added.

My father kept rocking back and forth over the book,[14] as though he were looking for help there and started talking as if to himself. "He is a pauper,

235

and he's supporting a bunch of hungry children. He even wanted to give me a few rubles," said my father and became thoughtful for a moment.

"And you gave them back to him?" my mother cut in angrily.

"How could I take them from him after I found out that he had borrowed these few rubles from Szymon to pay back his loan in the grocery store? They wouldn't give him anything more on credit. You should see those hungry children, how they threw themselves at the bread and herring he had brought home! Oh, well," my father said with tears in his eyes, "I didn't want those children on my conscience. I did not want them to die because of me."

My mother was moved by what my father had said, and tears glistened in her eyes as well. They didn't talk about this anymore. In the meantime, winter came with its gales and freezes. There was not much joy in our house either. We spent our last saved rubles for the rent. There was no income; there was nothing to buy coal with to heat the apartment. My father and mother walked around the house in their winter coats, and we children lay in our beds covered with our featherbeds and kept warm that way. Suddenly the door opened. The wind blew, and it became even colder in the room. The *melamed* came in,[15] stooped and embarrassed. After looking around the apartment and seeing our situation, he took off his coat and said, "Take this, Mr. Hersz, this is my entire fortune. This is a good fur; my father-in-law gave it to me as a wedding gift. This is what I have left from better times. What can I do when I have nothing to pay with? I am *a melamed*; many students have left me lately, and new ones aren't coming. You know what? Throw me out into the street with everything I have. Maybe someone will take pity and take me under their roof. I know you are not rich. So what am I to do? My wife even tried her hand at peddling, but instead of making money she put money into the business! It didn't work out. One could just tear oneself to pieces! Take my fur, please," and he shoved the coat into my father's hands. My father shuddered. "What are you doing, Mr. Dawid. For God's sake. In such freezing weather, how can I let a person out without a coat? Put it on, this second!

He walked the teacher to the door, and said in parting, "Be well, and may God help you!"

"A Jewish Home"[16]

Rajzla sits in a rocking chair, lost in thought and memories. Her whole life swims before her eyes, ever since her Michał went into eternity. She lives in her dreams and memories of the past. She had an intense life. She sees herself in a small town in Poland, where she was born in a very religious home, and she recalls the festive holiday celebration, the table beautifully set by her mother, the Shabbat candles, and she hears her father's prayers. All this has stuck forever in her memory. Then she thinks of daily life in her country [the United States—author's note], she is tormented by loneliness and abandonment, a longing for those close to her. Her face shines as she remembers Michał's proposing to her, but she was still too young, he was older and experienced. They decide to wait until her parents arrive here [the United States—author's note]. The beautiful days have passed. Love, theaters, concerts, operas—she visited them all. Dear children. Much joy. Her husband, Michał, also came from an Orthodox home. But he had long since walked away from that atmosphere. Travel in distant countries and eating in other people's houses moved him away from religion. He was an avid Zionist, and he loved his nation. He worked socially, but he wasn't religious. Religion, he would say, is an impediment in normal life.

What Michał said had an enormous influence on Rajzla. She was very young and slowly succumbed to Michał's influence. After the wedding, everything was kosher in her house at first, but Michał laughed at her. All these rules[17] had arisen in bygone, primitive times, even though they were invented by wise people. There were no sanitary conditions in those times. Jews were taught then to wash their hands before eating, to go to the *mikveh*, to use certain dishes[18] according to religion. All that was fine once, but now what do we need these superstitions for when we have hot water and soap? Well, understandably the rabbi didn't agree with him, but Rajzla nodded and worked out her own principles. For example, she bought meat at a kosher store, but she didn't soak and salt it.[19] She didn't mix meat and butter, and pork never appeared in the house. Michał also compromised. He pleased his wife, and he also respected her parents. He did not go to the bethel on Shabbat, but he came on holidays. He also went with Rajzla on Yom Kippur after the service to meet her parents by the synagogue to wish them a happy new year. The whole family gathered for the meal on Passover, and sometimes on Saturday evenings or on other holidays. That was the whole of his Jewishness.

Time flew, and children were born. Heated times ensued; Rajzla didn't complain but became active. She worked in Jewish organizations, studied, took classes, and read a lot of books. Often after hard work she would fall asleep with the children out of great fatigue. But she did not give up, thanks to Michał, who never refused to look after the children even though he got up very early for work. They spent Sundays all together. They took the children for a walk in the park; sometimes they went visiting, and sometimes they invited guests to their house. Rajzla grew spiritually and exceeded

Michał. She was active in organizations, sent the children to school and to declamatory classes. She herself studied a lot. Bitter years came, unemployment, crisis. Michał lost his job. It seemed that dollars had been saved. You had to eat, and there wasn't even money for the rent. Winter came, shoes needed to be bought for the children, and a doctor needed to be paid for. Michał would become despondent, anxious. But Rajzla kept comforting him. She repaired and remade old things. She borrowed here and there, and life improved again. Through the whole time her house was the most cultured in the whole neighborhood. Time did not stand still. Michał has not been among the living for a long time. He suddenly got a heart attack, and Rajzla had to manage on her own. The children left home, and then she missed Michał all the more. But by the end of the week the house would revive anew with laughter and conversations with the children, who came to visit their mother. The children often brought their guests, Jewish and Polish friends. The young people fell in love, and many of them married; that is when Rajzla noticed the mixed marriages among her children's friends. She became frightened. Her national feeling was revived. What will happen to my children now? This was during the time of Hitler. Her heart bled at what the Germans did to her nation. She saw and felt the indifference of non-Jews, their silence. A Jewish misfortune in a Christian world. She only then realized that she should have brought her children up differently. She wanted to consult Michał, she walked around shaken, and her lips murmured, "*Rabunu shel el.*"[20] She asked God for these children not to walk away from her nation. Her prayer was answered. Was it coincidence that her children married Jews and keep Jewish homes?

"Family"[21]

Around the year 1912, maybe 1913, my father became a subcontractor. He would supply the Russian garrison with food, mainly flour, sugar, fish, meat, and other products. I remember that my father would arrange the fish, ready to eat, in packages. They were seasoned with various seasonings and fried in oil. I still remember the taste of that fish, they were crispy and dry. My father once brought some fish home, because a barrel had broken open during transport and he could no longer sell them. But the main merchandise that my father provided was meat. In those times, one would buy cows directly from farmers and take them to the slaughterhouse. Those huge slaughterhouses in which meat was bought by the *pood* [a Russian measure of weight equivalent to about 35 pounds—trans.] did not exist yet. A Jewish butcher[22] had to buy a cow for his use at a butcher shop or buy kosher meat from my father. That's why my father would have his cows slaughtered at a Jewish slaughterhouse, at a ritual slaughterer's, and asked God that the meat was kosher.[23] For only then, when the meat was kosher, could my father exchange it with Jewish butchers. That's when he made money, when the butchers paid more for every kilogram of kosher meat, and my father would use the nonkosher meat for the army. The whole impoverished family benefited from the fact that the meat was kosher. In those days, a dish with a piece of meat was a rarity on the table. When my father happened on several pieces that were deemed kosher, he would bring all the offal home in a sack. The lungs, liver, intestines, heart, feet, and suet were all additional profit for my father. Doing something with them was a task that belonged to my mother, who placed many treasures on the table. She prepared bigger and smaller packages out of them right away.

"Bruchele, take this big package to Chana's. Her poor children will be glad," she would say, seemingly to herself. "And take this package across the street to Chaja's, she also has a room full of little children. A now you, Chaim, take this package to Leja's, and there's a package for you, Aronek, too. Run across and put this into Rachela's own hands."

We would already be on our way when we would hear our mother's voice, "And don't dawdle, children, but come right back! I still have packages to be delivered!"

And so my mother sent everyone out until the sack was empty. To this day I remember the children's joy when I would appear on their threshold. I remember the smiles, the clapping of little hands, when they saw me carrying a package. The children knew well that their mother would make tasty dishes from this package that they couldn't afford in those gloomy times. Even a piece of beef lard for frying kasha with sautéed onions made a heavenly dish. The children already knew that for Shabbat their mother would make cholent not with potatoes alone but with lungs, liver, intestines. A finger-licking delight. Oy! Then their mother would work miracles with that package. And I was wished all the best, and the big girl, the one that was ten, thanked me very much. I felt that I was doing something good and bringing joy.

"What I Remember"

I remember Siedlce as a clean, beautiful city with paved streets, asphalt sidewalks, boulevards, trees, and a beautiful park, the streets with stores and display windows. But most important were the cultural institutions and schools. The Russian Elementary School, the Russian Seven-Grade

Secondary School, the Polish Seven-Grade Secondary Business School. Jews constituted the majority of the population (almost all the Christians lived at the edges of the city), and the educational institutions and cheders surpassed the Christian schools in the variety of subjects taught in Yiddish and Hebrew. Evening classes were held for adults in both languages. Literature lectures were given. The Hazomir Society was very active. It had sessions in singing, as well as literature, and a library. Many talks were given and discussions held, which attracted many university students and secondary-school pupils not only from Siedlce. In those times Jews were subject to a quota.[24]Pupils from other parts of Russia and Vilnius took advantage of the fact that the Jewish residents of Siedlce and its environs did not fill the quota, and they came to the city to study. This was a great win for the city. The intelligentsia came mostly from Hazomir. A certain number of workers were joined to it, and classes were given so that they would not be exploited by their employers. Poor workers were taught, and special courses were created for them. From among them later came Zionists, socialists, and anarchists. They hid and held discussions secretly, relentlessly, with animated gesturing. Some were for, others against. The Jewish population at that time, during the German occupation in August 1915, numbered about 18,000, that is, about two-thirds of the population of the city.

Siedlce did not have any industry, but it had a pipe factory in which large sewer pipes were produced. I also remember a stamp factory. My husband, who was older than I, taught die engraving in this factory. He helped the revolutionaries when he was a young boy. He provided them with printing dies for their appeals. He was in prison for a while for this reason. Then he fled to Denmark and from there to America.

Shoemakers worked in Siedlce and made footwear that was sent to the depths of Russia. There was a certain group of gaiter makers, tailors, a few brokers who traded with the landowners, and two or three subcontractors (suppliers for the military). The majority were, however, small storeowners with low-priced merchandise. I also remember an iron warehouse, a mill, a hat shop, a photographer's studio, and so forth. There were also a certain number of carpenters, house painters, construction workers, upholsterers. They mostly lived in poverty. An interesting and real Jewish life pulsed in the city.

"MY FATHER'S FAMILY"[25]

From my father's side, I don't remember Grandfather Chaim Lejb and Grandmother Necha. But I know that my grandfather was a Talmudist butcher, and my grandmother kept house. She sold poultry and offal, fruit and goats. Sometimes grandfather helped her, but he didn't have a head for it; he only studied his books. They both earned only enough for water and kasha, only enough to maintain body and soul. They had a house full of children, three daughters and three sons. My father, Abram Hersz, called Herszke, was the fourth child. After the first three girls, my father was an unexpected guest. He was tall and had dark-blue eyes, blond hair, and delicate hands with long, slim fingers. He was a warm-hearted person, not only for his loved ones but also for strangers. When something had to be resolved, he decided and stuck with it. It always turned out that he was right. He studied until he was eighteen, but he couldn't look at the poverty in his house and the difficult life of his mother. He decided to act on his own. This was the first decision in his life that he made without the consent of his parents. He rented a large store in the Christian part of Siedlce. There he opened a modern butcher shop with non-kosher meat. He hired a worker who quartered the meat, put it on white paper surrounded by ice, and placed the whole thing into a white glass case. The merchandise prepared in this way awaited customers, who were looking at the clean and neat store with interest. In 1885 it looked not like a butcher shop but like a drugstore. Cleanliness and beauty, on top of a young salesman, drew the gazes of customers. Buyers increased by the day, so my father had to hire another helper. At first my grandfather and grandmother were shocked when they found out what my father had done. To abandon studying the sacred books and become a ritually unclean salesman was something that was revolting. But they slowly became convinced that he had done the right thing. My father was a good son; he gave all his earnings to his mother and studied the Torah and Talmud with my grandfather at night. He closed the shop on Saturdays and went to the synagogue to pray. The business prospered more and more, and the house revived. My grandmother stopped buying and selling, and my grandfather devoted more time to studying the holy books. The children grew like trees. After a time, they started saving. Now my father decided to hire a few workers and open a kosher butcher shop in the Jewish neighborhood. And this kosher butchery was also run in a hygienic way. It made a profit and brought prosperity. My grandfather slowly began to build a house. He finally built a house with four apartments and three shops. Now my father personally worked with several workers in the kosher butchery. Later he started working as a subcontractor, a supplier for the army, and he did only this. That took place when my father met my mother. Now I will describe their meeting.

My mother, the beautiful Rojzele (Róża), as they called her in the city, was being looked after for a few years by her grandmother Matl and grandfather

Szamaj [Lubelski] in Stara Wieś outside Siedlce. One day, her grandmother sent Róża, fifteen years old at the time, to the city to buy some meat for the house. She reminded her to buy it at the clean butchery that Herszke had just opened. My mother was a girl of exceptional beauty. When she appeared in the city, all the young boys turned to look at her. She came to the butchery her grandmother had told her about. My father recounted this episode to us children, and my mother always nodded in agreement. When he saw her, my father was so stunned that he injured several fingers while he was cutting the meat. He tried to keep her in the shop as long as possible and asked her about everything. Who she was, where she lived, and so forth. She answered all his questions. She was not shy. He, on the other hand, did not sleep all night after this meeting. On the next day he sent a matchmaker to my great-grandmother. And that's how it happened.

My father married my mother and didn't take a penny as a dowry. A beautiful wedding was arranged, and the young couple decided to live with my father's family. They took over the bedroom, and the whole family ate meals together at one table. This harmony did not last long, and disagreements arose between the mother-in-law and the daughter-in-law. The daughter-in-law wanted more privacy, and the mother-in-law wanted to be the only lady of the house as before. She told her daughter-in-law what to do, where to go, and so on. My father came home once and found the beautiful Róża in tears. He asked his mother what had happened. His mother took him aside and said that her daughter-in-law was bad and that he had "really been taken in," since she slept too long, didn't help enough around the house, and so on and so forth. My father interrupted her and asked, "Tell me, mother, did you bring a daughter or a maid into your house?"

After these words, she was stunned, and he left the house. He came home earlier than usual the next day and said, "Start packing, Rózia. We're moving out."

"What are you saying?" his mother asked in surprise.

"I've rented an apartment with everything we need," he answered with a smile.

"And what will happen to your parents?" she asked, worried.

"I have worked for them long enough. Now they have big, grown-up children. Let them help."

APPENDIX 17.

IDA JOM-TOW TENENBAUM—"THE WORST OF TIMES"

Some of the Jews [in Siedlce] were doctors, some were lawyers, and a few had large stores and were well-to-do. The great majority of Jews were poor; they were tailors or shoemakers or had little grocery stores.

The Jewish community had a great sense of unity. People knew each other so if somebody was in need people would get together to help. There was a special bank in which rich people deposited money that poor people could borrow without interest. These loans were not large but sometimes even fifty dollars helped. Poor people would go there and borrow money and pay it back when they could. One group of Jews was devoted to marrying off poor girls. They would assemble trousseaus and find husbands. Another group would walk around on Saturday mornings with a big basket and stand in the courtyards and call for people to donate bread. They would take this bread and distribute it to the poor. Another group organized a summer camp for children. There was a little Jewish hospital but only the poor went there because it wasn't great. If people really needed medical care they went to Warsaw. Some women would go there and bring chicken soup and food, or preserves to put into hot tea. There were a lot of groups like this. Sometimes they didn't even have formal names - people would just get together to help someone in need.

[...]

In 1918, when Poland came into existence, it inherited a lot of equipment from the Russian army which people didn't know how to use. Among these things were ropes of nautical thickness, mountains of them. These ropes were about six inches in diameter. Poland had no navy to use these ropes, but the army needed a lot of strong ropes because it used horses to pull cannons and in the cavalry. My father thought that the sisal or flax in the nautical ropes could be reworked, so he got the ropes from the government and hired some poor people to cut them into pieces with axes. He closed off some little streets and laid out the long ropes and the people cut them into shorter pieces. [...]

He also made backpacks for soldiers. The army needed hundreds of thousands of these so he opened a factory and hired a lot of people. When the workload got very heavy, they decided to use prisoners. The prisoners wanted to work because they got bored sitting doing nothing. The government allowed him to go into the prison and use the prisoners [from the Siedlce prison—author's note] as workers. Eventually he had several hundred prisoners working at his factory making ski shoes, running shoes with spikes—sprinting shoes they were called—boxing gloves, and other sporting goods.

In the 1930's some people at Astra, a company which made sport articles, contacted my father about making espadrilles. [...] Since people had to wear the soft espadrilles to play tennis there was a great demand for them. [...] The factory made ten to twenty thousand pairs of them each year.

[...]

When the prison factory got big, the union started opposing it because they didn't think that the prisoners should have the jobs. They figured that if my father employed several hundred prisoners, several hundred fewer people outside had work. The Sejm passed a special law allowing him to employ the prisoners. Prisoners would look to prison to learn a trade. They would go in as country boys and come out knowing how to make shoes or tennis nets. He rehabilitated many people, and he became very well known. He never wore a gun in the prison. The guards wore guns and suggested that he wear one, but he never did. He trusted those prisoners and he was never afraid to go in the prison. No one ever did anything to him.

I used to go to the prison a lot too. I helped in the prison office, and I learned to type there. The prison had a big theater and once a year, around Christmas, the prisoners would put on a play. I always went to the play, and my father would introduce me to everyone. We never had a problem. Before the war they voted to give him a medal for rehabilitating so many people. There was even a book written about him by a government official who was once sent to this prison for embezzling a lot of money. He got friendly with my father, and when he was released he wrote a book about his experiences in the prison. He devoted several chapters to my father. We had a copy of the book, but it was lost in the war.

My father was not really an ordinary man. He was a friend to the prisoners and they loved working for him. Twice a year at holidays he gave them packages. He would order lots of kielbasa—Polish sausage—and cakes and cigarettes and have them delivered to our house. We would make packages and wrap them and bring them to the factory for the prisoners. During the rest of the year he would give them premiums and they also earned money.

[...]

In the Jewish community there was a lot of cultural activity. We had two weekly Yiddish newspapers and a Jewish club with a small orchestra, an amateur theater and a big library. This club was supposed to be a cultural club; the only game was supposed to be dominos, but a few men got in who were card players and they turned it into a gambling club. People played a lot of poker there, and a lot of people lost money but the club kept functioning. The younger people didn't care too much about all this though, especially the educated ones.

I went to a government school for girls, the Queen Jadwiga School. It was a very fancy school but for a Jewish girl to get in was very hard. I got in because my father had friends in the Justice Department because of his work in the prison.

My brothers went to the equivalent boys school. There were only two Jewish girls allowed in each class - that was the limit. [...]

The career situation for Jews was almost hopeless. It was very hard for a Jew to make himself a place if he did not want to do what his father did, which meant have a little grocery or shop, and the feeling was that if you separated yourself and tried to mix in with the Poles your chances were better. Jews seldom converted, but they became reform Jews. My father, even then, didn't wear a beard. Poland had "numerus clausus" and "numerus nullus" in its schools. "Numerus clausus" meant that there was a certain quota or number of Jews allowed. "Numerus null us" meant that no Jews were allowed at all. Some universities had one rule, some the other.

So there were a lot of young people with nothing to do. There were young men who graduated from law school who didn't have the money to buy a cigarette. The father might have strained to send the son to school, and after years of work the son couldn't do anything, couldn't earn a dollar. It was a sad situation.

Source: I. Jom-Tow (Tenenbaum), *The Worst of Times* (New Orleans, 2002), pp. 38–39, 44–48, 73–74, 88–89. After consulting Helen Yomtov Herman, Ida's daughter, Tadeusz Kaźmierak selected and translated the fragments (Ida's surname in Polish documents is written Jom-Tow, but Helen uses the anglicized spelling Yomtov—author's note). [The text provided here is from Helen Herman's original work in English and is used with her permission.—ed.]

APPENDIX 18.
MARIAN TRZEBIŃSKI—"DIARY OF A PAINTER"

I was awoken by a loud hammering at the door—someone apparently wanted to enter my studio. When I went out to open the door, I saw two Jews, an old one and a young one. They were both dressed ritually, that is, in gaberdines, and they wanted to see me. I asked them in and got back under my quilt; after indicating some chairs for them to sit on, I waited for an explanation of this rather odd visit. The old man started, reminding me that he knew me when I was still a young boy, that he often sewed me new shirts and uniforms or remade old ones.

"I remember," he said, "how your mother would complain to me that her older son is a good student and will turn out well, but her younger only draws and draws and doesn't even think about studying. I laughed then, because no one knew that God would inflict the same punishment upon me."

I started to remember the popular school tailor Rynecki, who sewed and mended for half the secondary school. He had a chestnut beard and was always running somewhere, holding some clothing in his hands. I hadn't seen him in about 20 years. Now I had before me a sprightly old man with a grey beard who, pointing to his son, started spinning his woes to me:

"What trouble I've had with him! I've beaten him, I've starved him, but all he does is draw. He studied a little in Siedlce with Gajewski, but what could he have learned there? So I brought him to Warsaw, to Gerson.[a] And he asks me if the boy has finished any school. Maybe he doesn't even know how to read and write? He does know, I tell him, but in Yiddish. Then this Mr. Gerson says to me, 'You look like a smart man, mister merchant, and you don't know that nowadays even a tradesman must finish school, and you would have your son become an artist without any education?' How wisely he spoke to me, like a rabbi! So I sent my son to Międzyrzecz [should be Międzyrzec; perhaps a Russian/Yiddish mispronunciation—trans.] to study."

"To the Myezhiryecheskoye tryokhklasnoye gorodskoye uchilishche [Russian: Międzyrzec Three-Grade City School—trans.]," explained the young man, who until that point had been sitting quietly looking at my paintings.

Then the old man, wanting to find out about the material aspect of painting, started out by excusing himself for his boldness, justifying it by our old acquaintanceship.

"After all, I've know you since you were a just a boy this little (and he indicated with his hand about a foot above the floor). Please be so kind as to tell us in truth, how much you get for this business."

"More or less about 100 rubles a month," I answered.

"And nothing more?" Rynecki inquired futher. "So I see that this is no business. You studied in Kraków, in München, in Paris, and you earn barely 25 rubles a week. This is no business," the old man repeated several times.

"But I heard that if you study a few years in München, you can get a thousand rubles for a portrait," the young man interjected into the conversation.

Then they went on to the subject of artistic ability. "He can do anything for you that you ask for."

I pointed at a note pad and pencils lying on the table, which the young Rynecki picked up and asked boldly, "So, what should I draw?"

"Why don't you draw Jews arguing."

He went into the other room, returned after fifteen minutes, and said, "Why should they be arguing? I've drawn Jews praying."

The new painter-to-be gave the impression of a timid person; his face was in part that of a child, surrounded by brown fuzz, and he spoke with a slight Russian accent—after all, he'd studied in "Myezhiryechiye."

When my guests left me, walking down the covered stone staircase, they had the following conversation: "There you have your painting," said the old man. "Have you ever walked on a worse staircase? Did you see how that man lived? In a garret and without servants. He has to open the door himself! Did you see how he sleeps? Under a thin little quilt, doesn't even have a featherbed. Did you hear how much he earns? 25 rubles a week, what one of my senior apprentices makes. And how many years has he studied? And where has he not traveled? Listen, Moshele, I'll tell you this, this is no occupation, this is no trade, this is misfortune... You drop this abomination. I'll set up a paper store for you like the one Celnik has in Siedlce.[b] He already has eleven houses... He's not doing well? You will also be rich, drop this painting, it's for stupid goyim, not for a smart Jew."

But poor Moshele did not want to listen to any persuasions and only begged his father to sign him up to the School for Drawing.

"All right," the old man said, "but first I have to see what kind of business this is, this school for drawing."

And they went to Theater Square, where at the time Miłosz Kotarbiński was professor, a polite, cultured man.[c] In response to the request of his visitors, he showed them around the whole school, explaining that here one draws from patterns, there from plaster, and finally here the young people draw from real life. On the table at that time was a still life: old books and a large brass candlestick. The Ryneckis thanked him for his kindness, went out onto the street, and the old man again tried to discourage his son from painting.

"Listen, Moshele, I'm telling you this is no business. You drew patterns in Siedlce, plaster with Gajewski too. And that they finally toward the end show you how to paint a candlestick, this is no business. You already painted Napoleon in Siedlce, the one I sold to Dr. Frumkin for 12 rubles, and now they're going to teach you how to paint a candlestick."

A good couple of months passed when I was once again visited by the misters Rynecki around ten in the morning, and again they found me under my quilt. The old man was excited, and the young man was somehow sad and depressed.

"I've gotten rid of the whole bother," the old man started the conversation. "He didn't want to listen to me, so I married him off—let his wife take care of it."

The young man looked at his father with reproach and winced as though he was about to start crying. "And what will I do now? Why did you do this to me?"

The old man just stroked his grey beard and repeated, "Let his wife take care of it, and they won't have to live off the painting because I bought them a paper store on Krucza Street. His wife is from a merchant family, they'll do well. Why don't you visit them sometime?"

Poor Moshele's life did not turn out the way his practical father thought it would. The store did not do badly, but its owner did not give up painting and sat behind the counter in the store, painting. When his wife was minding the store, he'd go to the Jewish neighborhood with a thick notebook in one pocket and about a dozen sharpened pencils in the other. And he made sketches, from which he later made paintings sitting behind the counter in the store. He most liked to go to houses of prayer where he drew in his notebook, which was framed in an old prayer book, so he could pretend to be in prayer. He was once caught and almost beaten because it was suspected that he was doing this to make fun of them for the *Red Courier*.[d]

Rynecki had no foundations, he was undereducated, but he was a good observer with a certain comic dash. He rendered small Jewish weaving or lathing workshops or small children's toy factories. Here a hunchbacked Jew is finishing a cannon; there a Jewish woman is gluing feathers onto the tail of a wooden rooster. Rynecki developed a great observational sense, but he had a minimal fund of knowledge, so his works have little depth.

His father squandered him, for if he had allowed him even a year's stay in school and later facilitated his independent work, Rynecki would have been unrivalled as a ghetto painter and would have certainly become famous outside the country.[26]

Source: Marian Trzebiński, *Pamiętnik malarza* (Wrocław, 1958), pp. 170–173.

Editor's and Translator's Notes, Appendix 18

a. Wojciech Gerson (1831–1901)—a leading Polish painter of the mid-19th century, one of the foremost representatives of the Polish school of Realism during the period of the Partitions of Poland. He served as a long-time professor at the School of Fine Arts in Warsaw.

b. Hersz Celnik (1854–?)—merchant, publisher of first Siedlce postcards and photographs of Adolf Ganzwol.

c. Miłosz Kotarbiński (1854–1944)—Well-known Polish painter, sculptor, singer, literary critic, poet, and composer. A professor and later (from 1923) director of the Warsaw School of Fine Arts.

d. *Czerwony Kurier*—a daily tabloid with pro-Piłsudski political leanings published from 1922 to 1939.

Appendix 19.
Stories

Up to present times, four folk stories have survived among local Jews, passed on by word of mouth. One of them, "The Devils," was written down in Yiddish by Jehoszua Goldberg. The rest, that is, "Treif Fish," "The Pious Preacher," and "The Convert," were written down in Yiddish by Icchak Nachum Weintraub. These stories survived only because they were published in the Jewish press before the war. Adam Bielecki, an employee of the Jewish Historical Institute in Warsaw, provided a literal translation from Yiddish [into Polish for the first two stories], commissioned by the Society of Supporters of Podlasie in Siedlce. The remaining two stories are literal translations made by a group of students studying Yiddish. Paweł Śmieciuch made a substantial contribution to the endeavor. The author edited and annotated the Polish-language versions of these stories.

The story "The Water-Carrier" comes from Witold Duniłłowicz's (William Dunwill's) book *Three Colors of My Life* published by the Jewish Historical Institute in Warsaw in 2000 (pp. 12–13) [and in English in Melbourne, Australia (2004), translated by his son Julian Dunwill and reprinted here by his permission. The title was provided by Edward Kopówka.—trans.]. The water-carrier is presented in it as a real person. The story "Lewin's Torah" was written by Witold Duniłłowicz in a letter to the author. The title was provided by Edward Kopówka.

Icchak Nachum Weintraub—"The Convert"

The story I am telling here is, unfortunately, like many of the stories of old Siedlce, not written down anywhere. It was told by the elderly, who memorized it.

It was right after the 1863 uprising.[27] In the village of Wymysły[28] outside Siedlce there lived the Jew Icchak Josel, who leased a mill. Icchak Josel was a simple Jew and was considered to be a decent person. One day, the mill was damaged, and Icchak Josel brought a repairman from Germany, who fixed it. An argument arose between Icchak and the repairman, caused by the payment for the repair. During the exchange of views, the German said to Icchak Josel, "Just wait! You will remember me forever!"

From that time Icchak became a different person. He wandered off the upright path, started to drink and to do other improper things. Of course, he no longer paid proper attention to his business. But he made sure that his wife, who was very decent and virtuous, did not find out the truth. But Icchak Josel had a Jewish maid, who noticed the change that had taken place in her master and told her mistress about it. Icchak's wife did not know what to do, so she wrote a letter to her husband's family in Węgrów asking them to visit her and advise her about what to do to turn Icchak back onto the right path. Soon after, Icchak's two brothers arrived in Wymysły. Seeing that Icchak was moving away from the Jewish faith and crossing himself at every opportunity, they thought he had lost his mind. They tied his hands and left him in a separate room, believing that this behavior would pass after a time. No improvement was noted, however, quite the opposite. Josel, even with his hands tied, made the sign of the cross with his tongue on various books. It was with great difficulty that the brothers managed to convince Icchak Josel to go with them to Rabbi Icchak Neschiż.[29] The brothers told the rabbi about Josel's behavior. He listened to them attentively and answered that there was no longer any salvation for Icchak. They therefore returned depressed and left Josel in Wymysły. Several weeks later, Icchak changed his faith and adopted Eastern Orthodoxy. He had two sons—the older was 10 and the younger was 4. He took the older one with him and converted him. But his wife fled to Siedlce with the younger one. His wife's behavior enraged the convert. He went to Warsaw to the general governor, Count Berg,[30] and told him everything. The general governor gave strict orders to the Siedlce governor, Gromeka,[31] and the police chief, Madrach,[32] to take the boy from his mother and raise him in the spirit of Eastern Orthodoxy. Within a short period of time, the police chief, with the aid of threats, found the mother and forcibly took the child away from her. With the consent of the governor, the police chief adopted the child. But, since he was childless, he didn't have any experience in bringing up children, so he handed the boy over to the senior military medic. The medic lived at 11 Piękna Street[33] in Icchak Gad Kornblum's house. The child missed his mother and could not become accustomed to his new caregivers. His mother visited at Icchak Gad's every day to see the boy surreptitiously. The medic watched over the boy, however, and did not let his mother near him, although she had with great difficulty managed to receive permission to kiss her child at least once a day. After a time, the boy became accustomed to his new environment and started speaking Russian. And a hatred of Jews was instilled in him. The boy no longer wanted to speak Yiddish with his mother.[34] She, however, did not slacken in her efforts to take the child away from the goyim. At that time, the rabbi in Siedlce was Izrael Meisels.[35] The distraught mother came to see him every day and begged him to have the child returned to her. Rabbi Izrael Meisels gave her a letter to his father, Warsaw rabbi Berisz,[36] with a request for him to do something about this matter. Rabbi Berisz said, however, that he could do nothing. As we know, Berisz had taken an active part in the 1863 uprising. After the uprising was crushed, he was persecuted by the tsarist authorities, and for this reason he could do nothing. Rabbi Berisz did give the mother one piece of advice. Since she could not assure her rights through administrative channels, she should demand to get her child through the courts. The courts were Polish at that time. The mother indeed took the matter to court. As she had been advised, she claimed that her husband was not the father of the child, and so he did not have the right to convert the child. There was even someone who came in front of the court as the boy's father. Police chief Madrach claimed, however, that the child was Eastern Orthodox and no one besides him had any right to him. The mother lost the case due to lack of evidence. The child remained with the Eastern Orthodox medic. Seeing that all her efforts so far were for naught, the mother went for advice to Rabbi Dawid from Omszynów, the son of Icchak from Warka and a friend of Mendel from Kock. Rabbi Dawid was a great social activist and had a good heart. After hearing out the mother's sorrows, he promised her that he would come to Siedlce and that together they would consider what to do next.

Rabbi Dawid arrived in Siedlce so as to consider the solution to the problem along with Rabbi Izrael Meisels. Together they concluded that goodness wouldl not accomplish anything. Cunning subterfuge was the only way to save the child. During that time, the Jew Kalman Grajoncy lived in Siedlce. This was a very energetic and bold Jew for whom no matter was odious. Both rabbis, Dawid and Izrael, came to the conclusion that Kalman was capable of implementing the action they had planned. They therefore sent for Kalman and explained their intent to him, promising him good fortune in the next life if he concluded the matter successfully. Kalman promised them that he would not tell anyone anything. His task was to save the boy by breaking into the medic's house and kidnapping the boy. Grajoncy gathered his pals, divulged the matter, and swore them to silence. Then he introduced them to Rabbi Dawid, who instructed them in how to proceed. The conspirators started to observe the medic's house regularly. Once, when they noticed that he had gone to Warsaw for some medicine and only his wife and the child were at home, they decided to act. At night, they posted a guard around the medic's house, closed all the neighbors' windows and shutters so that they could not be opened from the inside. Then they did the same with the medic's doors and windows. They left only one window open, and through this they got into the apartment. The medic's wife, seeing an attack in the middle of the night, started to yell and resist. The attackers had no choice; they bound her, gagged her, and took the child. They left through the open window, which they closed behind them. The screams of the medic's wife could be heard in the apartment of Icchak Gad, who lived in the same building. Icchak Gad's household could not go out and check what had happened because the windows and doors were locked. The sounds of knocking and yelling brought the police, who opened the doors and windows.

On the basis of the police chief's order, Icchak Gad and his wife were put in jail because they were suspected of organizing this incident. Other respected citizens were also arrested then. Among them was Szymon Grynberg, about whom the old medic said that he had wanted to give him 1,000 rubles to enable the child's kidnapping. The Jews in Siedlce lived through difficult days. Governor Gromeka and police chief Madrach were the worst representatives of authority in Siedlce. And even though pogroms were not yet in fashion then, the Jews lived through much fear. An energetic investigation was launched against the arrestees, but in the end all but Icchak Gad were released. Every day an investigator would come to him and beat him, demanding information about the people who had kidnapped the child. Rabbi Berisz Meisels initiated efforts to free Icchak Gad since there was no evidence against him. These efforts were successful, and he was finally released.

You wish to know the further fate of the kidnapped boy? When the police found out that the child had been kidnapped, they surrounded all the toll gates of the city. Everyone leaving the city was thoroughly searched. He was hidden in a safe place. When the guards were removed from the toll gates, the boy was taken to Omszanów to Rabbi Dawid. There he was brought up in conformity with the dictates of the Jewish faith. Only a few people knew of this.

After many years, Icchak Gad received an invitation to a wedding in Brześć. On the invitation, on the fiancé's side, was the signature Dawid Momszanow [Hebrew, meaning "from Omszanów—ed.]. At first Icchak Gad did not know who the fiancé was, but then he surmised that it was the boy who had once been saved from conversion. The Omszanów rabbi wanted in this way to reward the suffering that had been inflicted on Icchak Gad. He was the one who had suffered the most from this whole incident.

Kalman Grajoncy and his pals kept the secret, and not one of them said anything. When after many years it came out who had kidnapped the boy, it was said that "even the common people who are among us are full of good deeds."

You are curious what end was met by the convert Icchak Josel? Well, in his old age he became a beggar and came to Jewish homes for alms.

Icchak Nachum Weintraub—"Treif Fish"

This was in the time when Eliazar Szalom was rabbi in Siedlce. The rabbi, along with the officers of the Jewish community council Nusbaum, Zalcman, and Zibercwajg created a committee that took care of buying arrestees out of the tsarist prison and of collecting money for social goals. The committee also imposed additional fees on yeast and salt since only the community council had a license for their sale.

Rabbi Eliazar often collected taxes from his faithful himself. One time, he came to a wealthy townsman whose name was Orzeł. He asked him for a large sum of money. He wanted to use it to buy out Jews who were in prison. Orzeł, however, started haggling with the rabbi and did not want to give him such a large sum. Then the angered rabbi walked up to the bookcase containing the Holy Books, took out the "Gemara,"[37] and started to read it. A rabbi contemplating this book could not be disturbed. The rabbi's contemplation dragged on.

"Why are you treating me like this, Rabbi?" the impatient Orzeł finally asked.

"Because your egoism is so great that it has disturbed the hierarchy of values! You place your own interest above the interests of your neighbors, which destroys internal order," replied the rabbi.

Orzeł gave Eliazar the appropriate amount of money and started thinking about the meaning of his words.

The rabbi didn't like the tradesmen who raised the price of fish before Shabbat. They sold their wares in the little square next to the synagogue of Przejazd Street.[38] One day, a new tradesman, hailing from Sokołów Podlaski, joined the local Jewish ones. The Siedlce tradesmen cursed the new arrival, and when that didn't help, they threw his wares onto the street. The distraught tradesman went to the rabbi with a complaint. The rabbi heard him out and went to the little square.

"These fish are treif!" he said to the leader of the dishonest tradesmen.

"These fish are treif!" he repeated loudly so that all the shoppers could hear.

"The fish are treif?" the tradesman asked in surprise. "Rabbi, what are you saying? How is that possible?"

"Your fish are treif because they have worms in them!" the rabbi replied angrily.

This news spread quickly throughout the city, and no one wanted to buy from these tradesmen. This situation lasted a few weeks. Finally the dishonest tradesmen were forced to apologize to their competitor for their shameful deed. When they did this, the rabbi publicly took back his words. A healthy competition prevailed in the little square.

Rabbi Eliazar Szalom had to leave Siedlce, however, because of... yeast!? Well, the merchant who held the license, signed by the rabbi, to sell it increased its weight dishonestly. For this reason the challah baked for Shabbat did not turn out well.[39] This was the cause of many marital arguments. Complaints were addressed to the city authorities requesting intervention. Finally, the rabbi was dismissed, and he went to Piotrków. From that time he started to be called Eliazar Szalom Piotrkower.

Icchak Nachum Weintraub—"The Saintly Preacher"

Magid[40] Manis lived in Siedlce before Eliazar Szalom Piotrkower was rabbi here. The city synagogue was made of wood then, but the prayer house was already brick and was located where the community council's office is now. It was in this Beit Hamidrash that Manis, the city magid at the time, spent day and night. He was a great scholar and also a great pauper. He received 80 groszy a week for his sermons, not in cash but in goods: from the baker he received bread, and from the shop he received kasha and candles. In addition to sermons, Manis also wrote his own Torah commentaries. Because he didn't have the money to buy a notebook, pieces of paper in which his food came wrapped were used for this purpose. His notes were collected, and the manuscript is held by Manis's grandson, Reb Goldberg. This collection, in addition to the commentaries, also contains a list of household expenses, which the magid wrote on these slips of paper. From this we know that his budget exceeded 80 groszy a week. The scholar, wanting to make up this deficit, very often fasted, and on occasion he would refrain from eating meat from Saturday to Saturday.[41] However, for all his poverty, he observed the principle of eating fish on Shabbat. The manner of buying fish for Shabbat was not what it is today, when everyone can buy them in a store. In those times in Siedlce, two inn owners would sell ready-to-eat fish for 5–10 groszy a portion. But not everyone could afford such a luxury. One of the two inns belonged to Etka Kawa, the mother of the later social activist Rachela Etkes. She was the one from whom the preacher usually bought fish for Shabbat, paying 5 groszy. Etka, being a pious Jew, was accustomed to give the learned magid the fish for free, thereby doing a good deed. With this goal, through her daughter, she would send fish over to him for Shabbat. It was not easy, however, to convince Manis to accept free fish, so as a mark of his gratitude he would bless the girl each time, since at that time Manis was considered to be endowed in some special way by the Holy Spirit. It was believed that he was capable of seeing into the depths of a person's soul.

The seer from Lublin, Jakub Icchak,[42] exerted a certain influence on Manis, advising him to open his soul and pass the grace on to others. Among the many stories that were passed on about Manis, it was said that Reb Wajnszenker and his wife, Róża, lived in Siedlce in those days. One day their daughter, who was already of marriageable age, came down with typhus. Her fiancé's parents sent for the magid so that he would pray for the girl's recovery. When Manis, who had just returned from the prayer house to rest, found out about the whole story, he advised him to place the engagement certificate at the patient's headboard, but he added that the girl would not live long. A while after this incident, the girl died.

It was also said that Reb Naftali Zejman, the fiancé whose beloved had earlier died of typhus, was to marry another. Before the wedding, he went to the magid for advice. The magid asked Naftali to write down his fiancée's name. When the reluctant young man did as he was instructed, Manis, after reading the name, immediately told him everything about his fiancée, including what dress she wore.

The pious preacher was an opponent of the Chassidim. They, however, told many stories that praised him. Among others, they passed on this story: Once the rabbi from Kock was traveling through Siedlce, and when he stopped on Warszawska Street, he went into the prayer house. Manis, who was engrossed in studying the Holy Scripture, didn't even notice him. Only after the tzadik left the prayer house did the magid sense that a great fervor of faith remained in the temple. When a while later he found out who had been there, he ran out of the prayer house. When after a few versts he caught up with the carriage in which the rabbi from Kock was traveling, he bowed to him. Magid Manis died in 1835 and was buried in the local cemetery.

Alter Drojanow—"Collection of Anecdotes"

A well-known tzadik once came to Siedlce. As was the custom, the Chassidim started bringing him gifts, requesting his blessing, and asking his advice. The next day, Rabbi Baruch Mordechaj Lipszyc went to see the tzadik. When the tzadik saw what a distinguished guest was visiting, he said to him, "Why did you trouble to come to me?"

Baruch Mordechaj answered, "I wanted to see how such a pious Jew could take money for nothing!"

Jehoszua Goldberg—"Devils"

A family lived in Siedlce called "Devils." These were not bad people before whom everyone in the city would tremble. On the contrary, these were very quiet people who wouldn't harm even a fly. They got the nickname as a legacy from their father, who had an extraordinary experience.

His name was simply Josel. He was called Josel Piekarz [Baker] because he owned a pancake and peasant challah stall right in the middle of the market square. Every Tuesday and Friday would be market days, and the peasants from the area would come and bring potatoes and vegetables.[43]

They would stop in at Josel's stall to buy a pancake or a piece of peasant challah, which was baked in large pans, oiled, and browned with onions.

Josel was a Jew of fifty or so with small, sharp eyes. Because his beard was always covered in flour, there was no way of telling whether it was grey or black. The peasants liked him a lot because he was a smart Jew and liked to have a friendly chat with them, pat them on the back, and give them good advice on various matters. He would be visited by Antoni, a tall, robust individual with watery-grey eyes and light blond hair. Antoni made himself at home at Josel's, and after the end of trading in the market he would come, unfasten his sheepskin coat, and shake all his takings out of his pocket onto the bed next to the drying noodles. He would count through the money he made and not be able to figure out if it all tallied. Josel would help him calculate his profit. After these operations, Antoni would calm down and buy a pancake and tea with sugar from Josel.

Once Antoni was very saddened sitting in Josel's alcove.[44] He stretched his hands out and rested them on his knees, eyes fixed to the floor, hat atilt.

"Why are you so sad, Antoni?"

He received no answer. Josel walked up to him, placed his hand on the peasant's shoulder, and asked quietly, "What's going on, Antoni? I see that you are very out of sorts. Are you out of money, were you robbed?"

Antoni slowly raised his watery eyes, looked ahead of him first, and finally said to Josel, "Disaster, my dear Josek!"

And he told him the whole story. Well, devils appear to him, they have been tormenting him for some time, they are ruining his property, his sheep and horses are dropping dead, milk from his cows is curdling. Hearing this, Josel thought it would be good to become a great and just man. And so he decided to do something so that Antoni would knock those devils out of his head.

"From what I see," he said to the frightened peasant, "you, Antoni, have news. I myself have more than once had to deal with this company, and thank God I've gotten rid of them. But you must know, Antoni, that their nature is such that if they settle in somewhere and become comfortable, there is no way to chase them out with stick or shovel. You should not neglect this but try to get rid of them as quickly as possible."

These words stuck in the peasant's head, and he asked Josel for some wise advice against devils. Josel advised Antoni, first of all, to apologize to the devils because maybe someone offended them unfairly with a word or a curse and that's why they're coming to seek vengeance. In order to apologize to the devils, you have to prepare a bottle of 96 percent alcohol, almonds, two eggs, two geese, and a black rooster. All this has to be placed in the ruins next to the old mill.

This advice very much appealed to Antoni. He sincerely shook Josel's hand and promised to do everything as he had been told. The appointed day arrived. Josel prepared a lantern wrapped in black paper, leaving only two openings with red paper taped over them. He placed a candle inside. He put on a sheepskin coat with long torn hair, a large cap, a hooded greatcoat, and went to the ruins by the old mill. He sat there and waited. And then he suddenly saw Antoni driving from a distance with a loaded wagon. So he quickly hid in a corner. Antoni stood waiting for the sun to drop lower in the west. Slowly he took everything off the wagon, entered the ruins from the back, and placed everything on the ground. He didn't even dare turn around. Then he got onto the wagon and waited for midnight. He fell asleep sitting on the wagon that way. Suddenly he heard wild murmurs, started awake bewildered, and almost fell off the wagon with fear. A phantom was standing in the ruins in front of him with a tall, pointed head and a pair of bloody red eyes. This being was not walking but jumping. Antoni took fright, his hands and legs started to shake, his teeth to chatter, and his eyes rolled in various directions. Suddenly he heard the call: "Antoni! Antoni!" And the muttering voice asked, "Did you bring the mother, the fiery water?"

Mobilizing all his strength to understand what was being demanded of him, Antoni answered, with beating heart and rapid breath, "Yes, yes, I brought it."

"From the 96th hell?"

"I guess so."

"And two birds that don't fly, you brought those?"

"I brought them."

"And three yellow-white almonds that live in peace and do not meddle?"

"I brought them."

"And everything is holy without a drop of blood?"

Here Antoni, confused, did not know how to answer. He was afraid to lie, and he himself didn't know the truth. The phantom came closer. Antoni became very frightened and began to scream in a wild, faltering voice, "Oh my God! Oh my God!"

People came running in response to these screams and found Antoni lying on the ground unconscious. They barely managed to revive him. Breathing heavily, Antoni kept pointing with his hand in the direction of the ruins in front of him. The people went inside. They looked, examined, and were all ready to leave with nothing, when suddenly one of them saw something moving in the corner. When they came closer, they saw a large bundle with two long belts. They themselves became frightened. When they recovered, they once again moved closer. They pulled the bundle toward them, stood it up, pulled off the sheepskin coat turned fur side out, and took off the head covering. Josel Piekarz appeared before them, mightily embarrassed.

He had much explaining to do for this trick. He had serious problems as a result, including a court appearance, and the nickname "Devils" stuck with him and his children.

Witold Duniłłowicz—"The Water-Carrier"

The water-carrier was a small, thin man dressed in old but always clean clothes. He wore old clothes given to him by his clients, who were sympathetic to his plight. He had no family. Someone generous allowed him to live in some cubbyhole for free. He seemed to be an example of condensed, intense, unmitigated misery and poverty. Everyone attempted to help him in some way. He became a recipient of the collective compassion of the neighbgorhood. He was fed by anyone who was able to do it. He was clothed by anyone who chose to do it.

His occupation was to supply the neighborhood with water from the local street pump. He made it his business to know when his customers were home, how much water they required, and when it should be delivered. He carried his merchandise in two large sheet-metal buckets hanging from each end of a wooden yoke, which was balanced on his shoulders. A delivery of two such buckets was counted as "one delivery" and was worth fifteen *grosz*. My grandmother and other clients usually recorded the tally on small blackboards or pieces of paper.

His income from such hard work was rather small, but sufficient for his daily needs. The neighbors often discussed the plight and poverty of the water-carrier, wondering about his continuing misery in spite of the fact that he did not have any family to support.

My grandmother was the only person who knew the real state of the water-carrier's finances. She was fed up with the situation, because Idel (such was his name) was depositing all his earnings in trust with her, yet living upon the generosity of the neighborhood. From a story that Grandma later told my mum, it was clear that this "very poor" man owned over two thousand *zloty*, all saved from his earnings. Such a sum coupled with a steady job—even a very basic one—was considered in those times to be a satisfactory financial situation. However, he was frequently heard complaining about his hard work and the hunger he frequently had to endure. As a result, he was fed by several people, who gave him any leftovers they could spare.

One day Grandma and some other tenants of Browarna Street hatched a cunning plan. When Idel delivered water and complained about his hard life, Grandma invited him into the kitchen, where in the presence of two other neighbors she suggested that he rest and eat a meal. Idel did not require lengthy enticement. He was surprised and delighted to see a large plate of chicken soup with noodles, followed by a half-chicken on a plate with a large piece of bread.

The food disappeared very quickly, accompanied by expressions of gratitude and deep sighs of pleasure. All three women observed this kitchen spectacle in silence. When the feast was finished, a very contented Idel thanked Grandma again for her generosity. Then the shocking news was broken to him: he was told that he might eat like this more often, since he could afford it! The women explained to him that he could afford such food and that the meal he had just consumed had been paid for with his money.

Poor Idel. He understood that he had eaten food bought with *his own* money! He did not want to accept the terrible fact that his hard-earned money had been spent on such an unworthy cause as his own food!

The shock was too great. Within a few days, he had moved out of Browarna Street. He was never seen there again. Browarna Street had a new water merchant very soon after, a businessperson who after a relatively short period swapped his water buckets for a small shop.

There are numerous career paths, and as many ways to save money.

Witold Duniłłowicz—"Lewin's Torah"

The house at 30 Asłanowicz Street was incorporated by the Germans into the area of the Siedlce ghetto and its occupants, Mr. and Mrs. Wierzejski, traded their house for that of the family of Julian Lewin at 58 Sienkiewicz Street on the third floor at the corner of Sienkiewicz Street and Świętojańska Street. Mr. Olszakowski's drug store was located in this house. Julian Lewin moved into the house on Asłanowicz Street with his wife, Anna, his daughter Rena [who later married Witold Duniłłowicz—author's note], his son, Jakub, and his younger daughter Marysia. They took up residence in two rooms with a kitchen. Lewin owned the motorized mill at 10 Luty Street. This mill was built at the end of the nineteenth century by the Lewin progenitor, Ischai Lewin, who began his milling career in the village of Paplin. He was an enterprising man, one who was progressive for those times. He was born in Paplin and felt a tie to the place, so to speak. The local farmers gladly brought their grain to Ischai, with whom they got along and whom they trusted, which was very important in times of scarcity and crop failure. Young Lewin did not go the way of his orthodox predecessors. He carried himself the way all the residents of the village did and thought the same as they. The only way he differed from his contemporaries was in his desire and striving for higher achievements. Paplin seemed "cramped" to him. For him, Siedlce at that time was "high society," so that's where he decided to move. He did so when he was already of mature years, when he had a wife and two young sons. He approached his objective in a very organized fashion. His objective was to build a modern, motorized mill. He implemented his dream very methodically. While still in Paplin, he bought property outside the city for a mill and an area in front of it. He brought an expert over from abroad as a consultant and an inspector to supervise the construction. With the help of contracted professionals and bank credit, he built what was for the times a large motorized mill that was the expression of the latest milling technology. The mill was at the time the largest establishment of this kind in Podlasie and remained one of the most modern up to the outbreak of the war in 1939. The direction of the mill after Ischai Lewin's death was taken over by his son Julian in the early 1930s. The establishment was run as a family business. Besides Julian, his three brothers worked there; his sisters were only shareholders.

The builder of the mill was aware of his achievement and felt very happy. An expression of this was his desire to help people, for which he was well known in the city, especially among the Jewish community. Siedlce at that time was starting to acquire a city look. As I have already mentioned, Lewin was not an active religious adherent, but he felt, how shall I say, "indebted" to the Lord God for his achievements. He therefore decided to set aside a space for a local bethel in the building of the mill, in which the family apartment was also located. He saw to the furnishing of the interior and decided to fund a Torah for "his" bethel, which was a large expense and needed the permission of the religious authorities. One has to realize that writing a Torah was a very complicated enterprise, since the preparation of the parchment, the selection of an authorized writer—and they were not numerous—and the preparation of the ink according to a strict biblical formula required tremendous preparations. And the writing itself took more than a year, after which the confirmation of the text and its verification took who knows how long. Bringing this intention to fruition took over two years in all. The confirmation of the Torah and its "introduction" into the bethel was a great holiday for the local Jewish faithful, and the bethel itself acquired a higher level of religious respect. Ischai Lewin took on this enterprise and was proud of doing so.

The Torah is one of the oldest lists of religious and secular laws and rules in the world; it is the model for the great religions of this world: Christianity and Islam. It is the list of the laws and precepts of the Pentateuch. This document is honored by all worldly chaplains of serious faiths and is respected by the people. One does not need to be a believing or practicing person in order to treat these scrolls written in an ancient script with respect.

The "bethel in the mill," as it was popularly called, functioned without a problem, serving the local pious Jews for whom the city's Main Synagogue on Piłsudski Street, opposite the municipal building, was too far.

In 1939, the Germans moved Treuhander into the mill, requisitioning all the grain and flour for the Wehrmacht. They also made the two mills in the city—Romański's mill on Kiliński Street by the railroad station and Lewin's mill—into delivery points for peasant levies. Of course, they simply chased all the Lewin brothers working there out without mercy. Julian Lewin tried to save what he could from the mill. He did not save much, but he did manage to carry the Torah out of the bethel.

Julian knew that the Germans brutally and sacrilegiously desecrated objects of Jewish religious worship. As I have already mentioned, one did not need to be a practicing person to respect the Torah scrolls. He managed to carry the Torah out of the mill, but he did not really have anywhere to hide it. And then he decided to hide it in plain sight of the barbarians who continuously robbed Jewish homes in the ghetto: he glued the scrolls to the wall and covered them with plaster and wallpaper. Unfortunately, Julian Lewin died in December 1941. His surviving wife and three children were occupied simply with the daily concern for a piece of bread. In August 1942, I was on the *Umschlagplatz* in front of the burned-down synagogue in Siedlce, where the entire Jewish population of the city had been herded before its mass murder and dispatch to Treblinka. I saw how SS and Ukrainian bullets killed religious Jews who were defending their Torah scrolls.

On 26 August 1942, at 11 AM, Julian's oldest daughter, the eighteen-year-old Irena, left her hiding place in some tiny cell behind the kitchen, got through the barbed wire surrounding the ghetto, and entered the apartment of the Wierzejskis, who let her wash. She rested a moment and went on to the fate that would allow her to survive this hell, passing through Pawiak and the concentration camps in Ravensbrück and Flossenburg. Her mother, Anna Lewin, born Botwińska, along with her son Jakub and her daughter Marysia, was discovered by the SS at 6 PM on that same day. Along with the other people who were in hiding, they were taken to the Jewish cemetery and shot to death. The mother and sister covered the brother, Jakub, with their bodies, and, although wounded, he survived the execution. He later died in 1944 in Lublin as a soldier of the Home Army using the name Jan Myrcha. My wife did not know about the Torah scrolls in the walls of the house on Asłanowicz Street. This was done in secret, and I suspect that only Julian and Anna knew about it.[45]

APOLINARY HARGLAS—"MILGRAM"

Shortly after settling in Siedlce, I experiences two humorous incidents, the second of which cost me 30 rubles. I had been living in Siedlce over a month already, when suddenly, at 4 PM, a young, handsome Jew comes to me dressed in a short coat [that is, in modern clothes, not the traditional long Jewish gabardine coat—trans.] and asks me if I'm the lawyer Hartglas. I answered that I was. Then he tells me that he was sent by police chief Sciepuro. I knew that the last name of the police chief was Sciepuro, but I didn't know him. Then my guest continues:

My last name is Milgram, Dawid Milgram. You don't know what it is in Siedlce to be a Milgram? We do not have a good reputation. We are robbers. I was also a robber and was sentenced to several years in prison. I was in the Chełm prison. One time, the prison Orthodox priest asks me, "Milgram, would you like to go free?" "Why not?" I replied. "Okay, you'll go free, but first you have to convert to Eastern Orthodoxy." "Why not?" I say. "And you won't be able to stay here; you'll have to leave, go somewhere far into Siberia." I had always dreamed of being able to live in the Far East, so I was glad and said, "Done." And in a few weeks I was already Eastern Orthodox, free, and settled in Nikolsk-Ussuriysky. I was happy there, made a lot of money. One day, I lost my passport [a domestic identification document, not a document for foreign travel—trans.]. So I go to the police to get a replacement, but at the station they say, "Eh, you're lying, buddy, you're a Jew." I tell them that, no, I'm Eastern Orthodox, and they say, "Where's your ID?" And where am I supposed to get and ID if I lost my passport? So they detain me and put me on a slow train to Siedlce. It has taken me about two months, I just got here at 1 o'clock, and I go straight to the police chief to register. The police chief wasn't in, and they tell be that he went to lunch and would be back at 3. So I come at 3, and the police chief knows me and asks, "How are you, Milgram? What's new?" I told him everything, and he asks, "Milgram, do you carry a cross?" So I says, "What the hell do I need a cross for? I need a passport." And then he says, "You know what, Milgram? You'd best return to Judaism. There's now a lawyer here, a Jew named Hartglas. He'll take care of it for you." So I came straight from the police chief to you.

Just last year, a statute about religious tolerance was passed, allowing christened Jews to return to Judaism. I advised Milgram to bring me his birth certificate, I took the matter on—for free, of course—and in six weeks Milgram was a Jew again. I doubt that this was a gain for my nation.

Source: Apolinary Hartglas, *Na pograniczu dwóch światów* (Warsaw, 1996), pp. 112–113. Title provided by E. Kopówka.

APOLINARY HARTGLAS—"THE PERSIAN RUG AND 30 RUBLES"

One day, at 8 AM, before I had left for court, a sergeant of the so-called convoy command, that is, the military unit serving to watch over and convey prisoners, appeared at my house. This personage was of a distinctly eastern type, with an impeccable uniform and an official book under his arm. He asked me with a clearly Georgian accent if I was an attorney and if he could entrust his case to me. I answered that I first wanted to know what the case was.

Then he told me that he was transporting by train a group of political prisoners from the prison in Wilno to the Siedlce prison. In this group was the assistant of a sworn attorney in Wilno, Mojżesz Wysocki, whom he knew from court. On the way, Wysocki told him that he had sent out a certain sum before his departure to be deposited at the Siedlce prison and asked him to feed the whole group of prisoners, about 30 people, on the trip and credit it to the deposit. Knowing that Wysocki was a decent person, he trusted him and spent the official travel funds he had with him, being sure that upon arrival Wysocki would use his deposit and reimburse him the money he had expended. They arrived in Siedlce around midnight, and it turned out that Wysocki's deposit had not yet arrived, but he had to submit an expense report for the monies that had been issued to him no later than noon that day. He would be 30 rubles short, so he'd have to be arrested and face criminal liability. So he wants to give me a retainer so that I could defend his case from the outset. He himself considers his case to be a good one, because Wysocki will testify that the embezzlement had taken place unintentionally at his, Wysocki's, request, and in the meantime the deposit would arrive, and it will become evident that Wysocki, too, was acting in good faith and that what had happened was simply an unforeseen and unfortunate coincidence. As for the honorarium, I could write to his brother-in-law, the examining magistrate of the fourth circuit in Wilno, Dżanibekow, as well as to his brother, the sworn attorney in Tyflis [Tbilisi—author's note], Eugeniusz Melikow, and they will pay.

During his narration, I casually looked over his official log, which was the convoy log for the transport of the prisoners. All the dates and stamps were in order, and I indeed found the name Wysocki among the names of the prisoners. I thought to myself that among the responsibilities of an attorney was not only to protect a client after the commission of a crime but to prevent one if that was possible. In the present instance it was possible, since the offence of embezzlement was a formal offence, and if the guilty party covers the shortfall, then the offence is considered not to have occurred. So it was only a matter of Melikow's having the 30 rubles. I decided to lend them to him, but since this sum was for me at the time a rather considerable one, I did not want to act too precipitously. I told him I would have to go out and check if something can be done for his case, so would he come back at 10 and I would accept the retainer then. He agreed and left. I then hurried to the district court and told everything to the clerk of the Civil Division, Nowacki, my university friend, a few years older than I, a clever and prudent man and quite a good lawyer. I suggested that we first check all the names and addresses Melikow had given in the court registry. Everything turned out to be completely in order regarding Wysocki, and regarding examining magistrate Dżanibekow, and regarding attorney Melikow in Tyflis. Nowacki suggested to me that he would make a business call to the prison office and ask if a group of political prisoners from Wilno had arrived during the night. He received a negative response. Then he expressed the opinion that the sergeant was probably a swindler, so I should not worry too much about his story. I went home. Melikow was already waiting at the door. I asked him in. Once inside, I turned to him with the following speech: "Sir, I believe that my conscience and my responsibility as an attorney dictate to me that I prevent your commission of a crime, that is, that I lend you 30 rubles. Thirty rubles is for me, an attorney just starting out, a considerable sum. So I went to the court to check if the story you told was true. The names and addresses checked out, but the prison responded that no group had arrived. I therefore suspect that you are a swindler. Here are 30 rubles, but I appeal to your conscience—if what you told me is not true, please tell me to ease my conscience and do not take these 30 rubles."

Hearing this, Melikow immediately exploded: "Who gave you right to butt into by business and my conscience? Did I ask you for money? I asked you to accept my retainer. And do you know that moving political prisoners from place to place is an official secret and the prison office may not confirm this? But now they will figure out that no one but I could have told you about this, and now they will have another, worse case against me: revealing an official secret. Now I don't want your defense, and I bid you farewell." He grabbed his log book and wanted to leave. I then ran to the door, locked it, and started to demand that he accept the money. "I know you are a swindler," I said, "but I want to have a clear conscience, because if it turns out that I was wrong and you are arrested, I won't be able to sleep because I failed to protect you from prison. So please take the 30 rubles." Melikow continued to protest for a long time, but finally he took the money and left. I went to court.

At 12:30, the court clerk came to me with the information that a certain soldier was asking for me and was waiting in the lobby. It turned out to be Melikow. He informed me that he had turned in the accounting in order, that he was leaving in half an hour, that he felt it was his responsibility to inform me before his departure that he had taken care of the matter and to thank me, and that the very next day, after his arrival, Dżanibekow would telegraph me the 30 rubles and an honorarium, which he would be able to determine more generously than I would, and that he would write about all this to his old father in Tyflis, and the father would send me a beautiful Persian rug as a souvenir. We said goodbye, and he left. As for the 30 rubles, honorarium, and Persian rug—I am waiting in vain for them to this day.

Source: Apolinary Hartglas, *Na pograniczu dwóch światów* (Warsaw, 1996), pp. 113–115. Title of the story provided by E. Kopówka.

Appendix 20.
Marian Pietrzak—"the Jewish Legion of 1920"

At the beginning of August 1920, the Bolshevik army marched into Siedlce. Its main forces pressed toward the capital of Poland. They marched not only to establish a new system in the conquered country. The leaders promised the soldiers that there was a "street of gold" in Warsaw, after the conquest of which everyone would take an appropriate amount of bullion. It was also said that there was lots of chocolate in this city and even more pretty ladies with whom the conquerors would be able to have fun.

The Bolshevik proclamations also maintained that the new government embraced the Jewish poor. In response to this slogan, the Jews of Siedlce started to form "their own legion."[46] It was to join the Bolsheviks in fighting against the Polish army led by Józef Piłsudski. Jewish volunteers started to flow into the legion from neighboring cities: Sokołów, Węgrów, Łuków, Łosice, and others conquered by the Bolsheviks. Within a week there were over a thousand of them. And one local Jew, a shoemaker by the name of Komar, living close to my grandma, said to the neighboring Poles, "Now I goes to army! I knows what I fighting for! I be walking on your heads like on pavement." [Komar's statement, although made in imperfect Polish, does play on the popular Polish term for cobblestones, which is "cats' heads" ("kocie łby").—trans.] Well, and he joined this legion.

For several days the Jewish volunteers underwent light training with weapons and helped in establishing the new system and order. A week later the Bolshevik offensive broke apart outside Warsaw, and they started on a disorderly retreat.

My mother, born Bukowska, was at that time 16 years old. She was living with her parents in Siedlce on Floriańska Street close to the intersection with Brzeska Street, which led eastward. She watched the infantry and cavalry divisions of fleeing Bolsheviks until late in the evening. Then they all ate dinner and went to bed. Around midnight, Bukowska woke her daughter, that is, my mother, and said, "Zosia, do you hear?" Her daughter listened. From outside the window some kind of loud rustling and whooshing that sounded like running water—a swift river—could be heard. Given that it was night, it was quite light both in the apartment and outside because there was a large gas lamp on a pole in front of the house. After a brief conversation, the mother and daughter, troubled by the strange sounds, decided to get up and see what was going on. When they carefully approached the window, they noticed that the whole width of the street was filled with Jews marching east, dressed in long, dark gabardines to their ankles, and that was what was making such a loud whooshing sound.

During the crossing of the Bug River near Brześć, the legion was attacked by Polish forces chasing the Bolsheviks. Most of the volunteers were killed and drowned. A few days after the pogrom of the Bolsheviks, the wife of that shoemaker Komar, when meeting her neighbors on the street, wailed in a tearful voice, "Ay, how stupid was my husband! What he need this legion for? What he need go for this Bolshevik!?" Complaining, she turned to her neighbors and offered to have their shoes fixed for free. She explained right away that she would take them to a "certain shoemaker she knew, who will fix them for free." There were those who gave her their shoes to be repaired. As it later turned out, the shoemaker did not die during the crossing of the Bug River. After several days, he returned at night to Siedlce. Then he stayed quietly in the attic of his house and repaired his neighbors' shoes for free in order in this way to apologize to them for insulting them and betraying the country. And in this he was successful.

Source: Marian Pietrzak, "Żydowski Legion z 1920 roku," in *Sokołów Podlaski dawniej i dziś oraz opowiadania podlaskie z lat 1863–1945* (Sokołów Podlaski, 2002), pp. 123–124.

The several-hundred-strong "legion" was crushed by the 7th and 8th companies of the First Infantry Regiment of the Legions commanded by Władysław Broniewski, a second lieutenant and poet.[a] He was awarded the Virtuti Militari Cross [cross of military virtue, the highest Polish military award, equivalent to the American Medal of Honor.—trans.] for the battle of Drohiczyn. (See W. Broniewski, *Pamiętnik 1918–1922* [Warsaw, 1984 and 1987]; unfortunately, they were not published in their entirety). The creation of the "Jewish legion" composed of volunteers was widely exploited by radical nationalist propaganda.

EDITOR'S NOTE, APPENDIX 20

a. Władysław Broniewski (1897–1962)—poet, soldier, translator, author of revolutionary and romantic poetry as well as threnodies.

AUTHOR'S NOTES, APPENDICES

APPENDIX 8

1. Organisation Todt—an organization functioning in the Third Reich and in countries occupied in 1938–1945, created and run by engineer F. Todt and then from 1942 by A. Speer, as an organization for technical support in the building of sites intended for the needs of the military. The Todt Organization had its own labor camps but also used prisoners from other camps.

APPENDIX 16

2. Bracha left Siedlce for the United States with her sister Anna (Chana) in September 1916 at the age of 17. The events described could have taken place in the first years of the twentieth century. This story appeared in print in the newspaper *Forverts* on 27 August 1967.
3. Rags that were wadded together and tied then used for games, such as kicking and throwing.
4. Literally, young men without principles, loose young men. In the original, the author uses an allusion that would be understandable to a Yiddish-language reader.
5. A. Liessin (1872–1938)—literary pseudonym of Abraham Valt, a well-known poet who wrote in Yiddish.
6. Literally, a *kopke*—a religious covering for the head.
7. Her mother died when Rojza was little. She was raised by her grandmother, Matl Lubelska, who probably adopted the girl. The rest of the siblings were with their father, Eli Osina, who was a *melamed*—a cheder teacher in Warsaw in the suburb of Grochów.
8. Reference here is also to rigorous cleanliness in preparing and consuming meals as an essential element in a person's life.
9. The author is describing events that took place in 1908–1910.
10. Since their religion prohibits Jews from creating sculptures and depictions of God, the very religious also avoid human depictions since they are made in the image of God.
11. Could also mean: legacy, inheritance, or the equivalent of the Polish patrimony. This house was located on Jatkowa Street, currently Czerwonego Krzyża Street. The story was printed in the newspaper *Forverts* on 17 October 1966.
12. Bracha Kahan was born in 1899, so the story takes place in 1905.
13. Literally, *sefer*—a religious book. In this case, Bracha's father applied the well-known method used by Jews to avoid conversation and argument. The responsibility of

a religious Jew is to study the Torah and Talmud. He is not to be disturbed during these activities.

14. Some orthodox Jews move their bodies back and forth while praying, which facilitates concentration and meditation. For it is written, "Study the Torah with all the limbs of your body."

15. *Melamed*—cheder teacher, called "rebe" by his pupils, taught children in his own home. In Hebrew, "cheder" literally means "room, chamber" and was actually a former primary school in which religion, reading, writing, and counting were taught. Parents often changed cheders.

16. Mixed marriages are something normal and common in the United States, and only those who have an extreme ethnic or religious bent object to them. Bracha's views may be dictated by the world view of the Jewish newspaper for which she wrote. The views of her sister Anna, however, were completely different. She wrote in Jewish periodicals with a leftist attitude and participated in the anti-racist movement.

17. Literally, rituals.

18. Separate ones for meat and for milk.

19. To soak so as to get rid of remnants of blood; it had to stay salted for a while, and then only after it was rinsed was it ready to prepare.

20. *Rabunu shel el*—Oh my God. [A shortened form of the more usual *Rabubu shel oylam*—O Lord of the World!—ed.]

21. For a better understanding of this story, it will help to add explanations from the diary and stories of Anna Kahan, Bracha's sister. Hersz Kahan was born in a village near Siedlce, where his parents owned a small farm. As a result of pressure from his mother, who wanted to assure her children a better future in the city, the family moved to Siedlce. For the money they received from the sale of their farm, they bought a small wooden house on Jatkowa Street, later called the *skheda*, and opened a butcher shop. Hersz learned the trade of a butcher by working with his parents. Since he came from the countryside, he was familiar with animals, particularly cattle. The work of a butcher consisted above all in buying cattle from surrounding farmers and bringing them to a ritual slaughterer (the so-called *shochet*). After the slaughter of the animal and the inspection of its innards, the slaughterer decided whether or not the meat was kosher. If it was, then the butcher divided it up and sold it to customers in his butcher shop. Hersz ran a butcher shop along with Josel. After a time, Josel independently opened a rival butcher shop on the opposite side of the street in which he sold meat at lower prices. He could afford to do so because he only paid attention to whether or not the meat was kosher and did not subject it additionally to veterinary inspections. Hersz's conscience would not allow him to report his former partner to the authorities. And so the rival, cheap butcher shop drove him to bankruptcy. He then worked part time in the butcher shops of other owners as a hired seller of meat, but the money he earned was not enough to support his family. Not having much to lose, he took part in a bid for supplying food to the Russian army stationed in the city by offering a very low bid. He won the bidding, but he did not have the capital for the initial purchase of inventory, so he had to take on Josel as a partner again. Because of the low margin and the partnership with Josel, he did not have much of a profit,

particularly since he was an honest man and took care that his inventory was of good quality. The events described here and the obtained meat was a kind of "bonus" for Hersz. What was involved was that Hersz would bring the meat he bought to the ritual slaughterer, even though the soldiers did not need it to be kosher. When the meat turned out to be treif, it went straight to the soldiers and there was no additional profit. But if the meat turned out to be kosher, then Hersz would exchange it for treif meat with other Jewish butchers who were not lucky and their cattle turned out to be treif. Since kosher meat was more expensive, the other butchers paid him the difference in price, and he provided the army with the treif product. And this was his "bonus," in addition to the offal and scraps with which his wife gifted poor families (explanation provided by Michael Halber).

22. He was engaged in ritual slaughter. It is worth explaining the difference among a number of related terms: a slaughterer or ritual slaughterer, *shochet* in Hebrew, is a person fulfilling the religious function of performing ritual slaughter; the *shochet* had to be a pious person, well versed in Jewish law, particularly that which related to *kashrut*; in smaller communities, this function was performed by the rabbi; in addition to the official slaughterer of cattle, there were also slaughterers of fowl, who serviced private clients; a butcher, *katsef* in Hebrew, was someone who traded in meat or was the owner of a butcher shop; a circumciser, *mohel* in Hebrew, was a specialist who was engaged in performing circumcision (cutting off of the foreskin) on male newborns.

23. The cow could not have any external or internal signs of disease or breakage.

24. Only a limited number of pupils as determined by the authorities could attend secondary school, the so-called *numerus clausus*.

25. The [previously] unpublished English-language short story "My Parents Elope Two Months after Their Wedding" by Anna Safran (Kahan), Bracha's sister, is based on the motif depicted here. Copy in the collection of the City Library in Siedlce. [Published in Polish translation in Anna Safran, *Dziennik Anny Kahan. Siedlce 1914–1916* (Siedlce, 2012)—ed.]

APPENDIX 18

26. Maurycy [Moshe—trans.] Rynecki died in Warsaw during World War II. [For information about Rynecki, including a gallery, biography, listing and photographs of his paintings in museums and collections, and his great-granddaughter Elizabeth's blog, see the website *rynecki.org.*—trans.]

APPENDIX 19

27. The action takes place in 1867 or 1868, for it was then that Siedlce County arose, and prior to that time Israel Meisels performed the function of rabbi in Siedlce. This period, like later years, was characterized by intensified Russification. Instances of forced conversion of Uniates to Eastern Orthodoxy are commonly known. This story testifies to the fact that Russification also attempted to encompass the Jewish population.

28. Wymysły—a place next to Chodów, where there was a water mill on the Liwiec River, more precisely between Chodów and Wyłazy. The mill functioned up to World War II.

29. Icchak Neschiż—surname read literally by the [Polish] translator, perhaps reference here is to Rabbi Icchak from Nieśwież.

30. Fedor Berg (1790–1874)—Russian general, last governor of the Polish Kingdom, famous for his ruthless suppression of the January Uprising.

31. Stepan Stepanovich Gromeka—first Siedlce general governor, held his post from January 1867 to 12 December 1875.

32. Madrach—major, police chief; held his post in Siedlce from 1868 to 1875.

33. Currently Kazimierz Pułaski Street.

34. That is, in Yiddish.

35. Israel Meisels—son of the famous Warsaw rabbi, held the post of rabbi in Siedlce from 1858 to 1867. He was an opponent of the Chassidim. After leaving Siedlce, he went to Warsaw and then to Kraków, where he died in 1876. He was known for his piety. After his death, a large prayer house was built in Kraków and named after him.

36. Rabbi Berisz-Ber Meisels—Warsaw rabbi known for his patriotic stance. In 1861 he was arrested for his solidarity with the independence movement and the closing of synagogues in protest. He was exiled from the Kingdom for this action. During the January Uprising, he was utilized by the National Government as a diplomat for talks with the representatives of the tsar.

37. Gemara—part of the Talmud, commentary to the Mishnah, that is, the collection of traditional Jewish law.

38. Przejazd Street does not currently exist; it used to connect Pułaski Street and Piłsudski Street, as an extension of Berek Joselewicz Street.

39. Challah—white bread made of wheat flour. It has symbolic meaning, as whiteness signifies purity and renewal. It plays an important role here, as it is the bread for Shabbat and other holidays, and blessings are said over it.

40. *Magid*—literally, "speaker, preacher."

41. According to the religion of Moses, one is not allowed to fast on Shabbat.

42. Jakub Icchak from Lublin (died 1815)—one of the Chassidic tzadikim who was gifted with second sight, was called the Seer.

43. This square was located next to the covered market, currently the area of the bus terminal.

44. An alcove is a small living space.

45. The Torah scrolls were discovered in 2000 during a renovation of the house.

Appendix 20

46. The story is based on fact. It refers to the march through of a 150–300 person Bolshevik detachment composed of Jews, which was broken up on 19 August 1920 by the Polish Army near Drohiczyn. There were 18 people from Siedlce in this detachment. See *Cud nad Bugiem*, ed. Z. Ruczaj (Drohiczyn, n.d.), p. 21.

Table 1. Residents of Siedlce in the Nineteenth Century

Year	Overall number of residents	Jews	% Jews
1820	4,399	3,072	70
1821	4,441	2,908	65.5
1827	4,414	2,908	66
1839	5,218	3,727	71
1840	6,471	4,359	67
1841	6,471	4,359	67
1846	8,000	3,032	38
1850	7,472	4,788	64
1855	7,263	4,804	66
1858	7,628	5,153	67
1865	9,710	7,094	73
1878	11,931	8,156	68
1897	15,131	10,094	67

Source: *Słownik geograficzny Królestwa Polskiego i innych krajów słowiańskich*, vol 10 (Warsaw, 1889); A. Winter, *Dzieje Siedlec 1448–1918* (Warsaw, 1969), pp. 41, 123–125; *Book of Remembrance of the Siedlce Community*, p. 52.

Table 2. List of Functioning Prayer Houses in Siedlce Compiled 6 December 1922

	Street	Year of founding	Number of seats	Owner
1.	38 Warszawska (currently J. Piłsudski)	1840	1,500	Jewish Community Council
2.	Warszawska (currently J. Piłsudski)	1856	900	Jewish Community Council
3.	10 Długa (currently Bishop I. Świrski)	1879	200	Jewish Community Council
4.	9 Browarna	1904	200	Jewish Community Council
5.	4 Stary Rynek (currently Bohaterów Getta)	1912	30	Srul Rzetelny
6.	6 Stary Rynek (currently Bohaterów Getta)	1918	25	Abraham Dawid Milberg
7.	6 Przejazd (no longer exists)	1887	12	Mendel Miodownik
8.	4 Żydowska (currently Berek Joselewicz)	1918	50	Joel Słuszny
9.	6 Mała	1900	20	Hersz Gordztejo
10.	4 Mylna	1907	20	Munysz Sukiennik
11.	4 Mylna	1918	50	Chaskiel Zylbersztajn
12.	4 Mylna	1916	40	Srul Blunsztejn
13.	4 Jatkowa (currently Czerwonego Krzyża)	1917	30	Ela Lib(h)aber
14.	11 Jatkowa (currently Czerwonego Krzyża)	1914	500	Joskiel Mandelbaum
15.	16 Długa currently Bishop I. Świrski)	1916	20	Matys Janerbaum
16.	16 Długa (currently Bishop I. Świrski)	1914	50	Mozes-Lejb Blubenkranc

17.	33 Długa (currently Bishop I. Świrski)	1888	40	Una Goldsztejn
18.	16 Warszawska (currently J. Piłsudski)	1902	25	Dawid Morgensztern
19.	7 Piękna (currently K. Pułaski)	1902	50	Mandel Mandelec
20.	27 Piękna (currently K. Pułaski)	1902	80	Abram Szaflan
21.	36 Piękna (currently K. Pułaski)	1920	20	Moszko Rydel
22.	37 Piękna (currently K. Pułaski)	1919	15	Szalim Mejer
23.	30 Piękna (currently K. Pułaski)	1906	40	Srul Szywak
24.	41 Piękna (currently K. Pułaski)	1920	40	Borach Rozenbaum
25.	42 Piękna (currently K. Pułaski)	1902	30	Rozengarten
26.	71 Piękna (currently K. Pułaski)	1887	200	Lejzor Gol(d)berg
27.	75 Piękna (currently K. Pułaski)	1907	30	Adler Dawid
28.	77 Piękna (currently K. Pułaski)	1912	10	Abram Ratyniewicz
29.	57 Ogrodowa (currently H. Sienkiewicz)	1912	30	Benjamin Bomblat
30.	6 Świętojańska	1919	15	Ela Morgensztern
31.	14 Kiliński	1902	50	Mordko Bronsztajn
32.	10 Szpitalna (currently J. Kochanowski)	1800	30	Jojna Popowski

Source: Archiwum Państwowe w Lublinie.

Table 2, Author's Note: The word *bóżnica* (*bożnica*) [prayer house—trans.] is used in the Polish language to designate a place dedicated to God. The word "synagogue" derives from the Greek and designates a "place of gathering." It is a house of prayer and religious services, as well as a place for studying the Torah and Talmud, a meeting hall, and the headquarters of the executive board of the community council and the rabbinical court. [To do justice to the variety of such places in the Jewish community, one would have to differentiate three kinds: (1) Synagogue—the principal large meeting place that served as a large prayer hall as well as meeting place and center of sacred study; (2) Besmedresh (beit midrash)—house of study—primarily a house of study but secondarily a place for daily prayer for those who chose to pray there, and also social meeting hall; (3) Shtibl (literally: a small room)—a room in a private dwelling or separate building used as a small prayer house for a small, specialized group of people, such as members of a common craft or friendship group or followers of a particular Hasidic sect.—ed.]

Table 3. Population of Siedlce by Faith as of 1 October 1940 (M = male, F = female)

	Faith								Total	
	Roman Catholic		Jewish		Eastern Orthodox		Lutheran and others			
	#	%	#	%	#	%	#	%	#	%
M	11,893	66.4	5,869	32.8	69	0.4	68	0.4	17,899	100
F	14,629	67.6	6,864	31.7	80	0.3	71	0.3	21,644	100
Total	26,522	67.1	12,733	32.2	149	0.4	139	0.3	39,543	100

Source: Archiwum Państwowe w Siedlcach, Akta Miasta Siedlce, sig. 2368; Kuligowski, "Liczebność mieszkańców Siedlec," p. 215.

Note: The number in column 10 is corrected from 17,894 to 17,899.—trans.

Table 4. Population of Siedlce in the Area of the Two Ghetto Neighborhoods by Race on 1 October 1940 and 7 November 1940

Street	1 October 1940			7 November 1940		
	Population			Population		
Neiborhood I	Aryan	Jewish	Total	Aryan	Jewish	Total
May 1st	402	614	1,016	38	777	815
Orzeszkowa	7	58	65	7	55	62
Stary Rynek	-	416	416	-	353	353
Kochanowski	120	340	460	30	292	322
Mała	-	-	-	-	-	-
Browarna	40	610	650	28	608	636
Jatkowa	22	327	349	4	377	381
Targowa	138	163	301	7	190	197
Asłanowicz	458	620	1078	216	564	780
Błonie	135	276	411	39	307	346
Pusta	1	55	56	-	66	66
Total	**1,323**	**3,479**	**4,802**	**369**	**3,589**	**3,958**
Neighborhood II	**Aryan**	**Jewish**	**Total**	**Aryan**	**Jewish**	**Total**
Sienkiewicz	1,218	1,177	2,395	228	493	721
Kiliński	455	595	1,050	56	262	318
Przejazd	-	31	31	-	19	19
Asz	5	115	120	8	103	111
Kozia	-	180	180	3	180	183
Poprzeczna	11	98	109	18	117	135
Pułaski	259	2,310	2,560	59	2,132	2,191
Przechodnia	-	-	-	-	-	-
Total	**1,948**	**4,497**	**6,445**	**372**	**3,306**	**3,678**
Neighborhoods combined	**3,271**	**7,976**	**11,247**	**741**	**6,895**	**7,636**

Source: Archiwum Państwowe w Siedlcach, Akta Miasta Siedlce, sig. 2362 and 2368; Kuligowski, "Liczebność mieszkańców Siedlec, stan z 1 X 1940," p. 218.

Table 5. Number of Jews in Siedlce at the Outbreak of the War and at Various Times during the German Occupation [collected from various sources, not normalized—ed.]

Year and date		Number of local Jews	Number of Jews from Elsewhere
1939	1 September	15,283	-
1940	1 October	7,976	15 March: 1,201
	7 November	6,895	-
	December	c. 13,000	December: 1,000
1941	March	12,000	-
	July	11,674	-
	November	12,417	-
1942	June	11,700	-
	26 September	2,000	-
1943	21 January	150	-
	13–14 May	200	-

Source: *Book of Remembrance of the Siedlce Community*, p. 705; T. Brustin-Berenstein, "Deportacje i zagłada skupisk żydowskich w Dystrykcie Warszawskim," in *Biuletyn ŻIH*, no. 1/3 (1952): 122; *Eksterminacja Żydów na ziemiach polskich w okresie okupacji hitlerowskiej. Zbiór dokumentów*, collected and annotated by T. Berenstein, A. Eisenbach, and A. Rutkowski (Warsaw, 1957), pp. 277–279; Archiwum Państwowe w Siedlcach, Akta Miasta Siedlce, sig. 2362 and 2368.

Table 6. Monthly Reports of Organizational Activity of Siedlce Jews in 1934

Month	Name of organization	Meetings		Gatherings		Recreational projects	
		Number of meetings	Total number of participants	Total number of gatherings	Total number of participants	Number of recreational projects	Total number of participants
1	2	3	4	5	6	7	8
January	Brit Trumpeldor					1	150
	Mizrachi					1	250
February	Zionist Org.					1	15
March	Agudath Israel					1	150
April	Zionist Org.					2	350
	Brit Trumpeldor					1	150
	Hechalutz					1	160
May	Zionist Org.					2	3,000
	Bund	1	120				
	R. Poalei Zion	1	300	1	300		
	Brit Trumpeldor					1	150
	Hechalutz	1	500				
June	Zionist Org.	1	40				
July	Zionist Org.					1	400
	Hechalutz	1	250				
	Kultur Liga					1	200
August	Zionist Org.					1	150
	Yiddishe Kunst					1	80
	Freiheit	1	40				
	Metal-Working Trade Guild	1	50				
September	R. Poalei Zion	1	150				
	Kultur Liga					1	130
	Yiddishe Kunst					1	120

1	2	3	4	5	6	7	8
October	Tarbut					1	200
	Soc. for the Care of Orphans					2	180
November	Revisionist Zionists					1	60
	Hechalutz					1	80
	Hapoel					1	500
December	Zionist Org.	1	40				
	R. Poalei Zion	1	60				
	Hechalutz Hatzair	1	25				

Source: Archiwum Państwowe w Siedlcach, Starostwo Powiatowe w Siedlcach 1918–1939, sig. 28–31.

NOTE: For explanation of abbreviations, see List of Abbreviations Used in Tables.

Table 7. Annual Report on the Activity of Jewish Organizations in 1934

Name of organization	Meetings		Gatherings		Recreational projects	
	Number of meetings	Total number of participants	Total number of gatherings	Total number of participants	Number of recreational projects	Total number of participants
1	2	3	4	5	6	7
POLITICAL PARTIES						
Mizrachi					1	250
Zionist Org.	2	80			7	3,915
Agudath Israel					1	150
Bund	1	120				
Revisionist Zionists					1	60
R. Poalei Zion	3	510	1	300		

1	2	3	4	5	6	7
ORGANIZATIONS AND SOCIETIES						
Brit Trumpeldor					3	450
Hechalutz	2	750			2	240
Hechalutz Hatzair	1	25				
Kultur Liga					2	200
Yiddishe Kunst					2	230
Freiheit	1	40				
Metal-Working Trade Guild	1	50				
Tarbut					1	200
Soc. for the Care of Orphans					2	180
Hapoel					1	500

Source: Archiwum Państwowe w Siedlach, Starostwo Powiatowe w Siedlcach 1918–1939, sig. 28–31.

Table 8. Monthly Reports of Organizational Activity of Siedlce Jews in 1935

Month	Name of organization	Meetings		Gatherings		Recreational projects	
		Number of meetings	Total number of participants	Total number of gatherings	Total number of participants	Number of recreational projects	Total number of participants
1	2	3	4	5	6	7	8
January	Tarbut					1	100
February	Agudath Israel	3	165				
	Hechalutz	3	137	1	80	1	200
	Freiheit	2	57			1	50
	Yiddishe Kunst	1	157			1	100

1	2	3	4	5	6	7	8
March	Agudath Israel	1	50				
	Mizrachi	1	42	1	30		
	TOZ	1	156			1	250
	Kultur Liga	3	47	1	25		
	Hanoar Haivri Akiba	1	20				
	Jewish Construction Workers Union	2	60				
April	Freiheit	2	77				60
	Yiddishe Kunst	1	157				60
	Zionist Org.	1	7				
	Poalei Agudath Israel	1	46				36
	Agudath Israel	1	100				87
May	Hashomir Hatzair			1	50		
	Kultur Liga			1	400		
	Hechalutz			1	150		
	R. Poalei Zion			1	200	1	100
June	Yiddishe Kunst	1	80				
	Tarbut					1	200
	Soc. of Fr. of Work. Pal.	1	700				
July	R. Poalei Zion			1	20		
	Soc. of Fr. of Work. Pal.					2	170
	Brit Trumpeldor					1	350
	Mizrachi					1	250
August	Brit Trumpeldor					1	100
	Hechalutz Hatzair	1	70				
	Beit Lechem	1	45				
September	no data						
October	Shomrei Shabbos	1	70				
	Hapoel					1	80
	Soc. of Fr. of Work. Pal.					4	320
	Freiheit					1	70

1	2	3	4	5	6	7	8
October	Soc. for the Care of Orphans					1	120
	Union of the Leather and Allied Industries					2	200
	Garm. Ind. Workers Union					1	120
	Coop. Joint-Stock Bank	1	132				
November	Linas Hatzedek	1	34			2	500
	Hechalutz					1	75
	Soc. of Fr. of Work. Pal.					1	80
	Soc. for the Care of Orphans					1	300
	Freiheit					1	90
	Tarbut					1	250
	Garm. Ind. Workers Union					1	200
	Food Ind. Workers Union	1	8				
December	Revisionist Zionists					1	200
	Agudath Israel					2	350
	R. Poalei Zion					1	70
	Brit Trumpeldor					1	180
	Hapoel	1	150				
	Kultur Liga					2	280
	Soc. of Fr. of Work. Pal.					1	130
	Tarbut					1	160
	TOZ					1	180
	Leather Ind. Workers Union					1	90

Source: Archiwum Państwowe w Siedlcach, Starostwo Powiatowe w Siedlcach 1918–1939, sig. 28–31.

Table 9. Annual Report of the Activity of Jewish Organization in 1935

Name of Organization	Meetings		Gatherings		Recreational projects	
	Number of meetings	Total number of participants	Total number of gatherings	Total number of participants	Number of recreational projects	Total number of participants
1	2	3	4	5	6	7
POLITICAL PARTIES						
Mizrachi	1	42	1	30	1	250
Zionist Org.	1	7			7	
Poalei Agudath Israel	1	46				36
Revisionist Zionists					1	200
Agudath Israel	5	315			2	437
R. Poalei Zion			2	400	2	170
ORGANIZATIONS AND SOCIETIES						
Brit Trumpeldor					3	630
Hechalutz	3	137	2	230	2	275
Hashomer Hatzair			1	50		
Kultur Liga	3	47	2	425	2	280
Yiddishe Kunst	2	394			1	160
Freiheit	4	134			3	270
Tarbut					4	710
Beit Lechem	1	45				
Shomrei Shabbas	1	70				
Soc. for the Care of Orphans					2	420
Hapoel						
Hanoar Haivri Akiba	1	20				
Soc. of Fr. of Work. Pal.	1	700			8	600
Coop. Joint-Stock Bank	1	132				
Linas Hatzedek	1	34			2	500
TOZ	1	156			2	430

1	2	3	4	5	6	7
LABOR UNIONS						
Leather Ind. Workers Union					3	290
Garm. Ind. Workers Union					2	320
Food Ind. Workers Union	1	8				
Construction Workers Union	2	60				

Source: Archiwum Państwowe w Siedlcach, Starostwo Powiatowe w Siedlcach 1918–1939, sig. 28–31.

Table 10. Monthly Reports of the Organizational Activity of Siedlce Jews in 1936

Month	Name of organization	Meetings		Gather-ings		Recreational projects	
		Number of meetings	Total number of participants	Total number of gatherings	Total number of participants	Number of recreational projects	Total number of participants
1	2	3	4	5	6	7	8
January	Hachalutz	1	52			1	70
	Hashomer Hatzair			1	55		
	Yiddishe Kunst					2	420
	Hapoel					1	150
	Tarbut					3	550
	Leather Ind. Workers Union	4	560				
February	R. Poalei Zion	1	40				
	Federation of Merchants	5	130				
	Tarbut					2	400
	Yiddishe Kunst					2	300
	Hapoel					1	130
	Soc. for the Care of Orphans					3	800

1	2	3	4	5	6	7	8
February	Garm. Ind. Workers Union					1	150
	Leather Ind. Workers Union	5	49				
March	Yiddishe Kunst					2	300
	Soc. for the Care of Orphans					1	120
	Transport Workers Union	1	30				
	Garm. Ind. Workers Union	1	25				
April	Zionist Org.					1	300
	Assoc. of Jewish Schools	1	65				
	Kultur Liga	1	12				
	Brit Trumpeldor	1	70				
	Soc. of Fr. of Work. Pal.					1	120
	Hapoel					1	260
	Yiddishe Kunst	1	92				
	Transport. Workers Union	1	34				
May	R. Poalei Zion	1	80				
	Zionist Org.			2	950		
	Yiddishe Kunst					2	600
June	R. Poalei Zion	1	300				
	Soc. for the Care of Orphans					2	560
	Hashomer Hatzair	1	64				
	Leather Ind. Workers Union	1	56				
July	Yiddishe Kunst	1	96				
	Leather Ind. Workers Union	3	85				
	Food Ind. Workers Union	1	25				
August	Bund			3	500		
	Zionist Org.	2	356	1	90		
	Kultur Liga	1	12				
	ZŻUWoNP	1	96	2	160		

1	2	3	4	5	6	7	8
August	Leather Ind. Workers Union	2	74				
September	Bund			1	200		
	Zionist Org.			1	250		
	R. Poalei Zion			1	300		
	Brit Trumpeldor	1	40				
	Leather Ind. Workers Union	1	45				
October	Zionist Org.			1	600		
	Soc. of Fr. of Work. Pal.					1	120
	Soc. for the Care of Orphans					2	500
	Hapoel					2	350
	Star					1	180
	UJWT	1	56				
	Garm.Ind. Workers Union	1	70	1	150		
	Retail & Office Work. Union	1	50				
November	Hechalutz	1	40				
	Star					1	200
	Yiddishe Kunst					1	250
	Hapoel					1	180
	Garm. Ind. Workers Union	1	34				
	Transport. Workers Union	1	16				
December	Bund	1	70				
	Zionist Org.					1	150
	Yiddishe Kunst					1	130
	TOZ					1	180
	Leather Ind. Workers Union	1	40				
	Garm. Ind. Workers Union	1	14				

Source: Archiwum Państwowe w Siedlcach, Starostwo Powiatowe w Siedlcach 1918–1939, sig. 28–31.

Table 11. Annual Report of the Activity of Jewish Organizations in 1936

Name of organization	Meetings		Gatherings		Recreational projects	
	Number of meetings	Total number of participants	Total number of gatherings	Total number of participants	Number of recreational projects	Total number of participants
1	2	3	4	5	6	7
POLITICAL PARTIES						
R. Poalei Zion	1	42	1	30	1	250
Zionist Org.	1	7			7	
Bund	1	46				36
ORGANIZATIONS AND SOCIETIES						
Brit Trumpeldor					3	630
Hechalutz	3	137	2	230	2	275
Hashomer Hatzair			1	50		
Kultur Liga	3	47	2	425	2	280
Yiddishe Kunst	2	394			1	160
Freiheit	4	134			3	270
Tarbut					4	710
Beit Lechem	1	45				
Shomrei Shabbas	1	70				
Soc. for the Care of Orphans					2	420
Hapoel						
Hanoar Haivri Akiba	1	20				
Soc. of Fr. of Work. Pal.	1	700			8	600
Coop. Joint-Stock Bank	1	132				
Linas Hatzedek	1	34			2	500
TOZ	1	156			2	430
LABOR UNIONS						
Leather Ind. Workers Union	17	909			3	290

1	2	3	4	5	6	7
Garm. Ind. Workers Union	4	143	1	150	1	150
Transport. Workers Union	3	80				
Food Ind. Workers Union	1	25				
Federation of Merchants	5	130				
Union of Jews in the Trades	1	56				
Retail & Office Work. Union	1	50				

Source: Archiwum Państwowe w Siedlcach, Starostwo Powiatowe w Siedlcach 1918–1939, sig. 28–31.

Table 12. Monthly Reports of Organizational Activity of Siedlce Jews in 1937

Month	Name of organization	Meetings		Gatherings		Recreational projects	
		Number of meetings	Total number of participants	Total number of gatherings	Total number of participants	Number of recreational projects	Total number of participants
1	2	3	4	5	6	7	8
January	Brit Trumpeldor	1	50				
	Leather Ind. Workers Union	1	60				
February	R. Poalei Zion	1	70				
	Bund	1	80				
	Brit Trumpeldor	1	60				
	Mizrachi	1	80				
	Freiheit	1	30				
	Tarbut					1	150
	Hechalutz	2	165				
	Soc. for the Care of Orphans					1	180
	Star					1	130

1	2	3	4	5	6	7	8
February	Hapoel					2	250
March	Zionist Org.					1	200
	Star					1	150
	Jewish LOPP Circle					1	250
	Leather Ind. Workers Union	1	51				
	Garm. Ind. Workers Union	1	264				
April	ZŻUWoNP			2	900		
	Hapoel					1	180
	Tarbut					1	60
May	TOZ					1	250
	Hachaluc			1	150		
	Soc. of Fr. of Work. Pal.			2	250		
	Yiddishe Kunst			1	200		
	Star					1	180
	Shoemakers Self-Help	1	22				
	Small Business Alliance	2	110				
June	Small Business Alliance	1	21				
	Soc. of Fr. of Work. Pal.			1	200		
	Shoemakers Self-Help	1	23				
July	Bund	1	50				
	Mizrachi	1	72	1	400		
	Brit Trumpeldor			1	1,000		
	Soc. of Fr. of Work. Pal.	1	75				
August	Federation of Merchants	1	70				
	Beit Lechem	1	21				
	Leather Ind. Workers Union	6	143	3	280		
	Garm. Ind. Workers Union	1	17				
September	Bund	1	45				
	Yiddishe Kunst			1	200		
	Hachalutz			1	250		

1	2	3	4	5	6	7	8
September	Freiheit					3	450
	Soc. for the Care of Orphans					1	50
	Star					1	75
	Hapoel					1	80
	Bank for Interest-Free Loans	1	40				
	Leather Ind. Workers Union	1	90				
October	Soc. for the Care of Orphans					1	120
	Star					2	82
	Federation of Merchants	1	78				
	Leather Ind. Workers Union	1	75				
November	Bund	1	150				
	Zionist Org.					1	130
	Hapoel					1	160
	Leather Ind. Workers Union	1	120	1	150		
December	Bund					1	300
	Hitachdut	1	32				
	Hapoel	1	47			1	120
	Star					1	150
	TOZ					1	100
	Freiheit					1	50
	Yiddishe Kunst					1	300
	Federation of Merchants	1	115				
	Shoemakers Self-Help	1	45				
	Union of Jews in the Trades	1	30			1	60
	Leather Ind. Workers Union	4	30				

Source: Archiwum Państwowe w Siedlcach, Starostwo Powiatowe w Siedlcach 1918–1939, sig. 28–31.

Table 13. Annual Report of the Activity of Jewish Organizations in 1937

Name of organization	Meetings		Gatherings		Recreational projects	
	Number of meetings	Total number of participants	Total number of gatherings	Total number of participants	Number of recreational projects	Total number of participants
1	2	3	4	5	6	7
POLITICAL PARTIES						
R. Poalei Zion	1	70				
Bund	4	325			1	300
Mizrachi	2	152	1	400		
Zionist Org.					2	330
Hitachdut	1	32				
ORGANIZATIONS AND SOCIETIES						
Brit Trumpeldor	2	110	1	1,000		
Star					7	767
Freiheit	1	30			4	500
Tarbut			2	210		
Hechalutz	2	165	2	400		
Soc. for the Care of Orphans					3	350
Hapoel	1	47			6	790
Jewish LOPP Circle					1	250
ZŻUWoNP			2	900		
TOZ					2	350
Soc. of Fr. of Work. Pal.	1	75	3	450		
Yiddishe Kunst			2	400	1	300
Alliance of Small Merchants	3	131	63			
Shoemakers Self-Help	2	90				
Federation of Merchants	3	263				

1	2	3	4	5	6	7
Beit Lechem	1	21				
Bank for Interest-Free Loans	1	40				
LABOR UNIONS						
Leather Ind. Workers Union	15	569	4	430		
Garm. Ind. Workers Union	2	281				
Union of Jews in the Trades	1	30			1	60

Source: Archiwum Państwowe w Siedlcach, Starostwo Powiatowe w Siedlcach 1918–1939, sig. 28–31.

Table 14. Monthly Reports of Organizational Activity of Siedlce Jews in 1938

Month	Name of organization	Meetings		Gatherings		Recreational projects	
		Number of meetings	Total number of participants	Total number of gatherings	Total number of participants	Number of recreational projects	Total number of participants
1	2	3	4	5	6	7	8
January	no data						
February	no data						
March	no data						
April	Zionist Org.					4	58
	Star					1	50
	Nat. Council of Trade Unions	1	27				
	Transport. Workers Union	2	328				
	Leather Ind. Workers Union	1	50				
May	R. Poalei Zion	1	120				
	Bund	1	150	1	200		
	Zionist Org.	1	300				
	Hitachdut	1	150				

1	2	3	4	5	6	7	8
	Leather Ind. Workers Union	1	80				
	Brit Trumpeldor			1	70		
	Star	1	50				
	Hechalutz Hatzair			1	65		
June	Brit Trumpeldor					1	800
	Retail & Office Work. Union	1	50				
	Leather Ind. Workers Union	1	160				
July	no data						
August	Brit Trumpeldor					2	220
	Leather Ind. Workers Union	1	49				
	Star					1	300
September	Zionist Org.					1	200
	Transport. Workers Union	1	36				
October	Zionist Org.	1	80				
	United Poalei Zion					1	30
	Star					1	80
	Hapoel					1	120
	Tarbut					3	450
	Brit Trumpeldor			1	150		
	Transport. Workers Union	1	6	1	50		
	Leather Ind. Workers Union			1	24		
November	Zionist Org.	1	150				
	Tarbut					4	800
	Transport. Workers Union	1	40				
December	New Zionist Org.	1	42				
	Brit Trumpeldor					2	360
	Soc. of Fr. of Work. Pal.					1	400
	Hapoel	1	70			1	50
	Shoemakers Self-Help	1	30				
	Tarbut	1	188			6	1,600

Source: Archiwum Państwowe w Siedlcach, Starostwo Powiatowe w Siedlcach 1918–1939, sig. 28–31.

Table 15. Annual Report of the Activity of Jewish Organizations in 1938

Name of organization	Meetings		Gatherings		Recreational projects	
	Number of meetings	Total number of participants	Total number of gatherings	Total number of participants	Number of recreational projects	Total number of participants
1	2	3	4	5	6	7
POLITICAL PARTIES						
Zionist Org.	3	530			5	258
New Zionist Org.	1	42				
United Poalei Zion					1	300
R. Poalei Zion	1	120				
Bund	1	150	1	200		
Hitachdut	1	150				
ORGANIZATIONS AND SOCIETIES						
Brit Trumpeldor			2	220	5	1,380
Tarbut	1	188			13	2,850
Star	1	50			3	430
Soc. of Fr. of Work. Pal.					1	400
Hapoel	1	70			2	170
LABOR UNIONS						
Transport. Workers Union	5	410				
Shoemakers Self-Help	1	30				
Leather Ind. Workers Union	1	209	1	24		
Nat. Council of Trade Unions	1	27				
Retail & Office Work. Union		50				

Source: Archiwum Państwowe w Siedlcach, Starostwo Powiatowe w Siedlcach 1918–1939, sig. 28–31.

List of Abbreviations Used in Tables

Agudath Israel—Union of Israel
Beit Lechem—"House of Bread" Society for Aid to the Poor
Brit Trumpeldor—Association of Jewish Youths, also Betar
Bund—General Union of Jewish Workers in Poland
Freiheit—"Freedom" Cultural-Educational Society
*Garm. Ind. Workers Union—Garment Industry Workers Union
*Hanoar Haivri Akiba—Hebrew Akiva Youth (Zionist religious socialist group)
Hapoel (Worker)—Jewish Workers Sports Club
Hashomer Hatzair—Young Guard, Scout
Hechalutz—Pioneer
Hechalutz Hatzair—Young Pioneer
Kultur Liga—"League of Culture" Educational Association
*Leather Ind. Workers Union—Workers Union of the Leather and Related Industries
Linat Hatzedek—Society for Watching over the Sick
*Metal-Working Trade Guild—Guild of Sheet-Metal Workers, Locksmiths, Boiler
Smiths, and Allied Trades
Mizrachi—Organization of Orthodox Zionists
*Nat. Council of Trade Unions—National Council of Trade Unions
Poalei Agudath Israel—Workers of the Union of Israel
*Retail & Office Work. Union—Retail and Office Workers Union
Shoemakers Self-Help—Shoemakers Self-Help Association
Shomrai Shabbos—Association for the Celebration of Shabbat
*Soc. of Fr. of Work. Pal.—Society of Friends of Working Palestine
Star—"Stern" Workers Physical Education Association
Tarbut—"Culture" Educational-Cultural Association
TOZ—Society for the Protection of Health
*Transport. Workers Union—Transportation Industry Workers Union
*UJWT—Union of Jewish Workers in the Trades
Yiddishe Kunst—"Jewish Art" Literary-Musical Society
ZŻUWoNP—Union of Jews Participating in the Battle for Poland's Independence

NOTE: * marks abbreviations added by translator. Alphabetical order of abbreviations differs from that of the original.

BIBLIOGRAPHY

MANUSCRIPTS AND ARCHIVAL MATERIAL

1. Archiwum Państwowe w Lublinie Wydział II Społeczno-Polityczny, Urząd Wojewódzki Lubelski 1919–1939 [National Archive in Lublin Social-Political Department 2, Lublin County Office 1919–1939, abbreviated as APL]
- Budżety i listy składek Gminy Wyznaniowej Żydowskiej w Siedlcach, sygn. 823 [Budgets and lists of dues of the Jewish Religious Council in Siedlce, sig. 823].
- Centralna Organizacja Żydów Ortodoksów w Polsce "Szlomej Emunej Izrael" (Agudath Israel)—Pokój Wiernych Izraelitów - informacja o oddziałach, sygn. 489 [Central Organization of Orthodox Jews in Poland "Shlomei Emunei Israel" (Agudath Israel)—Peace for Faithful Israelites—information about divisions, sig. 489].
- Działalność antypaństwowa Żydów oraz zajścia antyżydowskie 1924–1934, sygn. 498 [Anti-state activity of Jews and anti-Jewish incidents 1924–1934, sig. 489].
- Ewidencja czasopism żydowskich, sygn. 604 [Record of Jewish periodicals, sig. 604].
- Mapy wpływów politycznych poszczególnych stronnictw politycznych na terenie województwa lubelskiego, sygn. 19 [Map of political influences of individual political parties on the territory of Lublin Province, sig. 19].
- "Mizrachi"—informacja o oddziałach, sygn. 484 ["Mizrachi"—information about divisions, sig. 484].
- Monografia Stronnictwa Politycznego "Bund"—Algemeiner Jidisze Arbeter Bund in Pojlen—Ogólnożydowski Związek Robotniczy "Bund" w Polsce, sygn. 460 [Monograph of the "Bund" Political Party—Algemeiner Jidisze Arbeter Bund in Pojlen—"Bund" General Jewish Labor Union in Poland, sig. 460].
- Monografia Stronnictwa Politycznego "Centralna Organizacja Żydów Ortodoksów"—"Agudath Israel"—Związek Izraela, sygn. 485 [Monograph of "Central Organization of Orthodox Jews" Political Party—"Agudath Israel"— Union of Israel, sig. 485].

- Monografia Stronnictwa Politycznego "Jidisze Folkisze" "Folkiści", sygn. 470 [Monograph of "Yiddishe Folkishe" Political Party "Folkists," sig. 470].
- Monografia Stronnictwa Politycznego "Jidisze Socjalistisze Demokratisze Partaj Poalej Cjon in Pojlen"—"Żydowska Socjalno-Demokratyczna Partia Robotnicza Poalej Syjon w Polsce—Prawica, sygn. 459 [Monograph of "Yiddyshe Sotsyalistishe Demokratishe Arbeter Partay Poalei Zion in Poylen" Political Party— Jewish Social-Democratic Labor Party Right Poalei Zion in Poland, sig. 459].
- Monografia Stronnictwa Politycznego "Organizacja Syjonistów Ortodoksów "Mizrachi", sygn. 466 [Monograph of the "Organization of Orthodox Zionists" Political Party "Mizrachi," sig. 466].
- Monografia Stronnictwa Politycznego "Organizacja Syjonistyczna w Polsce", sygn. 465 [Monograph of the "Zionist Organization in Poland" Political Party, sig. 465].
- Organizacja Syjonistów Rewizjonistów "Brit-Hazohar" informacja o oddziałach, sygn. 492 [Organization of Revisionist Zionists "Brit-Hazohar" information about divisions, sig. 492].
- Organizacja Syjonistyczna—Al Hamiszmar, sygn. 462 [Zionist Organization— Al Hamishmar, sig. 462].
- Organizacja Syjonistyczna w Polsce—informacja o oddziałach 1923–1939, sygn. 487 [Zionist Organization in Poland—information about divisions, 1923–1939, sig. 487].
- Rewizje i aresztowania członków Ogólnożydowskiego Związku Robotniczego "Bund" w Polsce 1920–1921, sygn. 481 [Searches and arrests of members of the "Bund" General Jewish Labor Union in Poland 1920–1921, sig. 481].
- Sprawozdanie starosty siedleckiego o ruchu społecznym za rok 1926, sygn. 161 [Report of the Siedlce county administrator about the social movement for 1926, sig. 161].
- Stowarzyszenie "Hanoar Haiwri"—"Akiba"—Żydowska Organizacja Skautowa Akiba w Siedlcach, sygn. 1133 ["Hanoar Haivri" Association—"Akiba"—Akiba Jewish Scouting Organization in Siedlce, sig. 1133].
- Stowarzyszenie Kulturalno-Oświatowe "Freiheit", sygn. 1116 ["Freedom" Cultural-Educational Association, sig. 1116].
- Stowarzyszenie Robotnicze Wychowania Fizycznego "Jutrznia" w Siedlcach, sygn. 1190 ["Morning Prayer" Labor Association for Physical Education in Siedlce, sig. 1190].
- Stowarzyszenie "Żydowska Liga Oświaty Ludowej", sygn. 1115 ["Jewish League of Peoples' Education" Association, sig. 1115].
- Syjoniści—informacja o oddziałach 1929, sygn. 483 [Zionists—information about divisions 1929, sig. 483].

- Wybory rabina w Siedlcach 1933–1936, sygn. 747 [Election of the rabbi in Siedlce 1933–196, sig. 747].
- Związek Żydowskich Nauczycieli Szkół Powszechnych w Siedlcach, sygn. 1244 [Union of Jewish Primary School Teachers in Siedlce, sig. 1244].
- Żydowskie Stowarzyszenie Kulturalno-Oświatowe "Jabne" oddział w Siedlcach, sygn. 1117 ["Javneh" Jewish Cultural-Educational Association, Division in Siedlce, sig. 1117].
- Żydowskie Stowarzyszenie Kulturalno-Oświatowe "Tarbut", sygn. 1118 [Tarbut Jewish Cultural-Educational Association, sig. 1118].

2. **Archiwum Państwowe w Siedlcach [National Archive in Siedlce, abbreviated APS]**
- Akta Miasta Siedlce, sygn. 2364, 2368 [Records of the City of Siedlce, sig. 2364, 2368].
- Komenda Powiatowej Policji Państwowej w Siedlcach 1918–1939 [Headquarters of the County Natioanl Police in Siedlce 1918–1939].
- Siedlecki Gubernialny Zarząd Żandarmerii, sygn. 158, 192 [Siedlce Gubernia Gendarme Headquarters, sig. 158, 192].
- Siedlecki Powiatowy Zarząd Żandarmerii, sygn. 304 [Siedlce County Gendarme Headquarters, sig. 304].
- Starostwo Powiatowe w Siedlcach 1919–1939 [County Administrative Offices in Siedlce 1919–1939].
- Wykaz ilościowy ludności aryjskiej i żydowskiej w dzielnicach "Getta żydowskiego na terenie m. Siedlce" [Numerical list of Aryan and Jewish population in the "Jewish ghetto on the territory of the city of Siedlce"].
- Zbiór afiszy okupacyjnych powiatu siedleckiego [Siedlce County collection of posters from the occupation].
- Maksymiuk P.L., *Konspiracja w Siedlcach w latach 1907–1914* [P.L. Maksymiuk, *The underground in Siedlce in the years 1907–1914*].
- Kaleniecki Z., *Działalność KPP w Okręgu Siedleckim w latach 1918–1938* [Z. Kaleniecki, *Activity of the Communist Party of Poland in the Siedlce District in the years 1918–1938*].

3. **Sąd Rejonowy w Siedlcach Wydział Ksiąg Wieczystych [District Court in Siedlce Department of Real-Estate Registers]**
- Księga Hipoteczna nr 757, 682, 697 [Mortgage Register nos. 757, 682, 697].

4. **Archiwum Żydowskiego Instytutu Historycznego w Warszawie [Archive of the Jewish Historical Institute in Warsaw]**
Relacje [Accounts by]:
- Chwedczuk Grzegorz, sygn. 301/6366 [Grzegorz Chwedczuk, sig. 301/6366].
- Finkielsztein Hersz, sygn. 301/4506 [Hersz Finkielsztein, sig. 301/4506].

- Gorzeliński Ela, sygn. 301/6383 [Ela Gorzeliński, sig. 301/6383].
- Halber Izaak, sygn. 301/6407 [Izaak Halber, sig. 301/6407].
- Halberstadt Izrael i Rachela, sygn. 301/6436 [Izrael and Rachela Halberstadt, sig. 301/6436].
- Jontef Gitla, sygn. 301/4657 [Gitla Jontef, sig. 301/4657].
- Koć Lucjan, sygn. 301/6517 [Lucjan Koć, sig. 301/6517].
- Kowalski Witold, sygn. 301/5758 [Witold Kowalski, sig. 301/5758].
- Krawczyk Irena, sygn. 301/ 3998 [Irena Krawczyk, sig. 301/ 3998].
- Mieszyński Władysław, sygn. 301/5867 [Władysław Mieszyński, sig. 301/5867].
- Moszański Gabriel, sygn. 301/4357 [Gabriel Moszański, sig. 301/4357].
- Osiński Czesław, sygn. 301/600 [Czesław Osiński, sig. 301/600].
- Sulej Jan, sygn. 301/6134 [Jan Sulej, sig. 301/6134].
- Sądy Społeczne, sygn. 313/41 [Public Courts, sig. 313/41].
- Zarząd Miasta Siedlce, sygn. 301/4323 [Administration of the City of Siedlce, sig. 301/4323].
- Koć L., *Pomoc i współpraca z ludnością żydowską ludności miejskiej powiatu siedleckiego w okresie okupacji hitlerowskiej*, sygn. 301/6517 [L. Koć, *Help and Cooperation with the Jewish Population by the City Population of Siedlce County during the Nazi Occupation*, sig. 301/6517].

5. **Archiwum Akt Nowych w Warszawie [Archive of Modern Records in Warsaw]**
- Ministerstwo Spraw Wewnętrznych. Wydział Narodowościowy, sygn. 246 [Ministry of Internal Affairs. Nationality Department, sig. 246].

6. **Archiwum Państwowe w Krakowie [National Archive in Kraków]**
- Izba Zdrowia GG, sygn. 250 [General Government Chamber of Health, sig. 250].

7. **Archiwum Yad Vashem w Jerozolimie [Yad Vashem Archive in Jerusalem]**
- Zeznanie Agnieszki Widerschal, sygn. 2222/119-/ (03.2555) [Testimony of Agnieszka Widerschal, sig. 222/119–/ (03.2555)].
- Fritz Hoeft, sygn. 396/361 [Fritz Hoeft, sig. 396/361].

8. **Relacje w posiadaniu autora [Accounts in the author's possession]**
- Izaak Halber
- Hercel Kave
- Renia Pancerowa
- Henryk Rajze

9. **Biuro Badań i Dokumentacji Zabytków w Siedlcach [Office of Research and Documentation of Landmarks in Siedlce]**
- Sobczyk W., *Założenia projektowe na zagospodarowanie terenu cmentarza–pomnika* męczeństwa Narodu Żydowskiego w Siedlcach przy ul. Szkolnej. Materiały

historyczne *i zdjęcia opracował Jontel Goldman* [Sobczyk, W., Design Guidelines for the Development of the Territory of the Cemetery—Monument to the Martyrdom of the Jewish Nation in Siedlce on Szkolna Street. Historical material and photographs compiled by Jontel Goldman].

10. **Miejska Biblioteka Publiczna w Siedlcach, Czytelnia Regionalna [City Public Library in Siedlce, Regional Reading Room]**
- "Shedletser Wochenblat" 1934–1939 [*Siedlce Weekly Journal, 1934–1939*].
- Sztein M., *O cmentarzyskach żydowskich w Siedlcach. Referat odczytany na posiedzeniu miesięcznym Siedleckiego Oddziału Towarzystwa Krajoznawczego dnia 14 czerwca 1910 r.*, Siedlce 1910–2008 [źródło opracowane przez Adama Krzeskiego i powielone w niewielu egzemplarzach—author's note] [Sztein, M. "On Jewish Graveyards in Siedlce. Paper read at the monthly meeting of the Siedlce Branch of the Sightseeing Society on 14 June 1910," Siedlce, 1910–2008 (source compiled by Adam Krzeski and reproduced in a small number of copies)].

11. **Instytut Historyczny im. Gen. W. Sikorskiego w Londynie [General W. Sikorski Historical Institute in London]**
- S.P.P. [Studium Polski Podziemnej—trans.], teka 15, poz. 7 [Polish Underground Movement Study Trust, file 15, item 7].

12. **Instytut Pamięci Narodowej w Warszawie Główna Komisja Badania Zbrodni przeciwko Narodowi Polskiemu [Institute of National Remembrance in Warsaw Main Commission for the Investigation of Crimes against the Polish Nation]**
- Ankieta Sądów Grodzkich,sygn.49 [Magistrates' Courts Questionnaire, sig. 49].
- OKBZN w Siedlcach, *Pamiętnik Cypory Jabłoń-Zonszajn ur.w 1915 r. i zamieszkałej w Siedlach* [District Commission for the Investigation of Crimes against the Polish Nation in Siedlce, Memorial to Cypora Jabłoń-Zonszajn, born in 1915 and residing in Siedlce].

13. **Zakład Narodowy im. Ossolińskich we Wrocławiu [Ossoliński National Institute in Wrocław]**
- Koć L., *Pomoc i współpraca z ludnością żydowską ludności miejskiej powiatu siedleckiego z uwzględnieniem sytuacji zagadnień żydowskich na innych powiatach Podlasia w okresie okupacji hitlerowskiej w Polsce* (mikrofilm) [Koć, L. Help and Cooperation of the City Population of Siedlce County with the Jewish Population Taking into Account the Situation of Jewish Issues in Other Counties of Podlasie during the Nazi Occupation in Poland (microfilm)].

14. **Muzeum Walki i Męczeństwa w Treblince [Museum of Struggle and Martyrdom in Treblinka]**
- Relacja wideo Jana Michalaka, Bogdana Osińskiego [Video account of Jan Michalak, Bogdan Osiński].

15. **Zbiory Zbigniewa Wąsowskiego [Zbigniew Wąsowski Collection]**
- Grzymała W., *Wspomnienia*, Białystok 1982–1985 [Grzymała, W. *Memoires.* Białystok, 1982–1985.].

16. **Zbiory Jacka Jędrzejewicza [Jacek Jędrzejewicz Collection]**
- Relacja wideo Barbary Górskiej [Video account of Barbara Górska].

PRINTED SOURCES

1. *Archiwum Związku Żydowskich Stowarzyszeń Humanitarnych "B'nei B'rith" w Krakowie (1892–1938)*, opr. Czajecka B., Kraków 1994 [*Archive of the "B'nai B'rith" Union of Jewish Humanitarian Associations in Kraków (1892–1938)*, comp. B. Czajecka. Kraków, 1994].

2. Brückner A., *Słownik etymologiczny języka polskiego*, Warszawa 1957 [Brückner, A. *Etymological Dictionary of the Polish Language.* Warsaw, 1957].

3. Dmowski L., *Pod plecakiem 17 lat*, Warszawa 1998 [Dmowski, L. *Seventeen Years under a Knapsack.* Warsaw, 1998].

4. *Dokumenty życia społecznego Żydów polskich 1918–1939 w zbiorach Biblioteki Narodowej*, Warszawa 1999 [*Documents Relating to the Social Life of Polish Jews, 1918–1939, in the Collections of the National Library.* Warsaw, 1999].

5. Dunwill W. (Duniłłowicz W.), *Trzy kolory mojego życia*, Warszawa 2000 [Dunwill, W. (Duniłłowicz, W.). *Three Colors of My Life.* Warsaw, 2000; also translated into English by his son Julian Dunwill and published by iUniverse in 2005; reprinted here with Julian Dunwill's permission—trans.].

6. Fuks M., *Adama Czerniakowa dziennik getta warszawskiego 6 IX 1939 – 23 VII 1942*, Warszawa 1983 [Fuks, M. *Adam Czerniaków's Warsaw Ghetto Diary, 6 IX 1939 – 23 VII 1942.* Warsaw, 1983].

7. Grynberg M., Kotowska M., *Życie i zagłada Żydów polskich 1939–1945. Relacje świadków*, Warszawa 2003 [Grynberg, M. and M. Kotowska. *The Life and Extermination of Polish Jews, 1939–1945. Accounts of Witnesses.* Warsaw, 2003].

8. Hartglas A., *Na pograniczu dwóch światów*, Warszawa 1996 [Hartglas, A. *Between Two Worlds.* Warsaw, 1996].

9. *Interpelacja posła do Dumy znanego adwokata siedleckiego Stanisława Sunderlanda*, [w:] "Gazeta Podlaska", 1931, nr 25/26 ["Interpellation of Duma Delegate and Well-Known Siedlce Attorney Stanisław Sunderland." In *Gazeta Podlaska*, no. 25/26 (1931)].

10. Yon-Tov, I. *The Worst of Times*. New Orleans, 2002.

11. Karpiński E., *Wspomnienia z okresu okupacji*, [w:] Biuletyn ŻIH nr 1/149, 1989 [Karpiński, E. "Memoirs from the Time of the Occupation." In *Bulletin of the Jewish Historical Institute*, no. 1/149 (1989)].

12. *Księga Pamiątkowa Siedlczan*, Warszawa 1927 [*Memorial Book of Siedlce Residents*. Warsaw, 1927].

13. *Book of Remembrance of the Siedlce Community*, pod red. A. W. Jasny, Buenos Aires 1956 [*Book of Remembrance of the Siedlce Community*. Ed. A. Wolf Jasny. Buenos Aires, 1956]. [Original articles in Yiddish and Hebrew; Kopówka uses partial translation from Yiddish; not available in Polish or English in its entirety—ed.]

14. Lasman N., *Pięćdziesiąt kilometrów od Treblinki*, Warszawa 1994 [Lasman, N. *Fifty Kilometers from Treblinka*. Warsaw, 1994].

15. Lasman N., *Die Strasse. Erinnerungen eines jüdischen Zwangsarbeiters an eine "ganz normale Firma"*, New York/München/Berlin 1999 [Lasman, N. *The Street: Memoirs of a Jewish Forced Laborer at a „Normal Company"*. New York, Munich, Berlin, 1999].

16. Łętocha B., Messer A., Cała A., *Żydowskie druki ulotne w II Rzeczpospolitej w zbiorach Biblioteki Narodowej*, Warszawa 2004 [Łętocha, B., A. Messer, and A. Cała. *Jewish Leaflets in the Second Republic in the Collections of the National Library*. Warsaw, 2004].

17. Martyniuk Z., *Moje Siedlce. Wspomnienia z młodości*, Siedlce 2007 [Martyniuk, Z. *My Siedlce. Memoirs from My Youth*. Siedlce, 2007].

18. *The Diary of Anne Kahan. Siedlce, Poland, 1914–1916.* YIVO Annual of Jewish Social Science, vol. 18. New York, 1983, pp. 141–371. [Polish edition: Anna Safran. "Dziennik Anny Kahan." Siedlce, 2012. The volume also includes "Moje Pierwsze sześć lat w Ameryce" ("My First Six Years in America") and "Moi rodzice uciekli z domu w dwa miesiące po ślubie" ("My Parents Eloped Two Months after Their Wedding"—ed.).

19. *Słownik geograficzny Królestwa Polskiego i innych krajów słowiańskich*, t. X, Warszawa 1889 [*Geographical Dictionary of the Polish Kingdom and Other Slavic Countries*, vol. 10. Warsaw, 1889].

20. Ścisłowska Z., *Wspomnienia z przejażdżki po kraju*, Warszawa 1857 [Ścisłowska, Z. *Memoirs from a Drive around the Country*. Warsaw, 1857].

21. Weinstein E., *17 dni w Treblince*, Łosice 2008 [Weinstein, E. *Seventeen Days in Treblinka*. Łosice, 2008].

22. Willenberg S., *Bunt w Treblince*, Warszawa 1991 [Willenberg, S. *Rebellion in Treblinka*. Warsaw, 1991].

23. Witos W., *Moje wspomnienia*, Warszawa 1990 [Witos, W. *My Memoirs*. Warsaw, 1990].

Studies

1. Alexandre M., *Der Judenmord. Deutsche und Österreicher berichten* (brak miejsca i roku wydania) [Alexandre, M. *The Murder of Jews. German and Austrian Reports.* N.p., n.d.].

2. Arendt H., *Eichmann w Jerozolimie*, Kraków 1987 [Arendt, H. *Eichmann in Jerusalem.* Kraków, 1987].

3. Block, G., and M. Drucker. *Rescuers. Portraits of Moral Courage in the Holocaust.* New York, 1992.

4. Bobryk A., Kochan I., *Prawosławie w Siedlcach*, Siedlce 2007 [Bobryk, A., and I. Kochan. *Eastern Orthodoxy in Siedlce.* Siedlce, 2007].

5. Buber M., *Opowieści chasydów*, Poznań 1986 [Buber, M. *Tales of the Hasidim.* Poznań, 1986]. [Edition available in English: Buber, Martin. *Tales of the Hasidim.* New York: Schocken, 1947-48 / 1991—ed.]

6. Buber M., *Opowieści rabina Nachmana*, Paryż 1983 [Buber, M. *The Tales of Rabbi Nachman.* Paris, 1983]. [Translation used here is from Martin Buber. *The Tales of Rabbi Nachman.* New York: Horizon, 1956, pp. 12–13.—ed.]

7. Celiński A., Dmowski R., *Zarys dziejów ochrony przeciwpożarowej w mieście Siedlce*, Siedlce 2007 [Celiński, A., and R. Dmowski. *Outline of the History of Fire Protection in the City of Siedlce.* Siedlce, 2007].

8. Doktór J., *Początki chasydyzmu polskiego*, Wrocław 2004 [Doktór, J. *Beginnings of Polish Chassidism.* Wrocław, 2004].

9. Donath, G. *My Bones Don't Rest in Auschwitz. A Lonely Battle to Survive German Tyranny.* Montreal, 1999.

10. *Działalność Tajnej Organizacji Nauczycielskiej na terenie obecnego woj. siedleckiego w latach 1939–1944*, praca zbiorowa, Siedlce 1992 [*The Activity of the Secret Organization of Teachers on the Territory of the Current Siedlce Province during 1939–1944. Collective work.* Siedlce, 1992].

11. Eisenbach A., *Z dziejów ludności żydowskiej w Polsce w XVIII i XIX wieku. Studia i szkice*, Warszawa 1983 [Eisenbach, A. *From the History of the Jewish Population in Poland during the Eighteenth and Nineteenth Centuries. Studies and Sketches.* Warsaw, 1983].

12. Głowacka-Maksymiuk U., *Gubernia siedlecka w latach rewolucji 1905–1907*, Warszawa 1985 [Głowacka-Maksymiuk, U. *The Siedlce Gubernia during the Revolution of 1905-1907.* Warsaw, 1985].

13. Głowacka-Maksymiuk U., *Ulice Siedlec. Historia. Patroni. Zabytki*, Siedlce 1997 [Głowacka-Maksymiuk, U. *The Streets of Siedlce. History. Patrons. Landmarks.* Siedlce, 1997].

14. Gmitruk J., *Stefan Skoczylas 1918–1945 (Biografia dowódcy BCH na Podlasiu)*,

Warszawa 2008 [Gmitruk, J. *Stefan Skoczylas, 1918-1945 (Biography of the Leader of the Peasant Battalions in Podlasie*. Warsaw, 2008].

15. Gryciuk, F. *Siedlce 1944-1956*. Warsaw, 2009.

16. Grynberg H., *Dzieci Syjonu*, Warszawa 1994 [Grynberg, H. *Children of Zion*. Warsaw, 1994].

17. Heine H., *O Polsce* (brak miejsca i roku wydania) [Heine, H. *On Poland*. N.p., n.d.].

18. Hertz A., *Żydzi w kulturze polskiej*, Paryż 1961 [Hertz, A. *The Jews in Polish Culture*. Paris, 1961].

19. Jarosiński A., *Szkice z nadbużańskiego Podlasia*, Warszawa 1925 [Jarosiński, A. *Sketches from Podlasie by the Bug River*. Warsaw, 1925].

20. Kaszyński S.D., Tiliński H. H., *Gorod Siedlec, istoryko statisticzeskij oczerk*, Siedlce, 1912 [Kaszyński, S. D., and H.H. Tiliński. *The City of Siedlce. A Historical Statistical Essay*. Siedlce, 1912 (in Russian)].

21. Klugman A., *Izrael ziemia świecka*, Warszawa 2001 [Klugman, A. *Israel, a Secular Land*. Warsaw, 2001].

22. Kopówka, E. *Stalag 366 Siedlce*. Siedlce, 2004.

23. Kozaczyńska B., *Losy dzieci z Zamojszczyzny wysiedlonych do powiatu siedleckiego w latach 1943-1945*, Siedlce 2006 [Kozaczyńska, B. *The Fate of Children from the Zamość Region Resettled to Siedlce County in 1943-1945*. Siedlce, 2006].

24. Kozierowski S., *Badania nazw topograficznych archidiecezji poznańskiej*, t. II, oznań 1914 [Kozieroski, S. *Study of Topographical Names in the Poznań Archdiocese*, vol. 2. Poznań, 1914].

25. Kupfer F., *Ber Meisels i jego udział w walkach wyzwoleńczych narodu polskiego (1846, 1848, 1863-1864)*, Warszawa 1953 [Kupfer, F. *Ber Meisels and His Part in the Polish Nation's Struggles for Independence (1846, 1848, 1863-1864)*. Warsaw, 1953].

26. Krawczak T., *Kształtowanie świadomości narodowej wśród ludności wiejskiej Podlasia 1863-1918*, Biała Podlaska 1982 [Krawczak, T. *The Formation of National Awareness among the Rural Population of Podlasie, 1863-1918*. Biała Podlaska, 1982].

27. Król M., *Dr Wiktor Majerczak (1875-1919). Kronika Ruchu Rewolucyjnego w Polsce*, t. II, nr 4/12, 1937 [Król, M. "Dr. Wiktor Majerczak (1875-1919)." *Chronicle of the Revolutionary Movement in Poland* 2, no. 4/12 (1937)].

28. Lewandowska S., *Kalendarium ważniejszych działań bojowo-dywersyjnych*, Warszawa 1972 [Lewandowska, S. *Calendar of Major Diversionary Combat Operations*. Warsaw, 1972].

29. Lewandowska S., *Ruch oporu na Podlasiu*, Warszawa 1976 [Lewandowska, S. *The Resistance Movement in Podlasie*. Warsaw, 1976].

30. Martynowski S., *Pogrom w Siedlcach*, Łódź 1936 [Martynowski, S. *The Pogrom in Siedlce*. Łódź, 1936].

31. Michalec D., *Aleksandra Ogińska i jej czasy*, Siedlce 1999 [Michalec, D. *Aleksandra Ogińska and Her Times*. Siedlce, 1999].

32. Mierzwiński H., *Żydzi podlascy a powstanie styczniowe* [w:] *Rok 1863 na Podlasiu*, Siedlce 1998 [Mierzwiński, H. "The Podlasie Jews and the January Uprising." In *1863 in Podlasie*. Siedlce, 1998].

33. Moniewski, T. *Siedlce*. Siedlce, 1929.

34. *Naród. Kościół. Kultura. Szkice z dziejów Polski*, pod red. D. Walczewskiej-Belniak, cz. 2, Lublin 1986 [Walczewska-Belniak, D., ed. *The Nation. The Church. Culture. Sketches from the History of Poland*, part 2. Lublin, 1986].

35. Niezabitowska M., Tomaszewski T., *Ostatni. Współcześni Żydzi polscy*, Warszawa 1993 [Niezabitowska, M., and T. Tomaszewski. *The Last Ones. Modern Polish Jews*. Warsaw, 1993].

36. Ochnik J., *Rozkaz konspiracja*, Warszawa 1995 [Ochnik, J. *Command: Go Underground*. Warsaw, 1995].

37. *Obozy hitlerowskie na ziemiach polskich 1939–1945. Informator encyklopedyczny*, Warszawa 1979 [*Nazi Camps on Polish Lands 1939–1945: Encyclopedic Guide*. Warsaw, 1979].

38. Piasecki H., *Żydowska Organizacja PPS*, Wrocław 1978 [Piasecki, H. *The Jewish Organization of the Polish Socialist Party*. Wrocław, 1978].

39. Piłsudski J., *Rok 1863*, Warszawa 1989 [Piłsudski, J. *1863*. Warsaw, 1989].

40. Pinkus, O. *The House of Ashes*. London, 1991.

41. *Polski słownik judaistyczny*, opr. Z. Borzymińska i R. Żebrowski, t. 1 i 2, Warszawa 2003 [*Polish Judaic Dictionary*, comp. Z. Borzymińska and R. Żebrowski, vols. 1 and 2. Warsaw, 2003].

42. *Powiat siedlecki, ziemia, wody, człowiek*, pod red. Cz. Górskiego, Siedlce 1935 [*Siedlce County, Land, Water, People*, ed. Cz. Górski. Siedlce, 1935].

43. *Prasa podlaska w XIX–XX wieku. Szkice i materiały*, pod red. D. Grzegorczuk, A. Kołodziejczyk, Siedlce 2000 [*The Press of Podlasie in the Nineteenth and Twentieth Centuries. Sketches and Materials*, ed. D. Grzegorczuk and A. Kołodziejczyk. Siedlce, 2000].

44. *Prowincja noc. Życie i zagłada Żydów w dystrykcie warszawskim*, pod red. B. Engelking, J. Leociaka, D. Libionki, Warszawa 2007 [*Province Night. The Life and Extermination of Jews in the Warsaw District*, ed. B. Engelking, J. Leociak, and D. Libionka. Warsaw, 2007].

45. *Rejestr miejsc i faktów zbrodni popełnionych przez okupanta hitlerowskiego na ziemiach polskich w latach 1939–1945. Województwo siedleckie*, Warszawa 1985 [*Registry of Places and Facts of Crimes Committed by the Nazi Occupiers on Polish Territory during 1939–1945. Siedlce Province*. Warsaw, 1985].

46. Rusiński W., *Zarys historii polskiego ruchu spółdzielczego*, Warszawa 1980 [Rusiński, W. *Outline of the History of the Polish Social Movement*. Warsaw, 1980].

47. Sack J., *Oko za oko*, Gliwice 1995 [Sack, J. *Eye for an Eye*. Gliwice, 1995].

48. *Siedlce 1448-2007*, pod red. E. Kospath-Pawłowskiego, Siedlce 2007 [*Siedlce 1448-2007*, ed. E. Kospath-Pawłowski. Siedlce, 2007].

49. Singer I.B., *Rodzina Muszkatów*, Warszawa 1996 [Singer, I.B. *The Family Moskat*. Warsaw, 1996].

50. *Społeczeństwo siedleckie w walce o wyzwolenie narodowe i społeczne*, pod red. J.R. Szaflika, Warszawa 1981 [*Siedlce Society in the Battle for National and Social Independence*, ed. J. R. Szaflik. Warsaw, 1981].

51. Śliwowska W., *Czarny rok... czarne lata*, Warszawa 1996 [Śliwowska, W. *Black Year... Black Years*. Warsaw, 1996].

52. Tazbir J., *Protokoły mędrców Syjonu*, Warszawa 1992 [Tazbir, J. *Protocols of the Elders of Zion*. Warsaw, 1992].

53. Tomaszewski J., *Rzeczpospolita wielu narodów*, Warszawa 1985 [Tomaszewski, J. *Republic of Many Nations*. Warsaw, 1985].

54. Tyloch W., *Judaizm*, Warszawa 1987 [Tyloch, W. *Judaism*. Warsaw, 1987].

55. Wasiutyński B., *Ludność żydowska w Królestwie Polskim*, Warszawa 1911 [Wasiutyński, B. *The Jewish Population in the Kingdom of Poland*. Warsaw, 1911].

56. Ważniewski W., *Na przedpolach stolicy*, Warszawa 1974 [Ważniewski, W. *On the Outskirts of the Capital*. Warsaw, 1974].

57. Winter A., *Dzieje Siedlec 1448–1918*, Warszawa 1969 [Winter, A. *The History of Siedlce 1448–1918*. Warsaw, 1969].

58. Wodziński M., *Oświecenie żydowskie w Królestwie Polskim wobec chasydyzmu. Dzieje pewnej idei*, Warszawa 2003 [Wodziński, M. The *Jewish Renaissance in the Polish Kingdom vis-à-vis Chassidism. History of an Idea*. Warsaw, 2003].

59. Zawadzka A., *Szkoła siedlecka w okresie okupacji hitlerowskiej 1939-1944*, Warszawa 1986 [Zawadzka, A. *Siedlce Schools during the Nazi Occupation, 1939-1944*. Warsaw, 1986].

THE PRESS

"Biuletyn Żydowskiego Instytutu Historycznego" [*Bulletin of the Jewish Historical Institute*], no. 1/3 (1952), no. 17–18 (1956), no. 2 (1975), no. 1 (1992).

"Bund Młodych Duchem" [*Rebellion of Those Young at Heart*], no. 5 (2007).

"Gazeta Podlaska" [*Podlasie Gazette*], no. 25 (1931), no. 2 (1932), no. 24 (1933).

"Głos Gminy Starozakonnych" [*Orthodox Jewish Community Voice*], no. 1–2 (2003).

"Głos Podlaski" [*Podlasie Voice*], no. 35 (1934), no. 38 (1934).

"Hamelitz" [*The Advocate*], no. 149 (1900).

"Kurier Siedlecki" [*Siedlce Currier*], no. 2 (1991).

"Literatura na Świecie" [*Literature around the World*], no. 12 (1984).

"Nowa Gazeta Podlaska" [*New Podlasie Gazette*], no. 40 (1933), no. 51 (1933).

"Palestra" [*Bar Association*], no. 5–6 (2008).

"Prace Archiwalno-Konserwatorskie na Terenie Województwa Siedleckiego" [*Archival-Conservationist Work on the Territory of Siedlce Province*], no. 1 (1977), no. 3 (1988), no. 6 (1989), no. 10 (1997), no. 14 (2004).

"Projekt" [*Design*], no. 2 (1991).

"Shedletser Wochenblatt" [*Siedlce Weekly Journal*] (in Yiddish), no. 19 (1937).

"Siedlce" [*Siedlce*], no. 1 (1973).

"Szkice Podlaskie" [*Podlasie Sketches*[, no. 9 (2000).

"Tygodnik Ilustrowany" [*Illustrated Weekly*], no. 343 (1874), no. 38 (1906).

"Tygodnik Siedlecki" [*Siedlce Weekly*], no. 36 (1986), no. 27 (1988).

"Wysokie Obcasy" [*High Heels*], no. 3 (2007).

"Zeszyty Historyczne" [*Historical Notebooks*], no. 9 (1971).

"Ziemia Siedlecka" [*The Siedlce Land*], no. 2 (1938), no. 7 (1938).

"Znak" [*Sign*], no. 339–340 (1983), no. 396–397 (1988), no. 403 (1988), no. 404 (1989).

"Życie Podlasia" [*Life of Podlasie*], no. 9 (1934), no. 51 (1935), no. 52 (1935), no. 5 (1934).

ADDITIONAL BIBLIOGRAPHY COMPILED BY MICHAEL HALBER
(1 JULY 2009 [SUPPLEMENTED 17 MARCH 2014])

1. Block, Gay, and Malka Drucker. *Rescuers. Portraits of Moral Courage in the Holocaust*. Holmes & Meier Publishers: New York, 1992, pp.176–179, entry: Agnieszka Budna-Wiederschal (Agnieszka Budna hid six Jews in Siedlce; chapter written on the basis of an interview conducted with Budna by the authors; also contains artistic photographs taken by Gay Bloch). ENG.
2. Kaspi, Isaac. *Megilat praot Shedletz b-shnat 1906 [Chronicle of the Pogrom in*

Siedlce in 1906]. Tel Aviv, 1947. 44 pages. Historical study of this event, with a preface by Apolinary Hartglas. HBR.

3. Kaspi, Isaac. *Yidishe presse in Shedlets 1894–1939* [*The Yiddish Press in Siedlce 1894–1939*], *YIVO Bleter* 36: 361–362. New York, 1952. Kaspi's article on the development of the Jewish press in Siedlce. YID.

4. Donath, Gitel. *My Bones Don't Rest in Auschwitz. A Lonely Battle to Survive German Tyranny.* Kaplan Publishing: Montreal, 1999. 319 pages. Recollections of a Siedlce woman from the time of the occupation in Siedlce and mainly in Międzyrzec Podlaski. ENG.

5. Fainzilber, Melech. *Oif di khurbot fun main haim (khurban Shedlets)* [*On the Ruins of My House (the Extermination of Siedlce)*. Tel Aviv, 1952. 264 pages. (Considered the first book of remembrance of Siedlce Jews, it contains accounts from the mouths of survivors written down right after the war by a former teacher of a Hebrew school in Siedlce who left for Palestine before the war and visited his home town after the Holocaust with the aim of writing this book). YID. The book was digitized by National Yiddish Book Centre, Steven Spielberg Foundation, and is available for free download at https://archive.org/details/nybc209458. Table of Contents and Name Index are available in English from JewishGen Yizkor Buch Project http://www.jewishgen.org/yizkor/siedlce/Siedlce.html#TOC.

6. Finkelman, Yossef. *B'darchei ha-chaim* [*On the Roads of Life*]. Tel-Aviv, 2009. Translated from the Yiddish manuscript into Hebrew by architect Yechezkel Filon, son of the author. Memoir of life in Siedlce befor World War II and during the war in Russia. HBR.

7. Grynberg, I. P., ed. *Tsum 25 yorign iubilei fun der bibliotek bai der gez. „Yidishe Kunst" in Shedlets* [*Toward the Twenty-Fifth Anniversary of the Jewish Library at the "Yiddishe Kunst" Society in Siedlce* (translation in the original)]. Siedlce, 1926. 8,000 copies, 56 pages. Brochure published for the twenty-fifth anniversary of the Jewish library in Siedlce. YID.

8. Halbersztadt, Natan, and Chaim Rajze. *Vos s'hot pasirt mit undzer chaim-shtot Shedlets* [*What Has Happened to Our Hometown of Siedlce*]. 6 January 1946. 8 pages. An appeal of the Jewish Committee in Siedlce to compatriots in the United States for financial aid for survivors; a description of the extermination of the Jewish community in Siedlce and the circumstances of survivors right after the war. YID.

9. Knaani, David. *Mi Shedlets le Maagan Michael* [*From Siedlce to Maagan Michael*]. Israel, 1994. Private publication; memoirs of a Siedlce resident and kibbutznik. HBR.

10. Krawiec, Israel. *Der geheynom baim lebn (5 yor untern natsizm)* [*Hell on Earth (Five Years under the Nazi Regime)*]. Shabtay ben Michael: Tel Aviv, 1968. 356

pages. Memoirs of a Siedlce tailor from experiences in Siedlce during the occupation written down after the war on the basis of notes taken. YID.

11. Krawiec, Israel. *Hegehenom b-chaim (khamesh shanim takhat shilton hanatzim)* [*Hell on Earth (Five Years under the Nazi Regime)*]. Shabtay ben Michael: Tel Aviv, 1971. 248 pages. Hebrew translation from Yiddish original. HBR.

12. Lasman, Noach. *Die Strasse* [*The Street*]. Waxmann: Munich, New York, Berlin, 1999. Translation from Hebrew. GER.

13. Lasman, Noach. *Hakvish* [*The Street*]. Ministry of Defense of Israel: Tel Aviv, 1994. 190 pages. Translation from a manuscript in Polish; memoirs from a period of slave labor in a German camp on Brzeska Street. HBR.

14. Lasman, Noach. *Khamishim kilometer m-Treblinka* [*Fifty Kilometers from Treblinka*]. Moreshet: Tel Aviv, 1990. 304 pages. Translation into Hebrew from a manuscript in Polish. HBR.

15. Lasman, Noach. *Mistor b-bitzot* [*Marsh People*]. Moreshet: Tel Aviv, 1996. 164 pages. Translation from a manuscript in Polish; account of a group of Jews from the town of Mordy and environs who survived as an armed band by stealing food from local peasants. HBR.

16. Niezabitowska, Małgorzata. *Remnants: The Last Jews of Poland*. Friendly Press: New York, 1986. ENG.

17. Niezabitowska, Małgorzata. *Die Letzten Juden in Polen* [*The Last Jews of Poland*]. Stemmle: Schaffhausen, 1987. GER.

18. *Pinkas hakehilot* [*Encyclopedia of Jewish Communities in Poland*], vol. 7. Yad Vashem: Jerusalem, 1999. Entry: Siedlce, pp. 563–576. Outline of the history of the Siedlce community from its dawn until its liquidation. HBR.

19. Pinkus, Oscar. *Aschenwolken* [*The House of Ashes*]. F. Hopf: Waddewarden, 1996. Translation into German from the English edition. GER.

20. Pinkus, Oscar. *The House of Ashes*. Cleveland, OH: World Publishing Company, c. 1964. Translation from the Hebrew Ud Mutsal. ENG.

21. Pinkus, Oscar. *The House of Ashes*. I.B. Tauris: London, 1991. 282 pages. Revised edition. ENG.

22. Pinkus, Oscar. *Ud mutsal* [*The Surviving Firebrand*]. Hamatmid: Tel Aviv, 1957. 440 pages. Translation of a manuscript in Polish; recollections about the occupation by a Jew from Łosice, later a scholar and writer, containing fragments about Siedlce and its environs). HBR.

23. Rozen, Shlomo. *M'tokh hamapolet* [*From the Avalanche*]. Am Oved: Tel Aviv, 1944. 95 pages. (Recollections of a Siedlce-resident from the outbreak of the war in Siedlce and from the time of his life as a fugitive in Asia; translation into Hebrew of a manuscript in Yiddish). HBR.

24. *Shedletser Wochenblat* [*Siedlce Weekly*]. (Microfilm of almost all issues of the periodical from 1923 to 1939, located in the National Library in Jerusalem). YID.

25. Sheinfeld, Ilan. *Maase b-tabaat* [*Legend of a Ring*]. Keter Sfarim Ltd.: Jerusalem, 2007. 460 pages. (Novel about Jewish girls sold into prostitution in Argentina, having its fanciful beginnings in Siedlce). HBR.

26. Sheinfeld, Ilan. *Shedlets* [*Siedlce*]. Shufra for Fine Literature Ltd.: Tel Aviv, 1999. 235 pages. (Fanciful legends by the well-known Hebrew poet of the younger generation, based on the impression he gained during his childhood listening to the stories of his mother and grandmother from Siedlce). HBR.

27. Sheinfeld, Mina. *Perkei zikhronot 1916–1996* [*Fragments of recollections 1916–1996*]. Izrael. (Private edition; recollections of a Siedlce woman written down in her old age in Israel). HBR.

28. *Sprawozdanie Ochrony Sierot Żydowskich w Siedlcach, ul. Sienkiewicza No. 57/59 za rok 1926* [*Report on the Protection of Jewish Orphans in Siedlce, 57/59 Sienkiewicz Street, for the Year 1926*]. Ezrat-yetumim, Shedlets, Sienkiewicza 57/59. Bericht far'n yor 1926. (Original title in both languages [Polish and Yiddish—trans.].) Siedlce, 1927. 41 pages. (Brochure report about the activity of the organization Ezrat Jetumim [Hebrew for help for orphans], among which is mainly the construction of the new orphanage on Sienkiewicz Street [currently Podlaski Academy]; contains an architectural engraving of the building and a photograph at the stage of the end of construction). YID.

29. Stolovy, Beatrice. *From Bygone Days*. Unpublished, 197?. (Phonographic recording of some of the stories from *Fun fargange teg*, translated into English and read by the author). ENG.

30. Stolovy Broche. *Fun fargangene teg* [*From Bygone Days*]. Stolovy: White Plains, NY, 1978. 104 pages. (Short stories by Bracha Stolowy Kahan, sister of Anna Safran Kahan, collected from publications in the Jewish press in the United States, mostly relating to the time of the author's life in Siedlce up to 1916). YID.

31. Tsanin, Mordekhai. *Tel olam. Masa al pnei 100 kehilot nikhravot* [*Memorial— Journey to 100 Ruined Communities*]. Menora: Tel Aviv, 1952(?). 330 pages. Translation from Yiddish; notebook from a 1947 trip to Poland. HBR.

32. Weinstein, Edi. *Plada rotakhat. Sipura shel brikha m-Treblinka* [*Quenched Steel. The Story of an Escape from Treblinka*]. Yad Vashem: Jerusalem, 2001. 137 pages. Memoir of a Jew from Łosice who was deported to Treblinka from the square of exile in Siedlce, escaped from the camp in a wagon of clothing, and hid in the vicinity of Siedlce; Yiddish manuscript written in Latin letters edited by Noach Lasman. HBR.

33. Weinstein, Edi. *Quenched Steel. The Story of an Escape from Treblinka*. Yad Vashem: Jerusalem, 2002. ENG (translation from Hebrew). [Also published as *17 Days in Treblinka*, 5th ed. (Jerusalem: Yad Vashem Publications, 2008)—trans.]

34. Weissberg, Getzel. A chapter on Siedlce (chap. 3, Eye-Witness Report), in *From the Last Extermination: Journal for the History of the Jewish People during the*

Nazi Regime, ed. Israel Kaplan, no. 3 (October–November 1946), pp. 23–33; published in Munich by Central Historical Commission in 1947; eyewitness account of four days (27–30 Novomber 1942) during the liquidation of the last concentration of Siedlce Jews in Gęsie Borki and an escape from the train to Treblinka; chapter also includes translation into Yiddish from German of Fritz Hoeft's account and five of his photographs from the liquidation action on 22–25 August 1942. YID.

35 Yomtov, Ida. *The Worst of Times*. Private edition: New Orleans, 2002. Memoir of Witold Dunillowicz's sister, written down by her daughter on the basis of recordings as part of a master's thesis.

36. Zilberstein, Israel, ed. *Avot mesaprim Shedlets*. [*Our Ancestors Tell Us about Siedlce*]. Ziomkostwo Żydów siedleckich w Izraelu [Homeland Association of Siedlce Jews in Israel]: Tel Aviv, 2004. 271 pages. A partial translation of a Book of Remembrance translated from Yiddish into Hebrew. HBR.

ABBREVIATIONS: YID = Yiddish, HBR = Hebrew, ENG = English, GER = German.

Indexes

Index of Surnames

[* marks entry added to this translation.—trans.]

333

AUTHOR'S INDEX OF JEWISH TERMS

Editor's Glossary of Terms

Agudah—The name of the Orthodox religious organization in Poland, specifically anti-Zionist

Aron Kodesh—Holy Ark. An elevated alcove or cabinet on the wall of the synagogue in which the Torah Scrolls are kept

Beit [Ha-]Midrash—house of religious study, where religious Jews (particularly men) could gather at any time to study Talmud and other sacred texts

Bund—"Yiddishe Arbeter Bund" (Jewish Workers' Organization)—the Jewish Social Democratic movement, which served a dual purpose as a vehicle of political radicalism and Jewish national expression

Chalutz (pl. Chalutzim)—pioneer, specifically, one of the youthful avant-garde who trained themselves for innovative agricultural settlement in Palestine

Chassid—a member of the Chassidic movement

Chassidism (also Hasidism)—a charismatic Jewish religious movement, founded by Israel Baal Shem (1700–1760) and widespread in Poland, Ukraine, and other countries of Eastern Europe

Cheder—Traditional Jewish religious elementary school

Chevra Kadisha (Holy Society)—a volunteer society dedicated to the burial of the dead

Chevra Mishnayot—a society or club devoted to the study of the Mishnah, the concise law code (edited around 190–200), which is the basis of the Talmud = Brotherhood of Mishna Study

Gemara—the principal part of the Talmud, consisting of dialectical discussion of the laws of the Mishna (legal code) and incorporating biblical commentary

Hachsharah—training, specifically vocational and agricultural training to prepare prospective immigrants for agricultural work in Palestine

Haskalah—Jewish Enlightenment; specifically, the movement to spread modern European scientific and humanistic (hitherto strictly religious) education in the Jewish community to include modern secular subjects such as languages, literature, and sciences

Hechalutz Hamerkaz—Central Pioneer

Histadrut—Zionist Workers' Cooperative (see http://en.wikipedia.org/wiki/Histadrut)

Kahal—community; specifically, the Jewish community of a town or city as an official institution with its governing council

Keren Kayemeth—the Perpetual Fund for fundraising and investment in land in Palestine

Keren Kayemeth LeIsrael —Jewish National Fund

Litwak—A Russian Jew, as opposed to a native Polish Jew

Maskil—a supporter of the Haskalah (Jewish Enlightenment); a proponent of modern humanistic education among Jews

Matzah—Passover unleavened bread

Matzevah—gravestone, tombstone, monument

Mitnagdim—Religious opponents of Chassidism

Mizrachi—The principal Orthodox Zionist organization

Okhrana—Russian secret police during the tsarist period

Poalei Zion—Workers of Zion, i.e., Labor (Socialist) Zionists

Shavuot—Pentecost, Feast of Weeks, a holiday in late spring, counting 50 days from the beginning of Passover

Tarbut—"Culture." Specifically, a movement to foster Hebrew-language culture among Polish Jews through dual-curriculum schools and other cultural activities

Tzadik (pl. Tzadikim)—a Chassidic rabbi; the charismatic leader of a Chassidic congregation

The Jews in Siedlce 1850–1945

This work consists of eleven chapters. The first chapter, "Siedlce and the Jews through the End of the Nineteenth Century," presents the earliest traces of Jewish settlement as well as the development of Jewish and Polish communities in the city. The second chapter, "The Social and Political Life of the Jews of Siedlce at the Beginning of the Twentieth Century," describes the complexities of the economic and political situation during this period. The third chapter, "The Pogrom of 1906," includes information about this event, which was widely commented upon in the country and abroad.

The time span of the next chapter, "The Revival of Jewish Society during the Period 1915–1920," requires more detailed explanation. When the Russian occupation ended in 1915 and Siedlce was occupied by German troops, the political life of local Jews started to flourish. The Germans did not object to social, political, and cultural activities, although they were subject to control. Local Jewish activists immediately took advantage of that historic moment, which continued until the Bolshevik invasion in 1920. The political revival among Poles, however, did not commence until 1918, when the Polish state was established. Some earlier unprecedented political events did, of course, take place, one of which was the manifestation on 3 May 1916. This chapter exemplifies the fact that Polish historic periods do not always correspond to Jewish ones.

The fifth chapter, "Political Aspirations of Jews during the Period 1918–1939," provides an accurate description of all Jewish parties formed in the city. The sixth chapter, "Schooling," includes a listing of schools and teachers on the basis of two criteria: language of instruction, and school profile (secular versus religious). The language of instruction that was chosen for the child at school often testified to his/her parents' political, social, and ideological outlooks. The seventh chapter, "Cultural-Educational, Welfare, and Health Organizations and Sports Clubs," gives a broad account of the many organizations and their participation in the city's social life. The next chapter, "Internal Self-Rule and the Press," provides information about the Jewish community and the variety of newspapers available. The ninth chapter, "Self-Help Organizations," depicts both the history and the scope of activity of trade unions and cooperatives.

The tenth chapter describes the Jewish Holocaust, including the formation of the ghetto and its boundaries, health and sanitary conditions in it, as well as the stages of its liquidation. The account is supplemented by a register of labor camps for Jews, which served as sweatshops whose aim was the economic exploitation and physical exhaustion of workers. The last chapter, "After the War," concentrates on both the unsuccessful attempts to revive the local Jewish community and the disappearance of material traces testifying to four centuries of a Jewish presence in the city of Siedlce.

The book is supplemented by numerous appendices containing sources that have not appeared previously in Polish historiography (an interview with Hubert Pfoch and an account of Fritz Hoeft). The enclosed literary works, in particular the short stories by Bracha Kahan, depict distinctive types of Jews, their life stories, and the atmosphere of old Siedlce. The book also includes numerous tables relating the numbers of Jewish citizens living in the city in different periods. Enclosed also are lists of monthly and yearly reports provided by various Jewish organizations present in the city between 1934 and 1938. They provide information about the number of meetings and gatherings that took place in the city and how many members participated in them. The book is supplemented by numerous photographs. So many of them have been included in this book because of their uniqueness and their depiction of a reality that no longer exists.

The author would like to thank Isaac Halber of blessed memory, whom he met several times and who was a source of invaluable information. After his death, help was received from his wife, Maria Halber, who translated texts from Yiddish into Polish. Their son, Michael Halber, also gave the author many suggestions and provided him with various materials in English and Hebrew. Another source of information and inspiration were Jews from Siedlce who currently live in different parts of the world. The author communicated with them by mail and via the internet. These included Renia Pancer, Isabel Cymerman, Helen Herman, and Abraham Gome. In some cases, it is the second or even the third generation that has family ties with the city of Siedlce. They sent photographs and information that is included in this book.

Special thanks are due to the author's supervisor, Professor Zofia Chyra-Rolicz. This book owes its current form to the fruitful cooperation with her.

ŻYDZI W SIEDLACH 1850–1945

Praca ta składa się z jedenastu rozdziałów. Rozdział pierwszy, „Siedlce i Żydzi do końca XIX wieku", przedstawia najstarsze ślady osadnictwa żydowskiego w mieście i rozwój społeczności polskiej i żydowskiej. W rozdziale drugim, „Życie społeczno--polityczne siedleckich Żydów w początkach XX wieku", ukazana jest złożona sytuacja gospodarcza i polityczna. Rozdział trzeci, „Pogrom 1906 roku", zawiera informacje o tym wydarzeniu tak szeroko wówczas komentowanym w kraju i za granicą.

Wyjaśnienia wymaga zakres chronologiczny kolejnego, czwartego rozdziału, „Ożywienie polityczne i społeczne w latach 1915–1920". Po ustąpieniu okupacji rosyjskiej i zajęciu Siedlec przez wojska niemieckie w 1915 r. rozpoczął się bardzo ożywiony okres działalności politycznej wśród Żydów. Niemcy, choć w sposób kontrolowany, pozwolili na działalność społeczną, polityczną i kulturalną. Miejscowi działacze żydowscy od razu wykorzystali ten moment dziejowy. Trwał on do inwazji bolszewickiej w 1920 r. Natomiast wśród Polaków ożywienie polityczne nastąpiło dopiero w 1918 r., w chwili tworzenia państwa polskiego. Były oczywiście działania i wcześniej, chociażby wielka manifestacja patriotyczna z okazji 3 Maja w 1916 r. Przykład tego rozdziału pokazuje, że polskie okresy historyczne nie zawsze pokrywają się z żydowskimi.

W rozdziale piątym, „Dążenia polityczne Żydów w latach 1918–1939", opisane są wszystkie żydowskie partie działające w mieście. Rozdział szósty, „Szkolnictwo", zawiera wykaz szkół i nauczycieli. Jako wyróżnik przy podziale szkolnictwa, wzięto pod uwagę język, w jakim prowadzona była nauka oraz podejście do religii. Wybór języka, w jakim dziecko uczyło się w szkole, świadczył często o zapatrywaniach politycznych, społecznych i światopoglądowych rodziców. W rozdziale siódmym, „Stowarzyszenia kulturalno-oświatowe, opiekuńcze i zdrowotne", przedstawiono bardzo liczne organizacje i ich udział w życiu społecznym. Rozdział ósmy, „Samorząd wewnętrzny i prasa", zawiera informacje o gminie i różnorodnych tytułach gazet. Rozdział dziewiąty, „Organizacje samopomocowe", przedstawia historię powstania i działalność związków zawodowych i kooperatyw.

Rozdział dziesiąty zawiera opis zagłady Żydów, a więc utworzenie getta, jego granice, warunki zdrowotne i sanitarne, jakie panowały oraz etapy likwidacji. Zamieszczono też wykaz obozów pracy dla Żydów, które były przedsiębiorstwami służącymi do wyzysku ekonomicznego i fizycznego wyczerpania robotników. Ostatni rozdział, „Po wojnie", ukazuje nieudaną próbę odrodzenia społeczności żydowskiej miasta i zanikanie materialnych śladów czterech wieków jej tu obecności.

Praca zaopatrzona została w aneksy. Zamieszczono w nich źródła, które do tej pory nie były wykorzystane w polskiej historiografii (wywiad z Hubertem Pfochem i relacja Fritza Hoefta). Załączone utwory literackie, szczególnie opowiadania Brachy Kahan, ukazują charakterystyczne typy Żydów, ich sytuacje życiowe, klimat dawnych Siedlec. Praca zawiera tabele odnoszące się do liczby mieszkańców żydowskich miasta w różnych okresach. Natomiast na podstawie zestawień przedstawiających miesięczne i roczne sprawozdania z działalności organizacji żydowskich za lata 1934–1938 można dowiedzieć się o liczbie zebrań i zgromadzeń oraz ilości członków biorących w nich udział. Pracę uzupełniają liczne zdjęcia. Ze względu na ich unikalność i ukazanie nieistniejącej już rzeczywistości postanowiono umieścić je w tak dużej liczbie.

Autor chciałby złożyć podziękowania błogosławionej pamięci Izaakowi Halberowi, z którym wielokrotnie spotykał się i który był dla niego źródłem wielu informacji. Po jego śmierci pomocy udzielała Maria Halber, żona Izaaka, która tłumaczyła teksty napisane w jidysz. Również ich syn, Michael Halber, udzielał przez kilka lat wskazówek i dostarczył wielu materiałów, szczególnie angielsko- i hebrajskojęzycznych. Ważnym źródłem inspiracji i wiadomości byli Żydzi pochodzący z Siedlec, a mieszkający w różnych stronach świata, z którymi autor korespondował metodą tradycyjną, tj. pocztą, i przy pomocy Internetu. Byli to: Renia Pancerowa, Isabel Cymerman, Helen Herman, Abraham Gome. Część z tych osób stanowi już drugie, a nawet trzecie pokolenie, które związane jest tradycją rodzinną z Siedlcami. Osoby te przesyłały autorowi zdjęcia i informacje, które wykorzystane były w tej pracy.

Szczególne podziękowania autor kieruje pod adresem swojego promotora – prof. Zofii Chyra-Rolicz. To dzięki współpracy z Panią profesor praca ta nabrała takiego charakteru.

עבורו לפולינית טקסטים כתובים ביידיש. בנם, מיכאל הלבר, גם הוא סיפק למחבר פיסות מידע ומקורות אחדים באנגלית ובעברית.

מקורות נוספים למידע ולהשראה בכתיבת עבודה זו הם יהודים שבעבר חיו בשלדץ ואשר חיים כיום במקומות שונים בעולם, איתם נוצר קשר באמצעות הדואר ודרך האינטרנט. המחבר מבקש להודות לרניה פנצר, איזבֵּל צימרמן, הלן הרמן ואברהם גומא, שהם דור שני ואפילו דור שלישי של קשרי משפחה לשלדץ, ואשר שלחו לו תצלומים ומידע שנכללו בעבודה זו.

תודות מיוחדות מביע המחבר למנחה שלו, פרופסור סופיה קירה רוליץ, שעל פי הכרתו, בזכות שיתוף הפעולה הפורה איתה מוצגת התזה הזאת במתכונתה הנוכחית.

348

היהודים בשָׁדְלֶץ 1850–1945

התזה מתפרשת על פני 11 פרקים. הפרק הראשון, "שדלץ והיהודים עד סוף המאה ה-19" מציג את העקבות המוקדמים של הישוב היהודי בשדלץ כמו גם את התפתחותן של קהילה פולנית וקהילה יהודית בעיר. הפרק השני, "החיים החברתיים והפוליטיים של היהודים בשדלץ בראשית המאה ה-20", מתאר את מורכבותו של המצב הפוליטי-כלכלי בתקופה זו. הפרק השלישי, "הפוגרום ב-1906", כולל מידע על הפוגרום שפרסומו עורר תגובות רבות בפולין ומחוצה לה.

הפרק הבא אחריו, "התעוררות חברתית ופוליטית בין 1915 ל-1920", דורש הסבר מפורט יותר. עם סיומו של הכיבוש הרוסי בשדלץ, עברה העיר לשליטתן של יחידות צבא גרמניות, ומיד החלה אצל יהודי העיר פריחה של חיים פוליטיים. הגרמנים לא התנגדו לפעילויות חברתיות, פוליטיות ותרבותיות שבכל מקרה היו תחת פיקוחם, והיהודים ניצלו את הרגע ההיסטורי הזה, שהתמשך בפעילויות יהודיות מקומיות עד לפלישה הבולשביקית ב-1920. ההתעוררות הפוליטית של הפולנים עדיין התעכבה והחלה רק ב-1918 כשנוסדה המדינה הפולנית, אם כי כמה אירועים פוליטיים חסרי תקדים התרחשו בכל זאת מעט קודם לכן, ואחד מהם היה מצעד ה-3 במאי 1916. הפרק הזה מדגים את העובדה שהמהלכים ההיסטוריים התקופתיים של הפולנים לא תמיד חפפו את אלה של היהודים.

הפרק החמישי, "שאיפות פוליטיות של היהודים בין 1918 ל-1939", מציג תיאור מדויק של כל המפלגות היהודיות שהתגבשו בעיר. הפרק השישי, "השיטה החינוכית", כולל רשימה של בתי ספר ומורים בעלי שני מאפיינים, כמו שפת ההוראה וסוג בית הספר (חילוני או דתי). שפת ההוראה שנבחרה עבור הילד בבית הספר העידה בדרך כלל על תפיסת העולם של הוריו ועל עמדותיהם החברתיות והפוליטיות. הפרק השביעי, "אגדות של תרבות וחינוך, בריאות ורווחה", מציג בהרחבה ארגונים שונים ומעורבותם בחיים החברתיים בעיר. הפרק הבא, "מִנְהָל-עצמי פנימי ועיתונות", מביא מידע על הקהילה היהודית ועל עיתונים שונים שניתן היה להשיג בעיר. הפרק התשיעי, "ארגונים לעזרה-עצמית", מביא את תולדותיהם של האיגדים הקואופרטיביים של הסוחרים ואת תחומי פעילותם.

הפרק הבא עוסק בהשמדת היהודים, ומתאר את הקמת הגטו, את גבולותיו, את התנאים התברואתיים והסניטריים ואת רמות התמותה שהיו בו. התיאור מגובה ברשימה של מחנות עבודה בהם נוצלו היהודים בעבודה פיזית מפרכת עד אובדן הכוחות. הפרק האחרון, "לאחר המלחמה", מתמקד במאמצים הכושלים להחיות את הקהילה היהודית ועוסק בהיעלמותם של עדויות פיזיות על נוכחות היהודים בשדלץ במשך ארבע מאות שנה.

לתזה נספחים כמה פרקים חיצוניים ובהם מקורות שטרם צוטטו עד כה בהיסטוריוגרפיה הפולנית (ריאיון עם הוברט פוך, ושיחה עם פריץ הופט), וחומרים ספרותיים, במיוחד הסיפורים הקצרים מאת ברכה כהאן, המתארים את האווירה שהייתה בעיר, ומציירים דמויות של יהודים שחיו בה. התזה כוללת גם טבלאות אחדות המציגות את מספר האזרחים היהודים שחיו בעיר בתקופות שונות, וכמו כן נספחות לעבודה רשימות שסופקו על ידי ארגונים יהודים שונים, ובהן דוחות חדשיים ושנתיים שנעשו בין השנים 1934 ל-1938. קריאת הרשימות הללו מלמדת על מספר הפגישות והאספות שהתקיימו בעיר ועל מספר החברים שהשתתפו בהן. הנספחים האחרונים שחשיבותם רבה ביותר הם התצלומים המשלימים את התזה. תצלומים ייחודיים אלה מציגים מציאות שאיננה קיימת עוד ובשל כך הוחלט לכלול רבים מהם בעבודה זו.

המחבר מבקש לציין בתודה את יצחק הלבר המנוח, שאיתו הוא נפגש פעמים רבות ואשר היה עבורו מקור למידע רב ערך. לאחר מותו של הלבר ז"ל נרתמה אלמנתו, מריה הלבר, וסייעה למחבר כשתרגמה

וויפל ייִדן האבן געלעבט אין שעדלעץ אין פֿאַרשידענע צייטן און גיט אויך א ליסטע פֿון ייִדישע אָרגאַניזאַציעס און זייערע מאַנאַטליכע און יערליכע באַריכטונגען פֿון די יאָרן 1934-1938. פֿון די ליסטעס קענען מיר וויסן וויפֿל צחאַמענטרעפֿן זענען פֿאָרגעקומען און וויפל ייִדן האבן אין זיי אַנטייילגענומען. די לעצטע טייל איז זייער וויכטיק ווייל זי הענטהאַלט פֿיל פֿאָטאָגראַפֿיעס וואָס ערגענצן די טעזיס און מיט זייער זעלטנקייט ווייזן אונדז א ווירקלעכקייט וואָס איז מער נישטא.

דער מחבר וויל דאַנקען יצחק האלבער, ער האָט זיך מיט אים געטראָפֿן פֿיל מאָל און ער איז געווען פֿאַר אים א קוואל פֿון אינפֿאָרמאַציע. נאָך זיין טויט האָט אים זיין וויב מאַריא האַלבער געהאָלפֿן, פֿאַרטיייטשנדיק טעקסטן פֿון ייִדיש צו פֿויליש. זייער זון מיכאל האַלבער האָט אים געגעבן מאַטעריאַל אין ענגליש און אין העברעיש. נאָך א קוואל פֿון אינפֿאָרמאַציע זענען געווען געוועזן שעדליצער ייִדן וואָס זענען היינט צעזייט און צעשפרייט איבער דער וועלט. דער מחבר בין געווען אין קאָנטאַקט מיט זיי דורך דער פאָסט און די אינטערנעט. א טיפֿן דאַנק פֿאַר רעניא פֿאָנסער, איזאַבעל צימערמאַן, העלען הערמאַן און אברהם גאַמע. אָפֿגעשטאַמענע פֿון שעדלעץ, פֿון צווייטן און דריטן דור, האָבן געשיקט פֿאָטאָגראַפֿיעס און אינפֿאָרמאַציע וואָס דער מחבר האָט גענוצט אין זיין טעזיס.

א ספעציעלן דאַנק די אויפזעערן פֿראַפֿעסאָר סאָפֿיא קירא ראליק. די טעזיס איז דער רעזולטאַט פֿון איר פֿרוכטבאַרן מיטאַרבעטן מיט אים.

די יידן אין שעדלעץ 1850–1945

די טעזיס באשטייט פון 11 קאפיטלען. דאס ערשטע קאפיטל "שעדלעץ און די יידן ביז די ענדע פון ניינצעטן יארהונדערט" באשרייבט די אלטסטע שפורן פונעם יידישן ישוב אין שעדלעץ און די אנטוויקלונג פון יידישער און פוילישער קהילות אינעם שטעטל. דאס צווייטע קאפיטל "יידיש סאציאל און פאליטיש לעבן אין שעדלעץ ביים אנפאנג פונעם צוואנציקסטן יארהונדערט" באשרייבט די פערוויקלטע עקאנאמישע און פאליטישע סיטואציע אין דער אויבנדערמאנטער צייט. דאס דריטע קאפיטל "דער פאגראם אין 1906" גיט א באריכט פון דעם דאזיקן פאגראם וואס האט זיך געלאזט הערן אין פוילן און אויף דער גאנצער וועלט.

דאס פאלגנדיקע קאפיטל "יידישע פאליטישע שטרעבונגען צווישן 1915 און 1920 פאדערט א באזונדערע ערלקרונג. ווען די רוסישע אקופאציע האט זיך געענדיקט האט די דייטשע ארמיי פארנומען די שטאט און באלד האט זיך אנגעהויבן ביי די יידן אן אקטיוו פאליטיש לעבן. די דייטשן האבן זיך נישט קעגנגעשטעלעט צו די סאציאלע, פאליטישע און קולטורעלע אקטיוויטעטן וואס זענען געווען אונטער זייער קאנטראל, און די היגע יידן האבן אויגענוצט די דאזיקע היסטארישע געלעגנהייט צו זיין פאליטיש טעטיק ביז די באלשעוויקעס האבן אקופירט שעדלעץ אין 1920. די פוילישע פאליטישע אקטיוויטעט האט זיך אנגעהויבן יעצט אין 1918 ווען די פוילישע מדינה איז אנטשטאנען. א פריערדיקע פאליטישע פאסירונג איז געווען די דעמאנסטראציע פון 3-טן מאי 1916. דאס קאפיטל באווייזט אז פוילישע און יידישע היסטארישע אנטוויקלונגען זענען נישט געשען אין די זעלבע יארן.

דאס פינפטע קאפיטל "יידישע פאליטישע שטרעבונגען פון 1918 ביז 1939" באריכט גענוי אלע פאליטישע פארטייען וואס זענען געגרינדעט געווארן אין שעדלעץ. דאס זעקסטע קאפיטל "דער בילדונגס סיסטעם" שטעלט פאר א פולשטענדיקן רעגיסטער פון לערער און שולעס וואס באצייכענען זיך ביי דער שפראך אין וועלכער מען לערנט און ביי זייער גלויבן: רעליגיעז אדער וועלטלער. פון דער שפראך אין וועלכער מען האט געלערנט קענען מיר וויסן וועלכע זענען געווען די מיינונגען און גלויבן פון די קינדערס עלטערן און זייערע סאציאלע און פאליטישע דעות. דאס זיבעטע קאפיטל "ארגאניזאציעס פאר קולטור און בילדונג, געזונט און וווילשטאנד" באשרייבט פארשידענע ארגאניזאציעס און זייער טעטיקייט אין דעם שעדלעצן לעבן. דאס פאלגנדיקע קאפיטל "זעלבסטערגירונג און פרעסע" גיט א באריכט אויף דער יידישער קהילה און אויף די פארשידענע צייטונגען וואס מען האט געקאנט באקומען און לייענען אין שטעטל. דאס ניינטע קאפיטל "זעלבסטהילף ארגאניזאציעס" גיט א באריכט פון ארבעטער פאריינען און פון הענדלער קאאפעראטיוועס און זייער טעטיקייט.

דאס פאלגנדיקע קאפיטל באריכט די פארניכטערונג פון די יידן און באשרייבט דעם אויסשטעל פון געטא, זיינע גרענעצן, די געזונט און סאניטארישע אומשטענדן און זיין צעשטערונג. די דאזיקע באשרייבונג רעכנט אריין א ליסטע פון ארבעטס לאגערן וואו די יידן זענען אויסגענוצט געווארן אין שווערע פיזישע ארבעט ביז זייער אויסמאטערניש. דאס לעצטע קאפיטל "נאכן קריג" רעכנט אויס די נישט גערטאטענע באמיונגען צו אויפמינטערן די יידישע קהילה און דערציילט אויך פון דער פארשווינדונג פון מאטעריעלע שפורן וואס באשטעטיקן די 400 יאר פון יידיש לעבן אין שעדלעץ.

צו דער טעזיס זענען באגעלייגט עטלעכע עטליכע צחאצן וואס ענטהאלטן קוואל וואס זענען אומבאקאנט אין דער פוילישער געשריבענער געשיכטע (א געשפרער מיט הובערט פוף, א באריכט ביי פריץ האפט) און די אינגעשלאסענע ליטעראַרישע ווערק, איבערהויפט די קורצע דערציילונגען פון ברכה כאהן וואס באשרייבן פארשידענע יידישע געשטאלטן, זייער לעבן און די אטמאספער אין שטעטל. די טעזיס ווייזט

DIE JUDEN IN SIEDLCE 1850–1945

Die vorliegende Doktorarbeit besteht aus 11 Kapiteln. Im ersten Kapitel „Siedlce und die Juden bis zum Ende des 19. Jahrhunderts" wurden sowohl die ältesten Spuren der jüdischen Ansiedlung in der Stadt als auch die Entwicklung der polnischen und jüdischen Gemeinschaften dargestellt. Das zweite Kapitel „Das sozialpolitische Leben der Juden von Siedlce anfangs des 20. Jahrhunderts" schildert die komplexe wirtschaftliche und politische Lage der Stadteinwohner. Das dritte Kapitel „Der Pogrom vom Jahre 1906" enthält Informationen vom Ereignis, das damals sehr lebhaft im Inland und Ausland kommentiert wurde.

Die Zeitspanne des nächsten Kapitels „Die sozialpolitische Belebung in den Jahren 1915–1920" ist erklärungsbedürftig. Nach dem Ende der russischen Okkupation wurde die Stadt durch die deutschen Truppen im Jahre 1915 besetzt. Seitdem begann die Periode einer besonders lebhaften politischen Tätigkeit unter den einheimischen Juden. Die Deutschen haben zwar soziale, politische und kulturelle Tätigkeiten genehmigt, diese waren jedoch kontrolliert. Trotz der Kontrolle haben die einheimischen jüdischen Aktivisten den historischen Moment ausgenutzt, der fast bis zur bolschewistischen Invasion im Jahre 1920 gedauert hat. Unter den Polen fing der politische Aufschwung erst 1918 an als man begann den polnischen Staat zu gründen. Es gab jedoch frühere, nicht vereinzelte Ereignisse, wie z.B. eine große patriotische Manifestation am 3. Mai 1916. Dieses Kapital zeigt, dass polnische und jüdische historische Perioden sich nicht immer decken.

Im fünften Kapitel „Politische Bestrebungen der Juden in den Jahren 1918–1939" wurden alle politischen Parteien dargestellt, die in der Stadt tätig waren. Im nächsten Kapitel „Schulwesen" wurden Schulen und Lehrer zusammengestellt. Als charakteristische Merkmale der Zusammenstellung fungieren die Verkehrssprache in der Schule und das Schulprofil (säkular oder konfessionell). Die Auswahl der Verkehrsprache für den Schüler hat oft von der Weltanschauung seiner Eltern gezeugt. Im siebten Kapitel „Kultur-, Fürsorge- und Gesundheitsgesellschaften" wurden zahlreiche Gesellschaften präsentiert, die am Sozialleben der Stadt beteiligt waren. Das achte Kapitel „Selbstverwaltung und die Presse" enthält Informationen über die jüdische Gemeinde und verschiedene Zeitungen und Zeitschriften, die damals zu erreichen waren. Im nächsten Kapitel „Selbsthilfegruppen" wurde sowohl die

Geschichte als auch die Tätigkeit von Gewerkschaftsverbänden und Genossenschaften dargestellt.

Das zehnte Kapitel wurde Judenvernichtung gewidmet. Es berücksichtigt folgende Themenbereiche: Ghettogründung und seine Grenzen, gesundheitliche und sanitäre Verhältnisse innerhalb des Judenviertels, Stufen der Ghettoliquidierung. Beiliegend findet man auch eine Zusammenstellung von Arbeitslagern für Juden, die darauf abzielten, die Inhaftierten auszubeuten und zu erschöpfen. Das letzte Kapitel „Nach dem Krieg" zeigt die Misserfolge der Wiederbelebung der jüdischen Gemeinschaft in der Stadt und das Verschwinden von materiellen Spuren ihrer Präsenz, die vier Jahrhunderte dauerte.

Die Dissertation enthält Anhänge, in denen man Quellen angibt, die in der polnischen Historiografie noch nicht zitiert worden sind. Dazu gehören u.a. das Interview mit Hubert Pfoch und der Bericht von Fritz Hoeft. Die beigelegten literarischen Werke, insbesondere die Erzählungen von Bracha Kanan schildern charakteristische Judentypen, ihre Lebensgeschichten und die Atmosphäre der damaligen Stadt. In der vorliegenden Arbeit findet man auch Tabellen, die sich auf die Zahlen von jüdischen Einwohnern in verschiedenen Perioden beziehen. Anhand der beigefügten Zusammenstellungen von monatlichen und jährlichen Berichten über die Tätigkeit der jüdischen Gesellschaften in den Jahren 1934–1938 kann man erfahren, wie viele Versammlungen und Gesellschaften es gab und wie viele Mitglieder an ihnen beteiligt waren. Der Arbeit wurden auch zahlreiche Photos beigelegt. Wegen ihrer Einzigartigkeit habe der Verfasser den Beschluss gefasst, so viele von ihnen darzustellen.

Der Autor dankt sehr der seligen Erinnerung Isaac Halber, den er mehrmals getroffen hat und der für ihn eine wichtige Informationsquelle war. Nach seinem Tod hat dem Autor seine Ehefrau, Maria Halber Hilfe geleistet indem sie Texte aus dem Jiddischen ins Polnische übersetzt hat. Auch ihr Sohn, Michael Halber hat ihm über mehrere Jahre Hinweise gegeben. Außerdem hat er dem Autor viele Materialien auf Englisch und Hebräisch geliefert. Auch die aus Siedlce stammenden Juden, die zur Zeit in aller Welt wohnen und mit denen der Verfasser per Post und Internet kommuniziert hat, haben als wichtige Informations- und Inspirationsquellen fungiert. Dazu gehörten u.a.: Renia Pancer, Isabel Cymerman, Helen Herman, Abraham Gome. Manche von Ihnen vertreten schon die zweite oder dritte Generation, die durch ihre Familientradition mit Siedlce verbunden sind. Sie haben dem Verfasser Photos und Informationen gesandt, die er in seiner Doktorarbeit ausgenutzt habe.

Der Autor möchte sich besonders bei seiner Doktormutter, Frau Professor Zofia Chyra-Rolicz bedanken. Ohne Ihre Hilfe hätte die vorliegende Dissertation ihre jetzige Form nicht angenommen.

Hiermit möchte der Verfasser Beate Stollberg sowie Trägerkreis Shoah – Gedenkstätten beim Kirchenkreis Bielefeld seinen herzlichen Dank für Ihre Hilfe aussprechen.

Резюме

Евреи г. Седльце 1850–1945

Работа состоит из одиннадцати глав. В первой главе «Седльце и евреи в период до конца XIX века» представлены самые древние следы еврейского заселения в городе и развитие польской и еврейской общественностей. Во второй главе «Общественно-политическая жизнь седлецких евреев в начале XX века» указана сложная экономическо-политическая ситуация этого периода. В третьей главе «Еврейский погром 1906 года» приведены сведения об этом событии, широко рассматриваемом и коментированном тогда в стране и за её пределами.

Четвёртая глава – «Политическое и общественное оживление в 1915–1920 годах». После российской оккупации и захват в 1915 году города Седльце немецкими войсками, начался очень оживлённый период политической деятельности среди евреев. Немцы, хотя и контролируемым образом, разрешили им заниматься общественной, политической и культурной деятельностью. Местные еврейские деятели с самого начала умело использовали тот исторический момент. Продолжался он до вторжения большевитских войск в 1920 году. Зато, среди поляков, политическое оживление произошло лишь в 1918 году, в момент образования польского государства. Хотя, конечно, и раньше появлялись действия, хотя бы, между прочим, крупная патиротическая демонстрация по случаю праздника 3-го Мая в 1916 году. Пример этой главы указывает на факт, что польские исторические периоды не всегда совпадают с еврейскими.

В пятой главе «Политическое стремление евреев в 1918–1939 годах» описаны все еврейские партии, существующие в городе. Шестая глава «Образовательные учреждения» заключает в себе перечень всех школ и учителей. Показателем, который здесь использован, является язык, на котором велась учёба, и также отношение к религии. Выбор языка, на котором ребёнок учился в школе, чаще всего свидетельствовал о политических, общественных и мировоззренческих взглядах родителей.

В седьмой главе «Культурно-просветительские, опекунские товарищества и общества по охране здоровья» представлены многочисленные организации и их участие в общественной жизни. Восьмая глава «Внутреннее самоуправление и пресса» заключает в себе информацию о кагале и разные названия газет. Девятая глава «Организации взаимной помощи» представляет историю образования и деятельность профсоюзов и кооперативов.

Десятая глава, это описание уничтожения евреев, в частности, создание гетто, его границы, санитарные и медицинские условия, существующие там и этапы его ликвидации. Здесь я поместил также список лагерей труда для евреев, как предприятий, целью которых были экономическая эксплуатация и истощение работников. Последняя глава «После войны» описывает неудачную попытку возрождения еврейской общественности города и исчезновение материальных следов, существующих четыре века.

Работа снабжена приложениями. В них указаны источники, котые до сих пор не были использованы в польской историографии (интервью с Губертом Фохем и рассказ Фрица Гоэфта). Приложенные художественные произведения, в частности, рассказы Брахи Кахан, представляют характерные типы евреев, их жизненное и социальное пололожение, климат прежнего города Седьлце. В работе помещены таблицы, указывающее число жителей города еврейского происхождения в разных периодах. А на основании сводок, представляющих ежемесячные и годовые отчёты деятельности еврейских организаций за 1934–1938 гг, можно узнать о количестве собраний и количестве членов, принимающих в них участие.

Работу пополняют многочисленные фотографии. Учитывая их уникальность и тот факт, что они представляют собой уже не существующую действительность, решено было поместить их именно в таком большом количестве.

Автор хотел бы выразить свою благодарность блаженной памяти Исааку Гальберу, с которым он многократно встречался, и который оказался для него источником многих информаций. После его смерти, помощь оказала автору Мария Гальбер, жена Исаака, которая переводила на польский язык тексты написаны на идише. Также их сын, Михаэль Гальбер, на протяжении нескольких лет давал автору указания и передал много интересных материалов, в том числе на английском языке и иврите.

Важным источником вдохновления и сведений были евреи, происходящие из г. Седльце, а проживающие в разных сторонах мира. Автор с ними переписывался традиционным методом, т.е. по почте и, с помощью интернета. Ими были: Реня Панцерова, Исабел Цимерман, Эллен Герман, Абрахам Гоме. Часть из этих лиц является уже вторым, и даже третьим поколением, которых с городом Седльце связывает семейная традиция. Данные лица передавали автору фотографии и информацию, которые автор использовал в данной работе.

Автор хотел бы выразить особую благодарность своему научному руководителю – профессор Зофии Хыра-Ролич. Именно благодаря сотрудничеству с госпожей профессор эта работа приобрела такой вид.

SIEDLCE AND THE JEWS
UP TO THE TIME OF THE SECOND WORLD WAR

1. Synagogue built during 1856–1876 (photo from the collection of the Regional Museum in Siedlce)

2. Jewish hospital (photo from the collection of the Regional Museum in Siedlce)

3. Jewish workers during construction of the Brześć Road (source: *Rysy postawionych pomników i wybitych Medalów w Królestwie Polskim w roku 1825* [*Drawings of Monuments Erected and Medals Minted in the Polish Kingdom in 1825*])

4. Jewish neighborhood after the fire that took place on 12–13 July 1874. On the left, the earliest depiction of the synagogue (photo: *Tygodnik Ilustrowany*, no. 343 [1874]: 37)

5. Student strike committee from 1905 [at Państwowe Gimnazjum Męskie Klasyczne (State Secondary School of Humanities for Boys)—ed.]. Fourth from left standing is Kazimierz Stein, delegate of the Jewish community (photo Adolf Gancwol-Ganiewski)

6. Bullet holes in the headquarters of the Jewish executive council. View from Warszawska Street (currently Piłsudski Street) right after the 1906 pogrom (photo: *Tygodnik Ilustrowany*, no. 38 [22 September 1906])

7. Estera Ratyniewicz's house on Alejna Street (currently Kiliński Street) shot at and set
fire to during the 1906 pogrom (photo: *Tygodnik Ilustrowany*, no. 38 [22 September 1906])

8. House on Piękna Street (currently Pułaski Street) having sustained cannon fire during 1906 pogrom (photo: *Tygodnik Ilustrowany*, no. 38 [22 September 1906])

9. Victims of the 1906 pogrom (photo: *Tygodnik Ilustrowany*, no. 38 [22 September 1906])

10. On the left, Rabbi Pinkas Cukierman (c. 1840–c. 1914), nicknamed "The Droll," with his assistant, Abramele. Siedlce, in the vicinity of the synagogue in 1910 (photo from the collection of Isabel Cymerman)

Общій видъ

11. View of Siedlce, with synagogue in the center. Postcard by Tyliński from before 1915

362

12. Jewish family. Photograph taken in Adolf Gancwol-Ganiewski's studio (photo from the collection of the Regional Museum in Siedlce)

13. Jewish family. Photograph taken in Adolf Gancwol-Ganiewski's studio (photo from the collection of the Regional Museum in Siedlce)

363

14. Jewish family. Photograph taken in Adolf Gancwol-Ganiewski's studio (photo from the collection of the Regional Museum in Siedlce)

15. Jewish family. Photograph taken in Adolf Gancwol-Ganiewski's studio (photo from the collection of the Regional Museum in Siedlce)

16. Old Jews conversing in front of the synagogue (copy from author's collection)

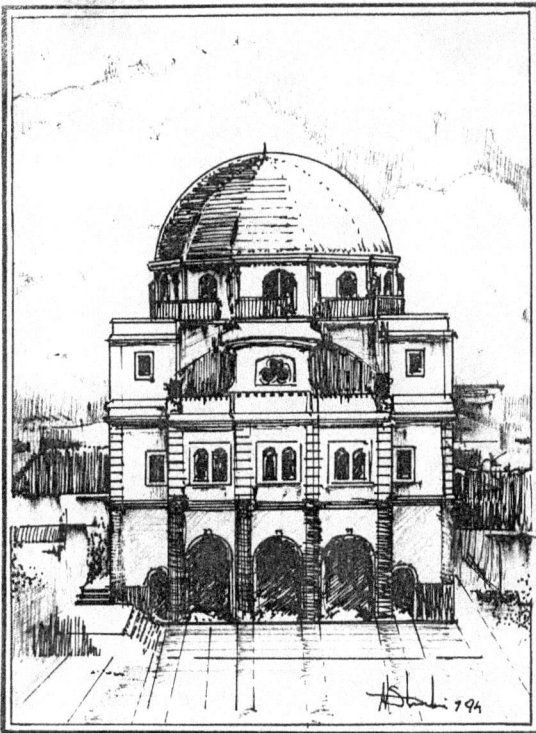

17. Reconstruction of Hurva Synagogue (ruins) (drawing by M. Starczewski)

18. Restored arch of the Hurva Synagogue in Jerusalem (author's photograph)

19. The old City Hall called Jacek. Postcard by B. Sadowski from the 1930s

20. Railroad station. Postcard by A. Gancwol from before 1915

21. Rural Credit Society. Postcard by A. Gancwol from before 1915

22. Prison. Postcard by H. Celnik from 1915–1918

23. Summer theater in the city park. Postcard by A. Gancwol from before 1915

24. Warszawska Street (currently Piłsudski Street)—the main street of the city. Postcard by A. Gancwol from before 1915

25. Pałacowa Street (currently Kościuszko Street). Postcard by A. Gancwol from before 1915

26. Polish Bank on Piłsudski Street. Postcard by B. Sadowski, 1930s

27. Market Square, currently bus depot. This is where Antoni and Josel did business in the story "Devils." Postcard by A. Gancwol from before 1915

SIEDLCE. VII-o klasowy Zakład Naukowy Żeński Konstancyi Zembrzuskiej.

28. Seven-Grade Konstancja Zembrzuska Girls' Educational Academy on Sienkiewicz Street. Postcard by A. Gancwol from before 1915

SIEDLCE. WIDOK OGÓLNY.

29. View of the city. Postcard by H. Celnik from before 1915

30. Ogrodowa Street (currently Sienkiewicz Street). Postcard by A. Gancwol from before 1915

31. [After 1918, Polish] Hetman Stanisław Żółkiewski State Secondary School for Boys on Konarski Street. Postcard by A. Gancwol from 1915–1918. [Prior to 1918: Państwowe Gimnazjum Męskie Klasyczne (Russian State Secondary School of Humanities for Boys)—ed.]

SIEDLCE.

Gesamtansicht.

Ogólny Widok.

32. View of Siedlce. Postcard by A. Gancwol from 1915–1918 (in upper right corner: Overview

SIEDLCE.

Rząd Gubernialny,

33. Ogiński Palace on Konarski Street. Postcard by A. Gancwol from before 1915 [in upper right corner: Provincial Administration]

373

Siedlce, Skwer pod Starym Ratuszem

34. Square in front of St. Stanisław Church. Postcard by B. Sadowski, 1930s [at bottom: Siedlce, Square by Old City Hall]

Siedlce, Gimnazjum im. B. Prusa

35. Bolesław Prus State Secondary School for Boys on Floriańska Street. Postcard by B. Sadowski, 1930s

374

Siedlce, Gimnazjum im. Królowej Jadwigi

36. Queen Jadwiga State Secondary School for Girls on what is now Bishop Świrski Street. Postcard by B. Sadowski, 1930s

Siedlce, Szkoła Rzemieślnicza

37. Trade School. Postcard by B. Sadowski, 1930s

38. New City Hall. Postcard by B. Sadowski, 1930s

39. Piękna Street (currently Pułaski Street). Postcard by H. Celnik from 1915–1918

Siedlec. Das Volkshaus. — Siedlce. Dom ludowy.

40. Community Center. Postcard by H. Celnik from 1915–1918

Siedlce, Kaplica Ks. Ogińskich

41. Aleksandra Ogińska's chapel. Postcard by B. Sadowski, 1930s

377

42. Advertising leaflet for F. Celnik's Paper Warehouse
[Paper Warehouse,
writing and drawing materials,
technical and surveying forms,
artists' oil paints and water colors,
fabric and relief paints,
brushes, canvases, cardboard, and painting liquids.
Canvases and decorative-bookbinding paper,
paintings, frames, and frame moldings
as well a huge selection of postcards
F. Celnik
Siedlce, 24 Kiliński Street]

43. Building of the Executive Committee of the Jewish Religious Council on Piłsudski Street (photograph from the collection of Bogusław Mitura)

44. In front of the synagogue (photograph from the collection of Bogusław Mitura)

45. An impoverished Jew (photograph from the collection of Bogusław Mitura)

46. Seal of the Executive Board of the Jewish Religious Council in Siedlce (from the collection of the State Archive in Siedlce)

47. Seal of the Siedlce Yiddishe Kunst Musical-Literary Society (from the author's collection)

48. Seal of the Siedlce Jewish Soup Kitchen (from the collection of the State Archive in Siedlce)

49. Imprint of the seal of Herszko Burchowicz Grynfarb's capmaker's shop (from the collection of the Regional Museum in Siedlce)

50. Protection of Jewish Orphans in Siedlce leaflet (from the collection of the State Archive in Siedlce)
[Remember the Jewish orphan]

51. Membership subscription with the likeness of Teodor Herzl. The Zionists, in order to gain funds for the realization of their goal, which was the creation of a Jewish state, distributed subscriptions—shekels (from the collection of Tadeusz Bohatyrewicz)

383

52. The Kahan family. Photograph taken in 1916 in the city park in Siedlce a few days before the departure of Anna and Bracha to the United States. Bracha, the author of the stories, is standing behind her father, and Anna, the author of a diary written in Siedlce, is standing behind her mother (photograph by Tuwie Siemiatycki from the archives of Rhoda Newman, daughter of Anne Safran)

52A. [Added to original] Photograph of Matl Lubelska described in the story in Appendix 16 (photograph from the archives of Edith Semiatin, daughter of Bracha Stolovy)

384

53. From the left, Bracha and Anna Kahan (photograph by S. Rozowski from the archives of Rhoda Newman)

54. Vignette of A. Gancwol's photographic studio (back of company card onto the front of which a photographs was glued)

55. Adolf Gancwol-Ganiewski (photograph from the collection of the Regional Museum in Siedlce)

56. Aaron Zelig Międzyrzecki (photograph by Adolf Gancwol-Ganiewski; photograph from the collection of the Halber family)

57. Froim Fiszel Halber (photograph by Adolf Gancwol-Ganiewski from the collection of the Halber family)

58. Sura Międzyrzecka (photograph from the collection of the Halber family)

59. Sura Gitla Halber née Celnik (photograph from the collection of the Halber family)

60. Mozes Międzyrzecki (photograph from the collection of the Halber family)

61. Dr. Henryk Loebel (photograph given to the author by Dr. Władysław Stefanoff)

62. Ida Jom-Tow (photograph from the collection of Helen Herman)

63. Dawid Jom-Tow in the uniform of the Polish Army (photograph from the collection of Helen Herman)

64. Next to the camera, Jakub Woda, who left for Birobidzhan (city in the Asiatic part of Russia, the capital city of the Jewish Autonomous Oblast); next to him, Maria Międzyrzecka, 1936 (photograph from the collection of the Halber family)

389

65. From the right, Maria Międzyrzecka and Hanna Apel in front of the Queen Jadwiga Preparatory School, 1937 (photograph from the collection of the Halber family)

66. In the middle, Kuba Międzyrzecki in the uniform of the Poznań Light Cavalry Regiment; on the left, Hela Radzyńska and Wowa Wiszniepolski; fourth person unknown, 1938 (photograph from the collection of the Halber family)

67. Izaak Halber in front of the liquor store on Piłsudski Street, 1937 (photograph from the collection of the Halber family)

68. Jewish youths during a swim in the Muchawka River, Sekuła suburb; first on the right is Izaak Halber (photograph from the collection of the Halber family)

69. Marchbein Upholstery Shop, in which Aszer Trzmielina worked, 1934 (photograph from the collection of Abraham Gome)

70. In the ice cream parlor on Kiliński Street. From the right: Emil Alberg, author of the later memoirs from the time of the occupation (writing under the name Jan Emil Karpiński), Aron Felzensztajn, and Bukier Alberg (photograph from the collection of the Halber family)

71. Dawid Tenenbaum (later Witold Duniłłowicz, author of the book *Three Colors of My Life*) with Maria Międzyrzecka in the Hazomir club, 1937 (photograph from the collection of the Halber family)

72. Aron Felzensztajn in his soda-water factory (photograph from the collection of the Halber family)

73. Cemetery on Szkolna Street (photograph from the work by J. Goldman)

74. Jewish cemetery on Szkolna Street, next to the gravestone of Josef Mendl Grynfarb (1860–1916), from the left: Zosia Grynfarb, Steffi Gleichgewicht (1882–1967), Leokadia Cymerman (1887–1971), Felicja Endler (1886–1942?); below, from the left: Adolf Endler and Bernard Cymerman (1882–1965). On the gravestone, next to the Hebrew inscription, the Polish inscription: B.P. Josef Mendel Grynfarb, d. 1 XI 1916 lived 53 year to our dear husband and father his wife and children. Photograph from 1917 (photograph from the collection of Isabel Cymerman)

75. Members of the cyclist division of the Zionist club Kadimah. From the left: 1. Unknown, 2. Unknown, 3. Keselbrener, 4. Bursztyn, 5. Abram Halber, 6. Zając, 7. Woda, 8. Aron Felzensztajn (owner of the soda-water bottling plant), 9. Lewin (owner of a barber shop), 10. Konopny, 11. Unknown, 12. Unknown. Members of the club wore white caps with a blue band (photograph from the collection of the Halber family)

76. Hashomer Hatsair troop, Siedlce 1929 (photograph from the collection of Abraham Gome)

77. Hashomer Hatsair summer camp outside Siedlce, 1935 (photograph from the collection of Abraham Gome)

WORLD WAR II—EXTERMINATION

78. Ruins of New City Hall. After German bombardment in September 1939 (photograph from the collection of the Regional Museum in Siedlce)

79. The center of the city after German raids in September 1939 (photograph from the collection of the Regional Museum in Siedlce)

80. Demolished and burned out houses, September 1939 (photograph from the collection of the Regional Museum in Siedlce)

81. Building of the City Council during the German occupation (photograph from the collection of the Regional Museum in Siedlce)

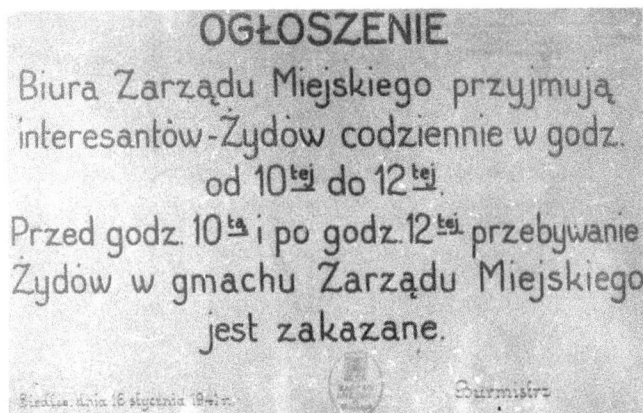

82. Announcement by the office of the City Council providing information about separate hours for dealing with Jewish and Polish petitioners (from the collection of Jontel Goldman)
[Announcement
of the Office of the City Council accepting
Jewish petitioners daily during the hours
from 10 to 12.
Before the hour of 10 and after the hour of 12 the presence
of Jews in the City Council building is forbidden.
Siedlce, 16 January 1941   (Stamp)   Mayor]

83. Warning: "Jewish neighborhood. Danger of epidemic. Entry to and departure from the Jewish neighborhood is permitted only with the written permission of the county administrator. Violation will be punishable by death. County administrator in Siedlce" (from the collection of Jontel Goldman)

84. The Germans burn the synagogue, December 1939 (photograph from the Regional Museum in Siedlce)

85. The Germans burn the community council buildings next to the synagogue (photograph from the collection of the Regional Museum in Siedlce)

86. "Souvenir photograph" of an officer commanding the operation of destroying the synagogue (photograph from the collection of the Regional Museum in Siedlce)

87. The synagogue in flames (photograph from the collection of the Regional Museum in Siedlce)

88. Synagogue after being burned (photograph from the collection of Jontel Goldman)

89. Ruins of the synagogue (photograph from the collection of Jontel Goldman)

90. The German occupying forces displayed a large map in front of the monument to Marshal Piłsudski and every day marked areas they had captured (photograph from the collection of the Regional Museum in Siedlce)

91. Two Jews with armbands. The photograph is from the time of the so-called open ghetto (photograph from the collection of Jontel Goldman)

92. Stary Rynek Street in 1940 (photograph from the collection of the Regional Museum in Siedlce)

93. Agnieszka Budna "Jadzia," Righteous among Nations (photograph from the collection of Yad Vashem)

94. Dawid Hochberg, born in Siedlce, member of Żydowska Organizacja Bojowa (Jewish Combat Organization), fell in Warsaw Ghetto Uprising in April 1943

95. Juda Koński, born in Siedlce, member of Żydowska Organizacja Bojowa (Jewish Combat Organization), killed before the uprising for smuggling weapons into the Warsaw ghetto

96. Cypora Jabłoń-Zonszajn, author of Siedlce ghetto memoir, with her little daughter, Rachela

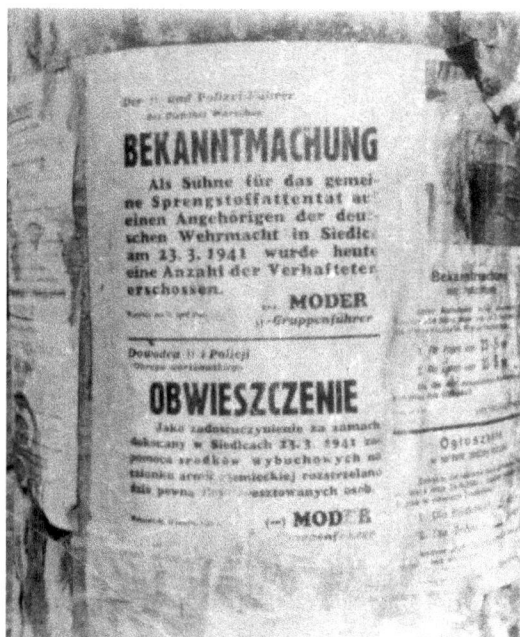

97. German announcement of an assassination (photograph from the collection of Jontel Goldman) [Commander of the SS and Police of the Warsaw District ANNOUNCE-MENT: As redress for the assassination carried out on a member of the German army in Siedlce on 23.3.1941 with the use of explosives, a certain number of arrested people were shot. Warsaw (date unreadable) (—) Moder (rank unreadable)

98. The entry gate to the ghetto on Stary Rynek Street. On the right, the remnants of the ruins of the synagogue (photograph from the collection of Jontel Goldman)

99. Gate to the ghetto on May 1st Street (currently Bishop I. Świrski Street) (photograph from the collection of Jontel Goldman)

100. The territory of the ghetto (German photograph, copy in the author's collection)

101. Commerce in the ghetto (German photograph in the collection of Łukasz Biedka)

102. Water-carrier in the ghetto (German photograph in the collection of Łukasz Biedka)

103. Commerce in the ghetto (German photograph in the collection of Łukasz Biedka)

104. Territory of the ghetto (German photograph in the collection of Łukasz Biedka)

105. Residents of the ghetto (German photograph in the collection of Łukasz Biedka)

106. Jewish workers under guard (German photograph in the collection of Łukasz Biedka)

107. The ghetto, a moment of respite (German photograph in the collection of Łukasz Biedka)

108. An old man and an "Übermensch" (German photograph in the collection of Łukasz Biedka)

109. Hearse used to transport corpses from the ghetto to the cemetery (photograph from the collection of Jontel Goldman)

110. Jewish policeman by the gate to the ghetto on Stary Rynek Street (photograph from the collection of Jontel Goldman)

111. Life behind the wires, Sokołowska Street, later the so-called triangle (photograph from the collection of Jontel Goldman)

112. Document issued by the Office of Labor (Arbeitsaust) in Siedlce to Izaak Halber, assigning him to compulsory labor (from the collection of the Halber family)

113. Post card sent in May 1941 from Siedlce to the USSR [Kiev] (from the collection of the Halber family)

114. Awaiting deportation. The residents of the ghetto were successively gathered in the former Jewish cemetery between Berek Joselewicz Street, May 1st Street, Stary Rynek Street, and Józef Piłsudski Street (photograph by Fritz Hoeft)

115. Awaiting deportation (photograph by Fritz Hoeft)

415

116. Awaiting deportation (photograph by Fritz Hoeft)

117. Final road of Siedlce Jews. The column is marching along Floriańska Street in the direction of the railroad station (photograph taken clandestinely by a soldier of the Home Army)

118. Final road of Siedlce Jews (photograph taken clandestinely by a soldier of the Home Army)

119. Final road of Siedlce Jews (photograph taken clandestinely by a soldier of the Home Army)

120. Final road of Siedlce Jews (photograph taken from under cover by a soldier of the Home Army)

121. Final road of Siedlce Jews (photograph taken from under cover by a soldier of the Home Army. The series of photographs of the liquidation of the ghetto was taken by a soldier of the Home Army on orders from his superiors. After the war, he also gave a set of prints to Izaak Halber. But he reserved anonymity. Izaak Halber passed the prints over to the Siedlce institutions in charge of the history of the city, but he never, in accordance with his agreement, revealed the name of the donor.)

122. Freight ramp, loading into railroad cars (photograph by Hubert Pfoch)

123. Freight ramp, loading into railroad cars (photograph by Hubert Pfoch)

419

124. Freight ramp, those who resisted or were weakened were murdered on the spot (photograph by Hubert Pfoch)

125. After the departure of the train, the bodies of those murdered during the loading were taken to the Jewish cemetery (photograph by Hubert Pfoch)

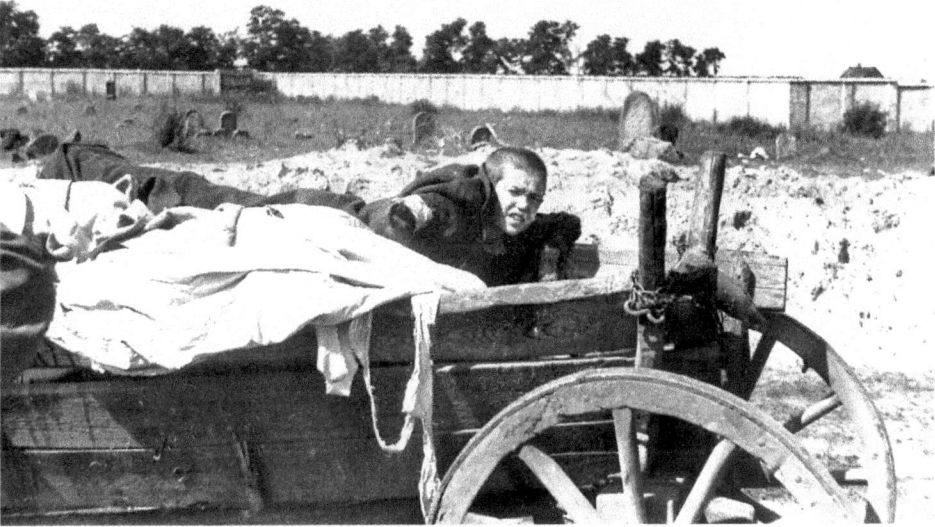

126. The bodies of those murdered during the liquidation of the ghetto were taken to the cemetery where they were buried by a group of Poles. Among them was Tadeusz Castelli, a member of the Home Army and a photographer. He took a number of photos documenting German crimes. Here is one of them. Out of a wagon full of corpses, a boy looked out from under a tarp. In the moment that he was looking around to determine where he was, Castelli noticed him and took the picture. Unfortunately, the Germans who were at the cemetery noticed him and shot him a moment later.

127. Fighting for the city in July 1944 (photograph from the collection of the Regional Museum in Siedlce)

128. Fighting for the city in July 1944 (photograph from the collection of the Regional Museum in Siedlce)

AFTER THE WAR

129. Jontel Goldman records headstones, which the Germans used as curb stones (photograph from the collection of Jontel Goldman)

130. Siedlce Jews who survived the Holocaust bury the exhumed human remains of those murdered in Opole near Siedlce. The circumstances of this crime have to this day not been explained (photograph from the collection of Jontel Goldman)

131. Design for a monument by Rappaport: "Rachel Crying over the Fate of Her Children." The monument was to have stood in the cemetery on Szkolna Street, but unfortunately it was never executed (photograph from the collection of Jontel Goldman)

424

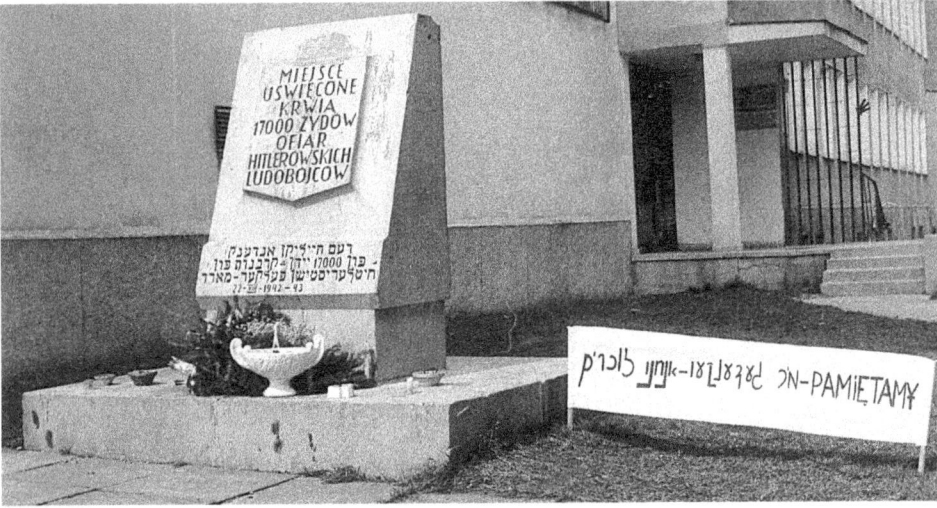

132. Monument honoring murdered Siedlce Jews on Berek Joselewicz Street. It stands where the synagogue was located (photography by the author)
[Place
sanctified
by the blood
of 17,000 Jews
victims of Nazi genocide]
[Yiddish script]
[22–VIII–1942–43]
[On banner at right: "We remember" in Polish, Yiddish, and Hebrew]

133. Grave of the Polish soldier artilleryman Zygmunt Hersz, born 15 February 1901 in Siedlce, died 17 May 1944 at Monte Cassino (photograph by the author)

425

134. Commemoration of Siedlce Jews at the cemetery in Holon in Israel. The gravestone's shape recalls that of the synagogue (photograph from the album *Siedlce before and after the Holocaust*)

135. Commemoration of Jewish population of Siedlce and Łosice at a cemetery in Paris (photograph from the album *Siedlce before and after the Holocaust* published by the Association of Siedlce Jews in Israel, August 1992)

136. Commemorative plaque at the cemetery on Szkolna Street (photograph from the album *Siedlce before and after the Holocaust*)

137. After the creation of the state of Israel, a social campaign was organized to plant forests. In the forest next to Jerusalem is a commemoration with the inscription: "Forest in memory of the martyrs of the Siedlce community")

138. In Jerusalem on Mount Zion there is a symbolic gravestone, a matzevah, with the inscription: "For eternal remembrance on Mount Zion, in memory of the Martyrs of Siedlce, a city in Poland, who were murdered, burned, and buried alive during the years of the Holocaust 1939–1945 by the cursed Nazis. May their name be obliterated. God will avenge the blood [of the Martyrs]. 1948. Union of Jews Who Originated from Siedlce in Israel, America, Argentina, and France" (photograph from *Book of Remembrance of the Siedlce Community*)

139. The inscription "Siedlce" in Polish and Hebrew (in the lower left corner) engraved in a block of bedrock on the territory of the Valley of Destroyed Communities in Yad Vashem in Jerusalem (photograph by the author)

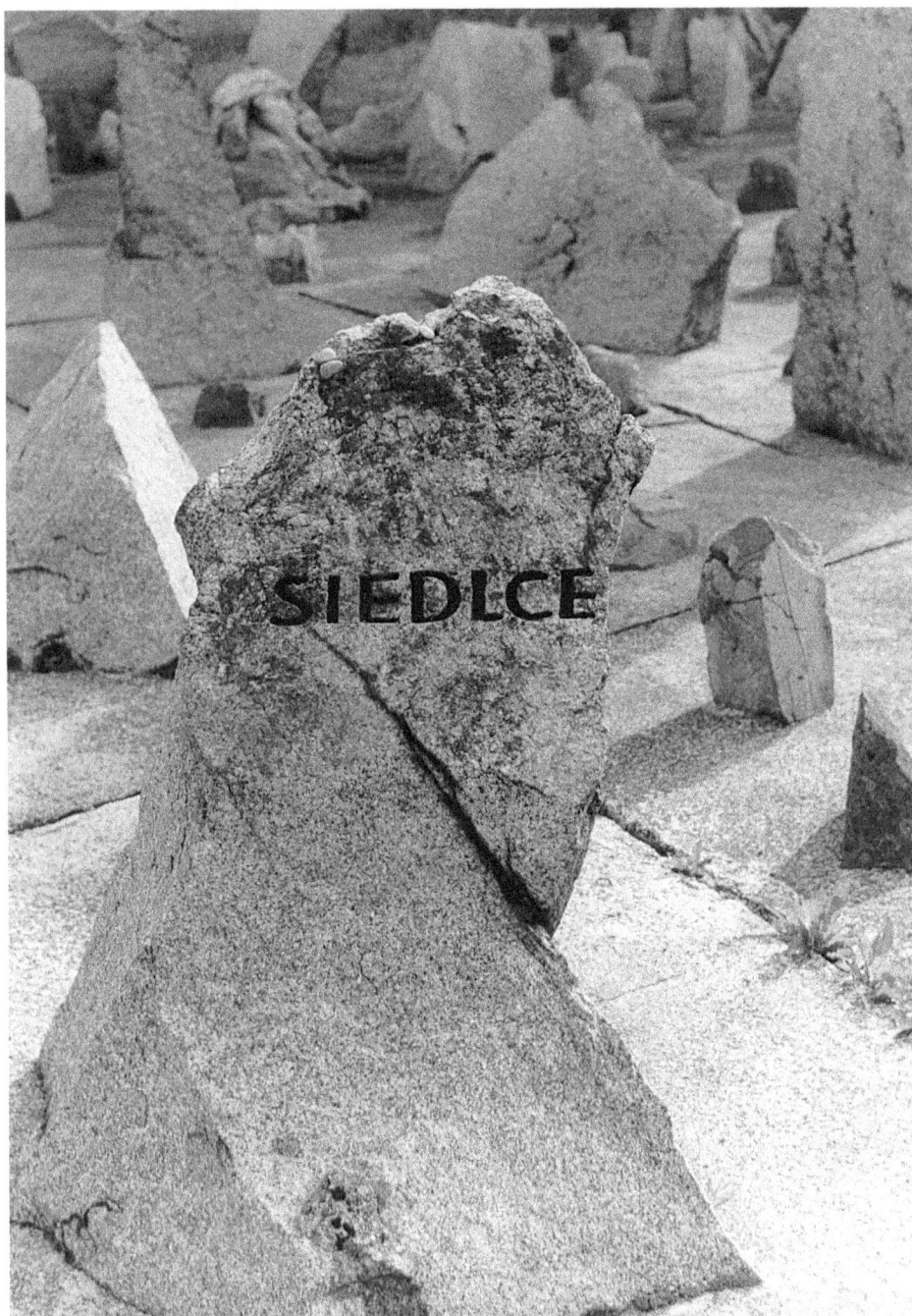

140. Rock with the inscription "Siedlce" on the territory of the former extermination camp in Treblinka (photograph by the author)

141. Torah found on the territory of the former ghetto. It currently serves the faithful of the Martyrs of Siedlce Yeshiva (religious school) in Bnei Brak near Tel Aviv in Israel (photograph from the album *Siedlce before and after the Holocaust*)

142. Fragment of exhibit showing the history of the Jews in Siedlce compiled by the author. The exhibit commemorating 450 years of Siedlce's city charter was organized in the District Museum (currently the Regional Museum) in 1997 (photograph by the author)

430

143. Izaak Halber (right) in conversation with the author (photograph from the collection of the author)

144. Butchers' prayer house. Photograph taken in 1980s; the building no longer exists (photograph by the author)

431

145. The Talmud-Torah building on Browarna Street (photograph by the author)

146. The building of the Jewish Home for Orphans and Seniors on Sienkiewicz Street (photograph by the author)

147. Bohaterów Getta Street (photograph by the author)

148. Berek Joselewicz Street (photograph by the author)

149. Fragment of Lewin's rediscovered Torah (photograph by Sławomir Kordaczuk)

150. Israeli and Polish teenagers at the Jewish cemetery on Szkolna Street in 2007 (photograph by the author)

151. At the end of May, beginning of June 2008, a group of volunteers worked on the territory of the cemetery and collected two containers of trash (photograph by Witold Bobryk)

152. Jewish cemetery. One of the few gravestones in Polish (photograph by Witold Bobryk)
[Jehuda
Suchożebrski
d. 2. XII. 1935
lived 66 years
remaining in deep
sorrow are his daughter and son]

435

153. Informational board on the wall of the cemetery on Szkolna Street (photograph by the author)

[Jewish Cemetery in Siedlce
Established in 1807
Jews settled in Siedlce in the XVI century,
contributing to the economic and cultural development of the city.
In 1941, German Nazis created a ghetto in Siedlce.
During World War II, Germans executed Jews in the cemetery.
Those who survived were deported to the extermination camp in Treblinka.
May their souls be woven into the knot of eternal life
Jewish Religious Council
in Warsaw]

154. Sign pointing the way to the Jewish cemetery (photograph by the author)

155. Place of executions. Imprints of bullet holes on the inside of the cemetery wall (photograph by the author)

156. Religious teenagers from Israel and Siedlce teenagers from General Preparatory High School No. 1 during a joint prayer at the Jewish cemetery on 19 March 2009 (photograph by Witold Bobryk)